WOMEN OF FAITH IN THE LATTER DAYS
Previously Published Volumes

Volume One, 1775–1820
Volume Two, 1821–1845

WOMEN OF FAITH
IN THE LATTER DAYS

VOLUME THREE, 1846–1870

EDITED BY RICHARD E. TURLEY JR.
AND BRITTANY A. CHAPMAN

DESERET BOOK

Salt Lake City, Utah

© 2014 Richard E. Turley Jr. and Brittany A. Chapman

All rights reserved. No part of this book may be reproduced in any form or by any means without permission in writing from the publisher, Deseret Book Company, at permissions@deseretbook.com or P. O. Box 30178, Salt Lake City, Utah 84130. This work is not an official publication of The Church of Jesus Christ of Latter-day Saints. The views expressed herein are the responsibility of the authors and do not necessarily represent the position of the Church or of Deseret Book Company.

DESERET BOOK is a registered trademark of Deseret Book Company.

Visit us at DeseretBook.com

Library of Congress Cataloging-in-Publication Data

Women of faith in the latter days. Volume 1, 1775–1820 / edited by Richard E. Turley Jr. and Brittany A. Chapman.
    pages cm
    Includes bibliographical references and index.
    ISBN 978-1-60641-033-2 (hardbound : alk. paper; v. 1, 1775–1820)
    ISBN 978-1-60907-173-8 (hardbound : alk. paper; v. 2, 1821–1845)
    ISBN 978-1-60907-588-0 (hardbound : alk. paper; v. 3, 1846–1870)
    1. Mormon women—Biography. I. Turley, Richard E. (Richard Eyring), 1956– editor. II. Chapman, Brittany A., editor.
    BX8693.W66 2011
    289.3092'52—dc23   2011035215

Printed in the United States of America
Publishers Printing, Salt Lake City, UT

10 9 8 7 6 5 4 3 2 1

For women who reach beyond
what they can see

Contents

Introduction to the Series . . . xi

Preface . . . xiii

Timeline . . . xvii

1. "Give Us an Expanding Faith" . . . 1
   Maud May Babcock
   by Laurel Thatcher Ulrich

2. "Do Some Little Good While We Live" . . . 13
   Martha Maria Hughes Cannon
   by Jonathan A. Stapley and Constance L. Lieber

3. "A Strong and Abiding Testimony" . . . 28
   Mary Elizabeth Woolley Chamberlain
   by Janelle M. Higbee

4. "Sow Seeds of Faith" . . . 43
   Ruth May Fox
   by Brittany A. Chapman

5. "Thank God That I Have Been Counted Worthy" . . . 57
   Susa Amelia Young Dunford Gates
   by Lisa Olsen Tait

6. "Wonderful to Me" . . . 69
Sarah Ann Taylor Howard
by Karol Gerber Chase

7. "Strength to Overcome Selfishness" . . . 82
Lorena Eugenia Washburn Larsen
by Loretta Luce Evans

8. "It Would Be Worth It" . . . 96
Mary Roselia Cook McCann
by Jeff Hillam

9. "Doing a Little Good for the Cause of Christ" . . . 107
Elizabeth Ann Claridge McCune
by Matthew S. McBride

10. "Courage to Follow Convictions" . . . 122
Tsune Ishida Nachie
by Ardis E. Parshall

11. "Truly Her Soul Rejoiced in Helping the Helpless" . . . 131
Emily Sophia Tanner Richards
by Andrea G. Radke-Moss

12. "Welcome the Task That Takes You beyond Yourself" . . . 146
Sarah Louisa Yates Robison
by Patricia Lemmon Spilsbury

13. "Guide Their Footsteps Aright" . . . 158
Annie Marie Woodbury Romney
by Barbara E. Morgan

14. "Those Who Love Most Tenderly Are Surely Most like Thee" . . . 171
Ellis Reynolds Shipp
by Susan Evans McCloud

15. "Hallowed Ground" . . . 183
Edith Ann Smith
by Janiece Johnson

16. "The Hand of the Diligent Maketh Rich" . . . 198
Ellen Johanna Larson Smith
by Christine T. Cox

17. "A Triangle of Happiness" . . . 211
Julina Lambson Smith
by Amanda Hendrix-Komoto

18. "Trying to Do a Little Good in a Weak Way" . . . 223
Lucy Emily Woodruff Smith
by Keshia Lai

19. "No Matter How Severe the Trial" . . . 237
Ida Frances Hunt Udall
by Kristin Owens

20. "Her Very Presence Is a Sermon" . . . 252
Mere Mete Whaanga
by Marjorie Newton

21. "If It Is the Truth, I Must Do So" . . . 263
Anna Karine Gaarden Widtsoe
by Kiersten Olson and Clinton D. Christensen

22. "The Power and Influence of Woman" . . . 276
Clarissa Smith Williams
by Andrea H. Maxfield

23. "How Thankful We Should Be" . . . 288
Cohn Shoshonitz Zundel
by Patricia Lemmon Spilsbury

Notes . . . 299

Contributors . . . 353

Image Credits . . . 361

Index . . . 363

Introduction to the Series

Although approximately half the people in the history of The Church of Jesus Christ of Latter-day Saints have been women, their lives of faith and dedication are just beginning to receive the attention they merit. This series, *Women of Faith in the Latter Days,* aims to enhance awareness of these women through inspirational accounts written for a general readership.

The seven volumes projected for the series will be arranged as follows:

> Volume 1: Women born between 1775 and 1820
> Volume 2: Women born between 1821 and 1845
> Volume 3: Women born between 1846 and 1870
> Volume 4: Women born between 1871 and 1895
> Volume 5: Women born between 1896 and 1920
> Volume 6: Women born between 1921 and 1945
> Volume 7: Women born between 1946 and 1970

Within each volume, the chapters are arranged alphabetically by the last name of each woman of faith.

We have sought to balance the preferences of general readers with the needs of scholarship by following common editorial conventions that enhance ease of reading but preserve the accuracy of historical sources and the personalities of the subject women. Briefly stated, in the historical sources we have preserved the original spelling and grammar, using square brackets [ ] to expand, correct, or clarify when necessary for readability. We have also silently added punctuation and capitalized the first words of sentences, using our best interpretive judgment to discern the writer's intentions. We have also altered capitalization when failure to do so might prove distracting to readers.

We have included chapters written by a range of authors, from well-established scholars to beginning writers. Some chapters adopt a scholarly approach, often quoting the subject woman's own words at length. Others follow a more popular approach, avoiding long quotations from the subject and replacing them with the author's own prose. Some of the subject women left few or no writings behind, making it difficult or impossible to quote them. Our goal has been to feature a diverse group of women, both those well known to readers and those who lived lives of faith in comparative anonymity.

We hope both scholarly and popular audiences will find value in these volumes. Our intent in producing them is to plant seeds for future work. If our series leads to better scholarly and popular works, we will feel rewarded for our efforts.

We invite you to join with us in celebrating the many Latter-day Saint women whose lives should be an inspiration to readers in the present generation and in generations to come. We hope these volumes will prompt readers to write about their own lives and will lead to longer works about past and present women of faith in the latter days.

Preface

Volume 3 of *Women of Faith in the Latter Days* features women of The Church of Jesus Christ of Latter-day Saints born between 1846 and 1870. The lifespans of the women featured in this volume extend from those who traveled across the plains of North America by wagon and handcart to those who lived to see a spacecraft land on the moon. The main body of Latter-day Saints left Nauvoo, Illinois, and surrounding regions in 1846, settling in camps across Iowa and along both sides of the Missouri River. In 1847, the first organized companies of Saints traversed the plains to settle in a part of the Great Basin eventually called Utah. Saints continued to migrate to Utah by animal- or human-drawn conveyances until the transcontinental railroad was completed in 1869, which allowed newcomers to travel by train.

All the women featured in this volume knew pioneer life firsthand. They also experienced the gradual transition to modern life, some of them living into the 1950s and 60s. Missionary work caused the Latter-day Saint body of believers to expand throughout the globe. The women whose stories are told herein hail not only from Utah but from other areas of the Americas and the world, including Japan, New Zealand, and Scandinavia.

Like the women of the first two volumes of this series, many of the women in this volume experienced polygamy, some growing up in plural homes, and most living also to see the abandonment of the practice in the years following Church president Wilford Woodruff's 1890 Manifesto. For many, the abandonment of plural marriage was as challenging as accepting it. Plural wives shared not only husbands and homes but also endured popular censure, particularly from an increasingly strident American public. Many also endured poverty, lived in exile on the "underground," and became the primary providers for their families.

The women who entered this form of marriage did so out of a belief that they were sacrificing the things of this world for greater blessings in the world to come. They thus provide an example for women and men of all ages who must likewise make earthly sacrifices for eternal blessings.

Women experienced growth in opportunities generally in society and participated actively in efforts to achieve equality for women by joining national and international women's organizations. They sought personal improvement, participated in clubs, and advanced the causes of woman suffrage, moral reform, and world peace. Often they became strong public advocates for the Church and its emphasis on education, industry, and self-reliance.

Several individuals aided in the preparation of this volume. We thank Beth Anderson, Betsy Crane, Jared and Carly C. Jakins, Angela B. Wagner, Jennifer Duqué, Sarah Jacobson, Andrea Ventilla, and Amanda Brown for their invaluable service. We give special thanks to our editorial assistant, Emily Simmons, for her talent and efficiency. This project would not be possible without the contributions of all involved. Again we wish to thank Sheri Dew and Cory Maxwell of Deseret Book, who encouraged us throughout this project, and our exceptional editor, Suzanne Brady, whose skills and suggestions continue to make this series accessible to a wide audience.

Once again, we extend our thanks to all the authors who have contributed chapters to this volume. The chapters contained in the physical book and the additional ones in the eBook provide insights into the lives of women whose faith carried them through afflictions, inspired them to create and embrace opportunities, and helped them expand their talents in the service of God and humanity.

Timeline

April 6, 1830	The Church of Christ is organized in Fayette, New York.
1831–38	**Saints in Kirtland, Ohio.**
July 20, 1837	First missionaries arrive in Britain.
July 30, 1837	First British converts are baptized in the River Ribble at Preston, England.
1831–39	**Saints in Missouri.**
1831–33	Independence, Jackson County.
1834–36	Clay County.
1836–39	Far West, Caldwell County.
April 26, 1838	Revelation declares the name of the Church to be The Church of Jesus Christ of Latter-day Saints.
1839–46	**Saints in Nauvoo, Illinois.**
April 1841	First plural marriage in Nauvoo is performed.
March 17, 1842	The Female Relief Society of Nauvoo is organized.
June 27, 1844	Joseph and Hyrum Smith are martyred in Carthage, Illinois.

July 24, 1847	Brigham Young, leader of the first pioneer company, arrives in the Salt Lake Valley.
December 27, 1847	Brigham Young is sustained as president of the Church.
1847–69	**Saints migrate to Utah by wagon or handcart.**
August 29, 1852	Plural marriage is announced publicly in Utah.
1868	Reorganization of Relief Society begins.
1869	Transcontinental railroad completed.
1870	Utah women receive the right to vote.
1872–1914	The semimonthly *Woman's Exponent* is the unofficial publication of the Relief Society.
1876	First colonies are established along the Little Colorado River in Arizona.
January 7, 1876	First missionaries arrive in Mexico.
April 6–8, 1877	St. George Temple is dedicated by Daniel H. Wells under direction of Brigham Young.
August 29, 1877	Brigham Young dies in Salt Lake City, Utah.
August 25, 1878	Primary Association for children is organized.
June 19, 1880	Eliza R. Snow is sustained as second Relief Society general president, Elmina S. Taylor as first general president of the Young Ladies' Mutual Improvement Association, and Louie B. Felt as first Primary general president.
October 10, 1880	John Taylor is sustained as third president of the Church.
1882	Edmunds Act is passed, intensifying legal action against polygamists.
1885	First Mormon colonies established in Mexico.
1887	Edmunds-Tucker Act further intensifies legal action against polygamists and revokes the right of women in Utah to vote.

December 5, 1887	Eliza R. Snow dies in Salt Lake City, Utah.
April 8, 1888– August 28, 1901	Zina D. H. Young serves as third Relief Society general president.
April 7, 1889	Wilford Woodruff is sustained as fourth president of the Church.
September 24, 1890	Wilford Woodruff issues Manifesto, leading to the discontinuance of the practice of plural marriage.
1891	Relief Society and YLMIA become charter members of the National Council of Women.
April 6, 1893	Salt Lake Temple is dedicated by Wilford Woodruff.
January 4, 1896	Utah statehood is granted, and women in Utah regain the right to vote.
September 13, 1898	Lorenzo Snow is sustained as fifth president of the Church.
October 17, 1901	Joseph F. Smith is sustained as sixth president of the Church.
November 10, 1901– September 20, 1910	Bathsheba W. Smith serves as fourth Relief Society general president.
December 14, 1907	Saints advised to discontinue migration to Utah and strengthen the Church in their native lands.
October 3, 1910– April 2, 1921	Emmeline B. Wells serves as fifth Relief Society general president.
January 1915	The *Relief Society Magazine* is launched as the official publication of the Relief Society.
November 23, 1918	Heber J. Grant is sustained as seventh president of the Church.
1919	Relief Society Social Services Department established.
April 2, 1921– October 7, 1928	Clarissa Smith Williams serves as sixth Relief Society general president.

October 7, 1928– December 31, 1939	Louise Y. Robison serves as seventh Relief Society general president.
April 6, 1930	Centennial celebration of the organization of the Church.
January 1, 1940– April 6, 1945	Amy Brown Lyman serves as eighth Relief Society general president.
May 21, 1945	George Albert Smith is sustained as eighth president of the Church.

Chapter 1

"Give Us an Expanding Faith"

Maud May Babcock (1867–1954)
by Laurel Thatcher Ulrich

Maud May Babcock, a petite young woman with a resounding voice, traveled to Salt Lake City in 1892 and soon secured a position at the University of Utah teaching "elocution" and "physical culture." By 1895, she had produced her first theatrical production at the old Salt Lake Theatre. In the 1920s, the Babcock Varsity Players were not only performing in Salt Lake City but also barnstorming through Utah and neighboring states in the summertime. When Miss Babcock, as her students knew her, retired from the university in 1938 after forty-six years on the faculty, the student newspaper, the *Utah Daily Chronicle,* pronounced her the "first lady of Utah drama."[1] A stage in the Pioneer Memorial Theatre on campus bears her name. Known nationally for her work in community theatre, she was revered locally as an inspired and inspiring teacher.[2]

Those who know Maud only through her theatrical reputation are often unaware of her work in promoting "physical culture," or what today we would call "fitness." Nor do many people know that in addition to serving as president of both Theta Alpha Phi, the national dramatics fraternity, and of the National Association of Teachers of Speech, she served for many years on the general board of the Young Ladies' Mutual Improvement Association or that she was an avid genealogist who, according to her own count, performed 21,234 vicarious temple endowments. Maud May Babcock was simultaneously iconoclastic and devout, imperious and kind. She could recite Shakespeare, climb mountains, stage plays, correct women's posture, and with equal aplomb serve gourmet meals in her home in Salt Lake City or steaming bowls of whole wheat mush to guests in her Brighton summer home.[3]

She used to joke that it was easy to remember her birthday, which was on May 2, because May was her *second* name.[4] In fact, everything about her was memorable. Born to William Wayne and Sarah Jane Butler Babcock in 1867 in East Worcester, New York, she seemed destined, even as a child, for the stage. After graduating from the National School of Oratory in Philadelphia in 1886 and the Lyceum School of Acting (now the American Academy of Dramatic Arts) in New York City in 1888, she explored the new science of physical culture, eventually joining other bloomer-clad women at the Harvard Summer School for Physical Training, a proprietary school organized by Dudley Allen Sargent. He was a pioneering educator who in the 1880s mounted classes in physical education for female students at the so-called Harvard Annex (later Radcliffe College) and then in 1887 secured the use of Harvard facilities for summer courses in "Physical Training," open to both sexes. According to Sargent, directors of Harvard's summer school were astonished at the variety of persons who showed up for classes, not only the gymnasts they expected but doctors, lawyers, and "members of foreign embassies." A female visitor from the West, astonished to see women in gymnasium bloomers performing on Sargent's gymnastic apparatus, exclaimed, "Well, this is a hell of a joint," then turned on her heel and walked out.[5] Measurements taken at Harvard's gymnasium on July 6, 1891, show that at age twenty-four, Maud stood five feet three inches high, weighed ninety-seven pounds, and measured

Maud May Babcock (1867–1954)

Maud May Babcock demonstrating an "educational gymnastic" used in her physical culture classes to improve posture, ca. 1894. A pioneer in the health sciences, Maud founded both the Department of Physical Education and the Department of Speech at the University of Utah.

twenty-two inches around the waist.[6] Although small of stature, she made an imposing figure in a gymnasium suit or a theatrical toga.

That summer, she met Susa Young Gates, the intrepid editor of Utah's *Young Woman's Journal*, who had traveled to Cambridge to study rhetoric and had become interested in what was going on in the gym. Among the small group of Latter-day Saints at Harvard that year was Joseph Marion Tanner, a teacher at the Utah Agricultural College in Logan, who had brought a group of students to study at Harvard. When Gates persuaded Maud to visit Utah, Tanner wrote letters of introduction to friends and relatives in Salt Lake City asking them to make her welcome.[7] After four months in Utah, she was baptized a member of The Church of Jesus Christ of Latter-day Saints—much to the dismay of her mother, who wrote, "I pray daily to God [that] if you open your lips to defend that cause in publick your tongue may be paralyzed."[8] Although her parents were never fully reconciled to her becoming a Mormon, they were proud of the honors she received among the Saints.

Maud's talents as a teacher come most fully to life in the descriptions left by her students. Former Utah governor Herbert Maw often told the story of how she saved him from his own insecurity when he was about to drop out of college. He had to work to support himself, and the only courses compatible with his schedule were in pre-law, but he couldn't imagine himself as a lawyer because he was shy and terrified of speaking in public. A friend took him to see Maud, who said she would help him if he promised to try out for her next play. To his astonishment she cast him as the king in *A Midsummer Night's Dream.* When he skipped the first rehearsal, hoping she would find someone else, she tracked him down in his morning class and insisted that he give it a try. Here is how he described her method of instruction:

> I had never taken a course in speech. I didn't know how to read. She had me read the lines, and I read them in a monotone. And she said, "Stress," and I didn't even know what she was talking about. She said, "The sentences that you are reading are meaningless until you begin stressing the words that put over the idea that you have in mind." Then she said, "You take this sentence, 'I love you.' Read it." And so I mumbled it out, "I love you," in a monotone. She said, "Why, if you should say that to your sweetheart, she wouldn't believe you, if you said it in that way. That sentence has no meaning until you stress. Listen to me now. If I should [say], '*I* love you,' the sentence takes on meaning, doesn't it?" And I said, "Yes." She said, "What is the meaning?" I told her that *I* and not someone else was the one that loved you. Then, she said, "If I read it this way, 'I love *you*,' it has a different meaning, doesn't it?" And I said, "Yes, it does. It means it's you and not everyone that I love." And then she said, "If I say, 'I *love* you,' it has still a different

meaning." In that way she taught me what "stressing" was. And then she said, "When you read your lines, pick out the words that put over the idea that you have in mind and *stress* them—make them stand out."

Well, for weeks I drove my family crazy and myself crazy . . . stressing words that I had to say. But that wasn't the worst of it . . . the worst of it was my walking. She had to teach me to walk with dignity . . . the dignity of a king. . . . She held me after every rehearsal. We walked up and down the stage hundreds of times with her by my side and showing me how to put forth my foot and to walk like a king would walk. I finally said, "Miss Babcock, I can't act like a king." And she said, "I don't want you to act like a king. . . . you *are* the king, so act like yourself!" Well, I did my best.

Finally one day I met her on the campus. . . . She said, "I have noticed you for five minutes. Here I have spent hours with you teaching you how to walk, and as soon as you get out of my sight, you walk like a nincompoop! I want you to know that every step you take—whether I am around or not—must be the step of a king!" Boy, what an assignment! I left her and walked down to Main Street to my work, and every step I took was the step of a king. She tortured me—trying to teach me how to walk and to read—but, do you know, after five or six weeks of that a miracle happened! For when I walked on the stage on the opening night of the performance with my queen on my side and lords and beautiful ladies dressed in beautiful gowns following me, I *was* the king! I had learned how to walk with self-control. If I hadn't learned that, I could not possibly have gone on with any success in any line of endeavor that I followed. . . .

To me she was a great woman. No greater person ever lived in my life. No person ever contributed to me what she contributed because she was as she was. She asked for no reward, except that I accept. Some of us resented the discipline she imposed. She talked to me more sternly and harshly than any woman or person has ever talked to me in my life, but I loved it for some reason or other.... I sought it because I knew she was wanting to develop me more than anything in the world.⁹

Clearly, Maud's method as a teacher focused on actions rather than theories. She believed that students learn best through doing.

Her concept of physical culture included healthful eating as well as exercise. An essay from the *Young Woman's Journal* shows her belief in demonstrating rather than simply asserting strong principles. That it includes a recipe for a dessert made with gelatin raises an intriguing possibility—could Maud have played a small part in creating the supposed craze for Jell-O in Utah? Although she surely wouldn't have approved the sugar-laden salads sometimes served in Utah and other parts of the United States today, she clearly approved of fruit-flavored "jellies" and the "moulds" that were their predecessors. Maud was progressive in her approach to nutrition; she participated in a Woman's Hygiene Reform Class and encouraged a healthful diet of light, fresh "hygiene" foods. An article in the *Young Woman's Journal* recounted:

> It was suggested by our dear sister, Maud May Babcock, that in order to prove to our friends we were not going to starve ourselves, or get cranky, because a departure from old customs was being made, that a banquet be given, and the menu to consist entirely of hygiene dishes.
>
> Sister Babcock took the matter in charge.... There were three courses served: First, soups—tomato, beans, peas; second, potatoes, green peas, green corn, cauliflowers, salads of lettuce and celery; third, fruits, lemon jelly, raspberry mould, whipped cream, cakes made of graham flower, etc.
>
> A few of the recipes are added for the benefit of those who are interested in this method of living....

Maud May Babcock (1867–1954)

Lemon Jelly
Soak half-box gelatine in a cup of cold water until soft. Then pour over it a pint of boiling water and stir until well dissolved. Add sugar and lemon juice to taste. Strain and put into molds previously wet in cold water, and place in a cool place to harden.[10]

Although Maud wrote several textbooks and a number of scholarly articles, she was much better known for her interpretation of other people's words than her own. When called upon, however, she knew how to compose and deliver her own texts. A speech she gave at a Mutual Improvement Association conference in 1904 recapitulates some of the themes in her life—her commitment to healthy living, including scrupulous attention to the Word of Wisdom, her ability to love her parents despite their rejection of her religion, and her belief in self-reliance as well as respect for authority:

> There is a general impression among people, as soon as you speak of loyalty, you mean a little Fourth of July effervescence—a few firecrackers, a flag, a few shouts, a turning out to see the President, to see the governor of the state, or something of that kind. Therefore, when this topic was given to me, I went to the dictionary to see what it said loyalty is. The Century dictionary says that "loyalty is to be true and faithful in allegiance; to be constant in service, in devotion." . . . Loyalty is not a passive thing; it is active; it is not to believe, but to do. It is engendered in the very heart, and we grow in loyalty by acting loyally, as we grow always by doing.
>
> The Lord, himself, has said, "Not every one that saith unto me, Lord, Lord, shall enter into the kingdom of heaven." There are many among our people—maybe I am wrong in this matter—by bearing testimony of their loyalty to the Church and loyalty to the founder of this Church, think they have absolutely discharged all obligation. When

they have stood upon their feet and testified that they know that the Prophet Joseph Smith was a prophet of God, and that all who have succeeded him have been prophets of God, they think that nothing more is required at their hands. And yet those same people, to take a simple illustration, will go directly to their homes, and the very first thing that will be placed upon the table, and of which they partake with blessing, is food that sets at defiance the Word of Wisdom—a law given through this same prophet, Joseph Smith, and which has been declared to be the truth of God by every prophet, seer and revelator who has stood at the head of this Church in this generation. These people, to my mind, seem not to be loyal, because we should "do the will of the Father which is in heaven," not say, "Lord, Lord," or "the Prophet Joseph Smith is a prophet of God," but acknowledge "in every act and every word that proceedeth from our mouth," that we are trying to live up to God's laws. . .

Loyalty is not servility. Many in the world think that we are a servile people—that we are led about by the nose—by the influence of those in authority. This is not true. We are loyal to our brethren, but not servile. Every true Latter-day Saint is loyal in this manner. Why? Because we know we have that knowledge within us that those in authority stand as prophets of God unto us, and, if we have the Spirit of God, we recognize his voice, and our loyalty and obedience proceed from that very knowledge; we know the right and act accordingly. . . . Is the college man "led by the nose" when he accepts the truth given him by a teacher, and proceeds to carry it out in life? No more are we. . . .

We should be loyal to our mothers and fathers; we should be loyal to our children. Now, again, it does not appear to me that loyalty means retrogression, not to gain any more than our mothers and fathers have gained. A basic principle of our gospel is Eternal Progression. If we were to

Maud May Babcock (1867–1954)

Maud May Babcock was a beloved drama teacher at the University of Utah. Maud is in dramatic pose, surrounded by (left to right) Margaret Caldwell, Eliza Pachard, Emily Bruition, Fay Cornwall, Billy Coleman, and Alta Jensen, ca. 1920.

follow the footsteps of our parents, neither the fathers and mothers of this audience, or this audience, would be here. . . . This does not mean, however, that because we have embraced the truth, that we are to throw the poor father and mother out into the street, that we are to consider that they have no claim upon us in the future, because we recognize the truth. Our religion should teach us to take care of our fathers and mothers. We are to do for them every thing that lies in our power to do; and, as true Latter-day Saints, we will be able to serve them far, far better than we ever could have served them had we remained, as they, perhaps, might have wished us to. . . .

Let us not be afraid, at any time or under any circumstances, to declare the truth which God has made known unto us. . . . Two years ago, a young lady who had never before been out of this state at all, was in the east, studying. She was at Chautauqua Lake, New York. There she heard Dr. Elliot, who had been to Utah, tell lurid tales of her people. When this girl, not yet twenty years of age, heard her people maligned by one who should have known better, she told the authorities of Chautauqua . . . that she had been brought up with this people; that this people were her people, and that their God was her God. . . . That young girl in all humility, with faith that God would assist her, said that she would be glad to defend her people in that vast theatre at Chautauqua . . . but the authorities stated that Dr. Elliot's story was the one the people of the United States wanted to hear, and they did not want to hear the other side—the truth.

Let us progress in loyalty, "be constant in service and devotion"; and may we take the admonition of the Savior, that "No man, having put his hand to the plow, and looking back, is fit for the kingdom of God."[11]

Maud also believed that teaching good literature and teaching young people interpretive or dramatic reading could build testimonies—that, in fact, everything could work toward that end if done in the proper spirit. A comment she made in the *Young Woman's Journal* in 1909 expressed that point:

I would like to state here that I think that there isn't any lesson that we ever had in Mutual Improvement work—it makes no difference what kind of a lesson it is, that cannot be forceful and become a testimony of the gospel. . . .

I feel that the great spirit of literature is the spirit of God—that God has moved these people to write and speak as they have done, and that we should bring that home to us, that it should be a testimony; that is one of the ways of getting testimonies . . . Perhaps I said something in one of our conventions that I want to explain here. I said that junior girls[12] were perhaps not able to have the lesson put in the same way . . . that some things we can see through and get the spirit of the gospel out of, are to them absolute nonsense. But I do think that if a teacher has the right spirit she can make things plain to them. And by all means I feel that the thing to be emphasized here is the importance of the teacher, and not the importance of the knowledge that she has, but the importance of the Spirit of God that she possesses, and the importance of seeing the Spirit of God in everything that comes up. Now, I believe in taking up all lessons in this way so we can get a testimony of God.[13]

After her retirement from teaching, Maud received an unexpected call to serve as chaplain for the Utah State Senate, the first time in the state's history that a woman had fulfilled that assignment. Handwritten copies of many of the prayers she delivered between January and March 1945 give us a glimpse of her patriotism, her concern for world peace, and her faith during the waning months of World War II, a time when the Allies began to close in on Nazi Germany but when fighting in the Pacific was especially vicious. The prayers she delivered on February 14 and March 7, 1945, seem as appropriate today as they were more than half a century ago:

> [February 14] Heavenly Father, ruler of the Nations of the earth, have mercy upon us, for our failure to achieve world brotherhood. Help us to all acknowledge the dependence of nation upon nation; give those nations that are now struggling, thine eternal assistance to create a better world order, an order with equal opportunities to all, in achievement and in service. We ask Thy divine blessings upon the United Nations. Speed the day of victory, when "good will" can replace enmity, faith overcome suspicion, co-operation be substituted for hostility, and may "universal peace lie, like a shaft of light across the land, and like a lane of beams athwart the sea."[14] We ask this and Thy help we need sorely, In His Name—our Savior, Jesus Christ, *Amen*.[15]

[March 7] Eternal Father, in this darkened, confused, and storm swept world, we need Thy ~~great~~ gift to man—Faith. May we have faith, which is sufficient to meet the needs and problems in these troubled days. Give us a living faith which will dare to venture into new and uncharted ways; give us a courageous faith which will mount all heights; give us an expanding faith, so deep, so wide and so high, that it knows no limits, until life has been mastered by Thy righteousness and Thy wisdom. ~~and we may can meet Thee.~~

We ask this greatest of heavenly gifts, in His name, who was the embodiment of Faith, our Savior, Amen.[16]

Maud May Babcock died on December 31, 1954, having demonstrated through her remarkable career an ability to integrate higher education, public service, and religious faith.

Chapter 2

"Do Some Little Good While We Live"

MARTHA MARIA HUGHES CANNON (1857–1932)
by Jonathan A. Stapley and Constance L. Lieber

In 1896, Martha Hughes Cannon ran as a Democrat for one of a handful of at-large Utah state senate seats. Among her opponents was her husband, who ran as a Republican. The Democrats prevailed in the election, and Martha became the first female state senator in the United States of America. That single event in Martha's life is sufficient to warrant the attention of historians and scholars; however, Mattie (her preferred appellation) was much more than her four years in the Utah state legislature. She was a dedicated physician, trained lecturer, suffragist, polygamous wife, mother, and Latter-day Saint.[1]

Martha Maria Hughes was born on July 1, 1857, near Llandudno, Clwyd, Wales. Her parents, Peter and Elizabeth Evans Hughes, members of The Church of Jesus Christ of Latter-day Saints, left for Utah Territory the following year. They stopped in New York in order to work for a living and for means to complete their emigration to the Great Basin. In 1861, the family obtained assistance through the Perpetual Emigrating Fund, and they arrived in Utah later that year. Peter died shortly thereafter.

When she became a teenager, Mattie began working as a typesetter for the *Deseret News,* which led to an opportunity to work on the publication of the *Woman's Exponent.* The *Exponent* was a women's newspaper that simultaneously promoted the Relief Society, defended the Church, advocated for women's rights, and provided a venue for women to publish fiction, essays, and poetry. It was an experience that shaped the course of Mattie's life. In the pages of that newspaper, she found examples of strong professional women and opportunities for education that inspired her to leave Utah for further schooling. A young, unmarried woman of significant intellectual acumen and ambition, she enrolled in the University of Michigan School of Medicine, graduating in 1881. She then attended the Auxiliary School of Medicine of the University of Pennsylvania in Philadelphia. The only woman in her class, she graduated in 1882 with a bachelor of science degree in pharmacy.

While in Pennsylvania, Mattie also attended the National School of Elocution and Oratory in Philadelphia from 1881 to 1882. In eighteenth- and nineteenth-century America, elocution was a popular field of study in which students were taught articulation, inflection, tone, and gesture with the goal of presenting educational lectures. At this school, she formed a deep friendship with her classmate Barbara Replogle.[2] After graduation, Mattie returned to Utah to practice medicine and Barbara went back home to Illinois, but they maintained a correspondence for years, and many of Mattie's letters to Barbara between 1883 and 1893 are extant.

Mattie's letters to her friend document her transformation from an anxious young romantic to a pragmatic polygamist and ad hoc single mother. The letters are saturated in passionate avowals of affection and memory and are superb examples of what scholars have identified as the rich and ritual-laden world of female relationships in Victorian America.[3] The following excerpts from this correspondence highlight these and other aspects of Martha Hughes Cannon's

Martha Maria Hughes Cannon (1857–1932)

Martha Hughes in Philadelphia, Pennsylvania, where she attended the Auxiliary School of Medicine of the University of Pennsylvania and the National School of Elocution and Oratory, ca. 1882.

personality and character. Because we have only one side of the conversation, we are left to deduce the context of Mattie's comments and questions; however, that context is frequently evident.[4]

Establishing a family and creating a fulfilling life were principal concerns to both Barbara and Mattie. Having a career was both a reality of nineteenth-century life and an important feature of female identity for many Latter-day Saint women. After returning to Utah from Philadelphia in 1882, Mattie, still single, became the house physician at the Deseret Hospital.[5] Practicing medicine, however, did not fulfill all her needs. She was not particularly close to any young women in Salt Lake City, and she longed for intimate personal friendships:

> This is a busy career I have entered upon, yet I like it but O how I long for some refining intellectual dessert to taper off with occasionally. If you were here, I should *take* time and practice elocution with you with a vim, and discuss with you our heroes in literature; as well as the living

masculine specimens we have come in contact with since our separation. Do not misunderstand me Dear that we have no intellectual people here, To the contrary I can truthfully assert we have some of the highest types in that direction to [be] found anywhere else, both among our people, as also among the so called Gentile population, but either I have not taken time, or else there has been a lack of that close sympathy which goes to form lasting attachments. Something however that those attachments have not been formed. I refer to feminine friends. Of course the time has not come, in my case at least, to make any definite progress in the masculine direction. Matrimony I refer to.[6]

Martha was never shy about her beliefs, and she frequently wrote about the roles of women and mothers:

After all it is natural for men & women to love and marry that is a part and parcel of the great plan of redemption. We never fully pay the debt to our parents until we bear children ourselves, providing it is within our power to do so—and mothers tell me there is no love on earth equal to a mother's for her child, and no joy surpasses that of nursing the tender infant. You remember what Lady Macbeth said "I have given suck and know how tender it is to love the babe that milks me"[7] &c. I admire your choice of a life work. Elocution and Literature. According to my ideas nowhere, outside the maternal circle, does woman shine in her full glory as on the platform. . . .

Now don't forget to let me know when that wedding is drawing to a "finale," describe the Champion to me. Do you love him as much as you are capable of loving? I suppose you think I ought to answer some of the questions you asked me. Truly the fates seem against all attempts at love and matrimony on my part. I fear I am doomed to maidenhood.[8]

In a subsequent letter, Mattie outlined her vision for married life, in which intellectual and professional advancement were completely harmonious with motherhood:

> When are you going to wed? After all, this to my mind, is the true state of womanhood[,] neither, if properly managed should it interfere with her true advancement, in whatever sphere she might cast her talents. 'Tis not the bringing of noble spirits into the world—to me, a mother's or woman's brightest glory—that dwarfs talent, and retards her intellectual advancement[,] but it is the multiplicity of household drudgery which only belongs to servants, and the conformity to the vile customs of modern Society.
>
> Barbara even if we have to be poor let us not waste our talents in the cauldron of modern nothingness, but strive to become women of intellect, and endeavor to do some little good while we live in this protracted gleam called life.[9]

Mattie was not destined for maidenhood, however, and her choice to marry a prominent, polygamous Church leader on October 6, 1884, was a risky one. Federal officials were actively prosecuting and incarcerating practicing polygamists, but she chose to marry Angus M. Cannon, president of the Salt Lake Stake and twenty-three years her senior, as his fourth wife.

Like many Latter-day Saints, Mattie tried to balance allegiance to her beliefs, family, and community with the exigencies of federal prosecution. She wrote to her friend:

> It has been widely rumored hereabouts, that I am third wife of one of the leaders of the Mormon Church, have actually been arraigned before the "Grand Jury" on the Charge of Polygamy but after I had given my testimony, that August body came to the unanimous conclusion that if the Mormon Chieftain *had* married a lady Doctor they had got hold of the wrong one.[10]

Angus Munn Cannon (1834–1915), about the time of his marriage to Martha Hughes, ca. 1885.

It seems clear that Mattie wanted to confide in her friend but feared Barbara's reaction, so she chose to present the fact of her marriage as a humorous rumor. Eventually, however, Mattie did write to Barbara about her marriage. Her extant letters highlight the great sacrifices that Latter-day Saints endured to practice their faith by engaging in polygamous relationships while the federal government actively prosecuted Church members who participated in such relationships. Mattie later wrote:

> The U.S. is *determined* to put down Polygamy, and the officials here are working like majors—or I suppose "beavers" would be more "appropos." I am having no peace, because I am considered a leading Mormon Woman. Barb you will hurt yourself laughing when I relate to you some of my experiences. . . .
>
> There are a number of cases that will shortly come up, where it is supposed that I have attended cases of confinement of Polygamous wives who are bearing children contrary to the Edmunds or Anti-Polygamy law.[11] Myself as

it is believed, being a staunch Mormon Doctor, it is naturally supposed that these polygamous families engage me. Hence I am considered an important witness, and if it can be proven that these children have actually come into the world, their fathers will be sent to jail for five (5) years. There is one case, that of Samuel B. Smith, which will come up on the 18 inst. and I am under two hundred dollars bonds to appear as the leading witness against him. After that is over with, I think I shall "skin out" for awhile before they Catch me on any others. By this time Barb you will think me a reprobate having so much to do with the courts, but this is the outcome of me being a Mormon, and living in a Mormon Community—but you will find me the *same* old Mattie.

Now dear by this time, you are tired of this strain. Please Keep this matter to yourself and simply state that I am coming on a visit, which really is the main object. Persons not understanding the circumstances, would be incapable of forming just opinions. To me it is a serious matter to be the cause of sending to jail a father upon whom a lot of little children are dependent, whether those children were begotten by the same or by different mothers, the fact remains they all have little mouths that *must be fed*.[12]

After giving birth to her first child, Elizabeth Rachel, on September 13, 1885, Mattie fled to Britain with her infant to escape federal officials. She could have remained in Utah Territory on "the underground,"[13] but she hoped that living abroad would give her more freedom. As she explained in a letter to her husband from England, she was intent "to breathe the Rocky Mountain air *freely* or not at all."[14]

Barbara also faced emotional turmoil during this period when her beloved fiancé passed away. After Mattie learned of his death, she wrote to console her friend and explicitly invoked divine providence and Mormon cosmology. First quoting a poem entitled "Whatever Is, Is Best"[15] by the popular American poet Ella Wheeler Wilcox, Mattie then quoted from Elder Parley P. Pratt's *Key to the Science of Theology*. She wrote:

> Of course *humanity* needs you. I truly believe that there is a great work for you yet to perform. As for your beloved "Emile," he died in his purity *let him rest*. Twill grieve him to witness your sorrow. Listen what is promised to those who die *pure* having kept their second estate here on Earth, having performed the work God assigned them. "A pure spirit free from sin & guile, enlightened in the school of heaven, by observation & experience, and association with the highest order of intelligences, and clothed with immortal freshness & beauty of eternal youth, alike free from pain, disease, death, and the corroding effects of time; looking back through the vista of far distant years and contemplating his former sojourn amid the sorrows & pains of mortal life, his passage through the dark valley of death, as we now contemplate a transient dream, or a night of sleep from which we have awakened, renewed and refreshed to engage again upon the realities of life.
>
> "Let us contemplate, for a moment, such a being, clothed in the finest robes of linen, pure & white adorned with precious stones & gold; a countenance radiant with the effulgence of light, intelligence & *love*; a bosom glowing with all the confidence of conscious innocence dwelling in palaces of precious stones and gold; bathing in the crystal waters of life; promenading or sitting 'neath the evergreen bowers and trees of Eden; inhaling the healthful breezes, perfumed with odors, wafted from the pinks and roses of Paradise, or assembled with the countless myriads of heaven's nobility, to join in songs of praise and adoration to the *Great Parent* of every good, to tune the immortal

lyre in strains celestial; or ~~to~~ move with grace immortal to the soul-inspiring measure of music flowing from a thousand instruments, blending, in harmonious numbers, with celestial voices, in heavenly song, or mingling in graceful circles, with joyous thousands immersed in the same spirit, and moving in unison and harmony of motion, as if one heart, one pulse, one thrill of heavenly melody inspired the whole."[16]

What more can I say for Emile? What more could you wish for him than to look upon him thus, and be happy? Banish sadness of heart, cherish pleasant memories of the departed *loved one*—and live so as to *meet him*. Think of the dead as gone to a brighter realm, and turn thy energies to the living & realities of life.[17]

Later Mattie wrote, reiterating:

> Of course humanity needs you, Satan knows this and will endeavor to give you the melancholy if possible, in order to thwart you, but *cheer up*. Emil is all right, just where God designs him, has some special work for him on the other side. He is far better off than on this little "span between the Eternities," the great past & future, where all is turmoil, "bubble bubble toil & trouble" with sprinklings of pleasure.[18]

By this time, Mattie had revealed to her friend that she was a polygamous wife, though she did not want that information made public. In fact, her letters are extant only because Barbara refused to follow her directions to "be *sure* you burn all my letters 'old chum' for I confide things to you that it would not do for *others* to see."[19] Elsewhere Mattie wrote:

> Be careful how you speak of my marriage as it is to be kept secret for three years, when it will be [illegible], and my

loved one out of jeopardy. You may state that I am married but do not mention to a ~~Polygamist~~ and that I am visiting Europe for my health.[20]

Mattie, suffering from poor health, was unable to practice medicine in Britain. She anxiously looked forward to returning home to her family, friends, and profession. She wrote to Barbara:

> I think when I go home I shall confine my work to office practice *only*, and engage in that branch known as "Gynecology" as the Diseases of women. In this way I would have control of and could regulate my time. Of course I won't make the means I once did, but money is not the goal I am striving for. I should like to prepare myself so as to give instructive lectures occasionally, but it will be some time before my head will permit the taxation of their preparation.[21]
>
> The persecution of our people still goes on and if I am ever blessed with strength & talent sufficient, I will give a series of lectures to aid those which this crusade has plunged in distress. Husbands are ruthlessly plunged into prison others are exiles, while their business goes to wreck and the families in consequence suffer. Dearest it will be like living again when I get home & can have you with me, & can be permitted to gaze on my loved ones once more.[22]

Among those whom Mattie sorely missed was her husband, and her romantic sentiments are an important window into polygamy as it was lived by many, including Angus and Mattie Cannon:

> Do you remember how proudly we used to quote, "Westward the Course of Empires Takes its Way, etc."[23] Our lives are intimately associated with its destiny. How proud, at school, were we of its rolling prairies and Rocky Mts. and how we used to think of its noble sons, and compare their manhood with the effeminacy of many of the eastern men.

> I have linked my fate with one that I love. One who seems all but perfection in my eyes, but I don't let him know it all. I think it well for a woman to keep a little reserve power in that line. And dearest I firmly believe there is a true Western Nobleman awaiting you somewhere when the right time comes.[24]

Mattie returned to Utah Territory in 1888 and started a new medical practice: "[I] have rented an office near Main Street and have a nice housekeeper. We keep house on a small scale, my little girl is with me, and she is such a jewel. I am building a neat little structure that will answer the purpose of office and residence when completed."[25] The realities of life were, however, altogether different from what she had imagined:

> My anticipations of happy associations with *loved* ones after my long exile were altogether overdrawn which is often the case with imaginative natures, and I find myself already simply *enduring* one of the veriest practical proxy of lives, which is the dryest *chaff* imaginable to a susceptible nature. Oh B look long and wisely before *you* chose a life *companion*, for tis deathly martyrdom to be linked to one who understands you not, and appreciates you less, their emphatic *verbal* statements to the contrary. A woman *knows & feels* when she is *appreciated*, without the interposition of mere *verbosity* this is to Keen witted woman but "a sounding brass & tinkling symbol." Dear B do not think me *absolutely blue*. No condition of life barring, the *poorest* of health could result that way with me. The reverses of love and fortune, I battle through *somehow*.[26]

The circumstances of living in polygamy in the 1880s appear to have altered Mattie's outlook on marriage. Giving advice to Barbara when she found a new suitor, Martha wrote:

Such natures as yours and mine Cannot exist without *love*, yet how hard to find our ideal—do we place our standard too high? I think not, in my own case at least. A man would not have to rank so far above the ordinary to satisfy me, if he only possessed that little key of sympathy that would answer ~~the~~ and call forth the corresponding congeniality in my nature. But to deal with, or have to face dignified(?) austereness, non-sympathetic "high-cock-a-lorum"[27] reserve—as much as to say in *all* things you must bend to *me*, Calls forth all the antagonism in my nature. Imagine the life I lead with such a *millstone*.[28]

Speaking of Barbara's impending nuptials, Mattie wrote:

'Tis one of the most important steps in life, and how few make it in the right direction. Few wed their affinities in this life. "What a pity" says H. Beecher Stowe, "to be truly mated only for *one* world (the next), when one, with the proper foreknowledge might be mated for *two* (this also)." "How many people (married)" says Beecher "who live in mere juxtaposition, without any mutual interpretation of soul. Simply as cattle might in the field."[29] But yours was all you could ask for as a lover. May the husband also meet your expectations. No reflexion on your ideal, whom I expect to respect as your honored husband,

> *But 'tis proverbial—man seldom proves*
> *As free from folly selfishness and guile,*
> *As is believed by woman, when she loves.*"[30]

After Barbara's marriage, Mattie wrote:

Now dear One, Friend of my girlhood days, let me wish you long long happiness in your wedded life. You are hardly initiated yet. 'Tis now nearly seven years since I launched forth on the great sea of matrimony, and I feel that I have not learned the a.b.c. of the great volume. Have scarcely culled from my sentimental nature, those romantic dreams, which are a "delusion and a snare" to young, or old wedded life, and the sooner they are rooted out and supplanted by the practical facts and conditions of the Mundane, the sooner we will attain those tranquil "shallows of contentment," far removed from those surging billows of life's ocean that cause us to "sound the heights and depths of human emotion."[31] 'Tis well to know what it is to *sound*, for to soar in the heights is to eat the Ambrosia of the God's, but we must learn to understand that such are but transient conditions, to want them to *always* last, is torment, for they *will not*. And the depths Oh may it be our fortune not to be there to often.[32]

Along with continuing her medical practice, Mattie Cannon campaigned for women's suffrage and became actively involved politically. Notably, of course, she was the first woman elected as a state senator in the United States, defeating her husband in the Utah state election of 1896. During her two terms in the state senate, she introduced several bills that continue to influence Utah health laws today, including providing for the first State Department of Health and establishing the State School for the Deaf, Dumb, and Blind. She was respected by her fellow legislators to such a degree that her name was suggested as a possible candidate for United States senator. The possibility of a woman senator in Washington, D.C., was so novel that it attracted attention in newspapers throughout the country.

Before that could occur, however, another widely publicized event eliminated that possibility and abruptly ended Mattie's political career: the birth of her third child, Gwendolyn Hughes Cannon, on April 17, 1899.[33] Gwendolyn's birth was proof to anti-Mormon activists that Mormons, despite the 1890 Manifesto, never meant to stop practicing polygamy. A flurry of newspaper articles appeared, Angus was fined, and Mattie and Gwendolyn fled to California.

Dr. Martha Hughes Cannon (front row, left) was the first female state senator in the United States. She served two terms in the Utah state legislature and made important improvements in public health. Elected on November 3, 1896, Martha, a Democrat, defeated her husband, a Republican, who ran for the same office. Two female clerks are also pictured, 1897.

Mattie thereafter immersed herself in her children and divided her time between Utah and California.

After her husband's death in 1915, Mattie moved permanently to California to be close to her children and to practice medicine, including volunteering to work with patients dealing with addiction. Mattie did not leave any formal declarations of faith written in her later life, and it appears that her family complied with her request that her diaries be burned after her death. But we have the declaration of her faith recorded in the actions of her life. And there is a resonance between Mattie's life with the sentiments she recorded as a twenty-year-old woman in the Young Ladies' Mutual Improvement Association of the Church:

> I have seen the power of God made manifest in my behalf, for which I feel to thank Him every day of my life. At times shadows cross our pathway while sojourning in this life; but they are directed for a wise purpose; it is at such times that I turn to my Father, with renewed strength, and strive to live closer unto Him, feeling determined to gain

some of those everlasting joys that are promised to the faithful, and which far surpass the pleasures of this world.[34]

In her later years, Mattie assisted her daughter Elizabeth Rachel with her children at Oasis Ranch, near Salt Lake City, and also lived with her second child, James, and his family, who had settled in Los Angeles. James's company, Cannon Electric, was well known because of his inventions and innovations. Eventually, James built a home for his mother, situated behind his own, in Los Angeles. Vivacious and beloved, Gwendolyn died of tuberculosis in 1928 at age twenty-nine. According to Elizabeth, when Gwendolyn died, part of Mattie died with her, as Mattie could not forgive herself for being unable to save the life of her own daughter.

Dr. Martha Hughes Cannon died on July 10, 1932, in Los Angeles, California. Beyond her legacy as the first woman to hold the office of state senator in the United States, she must also be remembered as an activist for the cause of women, a mother, a physician, and a devoted Latter-day Saint.

Chapter 3

"A Strong and Abiding Testimony"

Mary Elizabeth Woolley Chamberlain (1870–1953)
by Janelle M. Higbee

Mary Elizabeth Woolley was born January 31, 1870, in St. George, Utah, to Emma Geneva Bentley and Edwin Dilworth Woolley Jr. Mary, their second child, was named after both her grandmothers and called Mamie or Mame in her youth.[1] Characteristically active and high-spirited, Mary later wrote of herself, "I thoroughly enjoy life and see more beauty and grandeur in it every day that I live."[2]

Mary grew up in St. George and in the Kanab area of Kane County, Utah, where her father served for more than two decades as president of the Kanab Stake of The Church of Jesus Christ of Latter-day Saints. Throughout her life, she thrived on her involvement in social, civic, and Church affairs.

The following excerpts come from the life sketch that Mary Chamberlain wrote between 1934 and 1936 as a record for her sons and the rest of her posterity. "I have written the major part of this manuscript on my knees for a table in the quiet seclusion of the Kaibab Forest during my vacation there the last three summers," she explained. "Many of my strongest testimonies and choicest experiences are too sacred to commit to writing, hence do not appear here, but I do have a strong and abiding testimony of the Gospel of Jesus Christ and it grows stronger every day of my life. Without faith, life would not be worth living."[3]

Childhood in St. George

I was very plain and unattractive, with small "squinty" blue eyes, straight, coarse, dun-colored hair, with a "cowlick" so it never would part in the middle. Thus I started life handicapped from the beginning, but Mother would apologize for my looks by saying, "Well, she has a sunny disposition anyway," and for that one endowment I have been very grateful, as it has been a greater asset than looks possibly could be.[4]

One of my first teachers in Primary or Sunday School was Sister Lucy B. Young, wife of President [Brigham] Young and mother of Susa Young Gates. Among other things she taught us was that our Father in Heaven was real and tangible and that we should pray to him just like we would go to our earthly father and ask for whatever we wanted, but we must not feel badly if we did not get everything we prayed for, because it might not be for our good, so we should always say, "Father, if it is right, grant me this desire," or "Thy will be done." She explained the importance of partaking of the sacrament worthily. If we had done or said anything to injure another, it was our duty to go to them and make it right and ask their forgiveness and also to ask the Lord's forgiveness. If we would do this and then offer up a silent prayer as we partook of the emblems, asking for the Lord's spirit to be with us during the coming week, we would surely be blessed. Also that whenever we went to meeting, if we would offer up a silent prayer that something might be said for our particular benefit, we would never go away disappointed no matter how humble or unlearned the speaker might be. These and many other teachings I remember and bear testimony that insofar as I have lived up to them and put them into practice in my life, I have received the blessings and I advise all my posterity who may read this to try it for themselves and they will surely receive a blessing.

I don't remember paying tithing in my very early childhood, but we were taught to save every cent we got and donate it to the St. George Temple which was being built at that time. . . .

After the St. George Temple was finished, we began the same thing for the one at Manti, so "Saving" was my middle name, and I have carried it all through my life. Through its practice, I have been able to meet many emergencies, take advantage of many opportunities, and accomplish many things that would have been impossible without a few dollars held in reserve.[5] . . . Before we left St. George, I received my [temple] endowments, although only twelve years old. I was large and quite mature, etc.[6]

Youth in Kanab

In the autumn of 1889, Father sold his interests in Upper Kanab Ranch . . . and moved Mother and her family to Lower Kanab[7] as his stake duties required him to be there most of the time, and the children were growing and needed better schools than the ranch afforded. Also, more social advantages were possible in Lower Kanab. . . .[8]

There was no hotel in the town and we were about the only ones who had a spare room, and it was usually occupied. We never knew what it was to eat a meal alone, and the best of everything was always served for company.

We entertained all the General Authorities of the Church, including the representatives of the auxillary organizations who visited our stake conference for twenty-six years, and even longer than that.

Also, lords and noblemen from England, senators, congressmen, governors, Colonel Cody (Buffalo Bill) and party, railroad officials, drummers, post office inspectors, the exploring expedition of Benjamin F. Cluff and party to South America, of which my brother Royal was a member. They stayed sometime and fitted out from there. We also hosted cattle buyers, sheep and wool contractors, land commissioners and surveyors, artists, sectarian ministers, and novelists, including Zane Grey and others.

Very little remunerations were received. . . . But I feel that we were well paid with the opportunity of contacting such characters, which was an education in itself, and a privilege that few others have enjoyed. . . .

Being the ["]President's daughters" was not as easy nor as pleasant as some may think, for everything we did and said was watched and criticized, not constructively either, at time[s].

If the "Woolley girls" did anything, it gave all others a license to do the same, so that we had to be constantly on our guard, and while we never did pose as being superior in any way, we were expected to be an example. . . . Let one of us side-step the least bit and the whole town knew about it. . . .

When bloomers and divided skirts came in style, I was the first to don them in riding horseback and was criticized severely for being so unwomanly.

Old Brother Charles Cram appeared before the stake presidency at one of their council meetings with a complaint that "Mamie" Woolley had disgraced the town. They all gasped and wondered what ever was coming, and when told to proceed, he said, "Well, Sir, she rode down the streets of Kanab, Sir, straddle of a hoss, looking like a spread eagle, Sir!!" They all gave a sigh of relief, and a hearty laugh, and told him he had just woke from a Rip Van Winkle sleep.[9]

Latter-day Saints' College, Salt Lake City

In the fall of 1890 I went to Salt Lake City to attend the Latter-day Saints' College. . . . At the commencement exercises in June 1891, I was on the program to represent the lady students, and the following is my very feeble effort:

Board of Education, Faculty, Fellow Students, and Friends:

As has been said, we have met to end, in a formal way, our studies for the year. We trust, however, that they will not end indeed, but that we will continue to progress day by day, learning to value truth from whatever source it may come, or in whatever guise.

Woman's mission, though in a different sphere to man's, is nonetheless great. The influence which she wields is felt the world over, and it has been truly said: "The hand that rocks the cradle rules the world." . . .

The young ladies of this Institution stand on an equal plane with the young men and receive from them the respect which equals demand.

Sex with us is no distinction, if there is anything to be performed and a lady is capable, the fact of her being "fair" does not deter her.

Her opinion is expressed and sanctioned, her testimony borne and sustained the same as that of her brethren. She never feels that her efforts are depreciated, but that she is upheld and sustained by all around her.

> There exists between us, as a band of sisters, a feeling of deepest love and friendship which is manifest in our actions, and also by our faith and prayers.[10]

After graduating from college in Salt Lake City, Mary moved back to Kanab and worked as a clerk in the mercantile store, handling "everything from mowing machines to needles and pins," and working twelve or fourteen hours daily at a salary of thirty dollars per month.[11]

First Female County Clerk in Utah, 1896

A single woman of twenty-six, Mary was elected the first female county clerk in Utah. She wrote:

> In the fall of 1896, . . . [the] sewing for the family well under way, the canning, pickling and preserving for winter out of sight, my next venture was politics. Utah had just been admitted into the Union,[12] the first election under statehood was approaching; Democrats and Republicans alike were anxious for the honor of electing the first state officers. The precinct primaries and county conventions of each party were duly held. I was nominated on the Republican ticket for county clerk of Kane County. . . . Women had never held office in Utah and the propriety of her doing so was a moot question which was thoroughly "mooted," I assure you. The parties waged a vigorous campaign, and the last week before election, Henry E. Bowman, who was on the same ticket for county treasurer, Joe Robinson, the present deputy county clerk, my cousin Louie Woolley, and I, formed a quartette, and toured the county, holding rallies in every town. We had a book of current campaign songs, many of which we localized to fit our needs and all of which we sang with great gusto. . . . The halls were packed to the doors every night, some following us from town to town, as they said we were

staging the best show they had seen for a long time, and enthusiasm ran high.

I wish now that I had a copy of some of the speeches I made on the trip, but they were never written, being only spontaneous outbursts of my enthusiasm regarding woman suffrage and her right to stand shoulder to shoulder with man in public as well as private life, etc.

Election day finally came November 3, 1896, and excitement was rife, both parties working hard to secure votes, and each feeling sure of success. They literally carried people to the polls, the halt, the lame, the blind, none were overlooked.

That night while waiting for the election returns, a grand ball was held which lasted until nearly morning, before the last precinct was heard from. When reports were all in it proved that the county, state, and the nation had gone Republican, and I was elected on the ticket, headed by William McKinley for President of the United States, and I was the first lady county clerk in the State of Utah.... It was a valuable experience for me, which I appreciate, and have always considered profitable. The knowledge acquired during those two years has been a benefit to me in many, many ways throughout my life. It broadened my acquaintance with people, especially men, and taught me how to meet and deal with them, which I have had to do all my life.[13]

Courtship and Marriage

Mary Woolley married Thomas Chamberlain, the last of his six wives, in August 1900, ten years after Wilford Woodruff's Manifesto. Because plural marriage was illegal in the United States, they were married in Mexico and lived apart for most of their marriage.[14] To avoid detection and consequent persecution as a plural wife, Mary used the name "Mrs. Thomas" in 1901 and changed her pseudonym to "Howard" in 1904, meanwhile frequently moving between various Utah towns, with a brief stay in the Mormon colonies of Mexico. Mary recorded:

> During the winter of 1896–97 Brother Thomas Chamberlain of Orderville[15] purchased H. E. Bowman's interest in the Bowman and Company store in Kanab, and became the manager....
>
> I continued to clerk in the store, under his management. He was county treasurer, and I was county clerk; he was Father's counselor [in the stake presidency], and I their private secretary; he was stake tithing clerk, and I copied all the reports for him, so that we were thrown very much together, almost day and night at times, but everything was on a strictly business basis, so far as I was concerned at least, although there was an undercurrent flowing through it all of which I was totally oblivious.
>
> When, months later, he proposed marriage to me, it came like thunder from a clear sky, and was such a shock that I resented it very emphatically. I had never dreamed of such a thing! He already had several wives and a large family, of which any man might well be proud, and I thought he should be satisfied. I was not aware that he had declared when a very young man that he was going to have six wives and sixty children. And he had not reached the quota yet....
>
> The fact that he was a married man did not deter me in the least, as I had always been taught that plural marriage was a divine principle of our religion and I had been raised in it, so it was almost second nature to me....
>
> The following lines which I wrote during the "raid" of the eighties and nineties expressed my sentiments in a crude way, and while they would be considered treason today, and I would not think of giving such advice under present

Mary with her sons, Royal and Dee, ca. 1907.

conditions, as the whole order of things has changed, and we are no longer allowed to practice nor to teach the principle. I fully sustain the present leaders of the Church in regard to this question and advise all others to do so.

I simply copy these lines, which I find among my relics of the past, to show our thoughts and feelings of those days. . . .

> *Have courage, my girls, to say yes,*
> *Have courage, my girls, to say yes,*
> *If an Elder that's true, should come wooing to you,*
> *Have courage, my girls to say yes.* . . .

In spite of such sentiments in my heart, and the fact that I had always imagined myself as a plural wife, I was as cold and unyielding as steel to the proposal made to me, and resented every advance. He had already secured Father's and Mother's consent, which I considered very presumptuous, but he explained that he knew he would have a hard time to win me, and he did not want to make the struggle and then meet with opposition from them, so he paved the way beforehand. . . .

I made it a matter of earnest and humble prayer for days, and for weeks, asking the Lord to direct me and help me to know what to do. Finally one night before I left the store, I told him [Thomas] that if he would get the consent of each and every one of his five wives, I would at least consider his suit. His only reply was, "The Lord be praised!" . . .

Right here I want to pay a tribute of love and appreciation to those wives, than whom a better set of women never lived.[16] If they ever had any ill feeling or jealousy toward me, it was locked in their own hearts, and never came to the surface, for they have always treated me with the greatest love and respect. I love them as dearly as my own sisters, and there is nothing I would not do to help them if I could. While I had more advantages, social and educational, I have never felt myself superior to them in any way, but have learned many valuable lessons, and received inspiration from their lives. God bless them all! . . .

Ever since I had consented to accept his proposal we agreed to fast every Sunday and pray earnestly that if it were right for us to marry, the way would be opened up for the same. . . . The practice continued for three years before our prayers were finally answered.

The Manifesto had been issued several years previous to this time, in which President Woodruff advised the people not to contract any marriage contrary to the law of the land. There was no law against plural marriage in Mexico, however, and under certain conditions, and circumstances, marriages were still being performed there. So, in July 1900, he decided to make a trip down there to investigate and see if it were at all possible. Enroute he met President George Q. Cannon. . . . When he made known his errand, President Cannon told him what was necessary and just how to proceed, etc. He wrote for me to join him at once, which I did. . . . We were married August 6, 1900. The trip consumed a month, then we returned home (not together, however), and I resumed my work in the store as usual, and continued until July 1901, when it became necessary for me to quit work and seek seclusion.[17]

"Underground" Days

During the six and one-half years that I was away from home and my loved ones at this time, I corresponded with them regularly, never letting a week pass by that I did not write a letter to them, and they to me. . . .

It was a great trial to me to be separated from my husband and all my loved ones, and to drop completely out of sight with nothing at all to do; when all my life I had been so busy and so active in everything that went on around me, or took place in the community. Always working and planning for improvements, both public and private. No one who has not passed through such a sudden change can ever imagine what it meant to me and how I suffered! But I took the step which placed me thus deliberately and willingly, feeling that I was directed aright. Although I knew many and severe trials lay in my path, and that it would require unbounded courage and fortitude to fight my way through, I determined to make the best of whatever came my way (and plenty came). But I don't think anyone ever heard one word of complaint from my lips, nor an expression of regret for the step I had taken. I never have regretted it for one moment, but have ever been proud and thankful to be the wife of such a noble man.[18]

Mary and Thomas Chamberlain had two sons, Royal and Dee,[19] but Mary and her sons did not publicly use the name Chamberlain until 1916.[20]

Mary Elizabeth Woolley Chamberlain (1870–1953)

First Woman Mayor of an All-Woman Town Council

In 1911 Mary was elected chairman of the first all-female town council in the United States; that town council, in Kanab, served for two years. Even while she was mayor of Kanab, Mary proudly noted that she did "all [her] own house work" and was employed as "clerk in the store part of the time," while concurrently serving in Church callings as "local Supt. of Religion Class, Teacher of the 2nd Int[ermediate] Dept. in S[unday] S[chool], and Treasurer of Relief Society."[21] Mary wrote:

> In November 1911 I was elected president of the town board of Kanab, Utah, which office I held for two years, being the first woman in the United States, or even in the world to hold that office.[22]
>
> The entire board was composed of women, and a great deal was said and written about us at the time. . . .[23] I was elected under the name of Mary W. Howard, as I still went by that assumed name.
>
> Our election was intended as a joke and no one thought seriously of it at the time. When election day dawned, there was no ticket in the field; no one seemed interested in the supervision of the town, so the loafers on the ditchbank (of which there were always plenty) proceeded to make up the above ticket as a burlesque, but there was no other ticket in opposition, so, of course, we were elected. When Father came and told me about it, I was disgusted and said I would not think of qualifying and I knew others would not even if I did, etc., but he insisted that we take it seriously and put the job over as he knew we could, and he would give us all the support and backing possible. Brother Chamberlain also encouraged us and would not listen to our backing out. D. D. Rust, editor of the local paper, gave us a big write-up which was full of confidence in our ability, etc. So, after due

The Kanab all-woman town council served from 1911 to 1913. Left to right: Luella McAllister, treasurer; Blanche Hamblin, councilor; Mary W. Howard (Chamberlain), mayor; Tamar Hamblin, clerk; Ada Seegmiller, councilor.

consideration and much debating, we decided to tackle the job and see what we could do.

As soon as our election was published, we were besieged with letters from all over the country wanting to know all about it, how we managed, what we were doing, etc. and etc.

Sister Susa Young Gates visited Kanab while we were in office and was very enthusiastic over our work. Women's Suffrage was one of her many hobbies and she was delighted with what she saw and heard while here. She was then writing a book on what Utah women had accomplished and insisted that I write her all the details of our work, setting down the plain facts as best I could and then she would weave them into a story of her own. So, at the first opportunity, October 19, 1913, I proceeded to do so. When the letter reached Salt Lake City, she happened to be away from home in the East, and it fell into the hands of the editor of the *Improvement Era*, who published it verbatim in the July 1914 *Era*.[24] Imagine my surprise and embarrassment when

I saw what had been done, as I never dreamed of having the letter itself published. . . .

Aunt Susa always called me "Mayor" and shouted it out wherever she met me, on the street, in meeting, at the temple, or elsewhere, much to my embarrassment at times, but she took great delight in it.[25]

"Light and Love along the Pathway of Life"

After Mary's husband died in 1918, she supported herself in part by selling homemade baked goods to travelers.[26] In 1923, she accepted a position as a traveling sales representative and worked for ten years selling a line of ladies' silk knitwear throughout Utah, Arizona, Idaho, and Wyoming.[27] She continued to be active in Church callings and in the Daughters of Utah Pioneers organization while living in Provo and Salt Lake City.

Mary Woolley Chamberlain stayed active and alert until her death at age eighty-four. She died August 20, 1953, while visiting her granddaughter in Pocatello, Idaho.[28] Newspaper obituaries paid tribute to her domestic and her political achievements.[29]

> I hope that my influence will always be felt for good and never for ill among those with whom I associate, for my desire and constant prayer is that I may shed light and love along my pathway of life, and that I may be an inspiration to others as many of my friends are to me. I thoroughly enjoy life and see more beauty and grandeur in it every day that I live. The opportunities for advancement, self-improvement, and service are endless, and time is all too short for one to take advantage of those things which lie immediately in our path.
>
> I want to live just as long as I can be of service in the world, but my constant prayer is that I may never live to be a burden to anyone. I would much rather be called hence

before I am quite ready than to be left like "the Last Leaf"[30] upon the tree.

I have often remarked that I want to die while someone will shed tears at my funeral, and not hang on until they say, "What a blessing she has gone!"[31]

Chapter 4

"Sow Seeds of Faith"

RUTH MAY FOX (1853–1958)
by Brittany A. Chapman

Ruth May was born during a time of religious excitement in Westbury, Wiltshire, England, on November 16, 1853. Her parents, James and Mary Ann Harding May, joined The Church of Jesus Christ of Latter-day Saints five months after her birth. Left motherless at sixteen months of age, Ruth was cared for by relatives and Church members until she was eight years old, at which time she went to live with her father in Yorkshire. There they boarded with her future stepmother, Mary Ann Thompson Saxton, and stepsister, Clara, who was nearly Ruth's age.

In 1865 Ruth migrated to the United States with Mary Ann and Clara, her father having migrated several months earlier to secure work. He met them at the dock, and he and Mary Ann were married almost immediately. Eleven-year-old Ruth worked in a Philadelphia cotton mill and later as a dressmaker's apprentice to help the family earn money for their trek west. In 1867 the Mays joined the Leonard G. Rice wagon company and headed to Utah.

"At last the long journey was ended," Ruth recalled. "We had pulled up the hill out of Parley's Canyon just as twilight shrouded the valley. We could still catch a glimpse of the city below, but I confessed to some disappointment as I asked, 'Did we come all this way for that?' This, however, was my first and last disappointment."[1]

The family settled in Salt Lake City, the place Ruth would call home for the remainder of her life. She continued to work in textile mills until her marriage, acquiring formal education where she could and cultivating her active mind through literature. On May 8, 1873, in the Endowment House in Salt Lake, Ruth married Jesse Williams Fox Jr., the man she called "my companion in sorrow, my partner in joy."[2] They had twelve children over the course of twenty-three years.[3] In 1888, Jesse married a second wife, Rosemary Johnson. Although Ruth wrote very little about the event, her "convictions in the soundness of the principle" enabled her to "suppress every urge to jealousy,"[4] and Ruth's daughter described the two wives as "real friends."[5] Jesse made his primary residence with Ruth throughout most of their married life.[6]

Ruth was actively engaged with her family and church, but it was not until middle age that she awakened to her ability to contribute to an even wider sphere of influence. She stepped into public life in 1891 when she joined the Utah Woman's Press Club. "My willingness to work was soon discovered," she recalled, and that willingness opened opportunities for leadership in the women's club movement, the suffrage cause, political campaigns, moral reform, and other state and national organizations in which she became heavily involved.[7] Ruth celebrated womanhood and believed her roles as wife and mother were her most exalted positions. At the same time, she called for social progress, championing the enlargement of woman's sphere to include the public realm, challenging women to view themselves as citizens equal to men and with an equal voice.

Ruth devoted nearly forty years "full of rich experiences" in service to the youth of the Church.[8] She was called as a member of the Young Ladies' Mutual Improvement Association general board in

1898. She served as first counselor in the YLMIA presidency from 1905 until 1929 when, at age seventy-five, she became the third YLMIA general president.

In 1930, the Church celebrated its centennial year. To commemorate the event, Ruth May Fox wrote a rousing anthem, entitled "Carry On," for the young men and women to sing. The hymn became so popular in her lifetime that, after celebrating her own centennial, she observed, "Today I seem to be better known as the author of Carry On than for all other of my other achievements of one hundred years."[9]

As a general leader of the YLMIA, Ruth's primary responsibilities were to teach, minister, and preach to young women and their leaders in local wards and stakes. Visiting the young women of Zion, particularly in the nineteenth and early twentieth centuries, was an act of consecration on account of dirty, uncomfortable, and time-consuming travel conditions. Despite this, Ruth visited "most, if not all, of the stakes of Zion," also traveling overseas, first to Hawaii and then to Europe.[10]

A Tour of the Hawaiian Islands

"A most wonderful assignment came to me in August, 1936," Ruth wrote in her autobiography, "when I visited the Hawaiian Islands."[11] As presidents of the Young Women's[12] and Young Men's Mutual Improvement Associations, respectively, Ruth May Fox and Albert E. Bowen made "the first official visit in the history of the Church of an auxiliary head to a regularly scheduled conference of an organized stake outside the confines of continental America."[13] Ruth was eighty-two years old.

In Hawaii, she took her first airplane ride. There she continued to keep notes of her travels that exemplify her role as a leader of Mormon women, document issues in Church organization and administration, and give insight into the culture, people, and places she came to love during her sixteen-day sojourn in the Hawaiian

Ruth May Fox called her visit to the Hawaiian Islands in 1936 "the trip of my life."

Islands.[14] Her travel notes, written on seven loose leaves of paper, read as follows:

> *"My Hawaiian Trip," August 5 to September 3, 1936*
>
> Left Salt Lake Aug. 5, 1936. Arrived in Los Angeles next morning where Lester and Beryl met me with others of the family.[15] Staid all night at Lester's.
>
> Sailed on the 7th on the boat Malolo. Arrived at the Island of Oahu Thursday 13th at 8.30 a.m. I was well all the way enjoyed the voyage very much. Saw 1 unusual sunset.
>
> The Pres. of the [Oahu] Stake Pres. Ralph Woolly and many others were at the boat to meet us. 10 ~~lie~~ leis were put arround my neck. Reporters and camera men were there at the dock. My picture was taken but not used ~~so~~ I guess it

would not have done credit to the paper. ~~Pres. Woolly called a meeting of leaders to discuss M I A matters. Was somewhat discouraged at what I heard.~~ Sister Fred Lunt was at the wharf to take me to their lovely new home overlooking land and sea, the view taking in the Punch bowl and harbor. ~~Fri 14~~ We, Bro. and Sister Bowen were invited to Pres. Woolley's home. Sister Hyde was there just as happy and gay as any one.

We went out on the large veranda and soon about 12 young women were serenading us. They were invited in and continued singing. By and bye we heard male voices serenading. They also were invited in. They had several musical instruments with them so they all sang and danced their native songs and danced for 2 or 3 hours. They never get tired of those things no program was necessary it was all done spontaneously. No refreshments were served—which pleased me.

As we travelled to Bro. Woolly's we rode past a school surrounded by a wall and for a distance of one of our City blocks, or more running along the top and hanging down was hundreds of night blooming cerius. I considered myself very fortunate that I came in the Season of their blooming.

Fri 14 Was invited to a luncheon given by Sister Mary Tyler at the Lunchroom managed by the Salvation Army. A lovely garden and there too we went into a comfortable cabin built native style where Robert Louis Stevensen did a lot of his writing.

There were present 2 Relief Society members, 2 Primary Mem. and 3 M I A. officers. In the evening I had a lovely ride thro the bussiness section and a visit to a magnificent, spacious Hotel—the Royal Hawaiian ~~Hotel~~ with Bro. and Sister Lunt. ~~Pres Woolly Sat 15 Called a meeting of Leader to discount M I A work.~~

Sat 15. Bro Lunt took me down town to Luncheon his wife having an appointment. I had been invited to the Relief Society officer's meeting, but received word not to go—I don't know why. A long officers meeting with Pres Woolley on M.I A work in the evening. Visited great pine-apple Canning Factory, but could not get in. Sat eve. Meeting and social went on as much as usual notwithstanding Sister [Jeanette] Hyde's sudden death in the Relief Society meeting in the afternoon.[16] Pres. Woolly wished it so, as many visitors knew nothing of her death.

Sunday 16—Program brot forward 1 hr. so that we might all attend Relief Society Conference. Pres. and Counselor spoke very nicely. Pres. Woolly requested a sister to ask me to give the topic that Sister Hyde was to have given. 75 or more in the Choir ~~75 or more~~ sang the Temple [in Hawaii].[17] We truly had a wonderful con. There has never been a better Sunday evening meeting held in the church. Of course Sister [Emma Lucy Gates] Bowen sang,[18] but even without her the program was splendid—500 present in morning meeting and that many in evening, with out young children. Had dinner with Pres. and Sister Bailey[19] after 4:o clock also a ride to what is known as the Pola a scene no one can describe.

Mon 17. Sister Bailey took me down town to do a little shopping. We also went thro the Pine apple Canning Factory

Tue. 18 Sister Kapu 2nd c[ounselor] gave an Hawaiian dinner very sumptuous and very rich—Poi and everything, at 7 PM. In the afternoon went shopping, a ride and Luncheon at The Tavern on the Beach—my treat.

Wed 19 Bro. and Sister Bailey took us to Laie to see the temple almost 40 miles away. Another Hawaiian Feast. The table adorned with ferns and the petels of the marigold. Roast pig, cooked in the ground—Fish, Chicken, Poi,

Pine apple, Cake etc. etc. We then held meetings. Afterward I came back to Sister Lunt's. was given a fan and lei The Bowens staid all night Saw a water Buffalo going over. About 10 B[ee] H[ive] girls sang. 3 of my songs were sing. A sister gave me a fan and another a green and gold lei[20]

Thur. 20. Our Pres. called for me and took me to the home of her 2nd C. where we all prayed for the success of the work. This at the request of the President. Afterwards to my surprise The Councillors took of my dress and put on a holoku which I was to wear that afternoon at a mother and daughter party that afternoon to be given at Sister Bailey's. Singing, dancing, greetings and responses were given. As I often do, I wrote some verses—strictly religious, which I thot would please them. A long meeting for discussion of M.I.A. Program called was by Pres Woolley in the evening.

Fri 21. Got up at 6 a.m. Took Plane for Hilo.[21] Made one landing at Lania [Lanai] Another Island arrived 11. A.M. Met by Bro Hixon went to Missionary home. Ate at Honokaa, drove to edge of Waipio Valley drove thro Parker's Ranch to Waimea ate at resturant returned rested a little while at Sister Lindsays. Held meeting at Waimia M.I.A. meeting 6.30. Gen[era]l meeting 730. Staid at Arthur Lindsays all night. Returned to Hilo in the morning drove to Crater House for lunch saw sights. 3 miles around 1 crater walked thro the Lava tube, saw water-falls etc etc , saw Wonderful Palms and the Devils throat.

Returned to Hilo ate Relief S. dinner at Mission home, Sister Able Abel Mattoon responsible. Held meeting at 22 Hilo Saturday evening meeting not well attended—too many other attractions.

Staid all night at Hotel. Attended Sunday school sunday School. Class work, method, Seperation.

Sun. 23 Took boat at 4 P.M. Arriving at midnight in Kahului on Maui Island. Brother Cockilt, the County treasurer, met us and took us to his home gave us a glass of chocolate and a sandwich and we rested not more than 2 hrs.

24 At 3. a.m., now Monday morning, we got up and drove 30 miles to a height of 10000 feet to see the sunrise. It was a wonderful sight, but not what some of the party expected. We were favored by seeing a beautiful white rainbow and round rainbow or a halo which if one looked carefully at it he might see himself framed in an Halo, a wave of the hand might be mirrored. Returning we had breakfast at the Cockell's and undressed and went to bed for 3 or 4 hrs However On the way back we stopped at the very fine monument erected in 1851 in honor of the org. of the first Branch of the ch[urch] in that land by Pres Geo. Q. Cannon. There is a small meeting house close by, also the tree where Bro. Hugh J. Cannon received a manifestation when on his wourld tour with Pres. David McKay.[22] In the afternoon we visited Sam Alo—County Auditor, a beautiful home and a delicious dinner, a ride into a lovely canyon. Held a fine meeting then took a small boat, comparatively, at 9. PM. Were adorned with Leis and many farewells. This happened at Wailuku.

Tue. 25 Arrived at the Island Oahu at 6 a.m. Met again at the boat with friends and leis. Slept awhile then went down town to lunch with Sister Lunt a little—more shopping Met with B[ee] H[ive] officers in the evening at the mission home

26 Wed. eve Met 18 interested in Gl[eaners][23] members who will likely be made officers and gen. work at Sister Lunts and it rained in the afternoon Then Went with [illegible] and staid all night and until 3 P.M. Thur. she gave me a hkd. napkin ring and necklace

> 27 Thurs. evening a Chop suey supper at a fine Chinese restaurant on the Beach. Then to Bro. McBride's Collection of relics Sister [Maud] Mae Babcock[24] was with us.
>
> Fri 28. Went down town with sister Lunt. In the evening a party was given for us by the Mutual people. Dancing—native and song as usual refreshments. Br. Packer and wife gave me a [illegible] lei.
>
> Sat 29. Aug. Left for home Aloha and laeis golore Sister Mary Gave me a beautiful shell Lei., at the harbor next day
>
> 29 Sat left at 12. noon for home Alohas and Leis at boat. Monday a fire drill The sea quite rough for 2 days. picture shows.
>
> Sept 3d Landed about 9 am after a very pleasant Journey. Beryl Ed. Katharan[25] and children met me.

Ruth made notes on the back of her record, perhaps jotted down while she was in MIA leaders' meetings: "May Our Junior girls[26] continue to come; . . . Officers do not appreciate posittions and resign; Bishops new would help if fare was paid; Meetings disorderly."

A European Tour

"In 1937," Ruth wrote, "I had the great pleasure of returning to my native England for . . . a European tour to include the celebration of the centenary of the British Mission." "My participation in this historic conference in England was in many respects the crowning event in my long life of Church service."[27] She recorded:

> The trip to Europe was almost thrown at my feet. It was so unexpected and so wonderful that the memory of it will be a romantic vision all my days. My daughter Vida was taking a tour of about sixty people to Europe, the occasion being the great Latterday Saint [Centennial] Conference at Rochdale, England. . . . Eight countries were visited. France, Italy, Switzerland, Germany, Belgium, Holland, England

and Scotland. Last but not least the homes of my childhood—one in Bradford-on-Avon, Wiltshire and one in Rowden, Yorkshire. I found these homes almost exactly as I left them more than seventy-five years ago.[28]

Although she was not traveling on official Church business, "it was inevitable," she said, "that I should be recognized in all Church activities as the General President of the Y.W.M.I.A.," and she was asked "to speak at several meetings of the Saints."[29] By this time Ruth was nearly eighty-four years old. In a shaky hand, she kept a journal of her travels, including her experience at the centennial celebration of the British Mission.

"Travels" Diary

1937

June 14 The M.I.A conferins that ended yestreday was one of the most successful both for Program and numbers ever held[.] yestreday—Sunday The afternoon meeting in the Tab. was packed, I think there were more young people at the Con. than ever before. A genl. reception and usual Banquets were held.[30] . . .

June 15 on the way to chicago First lap toward Europe quite well. . . .

17) Ship sailed 2 P.M yestreday—'The Empress of Australia' Got settled slept well Cold this morning Vida on the jump every min. My good children sent telegram and lovely Corsage. . . .

22 The sun is going down at 9. P M No mortal can describe the beauty of sea and sky. . . .

On June 23, Ruth arrived in Paris and kept a faithful record of her travels through Europe. She arrived in her native England on July 21.

July 21 Rainy, London. . . .

24. have been out hunting trinkets Bot some Aft. staid in hotel 6 P M. went to a dinner Given by Bro. and Sister [Richard R.] Lyman in honor of Pres [Heber J.] Grant Nearly 40 people there including Am[erican] Ambassador altho he did not stay to dinner. . . .

Wooded land rivers Suny slopes and shady woodlands out peaks and rivers fair Tunnels dark and Fertile lowlands Spacious fields and blooming gar[d]en . . . lovely hamlets dome, and . . . Palaces of Kings and Emperors. . . .

July 25 [Illegible] 2 Chapels dedicated by Pres Grant 1 in No. London 1 in South London Attended both meetings houses packed. some came 70 miles. After meeting Pres. Jos J Cannon and wife invited us to their home for refreshments

Mon 26 Yestreday Went to Bradford on Avon A quaint old town founded by the saxons. Found every thing I wanted to see Mr. [W. H.] Watkins who now owns the Belcombe estate showed us all arround his beautiful grounds and a part of the mansion which was furnished as it now stands 200 years ago. The leaden lady that I used to look thro the fancy fence to see is on those grounds The gardener offered to take a picture for us of it

On our way back to London stopped at Westbury, where I was born and rode arround the town which is quite modern—The old Buildings are being replaced by new ones. The hillside shows a white horse which has been mad[e] by cutting away the turf I[t] was there when I lived Bradford.

Returned to London 27th

July 28 London In hotel all morning aft. Vida and I went shoping I bot a fur neck piece found express checks difficult to cash.

July 29 Went to ~~Preston~~ Nelson Lancashire and found Jane Perry and family they were all glad to see us and made us very welcome about 6. P.M Went out with a great many others to see the Duke of Gloster ride by. staid all night made plans to come back from Scotland on the 10th and visit Mary Johnson's relatives

July 30 Preston Left Nelson—for Preston. Mrs Park, Miles Perry Daughter, went with us ~~Did~~ visit Cock pit and the Hall where the Rev. Mr. Fielding. Meeting on the Ribble River where 1st Baptisms were performed. could not find accomodation for the night so went to Manchester with Luty G. Cannon my [YWMIA] Counselor and staid all night at Midland Hotel at Pres. Grant's Expense 5 missionaries with us on same terms

Sat 31 meetings morning and aft. Aft a M.I.A. meeting chorus by Gl[eaner] Girls fine speeches from about 6 Y. Men. Tea and speeches at Pioneer Hall to which Vida and I were late So missed toasts—one given to me to which Luty responded Gl. girls gave me Carnations In the evening a very splendid pageant put on in the Town Hall—hundreds turned away.

Aug 1 Aug 2 37 Rochedale Sat. morning was in the main a.m. M.I.A. meeting I spoke there and also at the River[31] at the meeting in the morning Pres Grant asked that the Congregation sing 'Carry On' One young man told me he never sings that song without having a choking feeling in his throat. My son Jesse M. had said the same thing.

Sunday. yestreday. morning Sunday School featured Bro George Pyper was there I was one of the speakers.

Aft. Pres. Clark and Grant the speakers. The Town Hall, a very beautiful building had been hired and Pres Grant had been well advertized a great streamer being placed on the front of the building There was seating capacity for 900 but hundreds were turned away. that was true of the pageant which was put on saturday evening. This was shortened and

Celebrating the centennial of the Church in England, Ruth May Fox stood at the edge of the River Ribble in Preston and "gave such an eloquent and stirring address that it thrilled the souls and touched the hearts of all . . . and brought tears to the eyes of many." Left to right: Ruth May Fox, unidentified, J. Reuben Clark Jr., and Heber J. Grant.

put on again Sunday night for those who had not seen it but still all could not get in.

9 a.m. Sunday was given over for testimony The Large hall was crowded and 5 or 6 people would rise at once

It was a splendid spritual Conference I was given full recognition Pres. Grant spoke well and sang quite well. It was a great time for the saints. . . . Gifts were freely given to many of us. A lovely silk British Flag to myself which I appreciate very much as I did my visit at this time. Carry On was sung several times once at Pres Grant's suggestion.

Ruth returned home at the end of August.[32]

"As my 84th birthday approached," wrote Ruth, "I gave serious thought to the termination of my service in the M.I.A. It seemed hardly appropriate for a woman in her eighties to be head of an organization emphasizing the word 'young' in its title."

After years of fruitful service and careful reflection, she composed a letter to Church president Heber J. Grant on October 20, 1937, stating in part, "In a short time I shall reach my 84th birthday . . . causing much comment, I am sure, among the young women of the Church as they connect my age with my position. . . . While I am not asking for release, I shall hold myself in readiness to withdraw whenever you think it advisable."[33]

Eight days later, she was released as general president of the YWMIA. In her last meeting with the general board, closing nearly forty years of service, Ruth said she had "done Church work all her life and had known nothing else and that the Lord had sustained her and been so good to her. It is a wonderful thing, she said, to have the privilege to sow seeds of faith in the hearts of the young people, which she had prayed and hoped all her life might be the case."[34]

Ruth May Fox's journey was lit by a religious conviction that fueled the actions of her entire life. Long years of experience taught her, "We can do anything we think we can."[35] The fruits of faith taught her, "God asks nothing of us that we cannot accomplish. He opens the way for every command."[36] She wrote: "Ever since I could understand, the Gospel has meant everything to me. It has been my very breath, my mantle of protection against temptation, my consolation in sorrow, my joy and glory throughout all my days and my hope of eternal life. 'The Kingdom of God or nothing' has been my motto."[37]

After decades of public and Church service, devotion to her large posterity, and consecration to the gospel truths she embraced, Ruth May Fox passed away in Salt Lake City, Utah, on April 12, 1958, at the age of 104.

Chapter 5

"THANK GOD THAT I HAVE BEEN COUNTED WORTHY"

SUSA AMELIA YOUNG DUNFORD GATES (1856–1933)
by Lisa Olsen Tait

Susa Amelia Young was born to Brigham and Lucy Bigelow Young, the second of their three daughters, on March 18, 1856, in the Lion House in Salt Lake City. Susa spent a happy childhood surrounded by her many siblings and "aunts" (her father's plural wives), all of whom were deeply committed to The Church of Jesus Christ of Latter-day Saints. She grew up in an atmosphere of complete faith and dedication to the gospel of Jesus Christ embodied in her parents and extended family.

"It would be impossible to paint a picture of Mother without the all-pervading spiritual light in her eyes, lingering in her smile and casting its halo over her whole personality," Susa recalled. "She loved the Gospel of Jesus Christ, she worshipped her Lord and Saviour, and she knew as she knew that she lived that Joseph Smith had seen the Father and Son and that the restored Gospel was the only plan by which she or any other could enter into the Kingdom of Heaven and partake of its glories."

Susa received a good education and training in music and dance. In 1870, she moved with her mother and younger sister to St. George in southern Utah. Lucy Young faithfully took her young daughters to church meetings and taught them to pray. "Long before words were easy on the childish lips, the tiny hands could be clasped in supplication, and the little bended knees beside her offered the childish symbol of prayer which was surely acceptable to God and was comforting to her own worshipful heart."[1]

Susa also credited her "other mother," Zina D. H. Young, with teaching her crucial lessons of faith.[2] "If you do not understand anything put it on the alter and leave it with God, he will answer your question in His own time and way," Zina testified. Beyond any specific lesson this great woman imparted, Susa felt that it was her gift of love that yielded the greatest influence:

> Above all things Aunt Zina impressed upon the value of love in the solving of all mental, physical and spiritual problems because she loved us and helped us to love her. She sympathized with our difficulties, and our dispositions and what she could not solve with her head, she soothed with her affectionate understanding. Like my mother, Aunt Zina *felt* religion and achieved it through her heart, not her head. After all, that is the only way any of us ever get a testimony—it is through the heart and soul, not through the mind and reason.[3]

The implicit faith and trust in God that Susa imbibed as she grew up carried over into her life as a young wife and mother. On December 1, 1872, at age sixteen, she married a young dentist, Alma B. Dunford, and gave birth to two children before initiating a painful divorce in 1878.[4] She then married Jacob F. Gates, a young man she had known in St. George, on January 5, 1880. This marriage was a great success: the Gateses had eleven children[5] and spent fifty-three years together, including three and a half years on a mission to the Hawaiian Islands.

As a young wife and mother in the 1880s, and especially during the years when she and her husband were missionaries in Laie, Hawaii, Susa spent every moment she could spare in her "beloved pursuit,"[6] publishing articles and stories in all of the local Latter-day Saint publications. Writing was her passion.

Susa kept a diary during her last year in Laie, frequently recording words of gratitude or supplication and calling upon heaven for help in her everyday tasks. "How very hard I have worked the last few days," she recorded in one typical entry. "It is because God has so blessed me. I am certainly blessed! How grateful I feel to my Heavenly Father."[7] Reading the diary, one can sense that Susa kept up a running conversation with the Lord as she went about her life, having her heart "drawn out in prayer unto him continually," as the Book of Mormon counsels.[8]

"Today arose at six, so grateful to my Heavenly Father for the quiet peaceful night's sleep I enjoyed," she wrote on October 28, 1888.[9] A week later she expressed the strain of relentless housework and childcare, lamenting both the burdens she was feeling and her own shortcomings in dealing with them: "I am often scolding the children and that makes him [her husband Jacob] scold me," she wrote. "Indeed, I am ashamed of being so cross, but there is so much for my one pair of hands. . . . The little boys are full of mischief and noise." Breaking off her complaint, Susa concluded, "Well, dear Father in Heaven help me to do better and be a joy to my dear precious family, not a bugbear."[10]

Susa's expressions of faith and reliance on the Lord were especially poignant in light of the great sorrow she and Jacob had experienced while on their mission: the deaths of their two little boys just a week apart in February and March 1887. Four-year-old Jacob and three-year-old Karl ("Jay" and "Karlie," as they were known) contracted "diphtheriatic croup," and the anguished parents watched helplessly as their children's lives slipped agonizingly away. It was an experience so painful that Susa could hardly bear to write about it a year later. Noting in her diary the "sad anniversary" of the tragedy,

Susa Young Gates and her husband, Jacob Gates, served as missionaries in Hawaii from 1885 to 1889. This 1886 photograph was taken only months before the deaths of her sons Jacob and Karl. From the left are children Jacob ("Jay") Young, Joseph Sterling, Karl ("Karlie") Nahum, and Emma Lucy.

she recorded: "Jacob had gone to Honolulu and that morning Jay said he was sick. I asked him if I could do anything, fix up his throat with coal oil and give him some catnip tea. No mama, he answered, only pray for me and put some oil on."[11] Then, still racked with grief and guilt on the anniversary of his death, she wrote about his final night:

> One year ago tonight! Oh, shall I wring my heart by recalling the sad sad time. It kills me to think of the little request my darling made that night one year ago. Are you going away Mama? he said. . . . Yes dear, I replied. Mama

must have some sleep. Don't leave me tonight mama dear stay tonight. And I, oh pain, I promised to stay. But when midnight came, and Jacob came over he insisted on my taking some rest. Our darling Jay seemed to be sleeping, so I was overpersuaded and left him to his papa. All the evening he had wanted me to rub his bowels, over his bladder, with oil, and to rub him. . . . His dear breath seemed to come harder and shorter, but oh I *didn't* dream, I couldn't *suspect* the awful truth. And so *I—I* left him. And all the rest of the night his papa admitted afterwards the little whispering voice called mama mama.

"Oh my darlings, my darlings, how my heart aches in thinking of you," she mourned. "How I loved you, and how I have missed you, only One knows. But it is the Lord's will, and blessed be the name of the Lord."[12] That anniversary was followed a few days later by another. "A year ago today Karlie was taken violently ill," Susa wrote on Sunday, February 26. "We have been sad today, poor Jacob had to weep."[13]

It was not just the grief that weighed upon Susa's heart. The experience was a severe test of faith. "I didn't dream people could die while on missions," she wrote, describing the many administrations, prayers, and expressions of faith exercised on Jay's behalf just before his death. "That night nearly every man on the place came over and administered to him. When they went out Bro. Allred said so firmly, Jay will be all right in a few days. I never saw more faith exercised for any one than was for my little lost love."[14]

But Jay was not "all right" in a few days, and that outpouring of faith was seemingly exercised to no avail. A year later, Susa still had not reconciled it in her own mind and heart, and throughout the remainder of her mission she frequently recorded moments of grief and anguish, especially whenever she passed the two little graves.

Ten years later, Susa wrote a lightly fictionalized account of the mission and the deaths of her boys for the *Juvenile Instructor*, adding new detail and showing how she had found some measure of peace with this great trial. In the account, Susa recounts the crisis of faith she and her husband had endured, intensified by their previous belief that if they strictly kept the Word of Wisdom, death and sickness would pass their family by: "Stupidly the mother sat. She was too stunned for tears, too heartbroken for noisy demonstration. Why was it? Had they not kept the Word of Wisdom? And what was the promise?"[15]

As depicted in the story, President Joseph F. Smith, in Laie at the time, tenderly helped nurse the boys and gave comfort to the grieving parents. A few weeks earlier, he had experienced a dream in which a double grave was being dug and when he saw the actual grave for Jay, he recognized it as a fulfillment of his dream. "I knew then that the grave would have to hold two," his character tells the parents in the story, "and I knew, too, why the Lord had sent me that dream. It was to show me that He wanted your two children. I wanted to tell you this, my dear friends, so that you, too, may draw comfort from the thought that God has taken your little ones for a wise purpose in Himself. Not for any lack or failing on your part, but because they were needed in the heavens."

Those words were a comfort to the parents. "And oh, how they needed it!" the narrator observes. "Over and over the mother said in her own heart to comfort and sustain her, 'The Lord wanted them both! It is no fault or lack of mine!'" Through this insight and the refinement of suffering, the parents came to see the purpose of their great loss. "Is it not possible, my wife, that our motives in coming on our mission were not as high and holy as they should have been?" the husband poignantly asks. "Have we not thought too much of ourselves, and too little of our fellow men?"[16]

Susa did not mention these conversations or insights in her contemporaneous letters or diary, which is not to say they did not occur,[17] but certainly they express the solace and insight that had come to her with years of reflection over this great sorrow—which was, as it turned out, only one in a long list of tragedies that left eight of her thirteen children dead before the turn of the century. Through her painful divorce, she lost custody of her eldest daughter, and her eldest son was taken away by his father several years later. She also suffered great anxiety and heartbreak over her sisters, Eudora Lovina Young Dunford Hagen and Rhoda Mabel Young McAllister Witt Sanborn, who both made hurtful and reckless marital choices.

While Susa had certainly imbibed the simple, implicit faith of her mother, she also identified strongly with her father, Brigham Young, who had taken a more intellectual approach and had studied the gospel for two years before committing to baptism. In a conversation with her father shortly before his death, Susa expressed a wish that she could know the gospel was true, "like he knew it, not hoped it, thought it, not in a sense believed it, but just knew it in every fibre of my soul as he did." Brigham's advice sank down into his daughter's soul. "He did not argue with me," she recalled. "He did not quote scriptures, he simply said: 'There is only one way, daughter, that you can get the testimony of the Truth and that is the way I attained my testimony and the way your mother got hers.— On your knees before the Lord, go in prayer and he will hear and answer.'" He then bore his testimony in memorable terms:

> So precious is the testimony of the mission of the Prophet Joseph Smith and the message that he delivered to this earth in reestablishing the Gospel of Jesus Christ to me that rather than do anything to lose that testimony I would be cut into inch pieces every night in my life and be put together in the morning to live out the day.

"The thrill that swept through me when I heard him say that was in itself my own testimony," Susa remembered.[18] This conversation took place in August 1877, and Susa determined to shape her life by this witness of truth.

As one of the most prolific and influential writers in the Latter-day Saint community, Susa repeatedly testified of her faith and encouraged others to gain the same witness for themselves. "My whole

Susa Young Gates and her daughters: Emma Lucy Gates (left), Leah Eudora Dunford (right), and Sarah Beulah Gates (center), who died in a tragic accident shortly after this photograph was taken.

soul is for the building up of this kingdom," she wrote when she was thirty-two years old.[19]

Susa had much to accomplish, and she remembered the 1890s as her "life's most crowded years." Susa had launched the *Young Woman's Journal* as the monthly magazine of the Young Ladies' Mutual Improvement Association (YLMIA) in the spring of 1889 and served as the editor and principal voice of this publication through the next decade. In addition to editing the *Journal*, she published work in many venues, attended a summer session at Harvard, taught and organized classes in domestic science and physical culture, served on the board of trustees of Brigham Young Academy (later University), founded a state chapter of the Daughters of the American Revolution and helped to organize the Sons and Daughters of Utah Pioneers, participated in the Utah Woman's Press Club, and promoted the kindergarten movement in Utah. She also developed a national presence, serving in the National Council of Women, speaking at the Chicago World's Fair in 1893, and helping to found the National Household Economics Association. She kept up a voluminous correspondence and entertained many visiting dignitaries, offering them, as she put it, "shelter and humble hospitality in our modest old-fashioned home."[20]

In the midst of her busiest years, Susa experienced a period of intense spiritual seeking. She did not have a crisis of faith in the sense that she doubted or wavered in her commitment. Rather, she went through the kind of process that many who have been born into the Church eventually do, realizing that she needed to stand on her own spiritually. As she later described it, she felt she had "just accepted every principle and practice at face value," and she renewed her desire to receive the certain testimony her father had described:

> So I began to pray for that testimony. I had always said morning and evening prayers, mother had carefully trained me to do so. Now, however, I began to pray for light upon the question of whether the gospel as taught in the scriptures and as revealed in these days to the Prophet Joseph Smith was in very deed true.
>
> I did not ask for a dream or any vision but I did pray to the Lord that he might show me the why and wherefore of every principle of the gospel. I wanted the glow and power of the testimony itself—oh yes—but I also wanted to know the reasons why this truth or that ordinance was established as parts of the Kingdom of God.[21]

Susa combined faith and intellect in her spiritual search. While she prayed, she also studied deeply, learning from the scriptures and other inspired sources while also investigating the beliefs and principles of other faiths. After some time, she came to feel that she had an intellectual testimony: "My prayer for the reason behind all these truths and principles had been answered but the glow and fire of that final testimony had not been given." She described the final phase of her conversion experience:

> But how, I asked myself, was I to get that flame and fire of testimony. I had studied out the principles of the Gospel and satisfied my reason. What more need I ask, or how get the spiritual testimony. I said my prayers, I paid my tithing, attended the sacrament service and was obedient to the counsel of my husband. It occurred to me that father had once told me that if I wanted any particular thing I must name that in particular words in my daily prayers. The Holy Ghost was the medium of communicating that testimony to me and to all others—I must pray for that Spirit to rest upon me and to communicate to me, in some way, the actual testimony of the Truth.
>
> During one year when I was nearly 40 years old, I disciplined my taste, my desires and my impulses—severely disciplining my appetite, my tongue, my acts, for one whole year and how I prayed!
>
> Then one day at the close of that year—about 15 years after father's death—it came to me in the simplest, homeliest environment possible to us humble women folk. I was sweeping the floor one day, and a voice within my soul—that same calm, deliberate, yet soul enlightening voice I had heard in the Lion House years before—spoke to my spirit these simple words: "You know it is true! Never doubt it again!"
>
> I never have! All other truths and facts and philosophies which came to my attention, and come today, I measure by one standard only: Does this or that idea or theory agree or does it conflict with the truths of the Gospel as taught in the ancient and modern Scriptures—if it agrees, it is mine!

The Jacob and Susa Young Gates family lived in Provo, Utah, for nearly two decades. In 1924, they revisited their old home.

If it does not, I cast it out, or lay it upon the altar of prayer till God reveals the truth to His Prophet at the head of His Church.

    I do not expect ever to learn all truth—not ever or ever. Progress—progress—study—learn—pray—these stepping stones upward and ever upward, are a part of my life here and hereafter! Faith, repentance, private and family prayer, baptism and confirmation by one having the authority of the holy priesthood, tithing, keeping the Sabbath Day holy, fasting and obedience to the councils of the priesthood, all have been and are living forces in my daily life.[22]

After recovering from a health crisis in the early 1900s, Susa increasingly focused her energies on genealogy and temple work. She created curriculum and taught classes on genealogy for the Relief

Society, wrote a column on the subject for the *Deseret News*, published a well-received reference work, *Surname Book and Racial History*, and worked actively to research names and perform temple ordinances for her ancestors. In 1914, she became founding editor of the *Relief Society Magazine*, a position she held until 1922. During the last decade of her life, she wrote an ambitious (but ultimately unpublished) book manuscript titled "History of Women." She also wrote a lengthy biographical treatment of her mother's life and compiled many autobiographical recollections. In 1930, she published *Life Story of Brigham Young*, a biography of her father written with her daughter Leah Dunford Widtsoe.

Susa Young Gates continued to proclaim her testimony until her death in Salt Lake City on May 27, 1933.

> I know it is true as I know that I live! We and our dear ones share in these joys as we do in our sorrows, knowing that all our trials are but stepping-stones to higher realms of achievement. And above all, I long to share that living fire and glow of testimony with every child and grandchild I possess, as well as with every friend within and without the church. My whole soul yearns to proselytize, with word and deed, tongue and pen, as long as my life shall continue! Thank God that I have been counted worthy of receiving this testimony![23]

Chapter 6

"Wonderful to Me"

Sarah Ann Taylor Howard (1856–1933)
by Karol Gerber Chase

Sarah Ann Taylor was born May 26, 1856, to Thomas and Mary Ann Danley Taylor near Mount Airy, Surry County, North Carolina. She was the eighth of nine children. Frugality and hard work were ingrained in Sarah's upbringing, and she was blessed with energy and quickness in body as well as mind. She was confident, caring, and bright with a passion for learning and leadership.

The United States Civil War began in 1861, when Sarah Ann was four years old. The family farm in Surry County, North Carolina, was caught in the middle of the conflict. Sarah remembered that when she was eight years old, "500 soldiers were returning from War and camped a half mile away from our house. Many of them came and wanted corn etc. for their horses. Mother, shivering at their demands and threats, finally gave up the keys [to the granary]. There was little corn or feed left when they got through taking what they wanted. Then out of the many who rummaged the house and took bacon and hams and other things, was one man who asked Mother to bake him some bread and he paid her for it."[1]

Earlier, around 1844, Latter-day Saint missionary Jedediah M. Grant had passed through the neighborhood preaching the gospel of Jesus Christ. "Father believed it and attended all the meetings," Sarah recalled.[2] Although the Taylors were not baptized at that time, Elder Grant "made a powerful impression" on them.[3] More than twenty years later, "Henry G. Boyle and Howard Coray came teaching the same doctrine," Sarah wrote. "Father said they taught the same doctrine that the Savior taught."[4]

"In March 1869," Sarah recorded, "my father, mother, one sister and 2 brothers joined the Church of Jesus Christ of Latter-day Saints."[5] Members of the Taylor family began making preparations to journey to the Salt Lake Valley. The family was divided, however, as four of her siblings had not joined the Church. Thirteen-year-old Sarah was "deeply moved in her feelings about leaving the home dear to her heart," and "very quietly she ascended a narrow stairway, leading to the small room above . . . and in front of a tiny window, poured out her soul in prayer."[6]

On July 9, 1869, the converted members of the Taylor family "started in company with a big crowd of Latter Day Saints to Utah," Sarah recalled.[7] Her family traveled west on the transcontinental railroad, which had been completed only two months earlier. Although riding on the train was less arduous than traveling on foot, the July journey proved hot and tedious. The Taylors arrived at their destination in Payson, Utah, on July 31, 1869, their journey having taken them twenty-two days.

The Taylors purchased a farm two miles west of Payson. Sarah attended school when possible, helped run the home and farm, wove carpets, and dried fruit for profit. On December 27, 1877, when Sarah was twenty-one years of age, she married Samuel Shelton Howard in the Endowment House in Salt Lake City. They settled on Howard Street in Woods Cross, Utah, and Sarah began her life as a wife, mother, and Church and civic leader.[8] She supplemented the family income by marketing her produce and using her skills as a seamstress. She soon found she was expecting a baby, but that did not stop her from planting a large vegetable garden and taking the produce to Salt Lake, where she peddled it door to door.

After her son's birth in September 1878, Sarah tucked her "Sammie" into a basket, put him beside her in their wagon pulled by a team of horses, and again drove to Salt Lake to sell her garden produce, butter, and eggs.[9] "A large orchard, flower and vegetable gardens were trademarks of Sarah all the years she lived in South Bountiful," recalled one family member. "The pride and joy of the Howard household was Sarah's elaborate vegetable garden. . . . She started her day at 5am to work in the garden."[10]

Sarah was tall for her time—five feet eight inches—and slender even after she bore seven children.[11] Samuel and Sarah worked side by side to create a welcoming home. A congenial and generous couple, they hosted many ward and social events and invited friends and foreign guests to their home, some of whom lived with them until they could find employment and a place to live.[12] In 1879, Samuel and Sarah started the Bountiful Dairy Company on land across the street from their home. They used a horse-drawn milk wagon to deliver their products. Sarah helped pump water for the twenty cows, and as the children grew, all family members participated. They also owned a brickyard and in 1893 organized the Bountiful Livestock Company. Although their days were filled with work, Sarah's daughter Lydia reminisced: "In the evenings the family would read and discuss the scriptures or play games. . . . Father played tiddlywinks, checkers, and dominos with the neighbor children, as well as the family, while . . . mother cored and peeled apples, popped corn and made molasses candy . . . They had a large home with a large kitchen and they held many parties and large gatherings there."[13]

Sarah strongly believed in and worked for woman's right to vote, and Samuel, along with many other local men, gave the suffrage cause his full support. Sarah served as the first president of the South Bountiful Woman Suffrage Association.[14] With other Utah women, Sarah "aided in 1896 in getting the Plank of Suffrage in the

Utah State Constitution."¹⁵ Active in the Democratic Party, she was elected Davis County recorder in 1900.

Although Sarah's formal schooling was limited by modern standards, she taught school for neighborhood children in her home.¹⁶ After her younger children were in public school, she seized the opportunity to continue her own education by traveling with her two oldest children, Samuel and Lydia, in "a little buggy and horse to Salt Lake City to the University of Utah (then known as Deseret)."¹⁷ "[I] attended the State University for 2 years," she wrote, "going 2 and sometimes 3 days each week for special studies. Much ecclesiastical work was given me, so in addition to my regular housework my time has been well occupied."¹⁸

Sarah served in numerous Church positions, including first president of the children's Primary in the South Bountiful Ward No. 2 and first stake Primary president of the South Davis Stake. After Sarah served as her ward Relief Society president, fellow suffragette Aurelia Rogers of Farmington asked her to be on her Davis Stake Primary board, where she served from 1907 to 1915.¹⁹

In time, each of her five sons received a mission call to the British Mission, all of them serving in the Birmingham Conference. When her husband was also called to serve in the British Mission in 1902 at age forty-six, his absence presented a huge challenge for Sarah and the family to maintain their businesses and home, but they supported his call.

In 1908, a few years after his return, Samuel rocked the family when he chose to marry a second, younger wife, despite the Manifesto of 1890.²⁰ Sarah Ann was devastated, and she and Samuel separated. Samuel lived in Salt Lake City with his second wife, and Sarah remained in South Bountiful.²¹ The period immediately after their separation was very hard for her; she deeply mourned the loss of her companion and the life she had known. Nevertheless, her faith and her children gave her the will to go on, although she never again wrote Samuel's name in her records, referring to him only by such indirect terms as "the father of my children."²²

Sarah Ann Taylor Howard (1856–1933)

In 1910, at age fifty-six, Sarah accepted a call to serve an eighteen-month mission to the Birmingham, England, Conference, where her sons and husband had served. She was one of the few sister missionaries in England at that time, and this mission restored her spirit and renewed her energy. Her zeal and love for missionary work was so strong that, despite health problems, at age sixty-three she accepted a second mission call to California, serving in San Francisco from November 18, 1919, to October 24, 1920. "Sister Howard" kept a daily handwritten journal of this mission:

> Friday Nov. 21 morn about 8:30 arrived at the [San Francisco] conference House,[23] 1649 Hayes St. San Francisco, California. Found all well there. The Pres. was [John Jarvis] Sellers, his wife [Emily Duke Sellers] was there & Sis. Delila Stoker, also 5 Elders. . . . Rested & did some writing . . .
>
> Saturday Nov. 22, 1919 washed & finished some letters to mail. Street meeting.
>
> Sunday Nov. 23, 1919. Attended Sunday school 10 a.m. Meeting 11:30 Pres. Sellers called me to speak. Visited Hospital & saw Sis. Greenwood. Attended 7:30 meeting in the Hall.
>
> Mon. 24 Class, & then went tracting with Elder [Wallace J.] Cook, visited Sis. Jones & another Sis. Jones Street meeting.
>
> Tues. 25 Class. Tracting from 10 to 12. Visiting from 2 until you get home. Mutual 7:30 P.M.[24] Program, debate & candy pulling. Tracting was with Elder [Joseph I.] Bodily.
>
> Thurs. 27 Thanksgiving Day. Class Subject: 11th Article of Faith: Visited with Elder [Oliver] Williams his Aunt, Sis. Williams, We certainly had a nice time & a good dinner. The Williams family are a fine, lot of people, and treated us royal. We returned home at 5:30 P.M. It was here that I learned a narrow piece of crochet edging.

Sarah Ann Taylor Howard as a missionary in Birmingham, England, 1911. She is pictured with missionaries who were also from Davis County, Utah.

Fri. 28 Spent 2 hours in class, Sis. Sellers made a nice plum pudding for dinner, Elder [Lynne C.] Layton gave a chicken, which had been sent to him, Sis Delila Stoker gave a chicken which had been sent her from home, so we all had a good dinner. Sis. Stoker & I went through a part of Golden Gate park to the Post Office. Also Elders [John] Wiscombe & Williams & I went to the Ocena Beach & Clift House. Saw a part of the town, San Francisco.

Sat. 29 Helped with Saturdays work. Was at Priesthood meeting at 2: P.M. Met many Elders & missionaries. It was a lovely meeting. There Were 31 Present. These meetings are held once a month & called Missionary Report meetings.

Sun. 30 Sunday school, meeting & then into Golden Gate Park along with Elder [Ralph L.] Mellor. Saw Museum Bldg. animals observatory. The skeleton of a whale 75 ft. long, 13 ft. deep weight 80 tons caught 1908 Sulpher Batton. Meeting in evening.

Sarah Ann Taylor Howard (1856–1933)

Sarah Ann Taylor Howard (second row, fourth from right) is pictured with missionaries in the San Francisco Conference, California Mission. This photograph was featured in a 1920 issue of Liahona, the Elders Journal, *a publication for Latter-day Saint missions.*

Mon. Dec 1 Tracting with Sis. Delila Stoker met a lady who said she had the message of Truth. Conversed freely with her, found another woman immensely rich who was desiring something, some spiritual food, she was a Catholic Mrs Davis

Tues 2 Rained so we all stayed at home, and studied. Had class at 8: a.m. . . .

[January 1920] Mon. 12 Had long conversation with Miss McCubbins, she took me with her to dinner then to Hippodrome which treats I enjoyed very much. Studdied in afternoon & evening.

Tues. 13. Tract well in morn. Relief Society meeting here at our apartments, it was work meeting & we had a good meeting & attendance. In evening went to Baptist services, home & to bed. . . .

Sun. 18 Got up & dressed, but did not feel well enough to go to Sunday school, so went to bed & rested all I could.

Mon. 19 Did not get up until nearly noon, but after I was administered to by Elders Larson, [Spencer C.] Taylor, Williams & [Henry M.] Stark I ate a little breakfast & slept a little & Sis. Kinsey brought me a new egg fixed up so it seemed also to help me & I soon felt better & stayed up the rest of the day. . . .

Wed. 21 Went to class. . . . Called to see some Investigators. Mailed some tracts to the folks at home. Bought Catholic Prayer Book to see & refer to for understanding 25 cts. . . .

Thurs. 29 Class, tracting & Visiting investiagors, made arrangements for a cottage meeting at Mrs. Teeples & Mrs. Potter's. . . . Went at 7 o'clock to the cottage meeting. Elder [Ezra E.] Larsen, Elders Cook & [George C.] Knapp & Sis. [Beatrice D.] Larsen & myself. Elder Larsen presided, Sang "Ye Elders of Israel" Prayer by Elder Knapp. Elder Larsen spoke at length concerning the Gospel, a few remarks by myself. Singing O My Father. Ben[ediction] Sis. Larsen. All felt well & we parted hoping we might have another such time in the future. Mrs. Mitchell was in attendance too.

[February 1920] Sun. 22 Pres. Heber J. Grant, Pres. of the church of Jesus Christ of Latter Day Saints was at San Francisco to speak to the People. So all here were up early . . . taking Buss . . . We attended Sunday school & meeting, where I met . . . a number of Saints, among which was Sis. Sears who when last she saw me was a small girl at Farmington, Utah, & had remembered me all this time. . . .

Between Sunday School & meeting Pres. Heber J. Grant, Pres. Wilford Richards[25] and a no. of Elders administered to me for my rheumatism. . . .

Thurs. 26 . . . Had a lovely ride out on st[reet] car, fare round trip 25 cts. Sis Weisgerber gave us a nice dinner, then Bro. Fred took us [on] a fine drive through Los Godas & Saratoga . . . he had a nice new Ford car. On arriving found Sis. Marie Weisgerber had prepared a warm supper, my! it was fine.

All came by O'conner Hospital & saw Elder Wallace Cook, Bro. John Cook & Sis Laron Cook. . . .

Sat.28 Studdied all morning.... went to Street meeting, Elders Bodily, Geo. C. Knapp, John Cook, Larsen & myself spoke, the first time in my life to speak on street. Hope the Lord will give me strength to speak again.

[March 1920] Wed. 3 Class, Tracting, & to Dr. Visited Mrs. Teeples 355 So. 4th St. Rear & Mrs. Powell with her, Mrs. Mitchell & asked them to our Relief Society quilting next Tuesday here at our apartment house, at 1 P.M. Called in to see Miss Myrtle McCubbins 296 So. 3rd St. had a visit with her & visited with Mrs. Prior. Attended the Priesthood meeting in the evening here at our Rooms....

Sun. 7 Could not go to Sunday school because I had rheumatism so bad, but felt some better in the evening & went to mutual, read a story from Young Woman's Journal "Aunt Rebecca's Observation." Our lesson Mormon Battallion....

[April 1920] Fri: 16 After class I tract & had fine success. Went to Dr. called on Mrs. Davis, Mrs. Prior & Mrs. Bada. Enjoyed all the time. Spent the evening with Sis. Kinsey all of us mssionaries.... She served refreshments, cake & cocoa.

Sat.17 Studied after I had straightened up the room. Went after my shoes. I paid $10.00 for them & $1.75 for a gusset in the backs, for my ankles were so swelled I could not lace them near together.

Sun 18 To Sunday school & services. Little Elton Yates come & went with us to S.S.... Mrs. Jury was at services also.... Sis Kinsey come up & we all studied the Relief Society lesson together. Then Sis. Larsen & I went with the Elders to street meeting....

[May 1920] Mon. 24 Visited Mrs. Copperfield & she had a Mrs. Peterson from Ill. visiting her. We all conversed freely on religion. Parted good friends. They did not believe in formal creeds or organizations. Said if we have faith, & love the Lord with all our souls, minds &c. we will be alright. I asked how we could show we had faith & love, only by obedience. Knowledge is promised us by doing the will of the Father. We the Latter day Saints believe in Organization as an outward evidence of the true church and combined with the doctrine that Christ taught makes the True church of which He said One Faith, one Lord & one baptism. Good night, I'm going to bed.

[June 1920] Fri. 4 class, Tracting with Sis. Stoker, 763 So. 2nd st. Man & woman railed out against us, against Joseph Smith & against our church. There was no reason in either one of them. We could not get to talk for their confusion until they got a little of the venom off their tongues. We tried to keep calm & when we did finally get a chance, we gave them something as straight as a line and although they resisted everything we said we stayed until they turned & shut the door with a bang in our faces. They said they were sorry for us. We told them to save their pity for themselves. We bore testimony to them that we had told them the truth & we knew our message was true. . . .

[August 1920] Sun. 15 Branch conference: Priesthood meeting at 9 a.m. meeting at 10. It was a splendid conference. Elders Mellor, Wiscomb, [Joseph E.] Larkin & Bro. & Sis. Alred had dinner here & then Elder [Merle G.] Stockdale & Sis. Lili Moss & Erma Rice come & we all spent a pleasant time together & all walked up to ST. James Park, listened to the Baptist preacher "Sullivan" awhile & then went to 5 o'clock conference meeting.

I was called to speak in this meeting spoke on "Resurrection."

Mutual at 7:30 good. I was asked to speak Spoke on "Obedience." Palo Alto Branch were here to all meetings.

Tues. 17 Class & Tracting, found one lady sitting on her porch, who is "Unitarian" Mrs. Upton She does not believe in the Bible, she thinks Christ was an inspired man, but only one of great characters, perhaps the greatest, but that is all. Told me I was not bright, said I was sincere & broad, but did not think right. We conversed for a long time, but could not get a head as she would not consider the Bible.

On leaving she invited me to stay & have dinner with her & she certainly treated us fine, gave me a hearty invitation any time. She is widely read and informed. . . .

San Jose. Sept. 1920

Tues. 14 class, Tracting after I had been in the store & gave tracts to Mr. Irvin & had a fine conversation with him. I went to Mrs. Guymires at Park Hotel gave her tracts & conversed with her.

Home at 1 P.M. had dinner & quilted with Relief Society on Sis. Harmons quilt. In evening Bessie Steinagel came & we all practised singing.

Wed. 15 class, Tracting, good conversation & 3 inv in homes. 2 good conversations in Park. Little Tommy & Mrs. Boyd, also a lady well cultured. Visited Mrs. Teeple & several Investigators. . . .

Thurs. 16 class, Tracting, to Dr. Ate dinner in St. James Park. Mrs. Boyd from Alexander Apts. 2nd & came with her fancy work as she had done the day before & we conversed a long time. . . .

6 o'clock when I arrived home for supper & after Elder Taylor, Sisters Larsen & I went & visited Sister Miller, her husband & children. Had a pleasant evening. They walked the way home with us, as far as through the St. Park. It was a beautiful evening. Full missionary work is true enjoyment. . . .

Sat. 18 Went to st. meeting, Elders Larsen, Williams & Taylor all of us spoke a short time. My remarks were on Free Agency. . . .

[October 1920] Thurs 21 After Pres. Iverson (Heber C.) & his son Grant had gone to Palo Alto to see Leland

Stanford University, I began Packing my trunks 2 in number, went to store & got ice cream & cake for the crowd . . . & I enjoyed it all together. The baggage man came & took my trunks & boxes for shipment. I rode to Post office with him, sent 3 boxes and then we went to the San Jose Station checked my trunks and I went to chiropractor for last time. . . . Then I called on several investigators & friends. . . .

I spent the time till after midnight washing my silk waist, under waist & stockings and ironing them dry, and fixing up everything for an early start next morning.

Fri. 22 Up early preparing to leave home, which had been my mission home for almost one year. 639 So 3rd st. San Jose, Calif. Mission Headquarters upstairs. . . . My feelings were of a very sad nature. I shall not attempt to express them now. It is more than I can do, for I was leaving . . . many good friends and the place that had sheltered me for a year from all kinds of weather, and above all those that were more dear than I can tell to me, my companions in the missionary work. . . .

I shall leave you to picture my feelings & I will leave you to Judge as if it were you. . . .

Sun. 24 Afternoon Conference. . . . I received my Release from Pres. [Joseph W.] McMurrin & was called upon by Pres. Richards to speak.[26]

I cannot describe the feelings on being released, but do desire it understood that I am grateful to my Heavenly Father for the wonderful privilege of being a missionary in the great cause of spreading the Truths of the Everlasting Gospel. . . . My! I do raise in praise to my Fathers name for these great opportunities. 2½ years in Missionary work. Wonderful to me.[27]

In her later years, Sarah was busy with family temple work; holding family reunions; marketing her cucumbers, pumpkins, and potatoes; having family dinners; seeking help for her rheumatism; and being the matriarch to her large family. Throughout most of her life, Sarah had moved with energy, but now she began to slow down. She was seventy-seven years old and knew her time on earth was growing short: she had been diagnosed with colon cancer. In January 1933, she and her daughter, Lydia, compiled a short history of her life. Sarah wanted her posterity to hear her testimony:

> I love the Gospel of Jesus Christ as revealed in the last days from heaven to Joseph Smith, and my life's work has been to help mankind to understand the principles of salvation and to make the world better by having lived in it. From childhood, I have desired to do good to all. Home and my own family have had my first attention and all my children are men and women of God, with love for truth and righteousness, desiring to be true latter-day Saints. Every one of them has helped to make my life sweeter and better. I still desire to be faithful and do all I can in the Church that was established by our Heavenly Father through Joseph Smith, the Latter-day prophet on April 6, 1830.[28]

On October 20, 1933, at the age of seventy-seven, Sarah Ann Taylor Howard passed away in the South Bountiful home where she had lived for fifty-five years.

Chapter 7

"Strength to Overcome Selfishness"

Lorena Eugenia Washburn Larsen (1860–1945)
by Loretta Luce Evans

Throughout her life, Lorena Eugenia Washburn Larsen had a strong testimony of the gospel of Jesus Christ as taught by The Church of Jesus Christ of Latter-day Saints. Dreams and other spiritual experiences comforted and guided her. When she decided on a course of action, she saw it through, despite opposition.

Lorena was born January 10, 1860, in Manti, Sanpete County, Utah, the sixth of seven children born to Abraham and Flora Clarinda Gleason Washburn. Because her parents had known many leaders of the Church while they were living in Nauvoo, visiting apostles often stopped at their Manti home. There Lorena heard stories of early Church history from people who had lived through the events. Those experiences strengthened her faith.

Lorena's mother was president of the Relief Society in Manti, and it was likely with her aid that Lorena and other girls formed a Junior Relief Society in 1869. Besides the fun of having their own organization, they collected scraps of fabric and bits of thread, enough to create two quilt tops, which they donated to the Manti

Lorena Eugenia Washburn Larsen (1860–1945)

Relief Society. The Junior Relief Society lasted for three years, ending in 1872 when Lorena and her family moved to Monroe, Utah.

Lorena's mother was the second wife of Abraham Washburn, and as a result, Lorena understood many of the challenges and blessings of plural marriage. When the time came for her to marry, she had opportunities to decide between monogamous marriage and plural marriage.

As a young adult, she was called to serve as president of the Young Ladies' Mutual Improvement Association (YLMIA) in Monroe; one of her counselors was Julia Larsen, wife of Bent Rolfsen Larsen. Sometime later, Bent, with the approval of both his ecclesiastical leaders and his wife, considered entering into plural marriage.[1] Julia said that Lorena Washburn would be a person she could easily love. Lorena recalled:

> In the early winter of 1879 I had no thought of marrying Bent Larsen, but one night I dreamed that we were at a dancing party, and he took me to his home, and pled with me to marry him. A short time after I had dreamed this, it happened just that way.[2]
>
> I had a lot of proposals before I accepted. I went into it hesitatingly, reluctantly. I could not think of hurting a man's wife, by marrying her husband, but Aunt Julia told me she would feel much worse if I did not marry her husband than she would if I did. She said that she and Bent had planned for a long time that if they could get my consent, they sure wanted me to be a member of thier family.
>
> On Feb. 25, 1880 I married Bent Rolfsen Larsen in the St. George Temple.[3]
>
> I did not fully realize until after I was married how great the trial was, ~~and~~ nor how greatly those tryals would touch the very center of ones heart.[4]

From the time I was married, Aunt Julia and I took turns milking the cows and doing the house work. She would do the cooking and kitchen work one week while I did the milking, and took care of that department, and then we would change for a week.

We did the washings together. . . . We made all our laundry soap, usually a years supply at one time, and stored it in the atic

We carded our own wool bats on hand cards and made our quilts and we had a goodly suply of them.[5]

I lived in that 3 roomed home with Aunt Julia for 7 years. And in all that time we never quarreled—not once, but I cannot say that we didn't sometimes feel like it; but we had gone into that order of marriage because we fully believed God had commanded it, and while we had human nature to contend with, we worked and prayed for strength to overcome selfishness and greed and live on a higher plain, learn to love each other, or there would never be happiness in ~~that order of marriage~~ our hearts and homes.[6]

In the summer of 1881 my husband was called to go on a mission to Norway, his native land. so we all went to work making preperations for his departure On Sept. 24, I and Aunt Julia had a surprise party at our home for him, (he had always said that no one could surprise him) I cooked the refreshments at our neighbors "Louis Andersons," and he was thouroughly surprised. . . . In those days money was scarce, and the price of produce low. To raise money to go on that mission my husband sold seven acres of land just north of Monroe for fifty dollars, he also sold some of the domestic animals.[7]

Bent left in October, just after general conference. "It was very hard to have him go," Lorena wrote, "as I had nearly died in Sept.

the year before with a premature birth. And I was pregnant again, and was afraid I would never see my husband again. On May 10, 1882, my son Bent Franklin was born. I was sick for 3 days and nearly died again, Thank heaven, it was the power of God which saved my life."⁸

Less than a month later, on June 4, 1882, Lorena wrote to Bent to report that the walls of the Manti Temple were almost finished. The Church was trying to raise $4,000 to put a metal roof on the temple so that work could continue through the winter, but cash was hard to come by at that time. "It will only be about 60 cts. to the family," she noted. "We have only 10 cts. in the house, but I hope the Lord will open the way, that we may donate our part."⁹

Lorena and Julia kept their spirits up while their husband was away. "We were glad that there were two of us, it kept the home more cheereful. And with Mutual meetings at our home once a week, we had . . . plenty of social life. The mutual girls thought it was sure an ideal life. And some of them said they would never marry unless there could be two of them, congenial like we were."¹⁰

Difficulties arose for the Larsen household after Bent returned home, however. Lorena described his mission as life altering:

> Our husband went on his mission in perfect health, but one cold stormy night in Febuary he and his companion were traveling out in the country. Night came on, and although they asked at every farm house they came to, no one would give them a nights lodging, because they were mormons. Finally with thier clothes wet from the storm they crawled into a barn, and slept on the hay. My husband took a heavy cold that night in Norway, his native land, which later developed into as[t]hma, from which he never did recover, but suffered from its effects the rest of his life.¹¹

Bent returned from his mission in the summer of 1883. Lorena wrote:

The years which followed were filled with work and anxiety. Our husband was home with broken health, and altho we kept up a happy appearance we did not know how long he could keep up, his health was so delicate he couldn't even chop the fire wood. Day after day Aunt Julia and I knelt together in prayer for him, we both prayed and cried together and tried to make life as easy as possible for him.[12]

Bent Franklin Larsen described his father's health this way:

> He was thirty-seven years older than I was. I knew him best when he should have been at the height of his physical manhood but his powers were lagging behind his hopes and desires. . . .
>
> I feel quite sure that he would have accepted the call to serve the Church even if he had foreknowledge of the sacrifice of health which would follow.
>
> It is difficult for the well person to understand how perpetual illness can blight ambitious hopes. Father seldom went to bed during the hours when men should work, but I have been with him many times when his breath failed him so he was compelled to lean against a fence or sit on a ditch bank to recuperate. During intermittent attacks, Father was quite helpless.[13]

Julia and Lorena continued to get along well, but a change to their living arrangements became necessary because of legal pressures. Lorena wrote: "As persecution of those in polygamy was increasing, Pa [Bent] decided it was no longer safe to have his two wives in the same house so he bought another home one block west, and a block south from Aunt Julia's home."[14]

Despite their precautions, Bent was arrested. Lorena wrote: "During the summer of 1888 my husband, Bent Rolfsen Larsen, spent 5 months in the Utah Penitentiary, for having two wives."[15] And though Lorena loved her new home, she was not able to live in it very long; she had to go on the underground to protect her family from legal prosecution.

"Late in the year 1888," she recorded, "I was pregnant and knew that I must go in hiding or my husband go to the Pen again. I couldn't tell just how things could be arranged, and I loved my little home so much. I and the children had been so happy there, and we had lived there only a little more than a year and a half."[16]

The Manti Temple had recently been dedicated, and each ward had been asked to provide temple workers. Manti, sixty miles from Monroe, thus provided a place of hiding, and Lorena was asked to help in the temple while Julia cared for her three children. "When the bishop said you are to leave your children at home with their father, it was almost more than I could endure, for my children were dearer than life itself. It sure was a test of my faith."[17] Lorena moved to Manti and worked in the temple. After a few weeks, her health broke (a miscarriage seemed imminent), and she was given an honorable release.

Bent next rented a home for Lorena and her three children in the town of Redmond, thirty-four miles from Monroe, where they used the alias of Thompson. Lorena and her children did not dare attend church or become friendly with anyone in town, for fear that deputy marshals might discover who they were. While living in Redmond, Lorena had a dream:

> I thought I had been away from my dear home a long time, and then I came home. It looked like the place had gone to ruin. My door-yard and front lawns were entirely overgrown with weeds, wild bushes, and vines. My heart ached at the sight. I immediately went to work on the north side of the front path pulling weeds and digging out the rubbish. I was very sad to think my place had gone to ruin while I was on the underground. While I was pulling at roots which went deep into the ground, suddenly I found myself by a beautiful tree completely covered with the finest

Lorena Eugenia Washburn Larsen with her children in 1896. Back row, left to right: Ida Lorena Larsen and Charlottie Eugenia Larsen. Front row: Bent Franklin Larsen, Enoch Rolf Larsen, Pearl Larsen, Floy Isabel Larsen, and Lorena, holding baby Ella Almeda Larsen. Lorena bore two more children thereafter: Clarence Abraham Larsen in 1898 and Fern Emma Larsen in 1901.

fruit I had ever seen. It stood a few feet from the northeast corner of the house, and had been entirely underground. And as I looked in astonishment, a voice said, 'The underground tree brings forth very choice fruit too.['] I looked and there stood a man leaning over the fence who had been watching me. Presently my children were there, grown, and the place was filled with people. My children brought me dishes, bowls, and small baskets. We filled them with that delicious fruit and they passed them around to the people.[18]

Lorena's dream greatly comforted her at that trying time.

To avoid further persecution, Bent decided to go to the San Luis Valley in Colorado. He left Julia and her children in Monroe and planned to take Lorena and her children to live with one of her brothers. Lorena fretted over the anticipated change and finally convinced Bent to take her and their children with him to Colorado;

Lorena Eugenia Washburn Larsen (1860–1945)

> In May [1889], as the time drew near for my husband to go to Colorado, and I must go somewhere farther away from my home, it was a great trial to me. I could scarcely endure it to be away from the little home which we loved so much, and from my mother and sisters and relatives who were very dear to me, and be confined among strangers, and my three sweet children who needed my care every hour. And money scarce, and where would the necessary help come from to take care of the children and me?[19]

So Lorena accompanied Bent, who built them a log cabin in Sanford, Colorado. Other Latter-day Saints moved there as well, hoping to start productive farms and provide a good living for their families. "New land did not produce well," Lorena lamented, "and the men who went out there to make their fortunes were glad to get enough money to get them back to Utah."[20]

The family lived in Sanford for one year, during which time, Lorena recalled, "My son, Enoch, was born 22, Aug, 1889, and at his birth I nearly lost my life. He weighed 14 pounds at birth."[21] Lorena developed a high fever, but thanks to priesthood blessings and her husband's care, she slowly regained her strength. Her older children were also a big help.

While she lived in Sanford, the Church asked members to fast and pray for relief from the polygamy persecutions. Lorena remembered:

> So great was our persecution that every man, woman and child was asked to fast for 24 hours commencing at sunset Saturday evening and continuing until Sunday night at sundown. We were instructed to neither eat nor drink during that time, and were to pray earnestly for help from the Lord. We were to keep our tempers and not scold a child, but have perfect peace in our homes. In our home we kept it strictly.

There were public prayer meetings in every ward in the church.

The people humbled themselves before the Lord and sought him earnestly, especially those who were suffering persecution.[22]

When the farmland at Sanford did not provide a living, Bent moved his family to Lightning Creek, near Durango. Throughout the summer of 1890, they scrimped and saved to return to Utah in the fall.

At the October 1890 general conference of the Church, members voted to sustain the Manifesto, President Wilford Woodruff's counsel that Latter-day Saints "refrain from contracting any marriage forbidden by the law of the land." Lorena and her family were returning to Utah at the time and heard about the announcement on their way. The news was devastating—they had made great sacrifices to live the principle of plural marriage. She described her agony of soul at the announcement:

> On our arrival at Moab we found several people there who were just returning from Conference. My husband went out and talked with them about the Manifesto.
>
> They told him that it was a fact that that principle [plural marriage] was dropped by the Church. They said that the first presidency and the apostles were all united on it, and that it should be practiced no more.
>
> My husband came to our tent and told me about it, and my feelings were past description. I had gone into that order of marriage solely . . . because I believed God had commanded his people to do so, and it had been such a sacrifice to enter it, and live it as I thought God wanted me to. And as I thought about it, it seemed impossible that the Lord would go back on a principal which had caused so much sacrifice, heartache, and trial before one could conquer one's carnal self, and live on that higher plane, and love

Lorena Eugenia Washburn Larsen (1860–1945)

one's neighbor as one's self. My husband walked out without saying a word, and as he walked away I thought, Oh yes, it is easy for you, you can go home to your other family and be happy with her, while I must be like Hagar, sent away.

My anguish was inexpressible, and a dense darkness took hold of my mind. I thot that if the Lord and the church athorities had gone back on that principle, there was nothing to any part of the gospel. I fancied I could see my self and my children, and many other splendid women and their families turned adrift, and our only purpose in entering it, had been to more fully serve the Lord. I sank down on our bedding and wished in my anguish that the earth would open and take me and my children in. The darkness seemed impenetrable.

A poignant spiritual confirmation, however, helped Lorena accept the new Church policy:

> All at once I heard a voice and felt a most powerful presence. The voice said, "Why this is no more unreasonable than the requirement the Lord made of Abraham when he commanded him to offer up his son Isaac, and when the Lord sees that you are willing to obey in all things the trial shall be removed."
>
> There was a light whose brightness cannot be described which filled my soul, and I was so filled with joy, peace, and happiness that I felt that no matter whatever should come to me in all my future life, I could never feel sad again. If the people of the whole world had been gathered together trying with all their power to comfort me, they could not compare with the powerful unseen Presence which came to me on that occasion.
>
> And as soon as my husband came back I told him what a glorious presence had been there, and what I had heard. He said, "I knew that I could not say a word to comfort

you, so I went to a patch of willows, and asked the Lord to send a comforter."[23]

Because of the Manifesto and the continuing danger from deputy marshals, a greater responsibility for providing for herself and her children fell upon Lorena, especially because Bent's health made it difficult for him to provide for both families. Bent and Lorena had nine children—three boys and six girls.[24] Lorena took in sewing, raised a large garden with fruits and vegetables, and purchased a machine to knit stockings. When a swarm of bees found her yard, she captured them and learned beekeeping. For a time she served as Monroe town clerk. In addition, her children worked for neighbors to help with family expenses.

Lorena's oldest son, Bent Franklin, wrote, "Probably no one, except some of Mother's children, can ever know of her fatigue, her heartaches, and ofttimes her humiliation with poverty and with the feeling of aloneness in the struggle to provide for her family and to secure the wherewith to make her dreams come true."[25]

And still she persevered. Her daughter Floy recorded, "No matter what the problem, she always seemed to find a way. Many times she seemed to accomplish the impossible by sheer force of will. But always with love and compassion and fasting and prayer."[26]

Lorena was determined that her children get an education. As her older children completed their own education, they helped the younger ones obtain more schooling. Bent Franklin left for Snow College with only sixteen dollars cash and some bedding and food.[27] He worked for Canute Peterson in exchange for bread. Young Bent said, "When my food supply dwindled to the bread and a handful of dried prunes I wrote Mother that I was intending to walk home if I could not catch a ride. The distance required two days by team."[28] Lorena insisted that he wait while everyone in the family fasted and prayed. For three days she contacted neighbors, hoping someone would lend her money enough that Bent could stay in school. Finally, on the third day, she was walking down the street when she heard her name called by Hugh Lisonbee, a rancher in town who had just sold a flock of sheep. Because there was no bank in Monroe in which to place his cash, he was looking for someone who might want to borrow some money.[29] God had answered her faithful prayers.

Throughout her life, Lorena was blessed with many spiritual manifestations, some of which aided her in family history and temple work. One night she awoke three times to find two women standing by her bed. One described a book in the Manti Temple containing her records. Lorena was sure she had seen her family's books at the temple, and the volume did not exist. The next time Lorena visited the temple, the recorder handed her a book he had just discovered—it contained the promised records.[30]

Another time Lorena worked to organize an excursion to the Manti Temple. She had the names of many family members who needed their temple ordinances, but as the day approached, relatives came to her with excuses why they could not make the trip. "By nightfall," Floy remembered, "not a person was able or willing to go. Lorena was very disappointed. . . . The next morning there was still no one to go with her, but Lorena went to the temple anyway. When she got there, nearly the entire population of the town of Annabel was there on an excursion, hunting names so they could do the endowments. . . . As the day was over she checked and found that over 80 people had worked for the names she had brought."[31]

Lorena continued to be closely involved with her children once they were grown. Her daughter Floy, after divorcing, found it necessary to support her two children by teaching school. Lorena was there to help. Glen Turner, Floy's son, recounted: "Through the years grandma lived with us a lot. When grandma was at our house, things were different. When she wasn't there, I would come home from school to a cold house. I'd have to build fires in the stoves and wait for mother to come home from school and cook supper. When grandma was there, the house would be warm, and the smell

*Lorena Eugenia Washburn Larsen in 1912,
age fifty-two.*

of cinnamon rolls or peach cobbler would greet me as I opened the door."³²

Lorena's touch continued to bless her family. In 1887 or 1888 Lorena had had a dream in which she met her deceased father. He showed her a beautiful city where everything was peaceful and orderly. She expressed a hope to stay in the city with her parents and loved ones but was told that she had a journey to take. A messenger took her outside the city and showed her the road she was to travel. She saw roaring rivers to cross and a steep, rough mountain to climb. The messenger told her that although there would be times when she thought the journey was impossible, he would be with her to sustain her. Despite this assurance, the road appeared too overwhelming, and she asked if she could go back to the city and ask her parents' advice before beginning. He agreed. However, when she returned to the city, she couldn't find anyone she knew. Finally she met Ann Tidd, a woman from her home town. Lorena described the terrible journey and asked Sister Tidd's advice. "She said, 'If you only knew the reward there is for traveling that road you would never hesitate.' . . . Then I decided I would go and do my best. I awoke."[33]

Truly, Lorena kept working and enduring until her life's end. In a letter to her son Bent Franklin, seventy-two-year-old Lorena described how she spent her time in the winter of 1932: "I made, and made over before Christmas forty-five articles of clothing, and since New Years have made fourteen dresses, and have eleven more to make. I am never out of work, am thankful I can work. I have written Father's history too, and made a suit for Pearl's baby."[34] This was in addition to taking an adult seminary course.

All in all, Lorena served in many callings in the Relief Society and the Young Ladies' Mutual Improvement Association over the years, and her love for genealogy and participation in temple work led to many spiritual experiences.

In 1932 Lorena reflected on the dream she'd had more than forty years before:

> I have traveled that road, and God has sustained me, and while traveling on the rough parts, at intervals, He sent to me the choicest gifts of heaven, my children, who have stood firm and true by my side in all the battles of life. And are still the same.
>
> Yes, I have been richly rewarded for traveling on that road, in the hard, yet rich experiences which I have gained, and my splendid children, and the great blessings spiritual and temporal, which God has showered down upon us. He has truly been with us to this hour.[35]
>
> L.E.W.L.

Late in life Lorena sold her home in Monroe and moved to Provo, Utah, where she died on August 2, 1945.

Chapter 8

"It Would Be Worth It"

Mary Roselia Cook McCann (1863–1945)
by Jeff Hillam

Mary Roselia Cook was born in Holden, Utah, on November 12, 1863, to Phineas Wolcott and Amanda Polly Savage Cook. As members of The Church of Jesus Christ of Latter-day Saints, both of Mary's parents had crossed the plains in the early years of the migration to Utah—Amanda in 1847 and Phineas in 1848. When Mary was eight months old, her family moved to Swan Creek, Utah, on the shores of Bear Lake.[1]

Mary reminisced about her youth in Swan Creek: "My child hood and girl hood was spent in this lovely buisy place on the shores of the beautiful Bear Lake. How I loved the dear old place. The creek the lake the hills every tree and shady nook was very dear to me."[2]

When Mary was eighteen, her father sold his business in Swan Creek, and she and her mother moved to "a little home and a small farme" in nearby Garden City. "My heart was almost broken," Mary recalled.[3]

Mary Roselia Cook McCann (1863–1945)

I lived with [my mother] till July 12th 1883 when I marr[i]ed Hyrum Johnston McCann. He had a home and small farme in Garden City and was the sole support of his widowed mother a widowed sister and her girl. So we did not intend to marry for a long time but he was very badley ingured in the canyon and we despared of his life for a long time. His mother was old and could not take care of him and his sister was handicaped in such a way that she could not either. I knew if he ever got well he must have care. So I married so I could nurse him back to health The Dr said he would never be strong but I loved him so much that I felt if I could only care for him even for a few years it would be worth it. We had a very hard winter that year with fences all buried in snow and a very late spring. His sisters had moved with their husbands the year before to the Ashley Vally Uinta Co. Utah and they wrote in glowing terms of the lovely climate and were so sure my husband would get well if we would only move there that we decided to go. . . .

It was very hard for me to leave my mother and all the dear ones and I feared the journey as I was expecting a baby in two months but felt no sacrefise was to great if it would be the means of restoring my husband to health. We were three weary weeks on the road. . . . We had three teams and two heavy wagons and one light spring wagon. I drove the team to that wagon and cooked three meals a day over the camp fire for seven persons. Our journey led through mountains over corderoy roads and steep dug ways. How I ever stood it is a wonder. I would drive all day and be in pain most of the night God must have taken care of me.[4]

Once in Ashley Valley, the McCanns secured a one-room log cabin on eighty acres of land "and raised enough wheat for our bread and for seed to plant in the spring." Mary remembered:

Two young women overlooking Bear Lake, the area that Mary Cook McCann always considered home, ca. 1910.

We sold a pair of twin steers to get alfalfa seed and to see me through my confinement. The water was very bad and I was quite ill for a week or more. I just laid on the cot and drank water and it would come up as fast as it went down On Sep 12 1864 my oldest child was born . . . and when I heard his lusty cry I can truly say I had never before been so happy. Yes lying there on a quilt on the little old cabins floore with the man I loved so well and his dear old mother and sweet sisters around me I know no one colud be any mor happy than I was. . . .

I soon became well and strong once more and that winter my husband and I joined the dramatic association in Vernal [Utah] which put on plays about every two weeks. . . . On the nights we played I took my precious baby with me. . . . My dramatic work and church dutes kept me very buisy but I was always home sick for my dear Mother and Bear Lake. . . . My husband did not become well and strong as we had hoped and some times he was not able to even do the out side chores when spring came I helped him all I could while he worked on the canal I plowed 16 achers of ground with a sulkey plow and three horses, part of the time with the baby in my arms I then harrowed it and got it ready for planting . . . We had about five cows. . . . One day . . . they were all bloted and we were only able to save one old cow. . . . This was surely a calamity and put me out of the cow buisness entirely. When we were at the end of our roap and did not know what to do next I happened through the reccomendation of my old teachers and good friend Charles Rich to get the pos[i]tion of teacher in the summer school. That ment very much to us all. . . .

That winter [1885] . . . the first mutual was organized in our ward I was chosen first counceler. . . . I enjoyed my work . . . very much. . . . My baby [Joseph Arthur] was borne on the 27 of Nov 1885. . . .

On Nov 11th 1887 I gave birth to a lovely little daughter [Stella] I had a nice time. . . . I had taken care of my self and so got along fine. . . .

[In 1888] my little boy Arthur was very ill all summer. . . . I know now it was just for want of propper food. We were very anxious to . . . go through the temple so we planned to do that in the fall. . . . We made the long journey [to the Logan Temple][5] all right but my little boy [Arthur] grew worse all the time we felt if we could get him to the Temple he would get well. On Oct 12 1888 we went through the Temple had our endowments and was sealed. My mother said she was afraid Arthur would not live till night. . . . The sisters took him and washed him and blessed him and he seamed much better. . . . He was much better in the morning so we started home.[6]

Mary had many more trying experiences during her young motherhood years. She and her family were enterprising and undertook several ventures, including a mercantile business, ranch, farm, and small orchard. Though they worked hard, the McCanns struggled with poverty. On account of Hyrum's frequently weakened physical condition, Mary bore a heavy load in supporting her family.

Although there were times that she despaired, she was quick to recognize and record the Lord's hand in her life:

> We were very hard up for days and days we had nothing to eat but dry bread and green corn I would say to Hy What would you like for dinner? bread and corn or corn and bread. He wass ill and each day grew worse I knew most of it was for lack of good food. at last I went out alone and praye[d] to the Lord to send me something to do, or open the way so that I could get nurishing food for my sick husband. In about an hour I heard a knock at the door and on opening it I saw a kneibor boy Alberto Bird with a large close basket on the step almost full of every thing good to eat Enough good things to last till my husband was well again. That was only one time in those four trying years that my prayers were answered.[7]

In 1890, the same year their daughter Rozella was born, the McCanns moved to Hams Fork, Wyoming, to begin ranching. In 1892, Mary gave birth to another daughter, Vera, and in 1894, she gave birth to a son, Laurence. "I enjoyed my baby very much," she wrote, "but all summer I felt a haunting fear that some thing awful was going to happen." Mary related:

> My boys were now olde enougt to be quite a help. . . . Arthur who would be nine in November . . . [and] was very anxious to get through with the haying as we had promised to take him to Garden City and have him baptised. He would be one of the first ones up and he would waken his father and say come dadie lets get the haying done so we can go to grandmas we took him over in August and he was baptised in the lake.[8]

Shortly thereafter, Arthur drowned in a creek near their home. "We did every thing we could to restore life but to no purpose," she grieved.[9]

> It was a sad winter for me. . . . I could not shed a tear at first and after a while I would cry all the time when I was alone and at night when every one else was asleep. . . . One night I went to bed thinking it could not have been worse no matter how it had been. At last I fell asleep and . . . [had a] vivid dream. . . . I saw Arthur. . . . He looked very sad and there was tears in his big blue eyes. . . . His lips quivered and he said I would be happy if my mamma did not cry so much. That dream also was so real that it made me feel that I was making m[y] loved one sad by greaving so I tried my best to get over my greaving and to once again be able to pray. It was a hard struggle. . . .
>
> After the New Year [1896] my baby Laurence was taken ill. He would run a temprature every afternoon that would last all night. . . . My mother and I did every thing we could for him but it was weeks before he got any better, at last I was prompted to give him a teaspoon full of caster oil with a few drops of terpentine in it thre[e] times a day for three days then repete the dose till nine mornings had passed I did this and he was soon well. . . .
>
> On October 1st 1896 a fine black eyed boy was born to us we named him Loys . . . That fall when we had our hay almost up and for the first time would have plenty. . . . I took a load of cheese to town [to sell]. . . . When I came [back] in sight of the house I saw a big smoke. . . . The children ran to meet me and I knew what was wrong before they told me. Their father had been burning brush across the river. . . . A breeze was blowing and sparks flue over into the stacks and before he knew it they were all ablase as he could not see the stacks from where he was when they did

see it it was to late to do any thing Hy stood and watched it burne and turned to John and said, "Well Im a damed smart man to work all summer just to make a bond fire. Well they gleaned what hay they cood and bought a stack. . . . If it had been an ordinary winter we would have had enough but it was not It began snowing and blowing the 1st of November [and didn't] let up till last of June. . . . We could not drive our stock to feed nor could we get feed to them One day we saw a man coming up the flat on foot. He had chanced it up from Kimmerer [Wyoming] part of the way and walked the rest. He loaned us money enough [to] get a load of corn and he took our team and sleighs and went to town for it That seen our cattle through till we could turn them on the hills. . . .

I became ill about the first of Jan. and was ill all winter I could not do any work and could not be up half the time. I was expecting a baby in Aug and that with all the worry was to much for me. . . . I became worse and was lying on the bed in pain and Hy said as soon as spring opens I am going to take you over to Dr Allquire. I said Allquire cant do me any good. than he said dont you think God can? I said no I dont think God knows any thing about me. If he ever did he has forgotten all about me. H went to the cupboared took the olive oil and poared some into a sawser He annointed me with the oil and blessed me. I became easy at once I had no more pain and s[l]ept fine all night The next morning I was perfectly well. . . . I never had another sick day. . . . On the 27th of August 1899 [m]y boy was born after three days labor. . . . His father blessed him named him Lorell. . . .

Every one was welcome at our house and time passed quickley we had dances quite often and the young folk did lots of horse back rideing and other sports. I my self loved horses and did lots of rideing Each morning I would rangle the horses while the men were having breakfast. . . . In the fall of 1902 I went to Garden City to send the children to school. . . . In July on the 6th of that month [1903] a little 5 lb baby girl [Jean] was born to me. She was very tiny and I had to be very careful with her. . . .

I was very anxious to live in civilization once more so we . . . sold the ranch . . . and bought a . . . farme in Garden City. . . . We had only been there a few weeks when Loys took Pneumonia he was then 10 years old I did every thing I knew and he grew worse I finaly sent for Dr JW Hayward When he stepped up to the bed Loys said Dr Hayward will you please administer to me? Sure I will the Dr said. He did so and then gave me instructions what to do and left medicine to give He said he is a very sick child I asked him if he had any hopes for him and he said O yes I have lots more hopes for him now than I did before I administered to him The night the Dr said the crisis would come I sat and knelt by his bed all night. He was so weak and exausted I would have to put my ear down to his face to tell whether he was breathing or not He was better in the morning and kept on improving God was very good to me and spared his life.

That spring Hy worked very hard to get his farme in shape for a crop. I was all ready following in mothers footsteps I began going as a nurse with the Doctors and it kept me very buisy. . . . I did a lot of nursing and the girls and I picked fruit on shares and for money We would go at 7 in the morning and pick till dark It was small fruit raspberries and goose berries we obtained our years fruit in that way we became efficent pickers and every one wanted us. . . .

I went about the middel of the month [December 1909] to Thomasesfork [Idaho] to nurse Toms wife Eunice[10] through her confinement when her baby was 10 days old a feeling came over me that I must go home. . . . I arrived there on Christmass eve and found every one well but very glad to have me home We had a quiet Xmass and Hy seamed as well as usulal. On the morning of the 2nd of Jan. he said how well he felt and insisted on going to the canyon. . . . That night he was taken ill with Pneumonia I did every thing I could but he grew worse He refused to let me send for a doctor at last I sent for one and did not tell him Hayward came and left medicine and instructions. On the morning he seamed better and said he would be able to be up to morrow but that afternoon he become worse and that night he died That was on Jan 9th 1910 he had been ill eleven days. . . . The rest of the winter was a very sad and lonely one. The girls did not go to a dance or place of amusment of any kind till the 4th of July. I took up the burden of life again and worked harder than ever. My mother wa[s] a great comefort to me and I knew I had a big job to do if I kept my family together and raised them as I should. . . .

I nursed all my girls in their confinements and nearly all the other wimmen in town my boys were growing up and were a big help to me. They had an Orchestra and played . . . for all the dances in Garden City. In July of 1915 I went to my brother Daves ranch and cooked for his hay men. On the 15th of Aug of July 1915 my mother died She was ill only four days. I felt like the last prop had been taken from under me and that I just could not go on with out her but I tried to gather up the broken threads of my life and live for my childrens Sake my little girl Jean was a great comefort to me.[11]

Mary bore nine children over the course of two decades.[12] She learned midwifery from her mother and delivered many babies, including several of her own grandchildren. Although she had little in the way of earthly goods, her door was always open, especially to young people. Mary and her family participated in many community activities, especially local theater and musical events. Her faith was expressed through years of service in her ward Young Ladies' Mutual Improvement Association and Relief Society and in the Logan Temple.

Several of Mary's grandchildren were born between 1915 and 1917, and she cared for her daughters, daughters-in-law, and the babies. After her daughter Rozella gave birth in October 1917, Mary wrote:

> I breathed easy once more for the baby crop in my own family was over for a while at least but other folks kept me buisy I nursed with Dr Hayward till he moved to logan and then with Dr Cooley and Dr Sutton The knollage I gained while working with these men was very valuble to me many time[s] I would have to be both Dr and nurse as the Dr could not get there in time.
>
> In April of 1917 just after the first world war was called Laurence went to the Post office and gave his name to be sent in as a volenteer. . . . I was so shocked. . . . I did not fully realize that there was a war. . . . In Aug 1918 [Loys] was called in the armey. . . . Lorell was very anxious to go that night [that Loys left] . . . I did not sleep any and I heard him moving about in his room Loys had told him his job was to stay home and take care of mother and Sissie meaning Jean. That night I knew how Abraham felt when God asked him to offer his son Issac as a sacrafise. I made up my mind to tell Lorell he could volenteer if he wanted to He was just 18. When he came down stairs in the morning he was very pale and I knew he had not slept. I went and put my arms around him and said, "Lorell if you want to volenteer I will not do any thing to stop you. . . . He hugged me tight and said It is because you are a real mother that you say that You are not like a lot of selfish ones who just think of self. He was very happy and went at once to try to inlist

but he found they would not let any one volinteer now so he would have to wait till the 18 to 45 draft came. . . .

How happy I was when the news [of the signing of the armistice] came and how a few of us did celebrate we road all over town in a ford and pownded tin pans and blew horns fired of[f] guns and made all the noise we could. . . . That night Jean and I got every thing of no value about the place and built a big bonfire in the lane by our place folks came from all over town and when that fire burned out we all went to John Hodges lane and built one there I surely was a thankful woman I knew my boys would come home in the governments own due time.[13]

Mary spent her last years in Logan, Utah. Ever longing for Bear Lake, she "tried to be contented" in Logan, where she stayed near much of her family. On October 20, 1927, Mary married Chauncey L. Dustin; she survived him also.[14] She began working in the temple, and she continued to serve her church, community, and family. She died on May 29, 1945, at age eighty-one.[15]

Mary endured hardship with aplomb, sturdiness, and faith. She spent years caring for her family and others through recurrent illness, poverty, hunger, and death, showing dogged courage in the face of adversity and undaunted faith in the Lord. Through it all, she took great enjoyment in that which mattered most: God and family. She is a witness to the strength that love can have, and, above all, the power of the Lord in the details of our lives. Though her life was full of hardship, she shone through it with a pragmatist's optimism. Her two cardinal virtues, evident in her actions throughout her life, were patient endurance and unremitting love. She navigated life with a successful marriage and family, love for the Lord, and zeal for his work.[16]

Chapter 9
"Doing a Little Good for the Cause of Christ"

Elizabeth Ann Claridge McCune (1852–1924)
by Matthew S. McBride

Samuel Claridge was a twenty-three-year-old grocer and baker living in Hemel Hempstead, England, when, in June 1851, he and his wife Charlotte Joy joined The Church of Jesus Christ of Latter-day Saints. Their second child, a daughter, was born eight months later on February 19, 1852. They named her Elizabeth Ann.

Elizabeth's parents soon answered the call to migrate to Utah and booked passage to the United States in January 1853 as members of the Ten-Pound Company.[1] After crossing the Atlantic, they traveled from Iowa and arrived in Salt Lake City on October 10, 1853. Some members of the company were asked to continue on to a new settlement called Salt Creek, eighty-nine miles to the south. So it was that in April of 1854, two-year-old Elizabeth Ann Claridge arrived at Salt Creek (later renamed Nephi), the small frontier town she would ever after think of as home.[2]

Elizabeth spent the years of her childhood on the edge of civilization, working with her family to eke out an existence and garner a few hard-earned luxuries. When the Utah Telegraph Company ran lines through Nephi in 1867, Elizabeth and two of her friends were trained as telegraph operators and assigned stations in Nephi and other nearby towns. They made use of the lines to keep in touch with each other.[3]

At age fifteen, Elizabeth was shocked when Brigham Young called her father to leave their comfortable life in Nephi and settle "the Muddy," a new settlement along the Muddy River near present-day Logandale in the bleak desert of southern Nevada. Elizabeth spent the next three years pioneering the Muddy with her father and his second wife.

Pioneer of Nephi and the Muddy

"There was no place on earth that was so precious to me as dear old Nephi," recalled Elizabeth later in life. "We were happy—perfectly so, and as proud of our station and of the parts we played as a people could be. The fact that everybody was poor didn't rob them of all the enjoyments of life. We proved in those days that it is not necessary to be rich to be happy. . . . Nephi was not large, not wonderful, but we had our occasions there, as we called them, just as much so as any big city of the land. And what is more, we got out of them every ounce of pleasure they would yield."[4]

Perhaps the most memorable of those occasions for Elizabeth was an 1867 visit by President Brigham Young. Accompanied by a party of Church authorities, he arrived in Nephi and was welcomed by Elizabeth's family and others. Elizabeth recorded the following account of the visit:

> The company having been taken to our homes the very best dinner we could provide was served. How we girls fairly flew about to make things look nice and stylish for these folks from the city! And I must confess that we did a little in the direction of making ourselves look as stylish as we could. . . .

During the afternoon we all attended the meeting, the girls in white having reserved seats in the front. The sermons were inspirational and grand. They made us very happy until well on toward the close of the meeting when President Young announced that he had a few names to read—names of men who had been selected to go with their families and "settle the Muddy." That almost stopped our beating hearts. Many of our people had been previously called to settle the Dixie country. But the Muddy—that was so much farther—so much more difficult. Then I heard the name of "Samuel Claridge," my father. After that I knew nothing for a moment and when I recovered myself again I was weeping bitterly. Tears were spoiling my new white dress but I sobbed on just the same. Said the companion who was at my side, "What are you feeling so badly about? My father has been called, too, but you see that I am not crying because I know he won't go." "That is just the difference. My father is called and I know that he WILL GO; and that nothing can prevent him from going. He never fails to do anything when called upon; and badly as I feel about it I would be ashamed if he didn't go."[5]

Elizabeth journeyed to the Muddy with her father, reluctantly leaving behind her friends, mother and sister,[6] and childhood home but inspired by her father's insistence on answering the call to "build up another waste place in Zion."[7] Elizabeth labored vigorously to help make a life for her family in the desert. Among her contributions was the work she did to help construct their new home:

My father built a house away down on the Muddy. . . . I helped my father build it. I worked just as hard as a man. Every adobe and every bucket of mortar that went into its walls I carried. Yes, every one. It was a hard task but I am not ashamed of it and would do it again under like circumstances if it were necessary. My father was a good man and

I was proud of the fact that I was able to lighten his burden in some measure.[8]

Her attitude toward work, wealth, and worldly attainments was forged by these pioneering experiences and remained with her throughout her life. Later, as a member of the Young Ladies' Mutual Improvement Association (YLMIA) general board, she was once asked to canvass the well-to-do women of Salt Lake for donations to a build a new building for the use of the women's organizations of the Church. She replied, "Well, I'll go. But I'd rather carry mortar in a hod to build it."[9]

After the Muddy Mission was abandoned in 1870, Elizabeth moved to St. George to work in the telegraph office. While there, she honed her dramatic talents as leading lady for the St. George Home Dramatic Troupe and became friends with Brigham Young's daughter Susa.[10]

During her sojourn in these southern settlements, Elizabeth maintained contact with her childhood friend and admirer in Nephi, Alfred William McCune, and on July 1, 1872, the two traveled to Salt Lake and were married in the Endowment House, afterward making their home in Nephi.[11] Between 1873 and 1891, Alfred and Elizabeth had nine children, eight of whom survived infancy. Their sixth child, Frank, died in a tragic accident at age five.[12]

Blessings of Success

The family moved to Salt Lake City in 1888 after living near Alfred's mining and timber interests in Montana for three years. By that time, a series of spectacular business successes had catapulted Alfred and Elizabeth into prominence as one of Utah's wealthiest families.[13] The contrast between her pioneer upbringing and her new situation could not have been greater; yet Elizabeth maintained her unpretentious demeanor, preference for simplicity, and do-it-yourself approach. She made regular and generous donations to a variety of causes and individuals and avoided hiring servants.[14] Her

Elizabeth Ann Claridge McCune (1852–1924)

Elizabeth Claridge McCune in Denver, Colorado, ca. 1880.

hesitancy to indulge in extravagance prompted Alfred to say that "the greatest fault he could find with her was that she would not spend freely enough what he so lavishly bestowed upon her."[15]

Elizabeth's generosity with her time and newfound wealth led to opportunities for service in high-profile settings. Between 1898 and 1920, Elizabeth shouldered a dizzying array of public and Church responsibilities: member of both the YLMIA and the Relief Society general boards, patron of the National Council of Women and the International Council of Women, vice chair of the Agricultural College of Utah board of trustees, board member of the Utah Art Institute, and committee member in the Genealogical Society of Utah and the Daughters of Utah Pioneers.

The McCune Mansion in Salt Lake City was completed in 1901. After residing in the home for nearly twenty years, the McCunes donated it to The Church of Jesus Christ of Latter-day Saints. It was used as a school of music and art. This photograph features the carriage entrance of the home, 1917.

After renting the Gardo House in Salt Lake City for three years, the McCunes built a home at 200 North Main Street.[16] Alfred gave Elizabeth carte blanche to design the house and insisted she spare no expense. Dubbed by her friends "the house that Elizabeth built," the stately mansion was completed in 1901 and would serve as the family home for nearly two decades.

Woman Missionary Forerunner

In 1897, Elizabeth and her family took a grand tour of Europe. She intended to spend some time in England doing genealogical research, and before leaving Utah, she went to President Lorenzo Snow seeking a blessing. Among other things, he promised her, "Thy mind shall be as clear as an angel's when explaining the principles of the Gospel."[17] With these words in her heart, Elizabeth assisted the missionaries in England by singing at their street meetings. Still, she "had an ardent desire to speak herself, feeling that as she was a

Elizabeth Ann Claridge McCune (1852–1924)

woman she might attract more attention than the young men and therefore do good."

At the same time, a former Church member named William Jarman was traveling about England promoting his anti-Mormon book. He reserved his most scathing criticisms for the way women were allegedly treated in Utah, depicting them as downtrodden and enslaved victims of their religion. These attacks were difficult to combat with a force of young male elders. At the October 1897 quarterly conference in London, William McMurrin of the European Mission Presidency spoke of "the base falsehoods which Jarman . . . had so industriously circulated regarding the Mormon women." He noticed Elizabeth in the crowd, and to her surprise, announced that she would speak that evening on the condition of women in Utah. Elizabeth later recalled:

> This announcement nearly frightened me to death. But the Elders assured me that they would give me their faith and prayers, and I added my own fervent appeals to my Heavenly Father for aid and support. . . .
>
> That night the hall was again filled and with a final prayer I arose to address the audience. . . . I told them I had been raised in Utah and knew almost every foot of the country and most of the people. I spoke of my extensive travels in America and in Europe, and said that nowhere had I found women held in such esteem as among the Mormons of Utah. Our husbands are proud of their wives and daughters; they do not consider that they were created solely to wash dishes and tend babies; but they give them every opportunity to attend meetings and lectures and to take up everything which will educate and develop them. Our religion teaches us that the wife stands shoulder to shoulder with the husband. . . . At the close of the meeting several strangers shook me by the hand and said, "If more of your women would come out here a great amount of good would be done."[18]

President McMurrin took special notice of the effects of Elizabeth's speech and invited her to accompany him to other conferences to share a similar message. After Elizabeth departed from England, McMurrin wrote the First Presidency requesting that they call sister missionaries. A few months later, the first single women to serve proselytizing missions were called to Great Britain. President George Q. Cannon cited Elizabeth's efforts as contributing to this momentous step.[19]

Elizabeth traveled extensively throughout her life and never shied from sharing her religious beliefs. "While abroad," she said, "I always had a burning desire in my heart to give our Father's children what I knew to be the Truth. Wherever I went to visit and had an opportunity to converse with the people I would lead up to this the uppermost topic in my mind."[20] In 1902 she visited Peru with Alfred. While he oversaw his mining interests, Elizabeth was busy, as she said, "doing a little good for the cause of Christ"[21]:

> I met the embassador from Brazil and explained the gospel to him. I said, "Mr. Alcoforada, I want to explain the principles of the everlasting gospel to you," and he very kindly listened, and remained conversing with me all the evening, being loath to leave, and he paid many compliments to our people. I related to him some of the history of our people and the trials they had passed through, and bore testimony to their purity and faithfulness. Tears streamed down his cheeks when I explained to him what our people had done; and I said, the time will come when there will be elders sent to this country, for they are commanded to preach to every nation, and I want you people, when they come, to treat them kindly when you meet them.

"I can testify," Elizabeth concluded, "that when we have a desire in our hearts to explain the principles of the gospel, our Heavenly Father comes to our assistance, and no matter how humble we are, when Father helps us, we make an impression. It is not ourselves, but the Spirit of God which enables us to do this."[22]

Wife, Mother, Friend

As exciting and demanding as her various public and Church assignments were, Elizabeth remained a very private, almost retiring person, and invested heavily in the deep personal connections she forged with her family and intimate friends. When her friend Susa Young Gates encouraged her to submit a biographical sketch to a publication highlighting prominent women, Elizabeth chided her friend: "You are always trying to promote me, but truly Susie I do not belong to that class. What little everyday things that I have done wouldn't interest any one, only a few of our own people." Yet she appreciated the compliment. "Bless your old heart no body sees me through your eyes."[23]

"Oh how she loved her family," wrote another of Elizabeth's friends. "What joy it gave her when the members of it manifested the faith in and love for the truths which inspired her heart! I think she would gladly have laid down her life as many times as there are members of her family, could that have insured their salvation!"[24]

Elizabeth's letters to loved ones open a window into her joys and reveal how her tender feelings for her family often left her vulnerable to pain and anxiety. Most distressing to Elizabeth was the way her husband, Alfred, and two of their sons distanced themselves from the Church as they became absorbed with their successful careers.[25] A letter to her half sister Julia contains this bit of marriage advice that grew out of Elizabeth's own experience:

> How thankful I was that you had such a good husband and that you were both so congeneal and happy. I thought of poor Fay while she has a good husband, there isn't the same hapiness as there is when you both see the gospel alike. I can see that Clarance will be a great man in the business world yet but tell him not to get so tied up that he will have to

give up any of his religious duties, there is where the danger creeps in. He has done such a wonderful work in the church, I don't want him to fall down and I don't think he will.[26]

Susa Young Gates, who experienced similar heartache over one of her children, often commiserated with Elizabeth and even wrote surreptitious letters to Alfred, goading him to rethink his relationship to the Church for Elizabeth's sake: "When I see the constant prayers of your loving single-minded wife, I am sure that they will, some day not far hence, be answered upon both your heads. You want her sweet society on the other side and she certainly would never be content in a heaven that did not hold you as its focus."[27]

Susa's letters of consolation to Elizabeth were deeply appreciated. One letter, containing a glowing report by a stake president of one of Elizabeth's genealogy lectures, elicited the following response:

> Your letter received and tears shed over it. My poor boy is still drinking and in to trouble. I had just been crying myself sick, when Alf brought up the mail and your sweet letter was one. Susan it seemed like the Lord sent that letter to comfort me. Say Sue, you certainly are my friend no one else would have written me that but you. You are so darn big and broad that it did you as much good as though he had said it of you. I know you through and through *girlie*. . . .
>
> I am trying to live up to my blessing and be cheerful it's hard when every thing I meet is opposite to what I like, but it's certainly a schooling.[28]

Genealogist and Temple Worker

In the midst of these spiritual trials, Elizabeth poured her energy into the twin causes of genealogy and temple work.[29] She shared a passion for them with her father, Samuel Claridge, who fulfilled a genealogical mission to England in 1877 and 1878.[30] Father and daughter worked together to perform thousands of temple ordinances for family members.³¹ Samuel once wrote to Elizabeth with some pride that his brother was "trying to get names but he says Lizzy [Elizabeth] and I have scratched over the straw so many times that he can hardly find a kernel."³²

Her father provided further impetus to Elizabeth's genealogical pursuits by linking them to that dearest of matters: her anxiety for Alfred's salvation despite his lack of interest in the Church. Samuel wrote her in 1902, "Now we must not grow slack in this great work . . . for I can see glorious blessings that will result from it, and let me tell you this will be one of the great means that will help your husband, for it will be seen that it has been through his means to a great extent that we have accomplish[ed] what we have."³³

As the Salt Lake Temple neared completion, Elizabeth persuaded Alfred to make a generous donation of $5,000 to its construction.³⁴ The gift was so large that Alfred had to borrow and pay interest on it in spite of his many business successes.³⁵ The gift was a testament to Elizabeth's earnest importuning, Alfred's generosity, and the couple's close attachment. Soon after the temple was dedicated, Elizabeth was called to be an ordinance worker, an assignment she cherished and fulfilled dutifully for more than two decades.³⁶

Elizabeth and fellow temple worker Susa Young Gates were the pioneers of an effort among the women of the Relief Society to expand genealogical work in the Church. The two spent over a decade as officers in the Daughters of Utah Pioneers and the Genealogical Society of Utah and as members of the YLMIA and Relief Society general boards, lecturing, creating training materials, visiting genealogical libraries in the United States and Europe, and providing branches and wards throughout North America with practical instruction in what was then an unfamiliar and daunting field.³⁷

In 1907, Elizabeth visited the Saints in Mesa, Arizona, where a new temple in the Church was to be built. A newspaper reported of her opening lecture:

The genealogical spirit is growing in leaps and bounds among the people of the country. She said this was to be expected, for the genealogical spirit "is nothing short of the 'Spirit of Elijah' that is working in the hearts of the people." . . . "Men and women of the earth are spending much time and money, gathering [and] compiling genealogical data, and publishing them in great family histories, and there are accessible to the Latter-day Saints from which to compile lists of their ancestors for whom they are being baptized in the temples of the Lord." Elizabeth said the four temples of the church are crowded to overflowing continuously. "We are now building two more temples, and I understand that you are to have a temple right here in Mesa. It is a grand and glorious work and we should prepare to do our full part in it."[38]

Elizabeth's work was not without its difficulties. A general lack of interest in genealogy, together with its technical nature, often made for an uphill battle. Elizabeth expressed her frustration with a branch in Brooklyn in a 1918 letter to Susa:

On Genealogical Sunday I don't think one of them would have remembered it if had it not been for your notice in the [Young Woman's] Journal or [Relief Society] Magazine. . . . If I do say it I gave them a good talk and certanly gave them something to think about, the few who were there. . . . I think I convinced them that genealogical Sunday was one of the most important days in the year. don't think they will forget it next year.[39]

Elizabeth credited her friendship with Susa for her zeal as a genealogist and temple worker: "I want to say right here Susan that what ever I do for the Salvation of the dead, you may not get it here but in the next world more than half the credit will be yours for you are the one that has spur[r]ed me on to attain the implicit faith that I have on

Alfred W. and Elizabeth Claridge McCune on their fiftieth wedding anniversary, 1922.

that subject."[40] Susa reciprocated, "Don't you imagine for a moment that I have helped you any more than you have helped me in faithfulness in the temple. Your influence and example has been one of the stimulants and brightest lights upon my pathway."[41] Through their Relief Society Genealogy Committee, the two friends significantly raised the quality and quantity of genealogical work in the Church.

Homebuilder and Philanthropist

During the almost twenty years that the McCunes lived in their distinctive mansion on Main Street, Elizabeth hosted countless board meetings, receptions, dinners, and other social events. The home was considered by many to be the finest in Utah. After attending a 1904 reception at the home, President Anthon H. Lund called it "the most elegant building I have ever been in owned by private individuals."[42]

But Alfred's business ventures kept him frequently on the road, and as their children began to leave home, Elizabeth grew lonely in the enormous mansion. She once quipped, "When you hear that I am rid of that big wickiup in Salt Lake you will know that it is the happiest day of my life."[43] As early as 1919, she discussed with Alfred the possibility of donating the home to the Church and finding a dwelling that required less upkeep and was more suited to their shrinking household. Her suggestion fell upon sympathetic ears.

Earlier plans to construct a building for the women's organizations of the Church had been postponed, and the auxiliary offices were instead housed in the Bishop's Building.[44] Elizabeth had the felicitous idea of earmarking their gift to the Church as a workspace for those organizations for which she had labored for the past two decades. Despite his lack of Church activity, the idea likely resonated with Alfred, as he had tremendous respect for the Relief Society and its mission.[45] On October 7, 1920, Elizabeth wrote a letter to the First Presidency on behalf of her husband, signaling their intentions:

> Dear Brehtren.—
> My husband and myself desire to give to the Church of Jesus Christ of Latter-Day-saints our home on North Main street, to be used, preferably, for a Woman's Building, thus providing quarters for the three Woman's organizations; or for such other Purpose as you deem best.
> Faithfully Yours
> [Elizabeth McCune][46]

President Heber J. Grant thanked the McCunes publicly in general conference.[47] The Relief Society general presidency sent Elizabeth a letter expressing their gratitude for "the magnificent gift which you tendered so simply, so unostentatiously."[48] Elizabeth had left it to the First Presidency to decide how best to use the building, and various possibilities were considered, including using the mansion as the residence for the president of the Church.[49] Ultimately, it was decided to convert the home into a Church-operated school of music and art. After Elizabeth's death, it was named the McCune School of Music and Art and served educational purposes in the Church for nearly forty years.[50]

After donating the mansion to the Church, the McCunes moved to Los Angeles. Separation from her friends and the temple was difficult for Elizabeth, and her health began to deteriorate. She returned alone to Salt Lake City in 1923 and stayed in the Hotel Utah while a small home was built for her. Before it was completed, however, Elizabeth Ann Claridge McCune passed away on August 1, 1924, surrounded by her family. Her funeral was held in the Assembly Hall on Temple Square, and her body was laid to rest in her beloved Nephi.[51]

Elizabeth's faith shaped her response to her life's experiences, whether enduring the privations associated with pioneering the desert or entertaining dignitaries at her lavish home, or visiting genealogical libraries in the great cities of Europe or teaching genealogy classes in the dusty settlements of southern Utah. Animated by a vibrant testimony and by gospel principles of hard work, kindness, and generosity, Elizabeth sought to accomplish "a little good for the cause of Christ."

Chapter 10

"Courage to Follow Convictions"

Tsune Ishida Nachie (1856–1938)
by Ardis E. Parshall

The first staffing problem to face Alma O. Taylor, the newly named president of The Church of Jesus Christ of Latter-day Saints' Japanese Mission in 1905, was finding a cook and housekeeper for the mission home in Tokyo. With the departure of Mary Ensign and her husband, President Horace S. Ensign, the only missionaries in Tokyo were proselytizing young men. Being only twenty-two years old himself and unmarried, President Taylor needed a housekeeper—and, to avoid gossip, a much older housekeeper to replace the young woman who had previously been working at the mission home. He interviewed several women in their forties—he referred to them as "old" and "elderly" in his diary—before engaging forty-nine-year-old Tsune Ishida Nachie, a widow, and her fourteen-year-old adopted daughter, Ei. President Taylor could not have known then that he had found more than a cook and housekeeper; he had found a woman who would become a mother to a generation of missionaries, a tireless missionary herself, and the first native Japanese temple worker.

Tsune Ishida Nachie (1856–1938)

Tsune Ishida Nachie was born in Tokyo on April 6, 1856, a daughter of Ando Tokizo and Cho Ishida. She married Sataro Nachie; they had no children, and he died in 1888. Sometime after 1892, Tsune took Ei, the daughter of Tsune's sister Fude, to raise as her own.

Before coming into contact with Latter-day Saint missionaries, Tsune had been a Christian, a member of the Episcopal faith for twenty years. She had worked as a cook in the homes of western businessmen for many years and could prepare both Japanese and western menus. She generally commanded a higher salary than the missionaries could afford, but she had a reason to accept the elders' offer that President Taylor did not learn until later: Tsune was quietly investigating Latter-day Saint beliefs.

A granddaughter of Tsune's older, deceased sister, Tome Sakazaki, had, like many other non-Mormon children of Tokyo, joined the Sunday School taught by the missionaries. Tsune visited the Sunday School several times and became interested in what she learned there. Once she moved into the mission home in July 1905, she continued to listen to the elders and carefully consider what she heard.

Unaware at first that their new cook was actually an investigator, the elders were simply delighted to have her services. "The new cook is all that we could expect," President Taylor wrote to others in the mission. "Her cooking reminds me of how mother used to do it. Some things she prepares are truly delicious."[1] Tsune introduced an element of civilization that the elders may have known at home but had forgotten during their days of keeping bachelor quarters: "We eat in style when viewed from the way we used to eat. We have napkins and the food brought on in courses."[2]

Tsune and Ei took care of all the housework at the mission home. With her many years of experience, Tsune must have been amused as Elder Taylor "swept and dusted the dining-room to show the new servants how it should be done."[3] But, Elder Taylor wrote, she was "very good natured," and she and the elders "get along swimmingly."[4]

Tsune had been at the mission home only a month when she approached Frederick A. Caine, one of the missionaries, to tell him about her interest in the gospel and to ask for baptism. "We felt that it would be better for her to wait a while and study the Gospel more thoroughly," Elder Caine wrote.[5] "She has heard during her short sojourn with us so many things that has given her new light," recorded Elder Taylor. "If after we test her sincerity a little more and teach her further about the church and its laws she is found worthy we will be greatly pleased to have her join with us."[6]

The missionaries' caution about Tsune's sincerity and worthiness was based on experience with the tiny handful of previous converts: The first man baptized had later been caught burglarizing the mission home,[7] and few converts had remained active. But Tsune would not be put off. On September 18, she called on her former minister. Learning that he was not at home, she left a message with his wife rather than waiting to call again, notifying him that she intended to become a Mormon and was withdrawing from his church. Then she returned to the mission home and told the elders that she was ready to be baptized.

On the afternoon of Tuesday, September 26, 1905, Tsune and Elders Taylor and Caine, along with Elder Daniel P. Woodland, two Japanese sisters, and a friend of Tsune's, boarded a streetcar that took them to the Shinjuku neighborhood of Tokyo. There they walked to a little stream that had been the site of earlier baptisms. They sang the hymn "Lo on the Water's Brink We Stand," Elder Taylor offered a prayer, and Elder Caine led Tsune into the water and baptized her. "The Spirit of the Lord was present with us and we indeed had a very happy time," recorded Elder Caine. "Our new sister seemed to be very much pleased that she had been allowed to enter the Church." The following Sunday morning, Tsune was confirmed at the fast and testimony meeting held in the mission home. "Sister Nachie is nearly fifty years old and she ought to know the

Tsune Ishida Nachie (1856–1938)

Tsune Ishida Nachie was hired to be a cook and housekeeper in the Tokyo Mission Home. After her conversion, she became a mother to a generation of missionaries in Japan, a tireless missionary, and the first native Japanese temple worker in Hawaii. Photo ca. 1910.

importance of the step she has taken, and I think she does," Elder Caine wrote. "We feel that she has a strong testimony and has been greatly blessed of the Lord so that she had courage to follow her convictions."[8] Elder Taylor reported her baptism to the First Presidency: "We . . . trust that our Heavenly Father will confirm the faith of our new sister, that she may grow in a knowledge of her God and in all the good graces of the Gospel."[9]

Tsune quickly assumed a significant role in Church activities. "Sister Nachie manifests a very good spirit,"[10] and "Sister Nachie always prays as though she were thankful for her home with us and her new-found faith,"¹¹ noted the elders. At the Christmas program a few months after her baptism, Tsune addressed the parents of the non-Mormon children attending Sunday School about the benefits of Church teachings to their children.¹² She became a Sunday School teacher herself¹³ and responded to Elder Taylor's assignment to "get our four native sisters working together in a sort of women's relief society-like way."¹⁴ When she learned of the practice of anointing and blessing the sick, Tsune asked that the elders consecrate a bottle of oil for her to have. Elder Taylor "spent part of the evening translating a prayer to be used in blessing a bottle of oil, which oil I blessed at evening prayer time. . . . It was Sister Nachie's oil, blessed for her," he wrote. "I am glad to see the saints manifesting their faith in the use of oil and the administration of the same in the household of faith."¹⁵

And Tsune became a missionary. By 1908, that calling was more or less formal when Elder Taylor "decided . . . to appoint Sisters Tsune Nachie and Nami Hakii as missionaries to visit the other sisters once a month and try to keep them in the line of their duty."¹⁶ But even before that formal appointment, Tsune had been an informal, and very successful, missionary. She frequently invited friends to stay with her in the mission home for several weeks at a time, during which time she taught them the gospel. She had taken one of those friends to her baptism. Another friend, Hisa Kato, asked for baptism in 1906.¹⁷ Tsune's sister Fude Tai, having been taught by both Tsune and the elders, was baptized in 1907. Katsu Ishikawa, a friend who stayed with Tsune in 1908, developed a testimony of the gospel; when her new beliefs became known to her former church, she was reprimanded, "but as she says, assisted by an unseen power, she defended herself and the Latter-day Saints and leaving the presence of her old teacher she came direct to visit her friend Sister Nachie."¹⁸ Tsune's niece Ei Nachie was baptized in 1908.¹⁹

Tsune became a trusted member of the mission family. Her decisions about housekeeping matters, whether in the Tokyo mission home or in other cities where the missionaries labored, were accepted by the elders without question.[20] She knew what property belonged to the mission and what belonged to servants who worked for the elders outside Tokyo,[21] she advised the elders on wages to pay other servants,[22] and she decided whether it was appropriate for a young member of the Church to seek employment with the missionaries.[23] She expected the elders to respect her position in the mission home: Year after year, as the elders made plans to attend conference in Tokyo, they were warned to be prompt for meals and that "whenever anyone i[s] going away and will not be here for any meal please tell Sister Nachie beforehand so that she can plan accordingly."[24]

But Tsune also became more than a housekeeper, more even than a sister in the Church, to the elders of the Japanese mission. She was their guardian: A lighter sleeper than the elders, she became aware of an intruder one night and raised the alarm.[25] She cared for them like a mother: When a homesick missionary in Kofu asked for his familiar breakfast "mush," elders in Tokyo were able to find it for him—but rather than mail it, Tsune boarded a train to Kofu, armed with a double boiler, to teach the elder how to cook the cereal like his mother had done.[26] Ever the missionary, Tsune took the opportunity of her visit to Kofu to speak in Church services in that branch about her experiences in the Church.[27] Realizing that holidays away from home and family could be difficult, Tsune tried to do for the elders as their mothers would have done: She prepared turkey dinners their mothers would have been proud of.[28]

The elders' love for Tsune was reflected in 1906 in an important Christmas gift they made to her of having her eyes examined and a pair of gold-framed glasses made for her. "She seems well pleased and will be sure to enjoy reading and sewing as she has not done for a long time," recorded one elder.[29] The missionaries learned to call her *Obaasan* ("Grandmother"), and as new elders replaced the ones Tsune had known in the beginning, their letters from Tokyo carried Tsune's *yoroshiku* ("greetings") to old friends resuming their lives in America.[30] "They [Tsune and Ei Nachie] send yoroshiku and are still

Tsune Nachie (standing, center) was a powerful member missionary among the Japanese in Hawaii. In part due to her dedicated efforts, a Japanese branch was organized in Laie in 1934. This photograph was taken during a visit by President George Albert Smith, ca. 1938.

staunch in the faith. I do believe it would [be] impossible to move Sister Nachie she seems so faithful," read one letter.[31]

As the years passed and Tsune matured in gospel knowledge and experience, she filled an ever larger role in Church service in Tokyo. She read parts of President Alma O. Taylor's translation of the Book of Mormon and commented on its clarity. After studying the translated title page and testimony of the witnesses, "she sa[id] that it is all very simple indeed, every word being perfectly plain to her."[32]

Minutes of Church meetings provide other glimpses of her service. She prayed at meeting after meeting. She often taught the theological class (today's Gospel Doctrine) in Sunday School, and whereas other teachers seemingly drew their topics at random, Tsune consistently taught from the Book of Mormon—scripture she had studied nightly with missionaries. She bore her testimony regularly, spoke in worship services and the Mutual Improvement Association, attended baptisms, and participated in other Church activities.[33]

Records show that Tsune was especially drawn to two gospel subjects: the Book of Mormon and work for the dead. She had learned of vicarious ordinances as early as March 1906, when one of the elders gave a Sunday School lesson on baptism for the dead.[34] Elder Caine, the elder who baptized Tsune, helped her compile a record of her ancestors.[35] At Tsune's request, Joseph H. Stimpson, president of the Japan Mission in 1917, wrote to Joseph F. Smith to ask about the status of Hisa Udagawa, a friend who had been on the point of baptism when she died in March 1915. "Just before she died she made our sister [Tsune] promise that she would see that she was baptised for in the temple," President Stimpson wrote. "How are we to proceed to have this work done?"[36]

Tsune Nachie served as the elders' housekeeper and surrogate mother for eighteen years. Her desire to visit the temple, as well as her increasing age, dictated that change must come. Early in 1922, elders in Tokyo contacted former missionaries, telling them of Tsune's desire to go to the temple at Laie, Hawaii, and soliciting donations to finance her transportation and retirement there. Lloyd O. Ivie, then president of the Japanese Mission, contacted the presidents of the Hawaiian Mission and the temple in Laie; "both of these gentlemen have given me assurance that they will do all within their power to see that Mrs. Nachie is taken care of and helped in every way necessary to accomplish the purpose of her mission."[37] Elder Ivie also called on elders throughout Japan to ask "whether there will be any of the Saints . . . who would want any names to go in to the temple when Sister Nachie goes."[38]

It is a testimony to Tsune and the affection she had won among the missionaries that they responded with contributions sufficient for Tsune to migrate to Hawaii, where she arrived on May 19, 1923.[39] The timing was providential: Tsune avoided the earthquake that devastated Tokyo later in 1923, and she was safely settled in the mission home at Laie when the Japanese Mission was closed in 1924, which otherwise would have left her without a home and without employment.

Tsune was the first Japanese convert to enter the temple, which she did on June 5, 1923, both for her own endowment and to be sealed to her deceased husband.[40]

Castle H. Murphy, who arrived in Hawaii as mission president in 1930, looked forward to meeting Tsune Nachie, of whom he had heard from elders returning from both Japan and Hawaii. "I was privileged for the first time to meet this far famed and much loved diminutive Nachie," he said. "My first impression was not unlike the lasting impression carried to the tops of the mountains by those who have felt the force of her great spirit and the tenderness of her love—Like a jewel, small in size but most precious thought I." He found her living in the Laie mission home, where she could "continue to be of service to the elders of Israel and to, as far as possible substitute for their mothers from whom they were separated . . . [and] to engage herself in the work of salvation for the dead in the temple, this being the paramount desire of her life."[41]

But redeeming the dead was not Tsune's only concern. Her service in Tokyo had also prepared her to take the gospel to the living. Without direction—impelled only by her testimony and her desire to share the gospel—Tsune left her home almost daily to proselytize among the Japanese of Hawaii, whom no one else was then teaching. Leaders of the Hawaiian Mission tried to persuade her to move to Honolulu near mission headquarters, where she could more conveniently be cared for during times of illness, but for many years she insisted on remaining at Laie, where she could go to the temple regularly and attend to her personal mission among the Japanese. She was *not* retired, she was a missionary—and she so identified herself even to a census enumerator.[42]

In April 1934, a small group of converts organized the first Japanese branch of the Church in Hawaii, and to Tsune's great joy, she lived to see the 1937 organization of a fully functioning Japanese Mission in Hawaii. Tsune was credited then as "a powerful influence in bringing about that organization," and "a saint, if ever there was one, a wonderful woman."[43]

Tsune Nachie, the mother of one adopted daughter and surrogate mother of innumerable missionary sons, passed away on December 3, 1938, at age eighty-two, after thirty-four years as a missionary.

Chapter 11

"TRULY HER SOUL REJOICED IN HELPING THE HELPLESS"

EMILY SOPHIA TANNER RICHARDS (1850–1929)
by Andrea G. Radke-Moss

Emily Sophia Tanner was born on May 13, 1850, in the South Cottonwood settlement of Salt Lake City, less than two years after her parents, Nathan and Rachel Winter Smith Tanner, and her older siblings left Winter Quarters, Iowa.[1] As one of the first generation born in Utah during the pioneering era of settlement, Emily grew up with a strong sense of connection to her family's religious past and the events of the Restoration. In spite of the roughness of the frontier, Emily "grew up in grace and graciousness, in knowledge and refinement, partaking as she did of the spiritual element in her devout parents."[2] It was said of her, "Truly her soul rejoiced in helping the helpless."[3]

Life on a farm in the irrigated agricultural areas in the Salt Lake Valley provided an idyllic setting for her childhood. At age six, Emily's father moved the family into Salt Lake City so that the Tanner children could attend school. Emily enjoyed great sociality with fellow students and was considered "a belle in the social life of the young people."[4] Among her teachers was the "independent, forward-looking school 'maam'" Sarah M. Kimball, pioneer Relief Society leader and suffragist, who no doubt strongly influenced her young pupil.[5]

In her late teens, Emily was courted by her former schoolmate Franklin S. Richards, the handsome and promising son of apostle Franklin D. Richards and Jane Snyder Richards, who was in her own right a great Relief Society and suffrage leader.[6] Perhaps the bonds of marital equality were built early for Emily and Franklin, for in Franklin's home there had been "no distinction between the girls of the family or the boys in the family."[7] Emily, age eighteen, and Franklin, age nineteen, were married on December 18, 1868, by his father in Salt Lake City. And on May 13, 1869—Emily's nineteenth birthday—they moved to Ogden to live with the Richards family.[8]

While living with her in-laws, Emily Sophia Tanner Richards gained the love and regard of her husband's whole family, and for Franklin's mother and father, Emily "was as their own child."[9] These happy times were not without their difficulties, however. Franklin's mother, Jane S. Richards, remembered these early years in Utah as times of trial in which "some of us were nearly all the time sick."[10] Men, women, and children in the Richards family, including Emily, united their faith in healing the sick. "Very many times they would all lay their hands upon me at once and pray in turn," Jane wrote, reflecting on a time of personal illness. "This afforded me the most comfort and added the most strength to my weak and feeble body."[11]

Emily and Franklin were kept busy as their own family grew. Three sons were born to them: Franklin Dewey, Joseph Tanner, and William Snyder, the last of whom died at one year of age. After a few years, the Richardses adopted two girls: Wealthy Lucile and, later, infant Emily Helen.

While in Ogden, Emily had her first experience in organizational leadership. She served as an assistant Relief Society secretary for Weber County, president of the Second Ward Young Ladies' Mutual Improvement Association, and first vice president of YLMIA for all of Weber County.[12] Emily loved those she served, especially

Emily Sophia Tanner Richards (1850–1929)

Franklin Snyder and Emily S. Richards with sons (left to right) Joseph Tanner, Franklin Dewey, and William Snyder, 1873.

the youth. At one YLMIA meeting in July 1882, Emily counseled the young women on the importance of duty in the Church: "If we had the spirit of our mission we would do a great deal different, we would attend to our duties better than we do now, if you were all president for about three months and felt the anxiety she does we would never fail to do anything when we are called on. . . . [L]ive nearer to the Lord and be more faithful in performing our duties and never shirk any duty."[13] Emily looked back on this time as a preparation for her activism for more expanded roles for women. The task required sheer strength and unstoppable energy.

In 1884, Franklin and Emily moved their young family to Salt Lake City, where Franklin put his legal skills to use for the Church during the decade of heightened troubles over polygamy. Franklin and Emily never entered plural marriage themselves, and her status as a monogamous wife benefited the Church when she later represented Utah in state and national suffrage leadership and spoke on behalf of Latter-day Saint women at world's fairs. Indeed, Emily became a public face for a younger generation of Mormon women; her marriage was an accidental public relations tool for the Church's transition from plural marriage toward monogamy and assimilation.

While in Salt Lake, Emily became involved in the Relief Society during Eliza R. Snow's presidency and served for more than thirty years as a board member under the presidencies of Zina D. H. Young, Bathsheba W. Smith, and Emmeline B. Wells. This service took her all over the Mormon settlements from Canada to Mexico, "organizing, teaching, exhorting and encouraging the women in the different stakes of Zion along the various phases of their work."[14] Emily gained a strong conviction of the Relief Society's "far-reaching purposes of charity, education and general helpfulness along every line of advancement in human welfare," but she did not limit that influence to Church service. Instead, she recognized the possibilities for great change in the world, as Relief Society service "furnished the base and background for all her varied and useful activities in every line of service."[15]

She learned well under the sound tutelage of her mentors in the Relief Society. Emily later recalled that "the first time Aunt Eliza asked me to speak in meeting, I could not. . . . She said, 'Never mind, but when you are asked to speak again, try and have something to say,' and I did."[16] This training certainly paid off as she moved into a larger sphere of public suffrage activism.

Emily had long held sympathies for suffrage, and like many other Mormon women, her entrance into activism came partly in connection with defending the Church against antipolygamy legislation. Her service extended beyond Church work to the territorial, state, and national stage of suffrage activism, promoting Democratic Party politics, and pursuing progressive causes for social welfare and peace. She did not end her suffrage activism when Utah women earned the vote in 1896 but continued to assist the cause in other states. She participated in the National and International Councils of Women, even traveling to Berlin in 1904 and Toronto in 1909 as a delegate.[17]

In 1882, Emily and her children accompanied her husband, Franklin, to Washington, D.C., where he was sent to lobby for Utah statehood. Over the course of ten years, the Richardses spent much time in the nation's capital as active members of a vibrant Latter-day Saint community there.

Living in the nation's capital, Emily was also able to make connections with national suffrage leaders.[18] In 1886, she and her sister-in-law Josephine R. West joined Emmeline B. Wells and Ellen B. Ferguson in presenting a Memorial of the Women of Utah to United States president Grover Cleveland and to the Congress in an effort to "allay the anti-Mormon feeling then at its peak in the city."[19] Still, their efforts did nothing to stop the Edmunds-Tucker Act (1887) from disenfranchising Utah women altogether. After that blow to Utah women's political autonomy, Relief Society and YLMIA leaders sought to join forces with national suffrage leaders.

In 1888, Emily proposed that Utah organize a woman suffrage group to be affiliated with the National Woman Suffrage Association. The Utah Woman Suffrage Association was formed on January 10, 1889, with Emily Richards and Margaret Caine—both monogamous wives—selected to represent Utah.[20] Emily soon went about creating local suffrage associations, mostly affiliated with individual Relief Society units in Utah, Idaho, and Arizona. That same year, in 1891, the Relief Society and YLMIA were accepted as member organizations of the International Council of Women and of the National Council of Women.[21]

Emily quickly rose to prominence in both Utah and national suffrage activities—giving speeches, lobbying on behalf of Utah women, and forming friendships with such leaders as Susan B. Anthony, Anna Howard Shaw, and Carrie Chapman Catt.[22] Emily's first appearance, in 1889, before the National Woman Suffrage Association in Washington, D.C., began inauspiciously— she was omitted from the program, whether intentionally or

Emily Sophia Tanner Richards and her husband, Franklin Snyder Richards, lived in Washington, D.C., in the 1880s. This photograph features those lobbying for Utah statehood in the nation's capital, ca. 1888. Back row, left to right: George F. Gibbs, L. John Nuttall, Charles W. Penrose. Front row: John T. Caine, Margaret Nightengale Caine, Joseph F. Smith, Emily S. Richards, Franklin S. Richards.

accidentally—but Anthony herself "went to the rear of the platform and conducted Mrs. Richards to the rostrum with every demonstration of respect."[23] Despite almost palpable tension in the room, Emily gave her speech, and one journalist described her speaking as "reserved, self-possessed, dignified, and as pure and sweet as an angel."[24] The results were evident, in that Emily's "appearance was a powerful antithesis to their preconceived impressions, and the change of feeling in the audience was almost instantaneous. . . . It was wonderful how sympathies were engendered and asperities removed."[25]

A Voice for Mormon Women

A highlight of Emily Richards's action on behalf of Utah women was her participation in the Chicago World's Columbian Exposition (or World's Fair) of 1893. Emily was appointed president of the

Utah Board of Lady Managers, which allowed her hands-on involvement in gathering information, organizing women, and preparing exhibits. She also received the express endorsement of the First Presidency, including "authorization to preach, teach, and expound the scriptures and doctrines of the Church of Jesus Christ of Latter-day Saints."[26] Together with other Relief Society and YLMIA leaders, she spoke at the World's Congress of Representative Women held in conjunction with the fair's opening to highlight Utah women's contributions to the nation and the world. Mormon women benefited from their membership in the NCW and ICW, with the primary goal being to forge a positive image for both the Church and its women by portraying them as they were: progressive, assimilated, and patriotic Americans who stood on the forefront of the most current activism for women's rights.

On the evening of May 19, 1893 Emily delivered an address entitled "The Legal and Political Status of Woman in Utah." This speech met both goals for Utah's women: "to defend themselves against unfair stereotyping and to show the strong connections between fair participation and women's broader hopes for legal and political rights."[27] The following is an excerpt from her speech:

> The legal age of woman in Utah is eighteen years. She possesses all the property rights enjoyed by man. She is not only his equal in this respect, but, if a married woman, she enjoys a marked advantage over her husband; she not only has power to possess property in her own right, which she can control and dispose of without consulting her husband, but she also has a dower right in his real property. All women of legal age [in Utah], whether married or single, have the same right as men to acquire, hold, and dispose of all kinds of property. . . .
>
> Under this statute a great many women have acquired and held title to property in their own right, and the

percentage of such property owners is large as compared with that in other States and Territories. . . .

Woman suffrage was conferred by an act of the legislative assembly in 1870. . . . This privilege was taken away by an act of Congress in 1887. . . .

Though repeated efforts have been made to restore the franchise, they have thus far been unavailing, as Congress has the exclusive power to change the law. The sentiment in the Territory favoring woman suffrage is believed to be as strong now as when we were enfranchised, and it may be confidently predicted that when the local government regains the power to do so, women will be restored to their political rights and privileges.

Socially, women enjoy all the privileges accorded to men. All our educational institutions are open to them. They are encouraged to practice law, medicine, and all the other professions. They are at liberty to preach the gospel, speak at public gatherings, visit the sick, and officiate at funerals. Important educational positions are occupied by them, and all the walks of life are open to them. Some are engaged in business for themselves; others, without opposition or prejudice, occupy places as clerks, saleswomen, typewriters, typesetters, bookbinders, factory operatives, telephone and telegraph operators, photographers, and other suitable positions, in many of which they are taking the place of men.

The influence of woman is fully recognized. Her cooperation is sought in nearly all undertakings of a public, political, or social character, and in whatever direction her energies have been employed her attainments compare favorably with those of men. The efforts and achievements of our women are appreciated by the men, who give them every encouragement and assistance in their various enterprises.[28]

Emily's talk was so well received that it was included in the official publication of the World's Congress of Representative Women. She also received public attention for the very fact that she was not a polygamist. Journalist Augusta Prescott from the Chicago *Inter Ocean* announced to her readers, "MORMON WOMEN Who Will Take Part in the Fair Congresses ARE NOT POLYGAMISTS," and highlighted Emily Richards and Electa Bullock as examples of this new face of the Church. Prescott seemed particularly smitten with Emily as "an ardent woman's suffragist [who] is interested in many forms of club and charitable work."[29]

Besides speaking at the World's Congress of Representative Women, Emily was also invited to speak before the Women's Branch of the World's Parliament of Religions. Her appearance there was significant because "the Parliament of Religions had refused admission to the male representatives of the Church, yet this gracious lady found opportunity for a hearing through the auxiliary."[30] In her typical fashion, Richards was "carefully prepared . . . and she gave a fine and sincere talk which carried its truths to the hearts of her audience."[31] Emily's success in Chicago led to her participation in other fairs; she represented Utah women in San Francisco in 1894, Atlanta in 1895, and Omaha in 1898.

"An Ardent Woman's Suffragist"

The momentum for equal suffrage in Utah only increased following the Chicago World's Fair. By the time of the 1895 Utah constitutional convention, debates arose about the prudence of including woman's suffrage in the new state constitution. Some argued that Congress would be less inclined to accept a constitution that included voting rights for women, or that an expanded female electorate would just maintain the theocratic power of the Church.[32] In spite of these concerns, Emily chaired a committee to prepare a memorial for a suffrage plank in the constitution.[33] After much lobbying by both women and men, including Emily's husband,

Susan B. Anthony (center) and Dr. Anna Howard Shaw (standing behind chair, left) visited Salt Lake City in 1895 to promote the cause of women's suffrage. To the right of Dr. Shaw stands Sarah Granger Kimball, Emmeline B. Wells, and Zina D. H. Young (sitting). On the second row, Martha Hughes Cannon stands on the far left and Emily S. Richards is fourth in the same row.

Utah's bid for statehood was granted on January 4, 1896, with universal suffrage included. Emily was chosen to represent Utah in Washington, D.C., at a victory event.[34] The following is an excerpt from the speech she delivered before the National Woman Suffrage Association convention on January 27, 1896, in which she celebrated Utah's suffrage victory:

> Equal suffrage having been incorporated in the organic law of the state, it cannot be revoked without the women vote for their own disfranchisement. As they constitute nearly half the voting population, it is not likely that the present order of things will be reversed.
>
> Thanks to the Giver of all Good, women have a chance in the Utah constitution to show their capacity for government, and help mold the institutions of society. Of course, the work is but begun; the cause is in its merest infancy. That which remains to be done opens up before us in an

almost endless vista. In a far away promised land we behold a perfected state wherein the heart and hand and intelligence of woman contribute their full share to the welfare of the race.

Thus far the progress of man has been deeply embittered and highly colored by the selfishness he has inherited from the dark ages, but now that education is more widely diffused, now that religion is taking on the hues of love and helpfulness, now that the spirit and inspiration of altruism are brooding more and more in the hearts of men, we find that an era of philanthropy and amelioration is setting in, that social life is rising into a region of reason, truth and sympathy, so that the gentler and nobler soul of woman can co-operate with man in achieving the higher ends of government—the attainment of true brotherhood, the inauguration of the kingdom of God on earth. Of course, we must educate and emulate. We must not grow weary in well doing; but, above all, we must learn to wait and spread our sails to the breezes of heaven, that in the providence of God, and in His own way and time, our ship of state may be wafted into the harbor of eternal truth, justice and righteousness.[35]

Once full suffrage was achieved in Utah, much of the strident suffrage activism of earlier years declined, especially as it had been tied to defending the Church against antipolygamy legislation. But not for Emily Richards—she saw the suffrage cause as an ongoing and important battle that did not end with Utah's victory. Emily soon organized the Utah State Council of Women "in order to keep up the interest and to help the women in other states in their suffrage work." She presided over this work until the ratification of the Nineteenth Amendment in 1920, and hers was "purely a work of devotion to the suffrage cause: Utah women had gained their victory, but for the women in other states Mrs. Richards still carried on."[36]

Emily also supported the League of Women Voters. She believed that women should put their voices and votes to the efforts of improving the state and the nation, especially in the context of the growing progressive movement in America. Emily Richards was a progressive through and through, and she found a home in the Democratic Party as the best vehicle for expressing her reformist views. She even attended the 1896 Democratic National Convention as an alternate delegate. She was considered for state political office herself but instead sought other ways to make changes in society.

Social Activism

Emily Richards's interests reflected the same passionate impulse toward social justice felt by many early Relief Society leaders. She placed her stamp on so many projects for public welfare that it is a challenge to list them all. The Orphans' Home of Salt Lake City was her first and perhaps most personal work because of her "tenderness in motherhood" and as a commemoration of her and Franklin's adoption of two daughters.[37] Appointed by the First Presidency on October 27, 1887, to represent the Church on the directorate of the Orphans' Home, Emily held this position for forty years. She took her passion beyond mere philanthropy to the next level of progress, that of legislative action, and "through her extensive acquaintance, too, with members of the Legislative Assembly she was able to obtain state aid in behalf of these helpless ones."[38]

These intersections of Church service and progressive reform gave this period in Utah a distinct mark, especially with the energy of such individuals as Emily Richards, who perhaps would have been an active progressive even without the Relief Society. She was instrumental in founding Salt Lake's Sarah Daft Home for the Aged and remained active as a vice president and member of its board. Her position gave her a strong voice with respect to building sites and architectural plans, overseeing employment and staffing, and financial management.[39] Emily also participated in the Mothers' Congress of

Utah[40] as its first president and as the Utah representative to various events of the National Congress of Charities and Corrections, including attendance at the International Convention held in Toronto, Canada, in 1904.[41] She was a member of the Utah Woman's Press Club, an advocate for the kindergarten movement, a trustee for the Agricultural College of Utah (now Utah State University), a member of the Utah Chapter of the American Red Cross and the Reapers' Club,[42] and a director of the Salt Lake City free library.[43]

Peace Activism

Emily's most passionate activism outside of suffrage was for the peace movement that grew in influence after the 1898 Spanish-American War and before the First World War. The peace movement took root between these wars as an honest ideological effort toward eradicating all global wars, and Mormon women immersed themselves in the movement. From her office in Salt Lake City in 1907, Emily called upon all Relief Societies and YLMIAs to engage fully in the work of peace:

Dear Sisters:

Acting under instructions of the Peace and Arbitration Committee for the National Council of Women and National Suffrage Association, we as General Committee, ernestly request that your organizations unite, and invite all citizens of your locality to join with you in holding Peace demonstrations in a Ward or Stake capacity, on or near May 18th. We suggest Sunday, May 19th, afternoon or evening, a fitting time for these meetings, when agreeable to Stake and Ward authorities.

It is also desired that you extend an invitation to the Ministers of all denominations in your vicinity to do likewise. . . .

RESOLVED: That the American Women assembled May 18th for the purpose of considering the fruits of war and the fruits of Peace, do solemnly pledge themselves to meet annually to hold a demonstration in behalf of peace and arbitration. They commit themselves to adopt as their own ideal that ideal of loving brotherhood which can be realized only by the cessation of International hostilities; they accept as a corollary of the universal Fatherhood of God the universal Brotherhood of Man. They send greetings to women of other countries who this day may be assembled to attest similar convictions. They rejoice that women throughout the world are beginning to feel their responsibility for human conditions outside of the home, as well as within its sacred walls. They ask all women every where to adopt as their own the task assumed by the International Council of Women, which is "The Application of the Golden Rule to society, custom and law." . . .

Respectfully,
Your Sisters,
Emily S. Richards, N.W.R.S.
Minnie J. Snow, Y.L.M.I.A.
General Committee, Peace Demonstration.[44]

Emily was active on the national scene, having served "as a member of the State Board for Peace and [as] one of the committee on the celebration of the 100th anniversary of Peace among the English speaking people 1914–15."[45] In the last decade of her life, she cut back on some of the more demanding travel and activism of previous years while still offering emotional and intellectual support to such cherished causes as the Salt Lake Orphans' Home and other movements for the welfare of mothers, infants, and children. She loved to travel, however, and enjoyed trips with her husband to California, Washington, D.C., and Europe, among other locations. She was a celebrated hostess who welcomed many distinguished visitors to her Salt Lake City home, and she remained always a devoted wife, mother, and grandmother.

Emily Richards died on August 19, 1929, of a cerebral hemorrhage. Her husband, Franklin, observed, "It seemed to me as though the light and joy of life had gone out of the world."[46] Her death certificate listed her occupation simply as "Housewife."[47] Historian Andrew Jenson recalled that Emily was "in no sense 'a new woman,' in the common acceptance of the term," but a "woman of the good old fashioned type, whose home is her earthly paradise."[48] Since she did not leave a journal, her legacy has sometimes gone unheralded in the usual telling of Latter-day Saint women's history, but she is nevertheless significant.

Emily Richards is a model of monogamous, companionate marriage in the nineteenth century; she was someone who balanced her public and domestic life and who was a model of both feminism and femininity. Her beliefs in change and charity fed into a vast movement of activism for peace and social justice, and she believed strongly in the restored gospel while also promoting progressive political views. Emily Sophia Tanner Richards was well traveled and well spoken, the model wife, mother, friend, hostess, and individual—a Relief Society and YLMIA leader, suffrage and peace activist, Democrat, and advocate for the helpless.

Chapter 12

"Welcome the Task That Takes You beyond Yourself"

Sarah Louisa Yates Robison (1866–1946)
by Patricia Lemmon Spilsbury

Sarah Louisa Yates Robison, who served from 1928 to 1938 as the seventh general Relief Society president of The Church of Jesus Christ of Latter-day Saints, was a woman whose name "rarely appears on lists of outstanding LDS women."¹ Though her decided preference was to work quietly in the background, this humble woman of great faith and quiet determination was the first Relief Society general president to speak in a regular session of the Church's general conference and the first to visit Church units in England and continental Europe. Her life is worthy of examination not only for her diligence and leadership during the great economic struggles of her service as general Relief Society president but also for the lasting contributions she made to the Church and to the lives of the individual women she served.

Born Sarah Louisa Yates on May 27, 1866, Louise (as she preferred to be known) was the second daughter of the five children born to Thomas Yates and Elizabeth Francis. Elizabeth was from Devonshire, England, the daughter of a British army officer; Thomas was from Somerset, the son of a gardener. Louise's parents experienced persecution for their chosen religion and overcame seemingly insurmountable challenges during their lives. Their examples of courage, determination, and service, as well as their great faith and reliance on the Lord, laid the foundation on which Louise built her life.[2]

Louise's parents arrived in the Salt Lake Valley in October 1863. The following spring they were called to help settle Round Valley (later known as Scipio), where Louise was born in the only log house in the valley.[3] Her father served as bishop of the Scipio Ward from 1882 until his health deteriorated in 1902. Her mother served as the Scipio Ward Relief Society president from 1877 until 1883, when she was sustained as president of the Millard Stake Relief Society.[4] The Yates children experienced a pioneering childhood, and they all learned to work—including washing, dying, and spinning wool, knitting stockings, and braiding straw hats.[5]

Louise felt her childhood was happy. Though means were scarce, her parents were resourceful and creative. Louise remembered the family Christmas tree, trimmed each year with molasses cookies and lighted with the ends of homemade tallow candles saved for that purpose. Birthdays were made special with handmade gifts found under breakfast plates—perhaps a pinafore, knit stockings, or a toy. The birthday child was given the opportunity to choose the dinner menu for the day, and birthdays were chore-free days, with everyone pitching in to cover the birthday child's responsibilities.[6]

As a result of her mother's Church service, Louise grew up with Relief Society. She participated in gleaning wheat for the Relief Society grain program, gathering "Sunday eggs" (the money from which was donated to the Perpetual Emigrating Fund), helping to care for the sick, and preparing burial clothing for the dead—all important life lessons for her.[7]

A favorite maxim of Louise's parents was "knowledge is never a burden; learn all you can." To that end, Louise attended a "better than the average pioneer school" at School Ma'am Martin's home school in Scipio. "Ann E. Martin set a high standard in her one room house that served as school room as well as home for a growing family," Louise remembered.[8] "When I was fourteen years old, [my sister] Lizzie and I went to the Brigham Young Academy at Provo—two little homesick girls. . . . Father took us to Provo, entered us in school, [and] found a lovely home where we were to live. . . . Both he and mother were eager for their children to learn how to use hands as well as heads—the old English desire for a 'trade.' . . . A[t] the close of the school year mother took us to Salt Lake and arranged for Lizzie to have a six month's course in Millinery, really making hats, and I to take dressmaking."[9]

After one year at the Brigham Young Academy and six months working with a dressmaker in Salt Lake City, Louise returned to Scipio in 1882. There she helped at home while her mother, as stake Relief Society president, traveled around the large area encompassed by the Millard Stake. "Home was the dearest place on earth so it was a great pleasure to stay there and help with the work," Louise recalled.[10] During this time, she met Joseph Lyman Robison, recently returned from his mission to England. Louise described her reaction to him: "The boys in Scipio were fine[,] but when this boy came with his dashing sideburns, a derby hat and caned umbrella, latest clothes—well. . . ."[11]

Though intrigued, Louise was not romantically attracted to him at first. Lyman was attentive, however, during a Scipio Christmas holiday dance and also called at her home. Louise described that visit: "When anyone passed away we showed our sorrow by staying up all night and sewing. This was one of those times. Early in the morning my father was in the kitchen and after a night of sewing I was a sight. There was a knock at the door and my father called to me. When I walked into the kitchen whom should I be face to face with but Lyman Robison. Well, to think he had caught me in such a mess I was angry at the poor man. . . . But we were married the following October [1883]." They became the parents of six children.[12]

Louise's marriage brought an end to her formal education, but she never stopped learning. While her children were in school, she studied their lessons. "By the time the youngest child was through school, Mother was better in his studies than any of us," her son Rulon related. "I remember her discussing . . . the various points of German, history, grammar, and mathematics. Not content with this, when her children were grown, she enrolled in university extension courses, and during the time she spent seven or eight hours a day in the Burial Clothes department of the Relief Society, she would arise at 4:00 each morning and work two hours on this extension work, doing her housekeeping and the work she loved in the garden between 6:00 and 7:30 AM, and again in the evening after work. This program went on, not for a few weeks, but for years."[13]

Louise and Lyman had a loving relationship, and their children remembered their home as "always full of understanding, happiness, and love." Their son Rulon recalled waking one morning while ill to find his mother bending over him "with the sweet, warm kindness that was so much a part of her."[14] Daughter Dorothy recalled her mother's "common touch." "We used to joke that we never could walk down Main Street with Mother if we were in a hurry, as she would stop and talk with everybody."[15] Daughter Gladys later related, "Although [we] were nearly grown when she was busiest in these organizations, we were never conscious of her responsibilities and accomplishments because somehow, she kept the home running smoothly and with very few late meals, and the cake we wanted to take to a party, or a special dress that we needed, was always ready."[16] Indeed, one of Louise's principal beliefs was that "a woman could claim no higher destiny than that of mother and homemaker."[17]

Louise took great joy in her children and recorded a number of amusing everyday interactions. She related, for instance, how her daughter Gladys, displeased with her name, decided at the age of six to change it. After thinking about it for several days, Gladys announced at kindergarten that her name would now be Buttercup, to the great consternation of her older siblings. Louise also related that her oldest son did not enjoy his responsibility of taking the new baby, Winifred, for walks in the carriage each day. He complained to

Louise, and she remarked that "he should be thankful the Lord sent this baby sister to him." He replied, "Well I do thank [the] Lord for her, but I wish He'd kept her until she could walk."[18]

One of Louise's maxims was "Welcome the task that takes you beyond yourself." Building on the example of her parents, she taught her children the importance of accepting callings in the Church regardless of their difficulty. Her son Rulon remembered that when they were growing up, Louise would leave the younger children with the older ones and walk the two or three miles to carry out her duties with the Young Ladies' Mutual Improvement Association (YLMIA), regardless of the weather or darkness. He knew she did not like walking across empty fields in the dark, "but she never hesitated."[19]

The Robisons lived in Fillmore for six years and then moved to Provo. There Louise noticed a sore on her face that was eventually diagnosed as cancer. She sought treatment and a blessing. Her bishop sent for the stake patriarch, who gave her a patriarchal blessing before administering to her. "Brother Pat Blackburn came to administer to me," Louise remembered, and "God healed me. Brother Blackburn told me in my blessing that my voice [would] be heard in many parts of the world, but until I moved to Provo, I had not held an office in the Church. There I was secretary of the Mutual." Her face healed without scarring or the need for surgery, and the patriarch's blessing was fulfilled through the service she gave over the remainder of her life.[20]

From Provo, the family moved to Logan and then to Salt Lake City. Louise continued her work with the YLMIA, and she served the community in other ways as well. During World War I, she worked with the Red Cross, teaching courses in gauze preparation for surgical dressings and heading the Red Cross volunteers who worked at the Gardo House.[21] For this service, she received the Red Cross pin, a recognition that meant much to her. After serving for years in the YLMIA as a worker, a teacher, president of the Salt Lake City First Ward YLMIA, and president of the Emerson Ward YLMIA, Louise was called to serve in the Granite Stake Relief

Society in 1914, initially as a stake board member and then as first counselor to stake Relief Society president Leonora T. Harrington.[22]

Louise's daughter Gladys recalled of her service: "In later years, I have realized the tremendous amount of energy and time that Mother used in these various activities . . . she would volunteer for the hardest, grubbiest work, as in the assembling and distribution of old clothes; or in meeting the earliest and latest trains in serving with the Traveler's Aid." Gladys described seeing her "in the middle of mounds of old clothes and old shoes sorting, sorting and matching pairs, and selecting and packing piles of clothing to be sent to . . . unfortunate refugees."[23]

Louise attended the Relief Society general conference in the spring of 1921 in Salt Lake City with her sister Lizzie Thompson. Her experience at this conference speaks volumes about how callings were issued then and about Louise's unassuming nature. "It had been announced there would be a re-organization of the Relief Society General Board," Louise's daughter Gladys related, "so when President [Heber J.] Grant released Emmeline B. Wells, and presented the name of Clarissa S. Williams as General President, Mother was delighted to give her a sustaining vote, as she had worked with her and knew her to be a fine, capable woman." As President Grant announced the names of Jennie Knight and Louise Robison as Sister Williams's counselors and asked for a sustaining vote, Louise raised her hand in approval. She "turned to her sister and said, 'I didn't know there was another woman working in the Relief Society who had a name so much like mine!' Her sister answered, 'Why Louie, that's you! You have just sustained yourself!' Mother nearly fainted."[24]

Louise was upset about the call for several days and finally paid a visit to her dear friend Annie Musser. Louise felt she was not someone the women of the Church would look up to. Annie advised her that it was the poor and humble people that made up the Church, advice that was echoed by President Grant when she was set apart.[25]

Gladys related that "when Mother went to President Grant's office to be set apart, she felt sure he had been misinformed about her abilities, so she told him she'd be happy to do her best in whatever he asked her to do, but she wanted him to know that she had a limited education, and very little money and social position, and she was afraid she wouldn't be the example that the women of the Relief Society would expect in a leader. She finished by saying, 'I'm just a humble woman!' President Grant answered, 'Sister Louisy, 85% of the women of our Church are humble women. We are calling you to be the leader of them.' Mother never forgot what she felt was a special call, and through her administration, her main concern was for those who were underprivileged because of lack of money or opportunity for education."[26]

While Louise served as second counselor to Sister Williams, she directed the Temple and Burial Clothes Department of the Relief Society, an assignment for which she was well prepared, as her training in this aspect of the work had begun under her mother's able tutelage. She also worked with the maternity welfare program. During the April 1922 general Relief Society conference, it was decided to put the money from all Relief Society wheat accounts into one central account. Louise was part of that effort, placing the wheat money in a fund in the presiding bishop's office. The interest derived from the wheat trust fund was used for maternity and child welfare work until 1940. In addition, Louise conceived and oversaw a Churchwide campaign for home beautification throughout the stakes of the Church.[27] She continued her interest in social welfare problems, serving in several organizations outside the Church, such as the Traveler's Aid Society and the Utah Tuberculosis Association.[28]

Called on the eve of the Great Depression, Louise Yates Robison was sustained on October 7, 1928, as the seventh general president of the Relief Society, a position she held for eleven turbulent years. She chose Amy Brown Lyman and Julia A. Child as her counselors.

Louise has since been described as a woman well suited for her time.[29] Always aware of her own lack of formal education and wealth, she reached out to others who struggled in similar circumstances. Her focus was ever on the individual. Belle Spafford, her friend and co-worker in the Relief Society, recalled, "Sister Robison was a humanitarian" who "stressed the volunteer compassionate services[.] 'Go where you're needed; do what you can.' That was her theme."[30]

Job loss was rampant throughout the United States at this time, and Utah was no exception. Louise reminded sisters that the purpose of Relief Society was to reach out to individual sisters with support and assistance. Throughout her service, she maintained direct supervision over the Welfare Department of the Relief Society. She worked with public health nurses, the state board of health, and other agencies in providing support and assistance to bishops in the Salt Lake area.[31] She taught that the purpose of Relief Society's work and meetings was to care for those in need. "This is the first requirement of our Relief Society," she instructed. "Cultural lessons must come on work days only when motherless children, or any children for that matter, are properly clothed. . . . Our program if carried out gives rounded development. Let us follow it and never become blind to the needs of the poor or deaf to their cries."[32]

She cautioned against dependence on federal aid for the relief of those in need. "There are many of our fine . . . people in every one of our communities who have the spirit of the pioneers in them, and who are trying to get along without Federal aid. We are asking you Stake Officers and Stake Board Members to encourage your Ward Presidents to see that these people are not allowed to suffer and are not forced to ask for Federal help if you can help them. . . . For ninety-three years Relief Society has been saying that we take care of our needy ones."[33]

During a Relief Society general conference meeting in October 1932, Louise encouraged stake and ward leaders to remember to seek out the "little woman who is so retiring that she does not come before the public. Try her out. One of the best pieces of work that can be done is to develop leadership! Some of these timid little women who have been called to office, and have done the best they could, have developed so wonderfully, that in a year's time they could hardly be recognized." Likewise, she stressed the importance of making all members feel comfortable and encouraging them all to come out to meetings, regardless of their ability to pay dues, which was a membership requirement at that time.[34]

Her board members described one of her outstanding strengths as "her ability to put the arms of her love around even the most timid and inexperienced women and give them confidence in themselves and create within them a zealousness for the cause." She was "able to draw out their best abilities and win their love and cooperation."[35]

One of her significant contributions was the establishment of Mormon Handicraft in 1937. The economic effects of the Great Depression forced many women to work outside the home to help support their families, but Louise felt strongly that, wherever possible, mothers of small children should be in the home rather than in the workplace. Mormon Handicraft was conceived as an outlet for women to market their home crafts. This was not a new concept to Louise; her father had operated a co-op in Scipio for many years, and Relief Society co-ops had existed in the early days when Relief Societies had their own halls. The Mormon Handicraft shop, located near Relief Society headquarters, was the most successful of these new ventures. It operated until 1986.[36]

Another of Louise's contributions was her support of the Relief Society Singing Mothers chorus. The Singing Mothers came into being in 1932 when Charlotte O. Sackett brought a group of 250 women from the Liberty Stake to sing at the Relief Society general conference. Eventually, the Relief Society sought a name for the choruses that sang at its general conferences, as well as in the wards and stakes. One of Louise's favorite quotations, "A singing mother makes a happy home," inspired the selection of the name Singing Mothers. True to her concern for the sister of modest means, she insisted on a uniform of dark skirts and white blouses, believing most women would own such a skirt and blouse and would not have to spend money on new clothes to sing in the chorus.[37]

Sarah Louisa Yates Robison (1866–1946)

Louise Y. Robison at the 1933 dedication of a monument in Nauvoo, Illinois, commemorating the organization of the Relief Society in 1842. Left to right: Mary C. Kimball, Julia A. Lund, Louise Y. Robison, Amy B. Lyman, and Julia A. Child.

At the prompting of Elder George Albert Smith of the Quorum of the Twelve in an address to a Relief Society conference in 1932, a monument was erected the next year at the Red Brick Store in Nauvoo to mark the site where the Female Relief Society of Nauvoo was organized by the Prophet Joseph Smith in 1842.[38] The unveiling of the monument was attended by members of the general Relief Society, YLMIA, and Primary presidencies, and other leaders of both The Church of Jesus Christ of Latter-day Saints and the Reorganized Church of Jesus Christ of Latter Day Saints (known today as Community of Christ). The event gave Louise great pleasure. The marker was later moved to the vacant temple lot and, in 1988, to the entrance of the Relief Society Monument to Women in Nauvoo.[39]

In her patriarchal blessing, Louise had been told her voice would be heard in many parts of the world. She was the first general Relief Society president to address the Church in general conference, speaking with an apparently impromptu invitation in October 1929. As she stood before the Church, she began, "My brethren and sisters, I am sure you will know that I need your faith and prayers, but I do love to bear my testimony."⁴⁰ The *Relief Society Magazine* reported, "Sister Robison was first [of the three women called on to bear testimony that day], and, as a result, had the least time to adjust to a situation wholly new. Yet she was equal to the occasion."⁴¹

Though she was described by a daughter as "the shyest and most self-effacing of women,"⁴² this humble woman time and again found herself in front of large groups of women and men, representing her sisters and her church in Utah, the nation, and Europe. As general president of the Relief Society, Louise was a participating member of the National Council of Women. As such, she traveled to Washington, D.C., for a conference and while there was entertained at the White House. When the council planned an international convention, she was asked to take charge of one of the meetings. Her first inclination was that she could not possibly do it, but then, she said, "The thought came to my mind to make the best of all opportunities. The names I had to pronounce were terrible. Most of them being foreigners. It was a wonderful thing."⁴³

In 1934, she traveled to Paris for an International Council of Women conference as one of nine American women chosen to be delegates. While traveling abroad, she made it a priority to visit branches and districts of the Church in England and Europe, thereby becoming the first Relief Society general president to do so.⁴⁴ She later traveled to Hawaii, which she described as "like Paradise." In 1939, she was appointed by President Franklin D. Roosevelt as Utah representative to the national Conference on Children in a Democracy.⁴⁵

After eleven years of diligent service as general Relief Society president, Louise was released on New Year's Eve 1939. Her husband had died in 1935, and so she went to San Francisco to live near her daughter and son-in-law Gladys and Stephen Winter. Louise returned to Salt Lake City on occasion, traveled to visit her children, and was active in genealogical work. She died on March 30, 1946, at the age of seventy-nine. As might be expected, the Singing Mothers performed at her funeral, which was held in the Assembly Hall on Temple Square in Salt Lake City.⁴⁶

Sarah Louisa Yates Robison (1866–1946)

Louise Y. Robison wrote on the back of this photograph: "To Greet me, upon arrival at Honolulu. Left to right. Sister Cummings, coun[selor] to Sister Salm; Sister Robertson R.S. Pres. Japanese Mission; Sister Salm, R.S. Stake Pres. Oahu Stake; Louise Y. Robison; Sister Bailey R.S. Pres. Hawaiian Mission; Sister Harmer (?) of Springville, Utah."

Louise indeed lived by the motto "Welcome the task which takes you beyond yourself." Her life of service was an embodiment of her maxim. She overcame shyness and a self-perceived deficiency in formal education to lead the Relief Society of the Church through an era of severe economic challenges. In a statement of appreciation from the Presiding Bishopric shortly after her release as general Relief Society president, Louise was described as one who has "truly been about her Father's business, feeding the hungry, clothing the naked, comforting the widow and fatherless and freely giving of her love and kindness."[47]

Perhaps her greatest gift was her understanding heart and firm conviction that every child of Heavenly Father needs the human touch. She was remembered by those who worked closest with her for her compassion and her service. Members of her Relief Society board proclaimed, "No leader has been more greatly loved, and few so loved."[48] Louise Yates Robison personified her theme "Go where you're needed; do what you can," a standard still relevant today.[49]

Chapter 13
"Guide Their Footsteps Aright"

Annie Marie Woodbury Romney (1858–1930)
by Barbara E. Morgan

Annie Marie Woodbury was born in Salt Lake City, Utah, on October 14, 1858, to Orin Nelson and Ann Cannon Woodbury. Three years later, on December 3, 1861, in obedience to the call of Brigham Young to help settle southern Utah's Dixie, the Woodbury family set up housekeeping in a tent in St. George while Orin built an adobe home. They experienced joy and sorrow as they carved out their niche in the new settlement, contributing to the community they came to love.

Childhood held both pleasant times and trials for Annie. She remembered her father taking her on his knee while they lived in St. George and singing her old, familiar songs. She remembered the lumber shanty where her mother carded and spun yarn to clothe her family. Candy, she remembered, was made from the skimmings of homemade molasses and was a great treat for the children.

One of her saddest childhood memories was watching her father's orchard and farmland wash away during a July 24 Pioneer Day celebration. She recalled:

Annie Marie Woodbury Romney (1858–1930)

My brother Orin and myself, with a number of other boys and girls rode down to the field to look at the orchard and the sight that met our gaze I shall never forget. The river was swollen to a raging torrent. Every few minutes we would hear a loud splash, and a large peach tree, loaded with delicious fruit, would fall as a large piece of the bank gave way and go rushing down the stream. Other trees would quickly follow. The entire orchard was completely inundated, and the young trees that were not swept down the river were bent to the ground and many of them were completely covered with mud or wet sand—while the beets, carrots, turnips, etc., that were growing between the rows of trees were buried to the depth of one or two feet."[1]

Even with the resulting financial difficulty, Annie's parents maintained the education of their children as a high priority. "I should like . . . to express my gratitude to my Heavenly Father for my parentage, and to my parents," Annie wrote, "for the way in which they toiled and sacrificed to give their children whatever advantages, in an educational way, that were possible at that time."[2]

One of the schools Annie attended was taught by Richard Horne, where her sister Eleanor was an assistant. Mr. Horne, who recognized the quick intelligence of his student and her interest in becoming a teacher, encouraged Annie, at age sixteen, to go to Salt Lake City to attend the University of Deseret and qualify as a teacher, an occupation that would become the hallmark of her life. The following year, Annie began her first teaching assignment in Harrisburg, Utah. Through teaching, Annie influenced the lives of Latter-day Saint children in Utah, Arizona, and especially the Mormon colonies in northern Mexico.

Annie was eighteen when she became the fourth wife of Miles Park Romney in August 1877 in the St. George Temple. Miles married five women in all: Hannah Hood Hill, Caroline Lambourne, Catharine Jane Cottam, Annie Marie Woodbury, and Emily "Millie"

Eyring Snow. He was the bishop in St. George and an architect by profession, but he also served in such other diverse capacities as attorney, chief of police, actor, newspaper editor, and superintendent of education.³

Two daughters were born to Annie and Miles while they lived in St. George: Ann, on January 15, 1879, and Alice, on April 6, 1881.⁴ That same year, Miles received a call from the First Presidency to settle St. Johns, Arizona.⁵ "I offered my property for one-fourth of cost, but looked for a buyer in vain, and therefore locked the doors and started on my return to this place hoping times of good business will revive in St. George," Miles wrote in a letter to the *Deseret News* on November 10, 1881.⁶

Annie became the first schoolteacher in St. Johns. In June 1882, she went into hiding with sister wife Catharine to avoid having to testify in court against their polygamous husband. While in hiding, Annie gave birth to her third child and first son, Orin Nelson Romney, on March 28, 1884. A few weeks later, in a letter to Annie's sister Eleanor, Catharine wrote that Miles had to run off "in the middle of the night" to "avoid the wicked men" seeking his arrest the "night before Annie's son was born."⁷

Two months later, Annie, Catharine, and their respective children were still in hiding: "Catherine and I are staying with Auntie Swapp in Luna Valley," Annie wrote to her sister Eleanor,

> as we were obliged to leave home in the night to avoid being subpoenaed to appear as witnesses against Miles. We arrived here a week ago today and have not heard a word from home since we left so you can judge how anxious we are to hear. . . . The Lord over-rules all things for the best in as much as we put our trust in him. . . . I realize more fully every day the truth of the saying 'we know not one day what the next will bring forth,' and it is probably a blessing that we are not permitted to know of the trials which are before

us, as we would no doubt shrink from coming in contact with them.

That evening, Annie added to her letter:

> I forgot to tell you about my baby; of course his Ma thinks there never was such a boy, and Alice says, 'He's the sweetest boy you've got hain't he Ma.' And of course I tell her yes, he is; though I think just as much of the girls. . . . Remember me kindly to George, Rose, the children and all our relatives and friends. That you may be blessed and preserved until we meet again, is the prayer of your loving sister.[8]

Annie and Catharine finally returned to St. Johns, but two weeks later they were on the run again. With a good sense of humor, Catharine wrote from Snowflake, Arizona, to describe their situation:

> Well my dear friend, we all have our trials, some in one way and some in another; and some of us have pleasures . . . for instance, Annie and I have been taking some lengthy pleasure trips around the country this summer. Last May some of our "kind" friends in "St. Johns" did us the "honor" of desiring to make our acquaintance and for that purpose issued invitations for us to attend a reception to be held at the court house, but strange to relate by some means or other the invitations failed to reach us, and unlike your letter have as yet failed to find us. Annie brought only Orin, but since this time [I] have added to our family.[9]

Two weeks later, still in hiding in Snowflake, Annie wrote:

> I suppose you have heard how we have had to spend the summer rusticating in different parts of the country. . . . It seems as though we have all got to be tried and proven,

some of us in one way and some in another, and we all think sometimes that we have almost more than we can bear, but our very trials often prove to be blessings in disguise, and if we can only have the strength and moral courage to bear them with resignation we ought to feel truly thankful.[10]

As the trials and persecutions continued for Miles and his wives, he took Catharine and Annie back to Utah in December to live until future arrangements could be made. A short time later, Annie chose to accompany her husband and their three young children to the unfamiliar country of Mexico.[11] Miles's other wives eventually joined them there.

Life in Mexico

Miles and Annie were among the first Saints to move to Mexico to escape prosecution for practicing plural marriage. They arrived in the spring of 1885.[12] Annie's letters, as well as the writings of others closely associated with her, give evidence of her faith and trust in the Lord, manifested in her own hard work and diligence. In July 1885, Annie wrote to her sister Eleanor:

> The last two and a half weeks we have been living in [a] small Mexican house about half a mile from town. The house is very cool in the daytime and warm at night, there being only one window and one door. I have all my cooking to do over the fireplace and very few things to cook in, but as we haven't much of a variety to cook, I manage pretty well. . . . I would find it very lonesome here if I had any spare time, but I have too much to do [to] think about it very often. I generally have a good cry, but I am getting hardened now so that I don't mind it so much. You never saw such a mischief as Orin is; he is into everything that he can lay his hands on. He chases the chickens and drives them off the roost at night. I forgot to say that we have four

hens and a rooster, also a good cow; and we find it such a help. I don't know what we would do without them.[13]

Much of Annie's busyness came less from her household chores and mothering duties than from her love of teaching. She started by instructing the children in her own dugout but, within a few months, moved to a one-room structure the Saints had erected to serve as a combination school, meetinghouse, and social center. Although the environment was not ideal for learning, Annie immediately took her place behind the handmade table, seated her students on split logs, and began a system of drill on the fundamentals of learning. Her interest in the boys and girls opened their hearts to her, and the basic principles she drilled into them motivated them to a proper use of knowledge and learning. She put one basic truth into simple terms by saying, "Be good, do good, and you will be happy."[14]

Annie gave birth to a second baby boy on March 13, 1886. She and Miles named him Erastus Snow Romney. To her sister, Annie described him as "the fleshiest and the largest baby I ever had." Within a couple of months after his birth, Annie was back in the classroom. In May of the same year she wrote to her sister:

> Well, Eleanor, I am at my old business again teaching school. It seems impossible to let it alone, but I am so thankful to be able to earn a little something, that I am willing to go along most any way. I have over 50 pupils, with all sorts of books and not enough of any kind; besides this we have to furnish our own seats, and it is quite a sight to see us starting off to school every morning with our books under one arm and a chair or stool under the other; but we get along very well considering that the children are very much better off than they would be running wild the way some of them have been allowed to do the past year.[15]

Annie Marie Woodbury Romney may have taught school in this building after her family moved to Colonia Dublán in 1904. It served as the first church and schoolhouse in the settlement.

By September, another wife, Hannah, arrived with her children and was able to ease the Annie's burden of teaching while trying to raise her own children. "I have taught one term of school and half of another," Annie wrote. "It is quite an undertaking with four little children, but I am thankful to be able to do it. . . . Hannah is good and kind about taking care of the children and helping me in whatever way she can."

In January 1887, Annie and the other colonists were informed that the original survey of the land on which they had settled was incorrect, and they were forced to move to a nearby township. It was also at this time that Catharine finally arrived from St. George. "Miles took Hannah, Catharine, and myself, and all the children that could crowd into the wagon up to the new town site, about two miles farther up the canyon. It is a beautiful location, far ahead of our present location as far as natural scenery goes, and in time will make a beautiful city." In this same letter, Annie expressed her feelings of inadequacy as a mother. "My constant prayer is that I may know how to rear my children and take care of them and guide their footsteps aright. I feel that it is a great responsibility and I sometimes feel that I am not capable to fill such an important position."[16]

Four months later, in May 1887, an earthquake shook northern Mexico. Annie described what happened: "We were in school at the time and the house shook so hard that I was glad to get the children out of doors for fear it would fall," she wrote. "It is reported that the earthquake has opened some springs . . . which will increase the water supply; if this is correct, it will prove a great blessing, as the scarcity of water has added greatly to our disadvantages. 'God moves in a mysterious way his wonders to perform,' and this earthquake may prove a blessing to us in more ways than one."[17]

On July 3, 1887, Annie described the joy of finally receiving her own home at the new town site in Colonia Juarez. "I have got a house at last, although a small one," she wrote. "I haven't seen it yet, but they say it is a small lumber room with a floor, and a porch in front; I name the floor because I have never had a floor or even stepped on one, for over two years. Miles and one of the boys built it last week in four days, so you can judge they must have worked. It is the first lumber house in [Colonia] Juarez, and what is better still, I earned most of the lumber myself, so I feel quite proud of it."[18]

On August 21, 1887, Annie wrote about her new home in a letter that captured her jubilation:

> Miles has now got us all moved on to the town lots at last and we feel much better than when we were scattered. . . . I will have to begin taking lessons in gardening, as it is a branch in which I have had no experience, even if my father is a farmer. . . . It seems so good to get out of the dirt. I got very tired of mud walls, mud roof and mud floor, that I know how to appreciate something better; of course, as I have only a lumber roof, the rain is sure to beat through some of the knot holes, but I am willing to stand a little clear water.[19]

Pioneering life was no easier in other ways. On February 12, 1888, Annie expressed longing for her family in St. George. "I should have enjoyed eating Christmas dinner at Ma's very much," she lamented. "I sometimes wonder if I will ever see you all together again. It seems as though I am doomed to be the stray sheep, and will always have to be separated from the rest of the family. I suppose, though, that it is for a wise purpose, and I know that I have so much to be thankful for that it is a sin to complain." She did not, however, allow this homesickness to ruin her Christmas. "My children had the best Christmas that they have had since we left St. Johns," Annie wrote. "Christmas eve I gave them my room to play in. Bro. Heleman Pratt's children came over and they had a fine time, eating molasses candy, popcorn balls, cake and cheese, and playing games, etc. The children each got a small present of some kind."

Nearing the end of her letter, Annie wrote, "I am still in school, but I think I shall quit in about three weeks." The reason for her quitting was the expected birth of her fifth child, Eleanor ("Ella") on March 28, but Annie took only a short, three-week break before returning to her young students to finish off the school year. She reasoned:

> I have either got to teach our own children or they must grow up without education, and if I can only teach them what little I know they will be able to make their way in the world. I have ten of our own in school, and sixteen others, and my room is only twelve feet square, so you can judge how crowded we are, but most of the children are learning so well that I hate to close.[20]

After a summer out of school, Annie again found herself doing what she did so well and loved. "I am at my old business, teaching school," she wrote to her sister in September.

Miles tells people some times that I wouldn't be happy if I wasn't in school. I haven't tried being out of school for more than a year since I first commenced teaching, but I certainly feel better to know that I am doing a little something to help along, than to depend on Miles for everything that I need. Besides we have eleven children to be taught this winter and we have no means to pay for schooling at present, and I came to the conclusion, that while I was teaching our own I might as well teach the rest of the children in town and so help myself a little.[21]

During the next few years in Colonia Juarez, Annie continued teaching as she gave birth to more children, ran the post office, worked at the family store, and served on the stake school board. She wrote, "I am always behind in my work and never have a minutes leisure unless I steal it, and then I can think of a dozen things I ought to be doing."[22] In her letters she wrote of trying circumstances, including economic challenges, illnesses within the family and community, natural disasters such as drought and flooding, the births of her youngest children, her husband serving a mission for over two years in Great Britain, and even the death of her father and brother. In a letter to her sister, she faithfully recognized that "the Lord knows best and we should try to acknowledge his hand in all things, which is however pretty hard to do sometimes."[23]

In 1899, nearly fifteen years after their move to Mexico, the Romney family was able to purchase a farm a mile west of Colonia Dublán, where they could all live in close proximity. In such a living arrangement, a division of responsibility among the wives became necessary. "My mother took care of the cream and made all the butter," Annie's daughter Ella recalled. "Except for a little to season something, we used no butter at all. The money from this went to buy clothes. . . . My mother also supervised the making of molasses. One year she made 500 gallons. I remember how she suffered with big open cuts on her frost bitten fingers."[24]

After living in the Latter-day Saint colonies in Mexico for more than twenty years, Annie Marie Woodbury Romney and her family fled their home in Colonia Dublán in 1912 during the Mexican Revolution.

Despite the challenges, life was not all work for Annie's family. In the evening while the children played, Miles, Annie, and the other wives would often "sit in front of the big house and sing such songs as 'Hard Times,' 'Mistletoe Bough,' and 'I'll take you home again Kathleen,'" Ella reflected. "What fun we had playing Steal Sticks, Pom Pom Pull Away, Base Rounders, Run Sheep Run, and many others."

Some of the liveliest family gatherings were around Miles's birthday, Christmas, and New Year's Eve. On these evenings the family often shared talents with each other, read stories, sang songs, and listened to Annie's recitations. Ella recounted, "I never prepared more consciously than I did for these home programs. . . . Never a grammatical error in our home that was not carefully corrected." With a spirit of gratitude, she remembered, "We grew up with all the advantages of poverty and surely were reared in a household of faith."

In 1904, still in Mexico, Miles P. Romney passed away, leaving his wives to decide their future course. Annie moved into a home built for her and her six unmarried children. In 1909, after more than twenty five years of separation, she had a joyous reunion with her mother, Ann Cannon Woodbury, who had been taken to Mexico by Annie's son Orin.[25] A few years later, in the summer of 1912, unexpected dangers associated with the Mexican Revolution led Church leaders to decide that all women and children in the Mormon colonies should leave immediately on the train for El Paso, Texas.[26] Annie's son-in-law Wilford Farnsworth escorted Annie, her three unmarried children—Erma, Frank, and Ann, a young widow, with Ann's daughter Lucile—to the train station to begin their journey. The move was so sudden that they reportedly "left hot bread on the table and most of their belongings in their home."[27]

Enduring to the End

Eventually, Annie and her family courageously found their way from El Paso to Provo, Utah. Annie kept house while Ann taught in Walsburg, Utah, and Erma, Frank, and Lucile attended school and worked at a variety of jobs to support the family.[28]

In 1918, Annie returned to St. George to help care for her mother. After their mother's death in 1921, Annie helped her sister Eleanor take care of the family home until Annie was called away to attend her daughter Alice, who was ill. Annie cared for Alice and her seven children in the nearby town of Lyndyll. When Alice passed away in December 1923, Annie remained in Lyndyll to watch over the children. The following May, Annie went to Douglas, Arizona, to assist her daughter Erma at the birth of her first child. Shortly after Annie's arrival, Erma's husband died of appendicitis. Heartbroken, Annie, Erma, and her newborn baby went to Provo, where Annie helped Erma in her widowhood.

Reflecting on her life, Annie expressed her faith that helped her endure years of difficulty:

> I still retain my membership in the Church of Jesus Christ of Latter-day Saints, and trust that I always will, because I know that it is true and my testimony grows stronger every year. My life has been controlled entirely by

circumstances of which I had very little control. I have tried at all times to do that [which] I felt to be my duty. I have raised a family of eight children . . . all of whom are loyal citizens and faithful members of the Church. My greatest happiness is in knowing that I have raised a good family, and in doing what good I can to them and to others.[29]

In 1929, Annie moved to Salt Lake City to live with her daughter Erma. While there, she contracted pneumonia and died on January 14, 1930, at the age of seventy-one.[30] Annie humbly and faithfully trusted in the Lord as she served her family and community throughout her remarkable life.

Chapter 14

"Those Who Love Most Tenderly Are Surely Most like Thee"

Ellis Reynolds Shipp (1847–1939)
by Susan Evans McCloud

Ellis Reynolds was born January 20, 1847, in Davis County, Iowa, to William Fletcher and Anna Hawley Reynolds. She was named after her grandmother, Ellis Hawley, and it was through the influence of Ellis and William Hawley that Ellis's young parents accepted the doctrines taught by missionaries from The Church of Jesus Christ of Latter-day Saints. After being baptized in 1851, the Reynoldses sold their property and joined with Captain James C. Snow's company to travel across the plains.[1]

Ellis was five years old when her family trekked west, and she long remembered the beauty of the landscape and the many games and pleasures the children experienced along the way. The valleys of the mountains were a wonder to the weary pioneers. When the Reynoldses and the Hawleys, Ellis's grandparents, settled in Battle Creek (later Pleasant Grove), Utah, in 1852, there was already a ward organized and more than one hundred people in the settlement. Grandpa Hawley and Ellis's father built the first gristmill, worked on the first schoolhouse, and constructed the first bridge across the Provo River.

At the outbreak of the Walker War, the settlers constructed a fort the size of sixteen city blocks with rock walls two and a half feet thick and six feet high.[2] They endured the hardship years with crickets and grasshoppers destroying their crops, but for ten years the Reynolds family lived a generally happy, peaceful existence. Then, on January 28, 1861, Ellis's mother died at the age of thirty-one. "Spiritually pure and strong," Ellis called her, and her example as a homemaker, wife, and mother became the ideal which helped to shape her daughter's life.

Though barely fourteen years old, Ellis gave all her energies to the management of her father's family and home. "In those early days work was joy," she wrote.[3] Yet within her heart were deep desires and yearnings: "Ever since light and intelligence began to dawn within my being, I had a love of knowledge. . . . Books in those early days were a rare commodity, and there was a hunger in my soul that never seemed satisfied."[4]

When Ellis was fifteen years of age, her father remarried, and the family moved to Sanpete County, Utah. Three years later, eighteen-year-old Ellis found herself dancing with Brigham Young at an evening's entertainment in Mt. Pleasant. He learned of her desire for education and kindly offered her a place in his household to study under the inspired tutelage of Karl G. Maeser, who was teaching the prophet's family at that time. The growth, understanding, and confidence she gained in the company of that great scholar and gifted teacher enabled her to seize the opportunities her Heavenly Father held out to her later in life. Ellis had nothing but praise for Brigham Young throughout her life. "I always loved Brigham Young," she wrote. "He was a father to me. I always thought he was just as near to heaven as any man could ever be in the world."[5]

During her studies, Ellis spent Christmas with her grandparents in Pleasant Grove. While there, she was reintroduced to Milford Bard Shipp, the cousin of her best friend. He had two previous failed marriages, and now he began to court Ellis. When Brigham heard of it, he warned her against the man, but she was determined, and on May 5, 1866, she married Milford.

This decision reflected the spiritual passions of Ellis's nature and the deep idealism that lit them. She believed she would be the most perfect of wives and that Milford would be a wise, noble, "perfect" husband. He could be supportive, but he was also at times harsh and controlling, and he tended to withdraw his affection and support when her actions met with his disapproval. He also struggled to make a living, and his efforts were interrupted by several missions, which he served honorably.

Their lives were always a financial struggle, and despite the consistent love and faithful support she showed Milford, Ellis later wrote: "Many many years of our wedded life had passed ere I could ever believe it possible for him to make one mistake—& always if ever one little mistake made to cause a ruffled feeling I always & ever blamed myself—& how I grieved over that one sad discovery! Poor blind child that I was. I should have known that every mortal is but human—& in this earthly probation we cannot expect perfection. *We should not*—for sooner or later we will be disillusioned."[6]

Ellis retained her idealism, however, perhaps because she possessed the rare quality of merging reality with an almost naïve longing for perfection. Upon the birth of her first child on February 24, 1867, Ellis wrote: "Our Father of Love devine bestowed upon me, His mortal child, the most gracious & sanctified gift within His storehouse of blessings—my glorious motherhood! sanctified in the birth of a beautiful son! . . . My being seemed transported to the realms of purest most perfect endeavor; an idealistic, heavenly inspired mother hood . . . what sacred mission for mortal woman to fill."[7] Ellis believed that motherhood was her most noble purpose and was intelligently dedicated to this role in life.

During the first busy years of their marriage, Milford traveled much on short missions or on excursions to earn money and discover new and better places to live, farm, and do business. These separations were bitterly hard for Ellis, and she suffered times of weakness and discouragement, especially during periods of ill health. In a sketch of her life, Ellis wrote: "Two years of this time I was almost a confirmed invalid, being unfit for physical exertion."[8]

One evening, Milford returned home from a trip and he "held me close," Ellis remembered,

> & whispered solemnly the words, "I have accepted the mandates of the celestial law of marriage & will soon bring to our home a sister & companion for you!["] . . . [I] firmly believed that [principle] of Plural Marraige to be a devine command of the Eternal Creator. Twas only this *solemn assurance* that enabled me to feel the holiness of peace that came to my surprised soul! Yes surprised for I had not dreamed this test of faith was so near—Although I knew it would in time be mine.[9]

Milford married three additional wives in the ensuing years: Margaret Curtis on December 31, 1867; Mary Elizabeth Hillstead on October 23, 1871; and Mary Catherine Smith on February 10, 1873.

Ellis loved her husband's other wives, Maggie, Lizzie, and Mary. For many years they lived in the same residence and raised their children together. Ellis bore ten children between the years of 1867 and 1889 and balanced a keen desire for learning with the demands of a growing family.[10]

"Early in my womanhood I marked out for my self a plan for study which served me well as the years passed on," Ellis wrote in her autobiography. "I began my studies at four o'clock a.m. & put in three solid hours before the household began to stir."[11] When her ambitious daily schedule was compromised by circumstances, Ellis maintained her focus. Under date of May 3, 1871, she wrote:

> The many practical duties that are mine preclude almost the possibility of intellectual study. . . . Of late my desire for

progress and improvement seems greater than ever before. I feel that gaining a deeper understanding of my inner nature . . . increases the desire to bring them into subjection. I know that can be accomplished in only one way—by the aid and assistance of the Holy Spirit.[12]

Maggie was the first member of the Shipp family to pursue a medical degree at the Woman's Medical College of Pennsylvania, leaving her children in the care of Lizzie, Mary, and Ellis in October 1875. After a month, however, Maggie returned to Utah, too homesick to continue. Ellis stepped forward to finish the studies Maggie had started.

The reality of leaving her children behind was almost unbearable. Ellis also feared that her education was limited compared to that of her peers. But she saw such a need for knowledge to save the lives of mothers and babies in frontier Utah that she chose to go. After all, two of her own babies had died. The death of her daughter Anna in 1872 was especially trying, as she had prayed and fasted for her daughter's recovery and felt the Lord would not take the child from her. Despite the challenges, Ellis felt confident she could succeed.

Ellis's youngest child was not yet two when she left for medical school on November 10, 1875. She left three little sons behind in the primary care of her "beloved sister Mary." "It was she," wrote Ellis, "my husbands youngest wife who made this effort possible for me . . . & [I] will ever love [her] eternally!"[13] "Oh, Heavenly Father," she wrote in her diary, "give me strength to endure the separation from my loved ones, and power to succeed . . . that my life may be noble and useful upon the earth."[14] To be noble and useful was the desire that lit Ellis's heart and empowered her efforts throughout her life.

As she experienced an almost unexpected taste of success, Ellis must have thought upon the encouragement of her husband, who had told her he *knew* she could succeed, as well as the words of

Brigham Young, who a year earlier had said: "Go on this mission and I say that you will be blessed. I say God bless you in your labors."[15]

"I was in the best school for women in the world for medical education," Ellis wrote.[16] She determined to take no money from the family, except what was offered her. She never spent more than fifty cents a week, ingeniously making trade arrangements with butcher, baker, and landlady to get by. In a letter to her granddaughter, she revealed the discipline of her routine:

> I never left my college until they closed in the evening. I remained in a cozy corner to keep comfortably warm when I studied and concentrated without disturbance. Then to my quiet cool room for a repast of bread and milk, then to bed to keep warm and with a coal oil lamp (turned low to save money) and my textbook by my pillow—so when one lesson was mastered I could go on with the others until the midnight hour—then laying books aside I began my five hours of sleep.[17]

Milford arrived in Philadelphia at the end of Ellis's first year of school. She had been experiencing ill health, and her husband insisted that she undergo a thorough examination. The results were not encouraging, and she was urged to return home. Concerned that if she left Philadelphia, she would not be able to go back to school, Ellis exacted a promise from Milford that she would return in the fall.

"September days of 1876 brought many hours of conflicting emotions," Ellis recorded, as the "very precious" summer months passed.[18] She had become pregnant, money was scarce, her little sons were tugging at her heartstrings, and yet

> the urge to complete that which under the circumstances seemed an impossible thing to do still lived within my tenacious soul. . . . I listened to the protests from those I loved which I felt were made in loving concern for me, & yet I

could not turn from inner convictions. . . . If only I had a shaddow of the chance I felt assured that I could overcome. . . . I knew the trying ways of strict economy & could endure cold & hunger—& mortal sufferings of motherhood which in the coming May time would come inevitably to me, my faith had driven every fear & dread from out of my soul.[19]

Milford was concerned about sending his wife, pregnant and alone, to Philadelphia. However, when he learned of a group of students leaving for the East the next day, he agreed that Ellis should go with them. The very next morning Milford doubted his actions, saying, "Well, I wonder if it's right for a husband to let his wife do things she shouldn't do." Ellis found herself replying, "What do you mean? Yesterday you encouraged me to go. . . . I'm ready to go and I'm going." "It was the only time in my life," she continued, "that I ever opposed my husband's desires. . . . It was hard to go the first time, but much harder the last."[20]

Her thoughts clung to home when she arrived for her medical schooling in the fall of 1876 and the potential challenges of her pregnancy bore in upon her:

> Oct. 8th Perhaps tis best I have a few days after my long weary journey to recuperate before College opens for our seasons work. & yet it gives perhaps too much time to think—time to survey the uphill trails I needed [to] climb. . . . I had no mortal soul in whom I could confide & often to relieve the mental stress I would walk & walk & walk & still walk on. At night I'd weep & pray & plead unto the Lord in much humility.
>
> One evening after a dreary day I was visited in my little room by . . . kind friends [from] my first last winter here at college work. We had a pleasant little chat when Mrs. W. remarked ["]we are wondering why you seem so sad—Last winter you were so smiling & content. You surely are not

like yourself." The other lady said. They both remarked, "& we have come to ask you why this change & [if] it may be possible to help or comfort you in any way."

For a time I tried to laugh & lightly pass it as a joke & then I thought—It will not be very long before the truth they will understand & then I told the secret of my fears in few & simple words. That I was just as loyal to my great desire to qualify as an M.D. as I had ever been indeed the hope was more intensified but in prospective motherhood I feared I overstepped the bounds of safety for my one unborn & also for my hearts best treasures left so far away—I had not one single fear for self—'twas all for those more precious than my life! Then in one voice they both exclaimed. Why you can never go on thus. You will surely fail in all your studies & can never graduate under such unfavorable conditions. You can easily rid your self of such an obstacle. You who know what you know of scientific ways to still the life of the unborn!!

To me such words were horrible beyond compare. I rose upon my feet—& never in all of mortal life did I ever feel such power and said: "No! No! Such crime is not for me, & here I testafy to you that I will prove my powers of success. I know that God, our Eternal creator, will pave the way for me & that his choicest blessings will be mine. My child shall live as proof of what I speak & both of us be blessed unto the glorious end!"

Soon I was left alone and there within that humble little room I fell upon my knees & there remained through many hours in nearness unto Heavenly, unto the Creator of the Universe of life. And then acknowledged Him & all His Providences for my weal—for blessings on my hearts beloved. And when the darkness of night had passed, the morning dawned, my feares had vanished, too. I soon [became] a woman filled with purest faith—& sweetest assurance that my Father was my ever loving true unfailing Friend! & never more could there come to me a single doubt—& here I testafy in all humility & joyousness of spirit that fear no more oppressed my soul!

I went my way through every Task, through every busy day. My lessons were but pleasant tasks. The stairways were Ideal and climbed with ease—I never hungered with my humble fare, need the longer hours of sleep . . . for which I humbly praise & thank my gracious God of Love.[21]

On May 25, 1877, Ellis's daughter Olea was safely born in Philadelphia. Ellis took care of herself and her baby, completed her course work, and graduated. She returned home bearing the credentials for which she had sacrificed—the precious medical knowledge and the precious new life that was her daughter.

With loving resourcefulness, Ellis contrived ways to keep her children with her or near her while she did her work. She set up an office on Main Street:

> Thus began the happiest hours of my life. The blessed companionship of intelligent, growing, developing minds; the loving helpfulness of two loving sons. They cared for my infants, kept our apartments in order, watched the telephone, carried messages to me. On one momentous day, through the aid of these two alert boys I attended five maternity cases in 24 hours. On returning from the last case, with a keen sense of satisfaction and sublimest gratitude, I found my beloved assistants still on the watchtower with everything ready for mother to find her needed rest. And while I slept behind locked doors, the entrance was guarded that I should not be disturbed.[22]

During this challenging decade from 1879 through 1889, Ellis bore two more daughters, Ellis and Nellie, who lived, and two more sons, who died as infants. She helped establish the LDS

Hospital, the School of Nursing and Obstetrics, and served on the general boards of both the Relief Society and the Young Ladies' Mutual Improvement Association. With other notable women, she represented the Church at the National Council of Women in Washington, D.C., and through her leadership in the Utah Woman's Press Club, entertained prominent women in her home, including Harriet Beecher Stowe. Her book of poetry, *Life Lines,* was published in 1910, when she was sixty-three years of age.

Ellis taught nursing in Mexico and Canada as well as in several western states. She also taught obstetrics and practiced medicine for fifty years, graduating five hundred nurses and delivering six thousand babies. Milford completed law school and eventually also obtained a medical degree. Ellis and Maggie were doctors; Lizzie and Mary, the other two wives, were trained by Ellis as nurses. Milford started a monthly journal called *The Salt Lake Sanitarian;* Ellis and Maggie were editors and frequent contributors. The following year, 1889, Ellis's last child, Nellie, was born; her eldest, Bard, was then twenty-two.

Ellis continued to pour her knowledge, conviction, and love into training nurses and also serving the general membership of the Church. In later years she was honored by her college and her profession, traveled, and even obtained additional education at the University of Utah.

In 1913, her youngest child, Nellie, was married. Three years later, Ellis and Milford celebrated their fiftieth wedding anniversary. A little less than two years later, on March 15, 1918, Milford died just shy of his eighty-second birthday. Ellis mourned him, seeing only the goodness in him, his endeavors, and his desires. But she had learned to understand herself and to stand alone.

Her children were her brightest treasures, and she cherished them while at the same time continuing to teach and give and serve others. Whenever she was called out on maternity duty, she would pray for help. "Pray in your soul as you hasten to your duty" was

Ellis Reynolds Shipp (1847–1939)

Dr. Ellis R. Shipp established a School of Nursing and Obstetrics and graduated five hundred nurses. This photograph features one of her midwifery classes in 1896. Ellis is seated on the second row, far right.

her motto. She acknowledged her Heavenly Father in every success, every achievement, of her life:

> And with these same principles I tutored all who sought usefulness, enabling them to usher new life into this world—that life so precious to the suffering mother and most sublime in the sight of God. I never yet have been able to express my satisfaction in this part of my life work, for thus have I been enabled to give and give of my knowledge and yet have more remaining to give over and over again.

In her later autobiography Ellis wrote: "Reverently unto God I give my gratitude for the successful practice of medicine for the span of more than fifty years. For more than six thousand times have I felt the exquisite bliss of seeing the mother's smile when for the first time she clasped her treasure in her arms."[23]

As her life approached its close, Ellis, who had kept meticulous records, told her children to burn the records of the thousands of dollars she was owed, believing that people who are suffering with illness have troubles enough.

Ellis Reynolds Shipp died on January 31, 1939, shortly after celebrating her ninety-second birthday. Many notable people paid tribute in the services held for her, including Annie Wells Cannon, Ruth May Fox, Levi Edgar Young, and George Albert Smith. But perhaps the greatest tribute is in the simple words of her daughter Olea: "Is there an end to the marvels you can tell about Mother? Love—endurance—sacrifice. She had absolutely *conquered herself.* Her every thought was for humanity—for you—what would *you* like? What do *you* need?"[24]

In conquering herself—her fears, her weaknesses, the intense feelings that sometimes set her apart—Ellis Shipp had learned what it means to live a Christlike life. This is evident in the lines from her poem entitled "Love Divine," which sums up the spirit of her life:

> *And if a heart is sore with sting*
> *From slight or words unkind,*
> *May I the balm of solace bring*
> *Their wounds to soothe and bind.*
> *Oh, help me love humanity,*
> *And all its virtues see,*
> *For those who love most tenderly*
> *Are surely most like Thee.*[25]

Chapter 15

"Hallowed Ground"

Edith Ann Smith (1861–1954)
by Janiece Johnson

In the early morning of December 18, 1905, a party left Salt Lake City on a pilgrimage to the hills of Sharon, Windsor County, Vermont, to attend the dedication of a newly erected monument memorializing Joseph Smith Jr. at his birthplace a century after his birth. Forty-four-year-old Edith Ann Smith conveyed the surprise she felt when she was given the distinction of unveiling the monument by removing the "immense" United States flag used to cover it.[1] One person who attended reflected:

> It was very appropriate that this ceremony should be performed by Miss Edith Smith, for no one in that numerous family is more worthy the honor. She has been for years the unpaid historian and Temple recorder for the Smith family; and what loving acts her brain has otherwise conceived, and her hand executed, only her friends, the poor, the needy, and the angels in heaven will ever know.[2]

Edith Ann Smith, born August 5, 1861, in Salt Lake City, Utah, was the youngest daughter of Lucy Brown and Elias Smith, a cousin of Joseph Smith Jr. One of fifteen brothers and sisters, some of them half siblings,[3] she was named Edith Ann—after Lucy's mother and grandmother, respectively—and her father deemed her "smart and healthy."[4]

Edith was educated in a family school, after which she attended the University of Deseret. She later worked as a cashier, wrapper, and bookkeeper at the Western Shoe and Dry Goods Company in Salt Lake and then as a cashier at the same cashier desk at ZCMI for thirty-two years. She was also employed cataloging books at the public library in Salt Lake City for a short time.

Service in The Church of Jesus Christ of Latter-day Saints was integral to Edith's life. In 1873, at age twelve, Edith served as secretary for the Juvenile Relief Society of the Salt Lake Seventeenth Ward before there was any Churchwide organization for children.[5] The Juvenile Relief Society was "spontaneously" organized by girls in the ward when they saw a need. Eliza R. Snow, general president of the Relief Society, later praised and blessed them for their initiative.[6] Participation in this organization became foundational for Edith's life of service. Over the course of forty years, Edith fulfilled a variety of Church callings, serving as counselor for the Young Ladies' Mutual Improvement Association, teacher, secretary, and family historian. She sang in the Eleventh Ward choir and was a member of the Mormon Tabernacle Choir for eleven years.

Edith found particular fulfillment in family history work and temple worship. Her father, Elias, noted in his journal that she received her temple endowment on a snowy day in 1876.[7] Elias detailed his faithful temple service, and Edith apparently continued that practice. She worked in the Salt Lake Temple for a number of years and attended several temple dedications, including that of the Cardston Alberta Temple dedication in 1923, where she helped record the first temple session performed. Called the "historian of the Smith family," Edith served as the "secretary/historian" of the Asael

Smith Family Organization and was honored for her "extensive" work.[8]

Edith, who did not marry, lived with her mother until her mother's death in 1895. At that time she moved into the home of her sister and brother-in-law, Lucy and John Acomb.

Sadly, few autobiographical documents remain to tell Edith Ann Smith's full life story, yet the variety of her writings disclose bits and pieces of her personality. She appreciated a good story and had a fun-loving and independent personality, as shown in the brief foray she made into the world of fiction when she wrote a Mutual Improvement Association play titled "A Sit Down Strike for Love."[9] Her writings, including what she chose to preserve, demonstrate what she valued. Her 1905 trip to Vermont and other historic sites were a high point in Edith's life, signifying her identity as a woman, historian, and believer. Within her two-page autobiographical sketch, the 1905 trip receives more attention than any other event.

Edith's 1905 journal is a testament to her belief in The Church of Jesus Christ of Latter-day Saints, as she followed the admonition of Church president Joseph F. Smith for each member of their traveling party to "sense the fact that they had some responsibility in spreading the truths of the gospel that had been restored after having lain so long concealed in this hill [Cumorah]."[10] Edith used her journal to testify and witness of Joseph Smith, thereby adding to the collective memory and shared conviction that he was a chosen prophet of God.

1905 Journal of Edith A. Smith

About December 14th 1905 I received an invitation to be one of a party to go to Sharon, Windsor Co, Vermont and be present at the Dedication of a monument erected in memory of the Prophet Joseph Smith in honor of the 100th Anniversary of his birth. . . .

Edith Ann Smith at the Joseph Smith Birthplace Memorial in Sharon, Vermont, dedicated on December 23, 1905, to mark the centennial of the Prophet's birth. She stands in the center of the second row to the left of her cousin President Joseph F. Smith.

Saturday. Dec 23. 1905

    All were instructed to be ready at 8 a.m for the Journey to Sharon [Vermont]. The porches of the Hotel held a very lively crowd. On account of the thaw of the previous evening the arrangements had to be somewhat changed.

    Bro Wells had secured all the sleighs in the neighborhood for this occasion and the snow had almost disappeared so most of the sleighs were changed for wagons, buggies etc.

    If the vehicles had gone over the road in a manner that all could be photographed it would have been an odd looking procession Phaetons—Surreys—bob-sleds—cutters, having been pressed into service. One crowd in a bob-sled with the driver standing all the way.

    Bro and Sis Easton, Eva Y Davies had a young driver who performed the act of tossing them out in the road without breaking any bones. . . .

Edith Ann Smith (1861–1954)

Passed several who had started on foot to be present at the services. Picked up an elderly gentleman who was quite chatty. he seemed to know a good deal about the people of the neighborhood. said he was studying French had some odd ideas about religion. Doctors he said prescribed different medicines for different kinds of disease—so religion, he said, was the "medicine for death."

Several newspaper men were in the party, to get memo and pictures for their papers. They seemed very anxious to get Pres Smith's photo. So he gave them one & also stood while they pressed the button. . . . By 9 a.m all were on the road. The Dairy Hill farm is about 3 ½ miles from Royalton.

The road led off in the same directions as Tunbridge but Just outside the town led off to the right. the sign post reading: "5 mi to Sharon;" an iron bridge spanned the river and the road followed the river almost the entire distance. It was a very narrow one, scarcely a foot of level ground was passed over, but up and down and around the corners we went. A Landscape artist would have found many subjects for his canvas, for the scenery was very beautiful. as on the day before, small groves of pine & spruce trees were seen on the hillside—straight-green-beautiful large shade trees were lying along the way the reason for which we afterwards found out. The Farm houses were close to the road, clean and neat in appearance. fences in good condition and everything showing thrift.

The snow was gently falling adding to the beauty of the surroundings.

As we passed from the main road onto the one that led to the farm, quite a steep hill had to be crossed. As we neared the top we obtained our first view of the monument to spire rising above the hills. As we reached the top and rolled around the west side of the house to the north we found ourselves in full view of the monument. It was a supreme moment. All felt they had reached their destination. The inscription die was covered with a very beautiful flag 24 x ft. This picture with the hills for a background and the falling snow was very beautiful

Although it was quite early many of the residents were in evidence, apparently desiring to miss nothing that was going on.

We ascended the steps on the east side of the house crossed the porch and entered the cottage.[11] The first thing which met our gaze was the historic hearthstone with its mantle decorated with carnations, chrysanthemums & pine boughs. A picture of the prophet Joseph Smith hung over the mantle.

The cottage was not finished but Bro Wells had succeeded in getting it in a condition to be used for the service. . . .

The neighbors had kindly loaned some of their furniture for the occasion and the interior was very comfortable & cheerful. . . .

The upper floor had a hall and four rooms one a bathroom, with tub, toilet & basin. This seemed to be somewhat of a curiosity to the people, as very few had bathrooms, if any were found in that neighborhood.

A furnace in the basement was also very much scrutinized.

The whole house was thrown open for the inspection of all. In one of the upper rooms Bro B. Goddard presided over a small bureau of information, where all who desired were provided with such literature as had been brought for that purpose. There were very few if any who did not secure a souvenir from this room.

I went to one of the upper rooms and addressed some souvenir postal cards to a number of the members of our

Edith Ann Smith (1861–1954)

Edith Ann Smith unveiled the Joseph Smith Birthplace Memorial, an honor for which her "heart was full of gratitude." December 23, 1905.

family who had not been permitted, for various reasons, to be present. . . .

Before the service commenced George A informed me that I had been chosen by Pres Smith to unveil the monument. I cannot describe my feelings, only that my heart was full of gratitude that I was considered worthy to fulfill this part of the exercises. Tears not of sorrow but of Joy would continue to flow

The announcement by Pres Smith to the people that being the oldest lady member of the family present I would have the honor of unveiling was not so great a surprise as it otherwise would have been.

All were invited to go outside and witness the unveiling.
Closed by Singing: "Praise to the man, etc"
Prayer by George Albert Smith.

Immediately after the close of the exercises most of those present moved to the outside no pushing, no hurry. but quietly and in order as though all recognized the solemnity of the occasion.

The exact time of the unveiling was 1.20 p.m; eastern time.

A great shout arose as the beautiful flag fluttered down onto the base.[12] After this a citizen of Vermont asked permission to propose three cheers for Junius F. Wells.[13] Then if at no other time Bro Wells must have realized that he had many friends in that section of the country.

I received many congratulations on the honors that had come to me. One great comfort was the unselfish way in which all expressed themselves, showing no envy nor Jealousy on the part of any whose right it might have been to receive recognition. . . .

A Mr Welcome Royalton's Photographer then took some pictures of the Utahans on the porch and at the base of the monument.

Pres Smith desired some songs sung. so all Joined in singing: "The Star Spangled Banner" and Sister Emma Lucy Gates sang: O Ye Mountains High" in her usual excellent style.

A lunch had been prepared by Miss Ala M Day by Bro Wells order some 300 people had partaken of the viands provided. The Utah people were served at the last table. A dinner which we have read about under the title of a "regular New England dinner," was served.

Hot chicken pie in generous portions. Meats—salads—olives—pickles. mince & pumpkin pie like "Mother used to make." all seemed to forget all else for a few minutes in the enjoyment of this spread. Apple cider made from the apples that grew in the orchard on the farm was served, another evidence of Bro Wells thoughtfulness.

Was introduced to Miss Day, the chef, who said she was a dressmaker by trade but enjoyed occasionally to cook a dinner. Several young ladies assisted in serving the dinner and seemed very anxious to please.

Tables had been placed around three sides of the basement and while all had to stand a general good time was had.

The Utah people again assembled in the room containing the hearthstone Pres Smith occupied a position in front of the fireplace and the party circled around him.

Pres A. H. Lund in behalf of the Utah Party presented a watch chain and charm to Pres Smith as a token of friendship and a memento of the occasion

Pres Smith very feelingly responded and the occasion was a very touching one. Tears filled every eye—and all felt the influence of that heavenly Spirit which seemed to fill every portion of the room as they feel the heat of a stove— or the rays of the sun.

By permission Bro Wells then presented each one present with a highly polished granite disc as a souvenir of the occasion. These discs or paper weights were made out of the piece of granite cut from the lower base.[14]

Tuesday, Dec, 26,

Arriving at Palmyra [New York], we found carriages waiting for the party and quite a number of people to see the "Mormons." Seven carriages were soon filled and the procession moved on towards the town which is some little distance away from the station. We drove to the home of Mr Wm. Avery Chapman once owned by Joseph Smith, Sr. . . .

It is supposed by the owners of the place that the Prophet received the visitations of the Angel Moroni here but the records show they took place before the house was built.

A little log house stood in the corner of the lot which was torn down after Mr Chapmans father purchased the place. This was evidently where the boy Joseph received the angels visits and received his instructions. . . .

Some postals and literature were passed to the people as a souvenir of the visit. The two parties then had their pictures taken in a group on the outside under one of the trees that is supposed some of the members of the Smith family planted.

From the home the party went to the sacred grove situated about a quarter of a mile away from the home to the west. As we crossed a small stream on the way we were informed that some of the first baptisms were said to have been performed here.

It was with peculiar feeling we all entered the Grove. Here some 85 years before, on a glorious spring morning, the boy, Joseph Smith knelt and prayed. Prayed for light and knowledge.

He had read James 1:5: If any of you lack wisdom, let him ask of God that giveth to all men liberally and upbraideth not; and it shall be given him.

He had sought the pages of the good old book, The Bible, to get comfort therefrom. after reading this passage he determined to ask for this assistance, for he felt he did lack wisdom and here was a divine pledge, to hear and give without upbraiding.

While engaged in prayer he was seized by some power and for a time it seemed he would be destroyed, but exerting all his strength he called upon his Father to deliver him. Above him he saw a pillar of light, which descended and fell upon him and as it did so this to him unknown power released him and fled

In this light standing above him were two personages, alike in form and feature and clad alike in snowy raiment.

EDITH ANN SMITH (1861–1954)

One of them, calling him by name, said pointing to the other "This is my beloved Son. hear him." As soon as he recovered himself he inquired of them as to which of the churches he should Join, for this was his heart's desire, never doubting but that one of them was right: The answer he received was that he should unite with none of them for they taught for doctrine the commandments of men having a form of godliness but denying the power thereof: After giving him other instructions they and their pillar of light ascended and passed from his gaze.

If there is any hallowed ground on the earth, surely the place where the Father and the Son appeared in person must be hallowed ground.

Many thoughts passed through our minds as we walked among the trees upon the ground strewed with dead leaves. We could not tell the exact spot where these holy beings stood but no one doubted that somewhere near the Father and Son did actually appear to Joseph Smith. The party gathered around the stump of a tree which by measurement was supposed to have been a sapling about 180 years ago. The song which then floated out on the stillness perhaps was the first that had ever been rendered in this sacred. Never before had it seemed so appropriate.

"Joseph Smith's First Prayer"

In speaking of the place as a grove it might be supposed that it was very small place with few trees, But it is several acres in extent and contains a large number of trees, principally maple and birch. There are a few walnut hickory and cottonwood trees among them. No ax has ever touched a tree in this grove. In 1859 Mr Chapmans father purchased the farm and although he did not believe in the religion Joseph Smith taught the world, he preserved the grove from destruction during his lifetime, never taking a tree from there except the ones that die naturally. His son, the present owner who had received instructions from his father to leave the grove in its natural state regards this place with a sacredness that was a pleasant thing for all to know. . . .

So we slowly retired from the grove which we hoped would still remain in the hands of friends and be a silent witness of the glorious manifestations that had been beheld within its sacred precincts.

We stopped in the road near the home to bid Mr Chapman, adieu and again thank him for his kindness. and then we rolled on to our next destination.

The Hill Cumorah

There was some little doubt as to whether Mr Sampson, who rents the farm on which the hill is situated, would allow the party to climb the hill or even linger on the outskirts. Our teamsters seemed a little dubious as to our success.

Arriving at the Sampson home near the foot of the hill, we were informed that the gentleman was not at home, but his wife, though somewhat reluctantly, gave her consent.

Pres Lyman suggested we climb the steepest part at the north end. It proved to be quite a climb, several halts were made for "more breath," while a few went to the top without a breathing spell. From the summit we found we had a fine view of the surrounding country Pres. Smith pointed to a spot on the west side where a depression was noticed and said from knowledge he had gained at a previous visit that was near where the stone box containing the plates had projected from the ground.

All inspected this spot and some pictures were taken.

Walking along the top of the hill toward the South where it gradually rolls off to the level, we approached a

Edith Ann Smith (1861–1954)

The traveling party on the "steepest part at the north end" of the Hill Cumorah near Palmyra, New York, on December 26, 1905.

small grove of trees where the party were called together and a song suggested. Here again a most appropriate selection was made, and all Joined in singing the hymn composed by Parley P. Pratt.

An angel from on high. . . .

After the conclusion of the Hymn Pres. Smith offered a most beautiful prayer. All eyes were filled with tears as each and every priesthood and auxiliary organization was remembered in its turn. Grateful for the oportunity for being present for the care that had been over us during our Journeying, he prayed that each one was sense the fact that they had some responsibility in spreading the truths of the gospel that had been restored after having lain so long concealed in this hill. The Prophets family were remembered that they might see and understand the truths of the living God. So broad and comprehensive did the prayer become that every one felt almost lifted above earth and seemingly enjoying the blessings of a holier sphere.

> That little party standing as it were in a double circle with uncovered heads will never forget the beautiful, heavenly spirit that accompanied that prayer and filled their hearts with Joy.
>
> We slowly wended our way back to the cottage some going down the roadway while others descend the steep side of the hill.
>
> A few arrow heads were purchased that had been dug up in the neighborhood of the hill. as there was not enough for all it was decided to draw for them.
>
> So we left what is now known as "Mormon Hill." In the Jaredites time it was called "Ramah" and in the Nephites day, "Cumorah." In the book of Ether we are informed that in the Jaredites day this hill was the scene of their final battle. after several terrible battles had been fought in which two million men had been sacrificed, this number not including women and children. Several hundred years later at this same place, The Nephites were annihilated. Thousand[s] of flint arrows have been found since 1825 by the farmers in this part of the country, when plowing and clearing the land.[15]

The members of the traveling party continued their trip through Kirtland, Ohio. After arriving home in Salt Lake City, Edith concluded:

> The Journey was a remarkable one. 5,500 miles had been covered in travel The special car Sofala had been transferred from one line to another as had previously been planned without loss of time. No accident happened.
>
> The party were as one family each vieing with the other to make the trip a pleasant [one].
>
> The results of this Journey, the dedication of the Joseph Smith monument and memorial cottage, the friends mad[e] the impression on strangers. etc cannot be estimated. All

were thankful for the oportunity afforded them and will ever remember the occasion as one of the most pleasant Journey of their lives.[16]

Susa Young Gates, in her account of the 1905 trip, wrote that those who knew Edith recognized her quiet, often anonymous, contributions. In her journal, Edith mentioned enjoying a Christmas tree in their train car on Christmas day; yet, her record did not point out the source of such thoughtfulness. Susa did: "Where has such a thing [the Christmas tree] come from, gay with shining balls, and loaded with paper parcels? Ask Edith! The girl who knows everything, and who does everything good and thoughtful." In her final poem about the trip, Susa continued to laud Edith:

> *While Edith is so fine and good.*
> *No harm can overtake her;*
> *In every thoughtful word and act,*
> *She is a record-breaker.*[17]

In 1954, then the oldest living Smith relative, Edith died on June 27, the 110th anniversary of the martyrdom of Joseph Smith and just before her ninety-second birthday.[18] She remains emblematic of many hard-working members of the kingdom whose efforts on a large or small scale remain less known than they deserve to be.

Chapter 16
"The Hand of the Diligent Maketh Rich"

Ellen Johanna Larson Smith (1868–1965)
by Christine T. Cox

Born in the final stretches of the rugged pioneer era before the railroad reached Utah, Ellen Johanna Larson Smith witnessed remarkable world changes in her lifetime. She was the daughter of Swedish handcart pioneers Mons and Elna Olsson Malmstrom Larson, who emigrated from Sweden in 1859, initially settling in a mud hut in Tooele. Seven years later, Mons took his family to the frontier town of Santaquin, Utah County, Utah, where Ellen, the youngest of eight children, was born on February 16, 1868.

Through the example of her parents, Ellen learned faith and obedience, virtues that she incorporated into her own life. Ellen's mother had "urged her husband to take a second wife because she was fully converted to the principle of polygamy," and she lived successfully in it.[1] In 1876 the Larsons, with two hundred other families, were called to colonize the untamed desert lands of Arizona. Their "property [in Utah] was disposed of . . . yet the thought of not honoring the call had never entered their minds."[2]

Ellen Johanna Larson Smith (1868–1965)

Ellen recalled that en route to Snowflake, Arizona, on Christmas Eve 1878, "We camped near the river under some cotton wood trees, so I hung my stocking from a crooked limb and Santa found it for in it was some candy and a can of lemon ade—sugar with lemon extract ready to be put in the water for drinking."[3] It was a simple Christmas but one that delighted her in every way.

Six days later, after a two-month journey, the Larson family arrived in Snowflake on December 30. "We set up our tent," she remembered, "and there we lived until the boys and father could get logs hauled from the mountain and build a house. And when we got the house built, they didn't have lumber for floors. Everybody just had dirt floors."[4]

"I attended every school taught within my reach until I finished the eighth grade," Ellen recalled. "I had a great desire for an education. . . . I once complained to my mother that if we had remained in Utah, I could have received a better education. She replied, 'My girl, you will never lose anything by your parents having obeyed counsel.'"[5] As a young girl in Snowflake, Ellen learned to be industrious and resourceful; every hand was essential on the family farm to obtain basic necessities. The skills she acquired sustained her throughout her life. Ellen's philosophy followed that of her mother, who "often remarked that poor people find so many more things to be happy over than the rich, because every common necessity acquired brings gratitude and joy."[6]

The Jesse N. Smith family settled on the lot across from the Larson home, and Silas Derryfield Smith invited Ellen to a dance. Thus began a lifelong romance of dedication and devotion. "I was in my 15th year," Ellen reminisced, "and had pledged my hand to Silas D. Smith with the stipulation that we wait three years at least."[7] As their courtship developed, they often "knelt in prayer asking our Heavenly Father to protect and guide us. We talked of the future and exchanged ideas; we both agreed that some day we would live the principle of polygamy." "I was sure," Silas wrote, "that with all the allurements of rivals, she would not break that promise."[8]

Ellen's family moved to Pima, Arizona, not long after she and Silas vowed to marry. The distance did not deter the building of a lasting relationship. Through correspondence, their love and commitment to each other continued to grow.

One day Silas wrote to Ellen of his admiration for a "splendid young lady, Maria Elizabeth Bushman, from St. Joseph, Arizona." Ellen responded tersely, "I have been thinking seriously about this matter of you taking a second wife and if you are determined to do so, I must ask you to excuse and relieve me now from going any further." Silas recorded:

> Well, I was sick and heart-broken. . . . Alone I pondered and visiting the little cedar trees, I poured out my soul in prayer. I really felt like saying, "Ellen, I will do anything or go anywhere for you." But my letter read thus, "Ellen, your letter breaks my heart. We have well understood this matter and have been in agreement in contemplating and planning a plural family; it is my purpose to continue in that determination come what will . . ." Sooner than I anticipated an answer came, a short note with this message, "Oh Silas, I love you, forgive me, I wanted to try you to see if you would give up a principle for a poor simple girl like me. I would not have wanted you had you not have proved to me that you are a man. The man I want my husband to be. I love you more than ever, Your Ellen."
>
> The load was lifted; at the little tree I expressed my thankfulness. Although Satan attempted to create anger for being played with, I finally wrote to her saying, "All is well, may God grant us courage to proceed."[9]

Ellen and Silas were sealed in the St. George Temple on November 10, 1886. "When we married," Ellen recollected, "we had to go by team to St. George, Utah, because we were determined to be married in the temple." The journey took sixteen days, and, according to Ellen, "We had a very good trip and everything went fine."[10] They returned to Snowflake in time to celebrate their first Christmas as husband and wife.

The newlyweds purchased Ellen's childhood home, where they set up their meager household and began a long life together. "We were so happy in this home filled with happy memories if not much else. We had a little cook stove, a goods box with shelves put in for a cupboard, a bedstead, table and chairs and a cheery fireplace. It was home and happiness indeed."[11]

Joy in Self-Reliance and Diligence

When Ellen and Silas chose to begin a plural family, it was not done naïvely. "Each of us was reared in polygamous families," Silas wrote. "We were not ignorant of the joys and sorrows and responsibilities and the importance of entering into that sacred order of matrimony."[12] One reality of the decision was the interference of the law, which was at its height in 1888 when Silas and Maria Bushman were married. Despite persecution, Ellen bore nine children over the ensuing years, and Maria bore ten.[13] They lived happily together for the better part of seventeen years. Silas recorded of this time, "We were poor as to worldly goods but rich in a peaceful, happy home."[14]

Over time "persecution abated somewhat,"[15] but "during the latter part of 1904," Silas wrote, "zealous politicians in Arizona began a campaign against . . . those who practiced the Church doctrine of polygamy. As a result of this persecution . . . I and many others were advised to get out of the state."[16] Silas and Maria and their family left for Utah. Ellen and her six children remained in Snowflake, where she became their primary economic support. Ellen had been apart from her husband in the past while she and Maria lived together and he "batched" wherever he could find employment.[17] This time apart, however, was of longer duration. Between 1893 and 1930, Silas was absent for twenty-one years: he was seeking employment in Arizona, Mexico, or California; serving a mission in Colorado; or living at intervals with Maria in Utah to avoid prosecution for polygamy.

Ellen did not murmur during her husband's absences. Instead, she kept busy. One endeavor she undertook to support her family was beekeeping. "One of mother's chief delights was the fact that she and the bee were on friendly terms," said Ellen's daughter. In one year, her bee colonies could bring in as much as "a thousand dollars which in that time was a wonderful asset for everyday living."[18]

Shortly after Silas and Maria moved to Utah in 1905, they found themselves in dire financial straits. A letter Ellen wrote to her husband shows her resilience and confidence in God: "Sell your land and lower lot and make your family there comfortable first there will be time soon enough to worry about us. The honey kept us last year and the year before, the prospects are much more promising this year. . . . I believe in making the best of the present, the Lord will come to the rescue in the future as long as one is not wasteful or lazy."[19]

Ellen had the enterprising ambition, skill, and trust in the Lord to make things work, whatever the situation. In addition to beekeeping, Ellen earned income by taking in boarders, cleaning the Snowflake Stake Academy, and operating a notions shop. She also ventured into photography with her daughter. In Ellen's words, "Professor [Joseph] Peterson had a camera and he came over and wanted to know if I didn't want to get it and so with a few lessons he gave and we took it over and soon had a thriving photography business."[20]

Ellen experimented with her newfound trade and developed her own informal style, documenting everyday people doing everyday things, breaking through the traditional boundaries of formal indoor studio photography. She created a social portrait of the community of Snowflake, Arizona, and captured life and humanity in ways seldom seen at that time.[21] She also expressed her love for nature in poetry and art, and she created intricate jewelry from beads and horsehair. She found beauty and joy in her common, everyday surroundings. By using her innate creativity, she left a significant legacy.

Her photographs provided a way for her to connect with Silas during his long absences. He described a photograph she sent to him in a letter, giving insight into Ellen's life:

Ellen Johanna Larson Smith (1868–1965)

Largely self-taught, Ellen Larson Smith captured a social portrait of Snowflake, Arizona, through her innovative photography. She developed a thriving photography business to help support her family. Photo is of Myrtle Smith at the washboard, Ethel Smith, Seraphine Smith, and an unidentified young man, ca. 1910.

My [the] pictures you send are fine. I can see every detail, the big fire place with the back log . . . the turkey for thanksgiving. My, such beauty and comfort. . . . it makes me ache for such a peaceful sleep . . . and then the picture of writing stories, poetry, and games—surely I feel now the fascination of it and can really see it all in my mind's eye—what a picture. . . . The two fires are so tempting one saying come fry your fish here the other you can fry your bacon better over here.[22]

Ellen's daughter Mae commented: "Mother was always busy, working in the dark room on photographs, tending the bees, making bread, churning, gardening, sewing and darning and waiting on customers in the little store. Now I realize how poor we were in material things and what a struggle Mother had to keep us clothed and fed, but I never heard her complain and I never had the feeling that we were poor."[23]

Of her mothering, Ellen said:

> My ambition was that my children should be well educated, not only in books but also in the practical things of life; that my sons should be worthy to go on missions, and become scientific farmers; that my influence on the formation of great characters might be felt even on my grandchildren. However the thing that counts and that should be emphasized and impressed, is to get a testimony of the gospel as taught by Joseph Smith.[24]

Ellen experienced her share of trials and sorrows, most significantly in the deaths of four of her children by accidental causes. In 1900, her six-year-old daughter, Charity, was fatally injured when "she fell under the wheels of a wagon loaded with stone." Reuel died in 1920 "when he too fell under the wheels of a wagon loaded with bailed hay. . . . Alof was killed in a mining accident at Bingham Mines in 1926, just a few weeks before he was to be married. In 1935 Josephine died in a car accident. Through all of these tragedies Ellen maintained her serenity."[25]

Ellen's namesake daughter, Ellen, remembered her mother's reaction when she received word of Josephine's death: "She said, The Lord giveth and the Lord taketh away, we have no choice. How thankful I am that I believe in the hereafter, that I shall see them all again. Yes she wept but was always so composed."[26]

Changing Times

In 1918 Silas, Ellen, and Maria moved to Salt Lake City. There, Maria developed a fascination with genealogy. In 1924 President Heber J. Grant called her to expand her research into the repositories of Washington, D.C., where she greatly forwarded the Church's genealogical work. She lived in the nation's capital for a number of years, and when she returned to Salt Lake City, Maria did not live with Silas. Instead, she spent her last years with daughters in

Ellen Johanna Larson Smith (1868–1965)

Portrait of Ellen Larson Smith's daughter Seraphine, ca. 1910.

Los Angeles, California, and Twin Falls, Idaho, where she died on January 9, 1953.[27]

By 1929 Ellen's children had married or were otherwise on their own. Two of her children, son Mons and daughter Seraphine, lived near Monticello, Utah, and she went to live with them. Silas was in California, hoping to create a lucrative new career and eventually have Ellen join him. Ellen wrote to him:

> Montecello July 17 1930
>
> My Dear Silas
>
> Yours of the 10 inst. at hand also the soap literature which I have carefully read, do hope you have found something at last that will prove remunerative but don't build your air castles to high so the fall won't jar us so much. You

Ellen Larson Smith's creative photography brought her subjects out of doors as she experimented with unconventional poses. Many of her photographs still hang in homes in Snowflake, Arizona.

see my castles are all on the ground floor so many of yours reach to the clouds and disappear. Let's hope this venture brings results somehow; that butterfly life doesn't charm me much but if we can make enough money out of it to accomplish our ends I am game for anything that is honorable.

I have helped the children hoe weeds, burn brush and nearly blistered my face and did blister the balls of my feet and hands, chased the turkeys, hunted eggs, and chased the cows and calves; slept under the trees, patched overalls and shirts for days, helped with the washing and moving, cooked, baked, made butter. That to me is real life, for beyond it all there is something real and tangable. Its productiveness, its bringing pleasure and joy to human beings, it broadens the imagination, it brings nature under the inspection of anyone who wants to see and learn and draw inspiration and it develops every mussle. It fills the system with pure first class air, and provides green groves or temples where we can commune with the invisable away from curious eyes; where we are monarch of all we survey and if the banks fail, if the railroads fail, if the merchants fail; yet we can live, for here we learn self-preservation for food can be garnered if we but put forth the effort. Comforts and beauty are likewise ours as well as love and health. What more do humane beings need. . . .

We have had very little rain, yet things keep on growing, boys are working ditch to fill the resever when it does rain. . . . Yes am wrinkled, grey and sunburned "yet can smile" can eat any thing and walk a mile.

It is now Supper time so will close for this time, better address me Montecello as I am in town part of the time sewing etc, etc.[28]

Affectionately
Ellen L. Smith

Ellen's tenacity and love for the land prompted her to move at age sixty-one to Tanglewood, a dry piece of property near Monticello, Utah, to homestead. She wrote to Silas:

I have been very humble and prayed that I might be guided as to the right step to take. I feel very impressed that we will be financially ahead if I go to Tanglewood by being there for planting. . . .

I can be there to get chickens and turkeys started and also supervise the building of the house. . . . I have had such a long rest that I am running over with energy, to be shut up in an apartment with nerve racking children would be suicide to my ambition.[29]

Starting over did not dampen her spirits. She wrote to Silas and urged him to leave his business ventures in California and join her at Tanglewood. "Our patriarchal blessings say we are to build up the waste places," she said, "so maybe it is time for us to begin."[30] Although Silas did not join her immediately, Ellen took to Tanglewood all the skills and knowledge gained over the years, and she made that little parcel of land blossom. Though it was hard work, she knew part of her life mission was to "build up the waste places," and she followed that counsel with all her heart. Tanglewood, she said, "gave us a wonderful feeling of independence and security."[31] She often wrote about it in her poetry, calling it the "Enchanted Ranch." "She believed in working with nature" and saw what the dry land could become.[32] "We can just make anything grow here," she said. "Look at this soil, the soil that God placed here for us."[33]

With that attitude, Ellen, with the assistance of her children and grandchildren, cleared the sagebrush and weeds from the land and planted a garden and fruit orchard—all from seed. Representatives from the State Department of Agriculture later called it "one of the most remarkable and diversified dry farms in the state of Utah."[34] Ellen also raised bees, cows, chickens, pigs, and the grain to feed them. She saw that members of her family had a daily supply of natural "vitamins," as she called them. They had everything they needed to sustain themselves.

Her grandson-in-law Hyrum A. Hendrickson, husband of Ellen's granddaughter Ida Smith Hendrickson, commented: "My first meeting with Grandma Smith . . . was at her home in Tanglewood. As we sat at the table, the only thing on the table that she hadn't raised was the salt and the pepper. We had a delicious meal. . . . She believed literally in the proverb, 'He becometh poor that dealeth with a slack hand: but the hand of the diligent maketh rich.'"[35]

Ellen Johanna Larson Smith (1868–1965)

Unwavering Faith

Ellen loved temple worship. She and Silas often dreamed of the day when they could devote their full-time efforts to temple work. On January 1, 1931, Ellen wrote to her husband, who was still in California:

> My Dear Silas
>
> A happy New year to you do hope your anticipations comes true: of course they will if you join us at Tanglewood we can't help but succeed: financially mentally and spiritually. Yes, I firmly believe that in a few years we shall be able to have means for research work and to spend time in the temples and then we can have a happy peaceful little nook to go where we can spend the summers. It just thrills me, this planning of the cosy new nest we shall build I have the plans all made out. . . . Melvin said it will sure take lotts of work to make Tanglewood the way you want it grandma. Since you are feeling so prime we will both be able to cope with any problem if we do have to exert a bit. . . .
>
> May the Lords blessings ever be with you. Extend the seasons greeting to the Robbins family, and your land lady and family. Yours affectionately
>
> Ellen L[36]

In 1939, Ellen, then seventy-one, and Silas fulfilled their desire to work in the temple. She wrote in her personal history: "We were called to be temple ordinance workers and we had our choice as to which temple we wanted to go to, so we went to the Mesa Temple. There we were officiators for 13 years, which work we greatly enjoyed."[37] Their children helped them get settled in Mesa so they could spend their later years together serving in the temple.

When World War II broke out, there was a scarcity of young men who could serve as missionaries. At the age of seventy-five, Ellen served a short-term mission to Placerville, California, with

Silas. "At their age," a daughter wrote, "it was quite a task for them, but being very young in heart and good in health, they found great pleasure in performing their mission."[38]

Afterward, they returned to temple service as officiators in the Mesa Temple. Of this experience Silas commented: "There is a most sacred and inspiring feeling in all the Temple activities. I thank God, my Heavenly Father, for this experience and the good health and vigor I enjoyed while doing this sacred work."[39] In the sunset of their lives they were blessed with peace, joy, and happiness by serving and helping those who could not help themselves.

"And as old father time crept upon them," a relative reminisced, "they began to feel the defects of this mortal body which was theirs. Aunt Ellen began to lose her eyesight and Uncle Silas began to lose his hearing. . . . [When asked] 'Well how are you today?' Ellen would say, 'Oh we're just fine, I'm getting a little blinder, and Silas is getting a little deafer, but we're just getting along fine.'"[41]

Ellen lived to see "wonders . . . accomplished" in her lifetime,[40] but, even in an ever-changing world, she continued steadfast in her love of the gospel and all of its principles. Her life was one of dedication and faithfulness to her family and the gospel of Jesus Christ. "Now in my old age [ninety-four] I can sit and listen to the radio and get all things that's transpiring in the church and out of the church," Ellen declared. "I'm visiting with my descendants down to the fifth generation."[42]

Ellen Larson Smith died in Mesa, Arizona, on January 12, 1965, four days short of her ninety-seventh birthday. Her thoughts and actions are incredible examples of optimistic diligence and obedience. She adapted as often as necessary to her circumstances, ever seeking to know and follow the Lord's will in all aspects of her life.

Chapter 17

"A Triangle of Happiness"

Julina Lambson Smith (1849–1936)
by Amanda Hendrix-Komoto

Julina Lambson was born on June 18, 1849, in Salt Lake City, Utah, the second daughter of Alfred Boaz and Melissa Jane Bigler Lambson. Her father had joined The Church of Jesus Christ of Latter-day Saints a few years earlier, in 1844, after being impressed with the charisma and presence of the Prophet Joseph Smith.[1] Alfred married Melissa Jane Bigler a year later. In 1847, they moved with their infant daughter, Melissa Jane (Julina's older sister), to the Salt Lake Valley, where Alfred built the small family a nice home, plastering the walls using a mixture that included hair from his oxen. In 1851, he was called on a mission to the West Indies, leaving his wife pregnant with their third daughter, Edna. In the years to follow two sons would also be born into the family.

Julina's mother, overwhelmed during her husband's absence, was relieved when her sister, Bathsheba Bigler Smith, offered to help care for her daughters. Julina stayed frequently at her aunt's house—eating dinner at their table and sleeping in one of their beds. She grew to feel as much a part of her aunt's household as her mother's and even lived with her aunt for a time.

It was at her aunt's house that Julina first learned about the day-to-day realities of plural marriage. Her aunt Bathsheba and her uncle George A. Smith accepted the divine origin of polygamy in 1845. In less than a year, George married five women. Bathsheba described them as "good, virtuous, honorable young women" and wrote that she had "joy in having a testimony" that she had done "what was acceptable in the eyes of my Father in Heaven."[2]

Because of Aunt Bathsheba, Julina's first experiences with polygamy were positive ones. When Uncle George brought home a new wife in 1857, Julina felt that Bathsheba welcomed her "as though she were her own daughter."[3] Julina wrote that her aunt frequently said "she knew her husband loved her and [that] the love he had for his other wives, did not lessen in the least degree that which he held for her."[4] The love Julina discovered in her aunt's home helped her deal with her father's own plural marriage. After he returned from his mission to the West Indies, he married twenty-seven-year-old Mary Jane Martin, who bore him four children.

When Julina married Joseph F. Smith as his second wife on May 5, 1866, she tried to be as accepting and gracious as her aunt Bathsheba in living the "Principle," as it was known. Her life was shaped and permeated by polygamy. She described her family as a "triangle of happiness" with her husband acting as "the center controlling bond of love."[5] Julina's descriptions of her life in reminiscences in the *Relief Society Magazine* and letters to her husband and sister wives offer insight into the lived reality of polygamy in the nineteenth century. Although she had been closely acquainted with polygamy since her childhood, Julina found that her family members initially advised her against marrying Joseph F. Smith, as he was already married to his cousin Levira Annette Clark Smith, an independent, vibrant woman he loved deeply.[6]

Julina's mother warned her that Joseph would never love her as much as he loved his first wife. The warning, however, did not deter her. "I love him," she said, "and if I am good he will learn to love me."[7] It happened that, despite their love for each other, Joseph and Levira had a tumultuous relationship, and their marriage ended in divorce in 1868, two years after he married Julina.[8]

Julina and Joseph had their first child on August 14, 1867. A year later Joseph married Sarah Ellen Richards, in 1871 he married Julina's sister Edna, and two other marriages followed a decade later—Alice Ann Kimball in 1883 and Mary Taylor Schwartz in 1884. Children followed in quick succession. Sarah Ellen and Julina gave birth to daughters just eight months apart. Julina described these years as filled with knitting, laughter, and kisses. Her diary provides a sense of her life's texture:

> Sunday Jan 2nd 1870 got breakfast washed and drest my little girls got dinner. Rhoda Knowlton, Martha Jane Coray called to see Sarah took dinner with us in the evening Joseph went to meeting in the 4th Ward. Abram Polly and Willard called in on their way to meeting. Aunt Lucy Kimball also called staid about an hour.
>
> Monday January 3rd 1870 . . . I also washed I have got another day's washing to do this week I did not wash last week because my baby had the chicken pox. I have been writing to Edna this evening she is in Fillmore. Edward started to school this morning to Mary Jane.
>
> Tuesday Jan 4th 1870 I made my baby Mary a rapper, mended Joseph's slippers, and ironed to day. Sarah is considerable better did the work to day.
>
> Wedensday Jan 5th 1870 I did a big wash to day washed 105 peaces. in the evening Joseph and Sarah went to the Theatre. Willard come over and staid two hours I partly worked a little sack for my baby. . . .
>
> Thursday Jan 6th 1870 I made a comforter for Edward's bed to day which has kept me quite buisy. Sarah helped me

to finish tieing it this evening. Aunt Lucy Smith called to see me this after noon.⁹

Filled with references to slippers and dress patterns, Julina's diary shows the meaning she found in her daily activities. As a member of the general board of the Relief Society, Julina emphasized the importance of the work women did within the home, telling them that their first responsibility was to their children. There were many things, she said, "which can be taught in no other place as effectively as in the home, such as praying and paying tithes."¹⁰

The letters she wrote to her sister wives throughout their lives together were filled with details about the daily lives of their children and the work that needed to be done around the house. "Baby is getting to be a good boy," she wrote in a letter to Sarah while the two were temporarily separated by one of Joseph's missions. "I did a large wash yesterday, and have been sewing for Robert today, have mended his breeches, made some valences for his bed, and curton, and cover for his (*box*) wash stand and a pair of pillow cases. The prayer bell has rung and baby is awake."¹¹

Julina found happiness in these quotidian activities of home life. When she was in her mid-sixties, Julina wrote that her "large dining-room was always the personal property and common gathering place of all." "Even now," she reminisced, "I can hear the laughter of our children as they played about us before being kissed, and tucked in their beds. There, too, I can see the evening picture of three tired but happy mothers, often busy with kneeless stockings, seatless trousers or other articles of clothing needing buttons or stitches; or with, perhaps, something good to read or ideas to exchange."¹²

The affection Julina expressed for her sister wives was echoed in the fondness with which Joseph wrote to each of them. He told Sarah Ellen, "My family, my beloved companions and our little ones, one and all, form the center of attractions for me on this earth."¹³

Julina rarely mentions her husband's later two wives in her letters or writings, suggesting that she felt closer to Sarah Ellen and sister Edna than to Mary or Alice, who were several years her junior. Her affection for Sarah and Edna was also born out of their experiences in living together and helping each other in their husband's absences. In letters they wrote to Joseph while he was presiding over the Church in England, attending to southern settlements in Utah, and traveling on Church business, Julina, Edna, and Sarah described attending balls together, watching each other's children, and helping each other sew and mend clothing. While Joseph was on a mission to Great Britain, Julina and Edna "clubbed together," in Julina's words, with their mother and Sister Grant "and got a five dollar . . . box of *soap*." As a result, Julina told Joseph, "we have got something to wash with."[14]

Joseph's missions and leadership responsibilities frequently interrupted their family life. Because of the close relationships between Joseph and his family, his absences affected them deeply. In a letter written just a few weeks after Joseph left for Britain, Julina described their daughter's distress: "Before going to bed . . . the first night after you left," she wrote, "[Mamie] put her arms around my neck and cried before she could finish her prayers. In the morning when she awoke she said, mama I woke up in the night the *tears* were on my cheeks I thought I was crying, but I was not. I wiped my eyes and went to sleep again."[15] The little girl's feelings matched her mother's. In a letter written a week later, Julina told Joseph that she was only "just begining to realize what it is to have responsibilities rest upon me."[16]

Joseph's missions were made harder for his wives by the fact that he often took one of them with him. Although having one of his wives present provided Joseph with comfort, it meant the wives he left behind were deprived of the labor and affection of two adults while also caring for additional children. Julina, however, felt it more difficult to be the one absent than the one left behind. In 1886, Julina was living in Laie, Hawaii, with Joseph when she received news that Mary might be able to come to the islands, freeing Julina to come home. Julina wrote a letter to Sarah expressing her feelings.

Although she was not "willing to leave him alone," Julina "would rejoice to go if somebody else could be with him, or if there were any hopes of his returning soon." "Just let me get home once again," she told Sarah, "and I will never be as eager to leave it as I was once. Will we ever be happy and permitted to live in peace again?"[17]

The last line of Julina's plea refers to the disruption that had occurred within Joseph's family as result of intensified efforts of the United States government to prosecute Latter-day Saint leaders for polygamy. The continued presence of federal officials outside Joseph's home and frequent raids of Mormon communities had forced Joseph to flee Utah. In 1885, he had taken Julina with him to Hawaii, which was then outside the United States and thus a place of refuge from the federal marshals who wanted to arrest them for breaking the law. They remained on the islands for two years.

Julina found it difficult to be separated from her sister wives and children. On the first anniversary of her departure from Utah, she wrote a letter bemoaning her absence. "It was one year yesterday morning since I left my home and children for this far off clime," she wrote sadly, "little did I think then that I would be away so long, and now I know not how much longer before I return if ever, though the circumstances in which I left is still as fresh in my mind as though it were but yesterday. I both see and feel how much I am needed there."[18]

In another letter to Sarah, she wrote, "Oh, emagin what a mother's feelings are when so far from her children?" "Especially," she added, "when she hears of them being sick. How I long to see my pets."[19] Although Julina constantly worried about her children, she also feared placing too much responsibility on her sister wives or troubling them with her own worries and concerns. She told Sarah she was "sorry that you should give your self one moments trouble either Sleeping or waking about my affairs, farther than the care of the children. I know they are a great responsibility on you." She added, "And as for money or orders I care not for either, so that the children are comfortable, and you all keep well, till we can meet again."[20]

Her anxiety represented a desire not to further burden her sister wives who, she knew, were still being troubled by federal agents. While Julina and Joseph were living in Laie, federal officials ransacked the Salt Lake City house where Edna and Sarah Ellen lived, uprooting their families as they searched for evidence that Joseph was a polygamist.[21] When Joseph heard this, he was irate. "I would give all I am worth and borrow to the extent of my credit to be at home in possession of my liberty and power to execute my judgement or rather Gods judgement upon the damned villains who have expelled my wives and little innocents from their homes in the dead of winter.... If I could curs them until the elements were white-hot and their miserable carcases were consumed to ashes, it would not do justice to my feelings."[22]

During Julina's absence, one of Edna's children died. On that day in February 1886, Julina wrote in her diary:

> Sunday 21st [1886] Attended meeting this morning. Took a nap and wrote to my children in the afternoon. Albert [a missionary] came early in the evening bringing the Sad news of little Roberts death, Joseph met him at the barn. I stepped out of the door I could see by their looks that something was rong they both looked so sad. I asked what is the matter you have brought bad news. Albert answered "your Children are all right.... it is Robert he is dead.["] I burst into tears. I felt that it was too hard. Oh my poor Sister Edna in her touching letter she says, "I am so lonesome no baby to love." Poor girl how my heart aches for her, and poor papa to see his grief seems more than I can bear. O, Lord comfort their hearts.[23]

For the next few weeks, Julina dreaded receiving letters from home because it was possible that they would bring bad news. On March 7, 1886, she wrote, "I fear all is not well. It has been a sad long two weeks since we got our last mail and since I wrote in my journal. Jos[eph] has fretted so much and felt so very bad over the loss of his little Robert one of the nicest children we had."[24]

It was not the first time the family had lost one of their children. Just four years after Julina's marriage to Joseph, they had lost their firstborn, a two-year-old daughter named Mercy Josephine. They had nicknamed her "Dodo," and her death affected them for the rest of their lives. Julina sorrowfully marked the anniversary of her daughter's death whenever she was keeping a journal. Her entries were always terse. In one, she wrote simply, "It is sixteen years to day since our precious 'Dodo' died."[25] Another time she copied the more florid prose that her husband had written about the child's death into her journal, which lamented the loss of "the beaming little black eyes" and "the sweet little eunquiring voice."[26] The brevity of her entries, however, did not diminish the pain she felt over her daughter's death or the memories called forth by the death of her sister's child. When Julina read about Robert's death, she likely remembered her own daughter's and worried for the children she left behind.

Her time in Laie, however, was not all sorrow and heartbreak. She sunbathed in the ocean, planned birthday parties, and wrote about native customs. The trip deepened her relationship with her sister wives as she came to feel a deep sense of gratitude for the two women who had willingly taken her children into their homes and cared for them as if they were their own. "I love you more than I ever did," she wrote to Sarah after the latter had cared for her children for nearly two years, "and you know I always loved you as much as it is possible for one woman to love another. I know my pets are as safe in your care as they would be in mine. . . . And I know I can never repay you in this world."[27]

Julina ultimately found that separation from her sister wives and children was too difficult to bear and asked to return home to be with them. She left the islands in March 1887 with three of her children, two who had been born in the islands and a fifteen-year-old

The Joseph F. Smith family in 1898. Seated in the middle of the photo are, left to right, Mary Taylor Schwartz (m. 1884; seven children); Sarah Ellen Richards (m. 1868; eleven children); Julina Lambson (m. 1866; thirteen children); Joseph F. Smith; Edna Lambson (m. 1871; ten children); and Alice Ann Kimball (m. 1883; seven children).

daughter who had arrived in Hawaii the previous year to help care for her siblings.[28] Joseph described his sorrow at their leaving: "The steamer cut loose at 12 p.m. and at exactly 12:15 she commenced her course out of the harbor; and I took the last look at the receding forms of my loved and loving ones until God in his mercy shall permit us to meet again. . . . Once alone, my soul burst forth in tears and I wept their fountains dry and felt all the pangs and grief of parting with my heart's best treasures on earth."[29] Joseph returned to Utah a few months later in response to a letter advising him that President John Taylor was gravely ill.[30]

For Julina, the most satisfying part of her life remained the years in which she had lived with Sarah Ellen and Edna in a single home, together raising their children. But Julina was unable to recapture the happiness of those early years upon her return to Salt Lake City.

Although Julina remained close to Sarah and Edna, Joseph had married two additional wives—in Julina's words, changing their family "triangle" into a "star."[31] Because of the growth of the family and the demands of the federal government that polygamists no longer cohabit with their plural wives, the family decided to move into separate houses. Joseph publicly defended his right to live with his wives and to continue to support them emotionally, financially, and physically, but Julina felt her husband had been torn from their family. After he returned from Hawaii in July 1887, Joseph lived in Salt Lake City as a virtual prisoner in the Gardo House while Julina and Sarah lived on west First North. Edna and Joseph's other two wives lived in separate households on the Wasatch Front.[32]

Though some Latter-day Saint women greeted the 1890 Manifesto as a blessing, for Julina it was a palpable loss that ended the practice that had shaped her life and given it joy. The forced separation from Joseph, Julina wrote, "was the greatest trial of all, but I suppose such happiness could not last forever."[33] Little evidence remains of what Julina experienced in the later part of the nineteenth century. In the *Relief Society Magazine,* she describes it with just a few phrases: "Our babies grew into manhood and womanhood, our hair turned gray."[34]

Throughout her life, Julina cultivated her roles as a wife and mother. She eventually bore Joseph eleven children and adopted two others.[35] The leadership positions she filled within the Church and the local community focused on the domestic sphere. She worked as a midwife and nurse for decades, helping thousands of women bring their children into the world. She served in the Young Ladies' Department of the Ladies' Cooperative Retrenchment Association and on the general board of the Relief Society. She also served as second counselor in the general Relief Society presidency to Sister Emmeline B. Wells from 1910 to 1921. In these responsibilities, she encouraged women to shun modern fashion, rekindle their spirituality, and place their primary focus on motherhood. Like many late nineteenth- and early twentieth-century women, she saw her public

JULINA LAMBSON SMITH (1849–1936)

Julina Lambson and Joseph F. Smith on their fiftieth wedding anniversary, 1916.

advocacy as an extension of her domestic life. In an autobiography she wrote for the Daughters of Utah Pioneers, she wrote that she "felt again the thrills" of "looking in to my own babies' faces" whenever she placed "a tiny one for the first time in its mothers' arms."[36]

As family was central to her life, Julina's writings reveal profound insights into the relationships between sister wives within a polygamous family. The joy she found within her marriage provides a counterpoint to the assumptions of many historians that women could not find meaning within polygamy. Although her story does not negate the stories of women who found plural marriage to be lonely and alienating, her life should remind us that women's experiences within polygamy varied. Some women found heartbreak and sorrow; others developed loving relationships with their sister wives.

In 1915, Julina Smith published a tribute to sister wife Sarah Ellen Richards, who had died just a few months earlier. She spoke to Sarah as though she were still alive. We were "mere girls," she reminded her, "when we started life together. I the mother of one little one, when two years after my marriage, 'Papa' brought you home [as] his wife." Julina reminisced about their time together—mending worn clothes as dozens of children, who needed to be kissed and put to bed, played around them.[37] Julina's tribute ended with a poem to her beloved Sarah:

> *We miss you tonight, Aunt Sarah,*
> *We miss you at noon, and at morn*
> *Our eyes are heavy, our hearts are sad,*
> *The companion we loved is gone.*
> *Yet a voice of sweet comfort whispers—*
> *"Lift up thine eyes! Weep not!*
> *The sister thou lov'st is smiling on thee,*
> *Thou shalt not be forgot."*

When Julina died on January 10, 1936, in Salt Lake City, the *Relief Society Magazine* described her as "firm in her conviction, kindly in her attitude, devoted to her family, friends and the Church."[38]

Always loving, Julina Lambson Smith left a legacy of active service in her local community and in her family. She "look[ed] forward with joy to the happy reunion which will come when we, who remain for a season, will join you on the other side." Julina believed that in the end, she would be together with her family. "All the bliss that ever comes to earthly human homes," she wrote, "has been ours and perfect happiness will be ours in eternity."[39]

Chapter 18

"Trying to Do a Little Good in a Weak Way"

Lucy Emily Woodruff Smith (1869–1937)
by Keshia Lai

On January 10, 1869, Wilford Woodruff Jr. and Emily Jane Smith welcomed their first daughter, Lucy Emily Woodruff, into their home in St. Thomas, Arizona (now Nevada). In 1878, when Lucy was still a young girl, her mother died, and Lucy took comfort in the care of her grandparents: Wilford and Phebe Whittemore Carter Woodruff and Elias and Lucy Brown Smith.[1] Young Lucy resided with each set of grandparents in Salt Lake City from her mother's death until her marriage.[2]

As a young girl, Lucy Emily could hardly have fathomed marrying her childhood nemesis, George Albert Smith, much less that he would eventually become the eighth president of The Church of Jesus Christ of Latter-day Saints. George was "instinctively drawn" to the "pert and pretty" little girl when she moved to Salt Lake City. Unfortunately, the awkward boy "resorted to teasing and tormenting her" to gain her attention. A highly annoyed Lucy no doubt welcomed the respite from his teasing when George, at age twelve, moved to Provo to attend Brigham Young Academy (BYA). His time at BYA changed him, however, and when he returned home to Salt Lake City a year later, Lucy was incredulous to discover that he had matured into a gentleman.[3]

Although George single-mindedly pursued Lucy for years, their marriage was anything but guaranteed. She had other admirers, and one suitor in particular competed with George for her affections. George was also frequently away, which didn't help his campaign. First he was a traveling salesman for Zion's Cooperative Mercantile Institution (ZCMI), and then he became a missionary from September to November 1891 to recruit members for the Young Men's Mutual Improvement Association.

Despite these circumstances, Lucy chose to marry George. Years before, she had recognized in him a companion who inspired her to be a better person, one whom she loved and regarded with the highest esteem. On February 5, 1888, she recorded in her journal, "Tonight I retire with a thankful heart to God . . . and pray that he may give me strength to be more deserving of the love of one whom I firmly believe to be one of the best young men that was ever placed on the earth."[4] Three years later, Lucy wrote George a letter expressing this same sentiment. Tender, romantic, whimsical, even a little idealistic, Lucy's letter reflects a young woman in love and also a young woman of faith, ready to support her future companion in his vocation and Church callings.[5]

> Salt Lake City June 28/ [18]91
> Dear George
> I received a very welcome letter from you yesterday and was awfully glad to hear from you, if it was an awfully short one. George don't go without sleeping or eating for the purpose of writing to me although I believe I would be selfish enough to have you do that if it were the only way I could hear from you. I wonder what you are doing this evening. I believe you are writing me a letter which I will receive tomorrow. Does your traveling companion receive

as many letters as you? You remember once you were jealous of Mr Patrick because his wife wrote him so much more often than I did you. I have been thinking last night and to-day of the happy future you refered to in one letter. I hope and pray earnestly nothing will separate us because I know I shall be so happy if God permits me to be your wife. You won't blame me if I dream of a happy home with you where you can always help me to do right. To look forward to the time when your home coming, whether it be of a long or short duration, shall be to me; and that when there you won't leave me. Today in my heart believe I love you more than I ever did and think of you until it seems if I turn you will be standing by me. I guess you think this is enough building air castles but I don't very often write or talk in this manner. I wish you were here now for a short time at least that I might see you. I think I have felt better to-day than I have since you left although I am very weak. I have been to Sunday School and afternoon meeting but think I won't go again to-night.

Who was kind enough to remember me in Provo and what were their enquires regarding me[?] Have I just spelled a word wrong I think I have. I attended Y.L.M.I.A conference last night which I enjoyed very much but I very nearly lay in a reclining position most of the time. Bro Beatie this morning came to me to find out when you would return. Next Sunday at S[unday] S[chool] we are going to have some kind of a programme. I don't know what else to call it. J. S. Tingey represents the theological class. Lizzie & May the Primary and Vickie and myself the intermediate. Vickie was chosen in your absence. I don't know what kind of a response it will be from me. I scarcely feel equal to the task as it must be orally given. . . . I will quit and go post my letter. I hope you read my letters in rotation but it makes no difference. Good night and God bless you. I would rather receive a short letter than none but don't work so hard as you are doing. With love I am

                    Yours Lucy[6]

Nearly a year after the date of this letter, Lucy and George were married on May 25, 1892, in the Manti Temple. But marriage did not bring the long-anticipated relief from separation. George received a mission call to the Southern States while they were engaged and was scheduled to leave less than a month after their wedding. When Lucy joined her husband in the mission field in November of that year, she was dismayed to discover that he, as mission secretary, accompanied the mission president, J. Golden Kimball, on his tours around the mission and would often be away. The new bride poured her feelings into her journal, one that she faithfully wrote in every day of her mission. Her entries reveal her feelings of loneliness and insecurity while making clear her adoration and support for her husband. Separation, however, was not the only trial Lucy faced, for she suffered from ill health and homesickness during the entire mission. Nonetheless, she had many sweet experiences that helped her grow in knowledge, faith, and character. As the following journal entries show, Lucy recognized the hand of God in her life and frequently expressed gratitude for his love and tender mercies.[7]

Southern States Mission Home, Chattanooga, Tennessee[8]

January 1893

    Sunday 1st Was just recovering from a very severe headache the worst I had had for a number of years. Remained quietly in the house all day. Mr Neff a transient boarder arrived the night before from Mexico.

    Tuesday 3" Went out for a short walk and helped in the office.

    Wednesday 4" Grandma Lucy B Smith was seventy two years old today and we are 2300 miles apart. I like

Lucy Emily Woodruff Smith (1869–1937)

Lucy Emily Woodruff in her wedding dress about the time of her marriage to George Albert Smith on May 25, 1892.

Chattanooga Tenn my present location very much but like my mountain home better

Thursday 5 Bro D. H. Doxey, E. J. Jones and John G. Ellis of Ogden & H. W. Findlay of Fishaven arrived in Chattanooga perpartory to leaving for their fields of labor. They spent the evening with us and were pleased as we always are to meet with people from home.

Saturday 7 Posted up the books and read correspondence.

Tuesday 10" My birthday and my darling remembered me with a beautiful silver glove box. I also received a parcel from home and spent a very happy birthday.

Lucy Emily and George Albert Smith served a mission in the Southern States beginning shortly after their marriage in 1892.

Wednesday 11" Was reading letters nearly all day. Went for a walk with Geo.

Sunday 15" Went to the Cumberland Presbyterian Church & Mr Cole introduced us to the Rev Mr Bushnell. Enjoyed the sermon very much. The streets were like glass & Jennie & Mr Münster fell down.

Wednesday 18" Helping Geo with mail orders. In the afternoon we went down on the lower floor and examined the contents of a trunk belonging to the mission. The mice had very evidently enjoyed themselves among the letters. Feel some better. The water pipes are all frozen. The snow has fallen here 10 inches.

Sunday 29 Attended communion service at the episcopal church. It was very long and I got very tired.

February 1893

Thurs 2 Was reading correspondence nearly all day and writing some. Fast day. Would like to once more meet with the saints at home.

Thur 16 Felt some better. The rain has poured in torrents. I never in my life saw so much.

Fri 17" . . . Geo brought me five letters from the P[ost] O[ffice] and how happy I was. I was just sick to hear from home.

Sun 19 In the morning we went to Church at the Baptists and heard the Rev Mr Jones. Enjoyed the sermon very much.

Sun 26 In the morning Mr & Mrs Mason Geo & myself went to the Methodist Church and hea[r]d a very good discourse by Dr Payne from New York.

Mar 1893

Sun 12 A beautiful day. George Mr Shelly and myself went to Cassandra Georgia[9] to spend the day and had a very nice time. My first walk in the mission field. We called at Bro Fawcetts and then went on to Mrs Baileys where we spent the day. I had a ramble on the hills and enjoyed it very much.

Fri 17 In the office all day working. Am so happy here and have such a good home.

Mon 20 Four months since my arrival in Chattanooga. Can scarcely believe it. How contented I have been.

April 1893

Tues 4 Today is my *husbands* birthday. We both spent a very happy day. Davidson & Son remembered the *Dr* Smith. A lovely summer day.

Thurs 6 Today at home is a day long looked for by old & young the dedication of our beautiful temple.[10] To think of living so near the temple for a number of years and at its completion I am 2300 miles away. I am trying to do a little good in a weak way but don't know I shall succeed.

May 1893

Fri 19 Arrived in Chicago at 8:20 and were met at the depot by father and mother. We then boarded the elevated R.R and started for the [World's] fair. As the buildings appeared in sight I couldn't call it anything but miracle that I should be there. I scarcely dreamed of such a thing when the fair was being built. We spent most of our time in the manufactures & liberal arts building. We went to the Utah building where we met Mrs. [Emily S.] Richards[,] May Preston, Priscilla, Rachel & Mr Richards and how happy we were at meeting them. I went home or to our room at night weary and tired. I could scarcely stand.

Sat 20 We went in early at the fair and remained until nearly 11 P.M. The electral display was magnificent and thoroughly enjoyed by me. Never will I forget so long as I live the beautiful sights I gazed that night. When we returned to our room I was nearly worn out and quite sick.

Thurs 25 . . . Our wedding day and we are on the train coming from the fair. It hardly seems possible that we have been married one year but so it is and how happy I am.

Sat 27 Geo was very busy in the office. I am just realizing how tired I am. The fair was wonderful and grand but it takes a great amount of strength to rest up or rather to go on.

June 1893

Sun 11 . . . Word has been received from Alabama that two of our elders have been badly whipped but not killed for which we are truly thankful.[11] Geo & I went to the 2nd Presbyterian church and remained home the rest of the day.

Mon 19 Sick in bed all day long. I have suffered terribly. The day was just awful warm and how tired I was. I sometimes wonder if I ever will get well. Geo is so good to me or I could not stand it.

Thur 22 A little better. Helping Geo some in the office. Went for a ride & Geo showed me where he used to board. He showed me where he wrote me his first letter from Chattanooga.

Mar 26 Sewing nearly all day long. In the evening my sweetheart & I went for another ride. The Lord is very good to us.

Tues 27 Helping Geo in the office. In the afternoon I had an examination by Dr Key. I was frightened almost to death. I didn't get hurt but the most terrible thing is to think I must undergo an operation.[12] Have nearly made myself sick crying. Geo took me for another ride in the evening.

Wed 28 Last night I worried all night and tryed to make up my mind to be treated. Came over to Dr Keys in the morning and cried like my heart would break. I don't know how I can stand it. My nerves are all shattered. If I was only home I think I could stand it.

Thur 29 Am almost wornout with weakness. I realize God has blessed me very much. My operation was performed today and I was put to bed. Can I ever thank my Creator for His goodness to me.

Fri 30 It seems to me I have been at the sanitarium[13] for weeks but I must be patient. I am doing nicely I guess. All day in bed & so warm.

July 1893

Sat 1 Still in bed but I do not suffer for which I am truly thankful. The weather is very warm but I rest at night better than I did & that is something to be thankful for.

Sun 2 In bed until afternoon. My sweetheart comes often to see me or I couldn't stand it. Got up in the afternoon and went down stairs. In the evening Mr & Mrs Mason came to see me.

Mon 3 Out of bed all day but O my how I wish I was home. God can take care of me just as well in one place as another. I have been wonderfully blessed of God to get along as well as I have.

Tues 4 The fourth and here am I in a hospital. Geo was with me nearly all day and that was better than last year. He is the dearest noblest man and so good to me. . . . I know God has helped me very much.

Wed 5 . . . At noon Dr Key said I could go home for awhile & now I can scarcely wait for my darling to come. T. W. Sloan & Geo came to see me & took me home. My joy knew no bounds. Home again & how I appreciate it.

Aug 1893

Tues 22 Am still feeling very badly. It seems that ill luck is mine but today I met an object lesson. I went down over the hill & found a family starving & dying. The sight made me sick. To think some in this world have so much & others so little.

Sept 1893

Thurs 14 Geo has gone with Bro [J. Golden] K[imball] to the East Tenn[essee] conference & left me in the office alone. I must try and be brave but O I am lonely without my sweetheart.

Tues 19 Bro K came back in the middle of the night, and this morning gave me a letter from Geo. How happy a few lines on paper can make me feel. My sweetheart is coming home tonight.

Thurs 21 . . . I am one of the richest women in the world. I have a pure honest man for a husband. God bless and protect him.

Lucy Emily Woodruff Smith (1869–1937)

Tues 26 My sweetheart left this morning for Atlanta and how lonely I am. Have been partway to the depot with him and returned with the mail. The Dr called on me but I have been sick all day.

Oct 1893

Sun 1 Another month has gone which brings us that much nearer home. I wonder if my darling will come in the morning. I want to see him very badly but also want him to have his out. I am so lonely. Jennie has been so kind to me and remained with me at night.

Mon 2 My darling came home early this morning and surprised me. I was so delighted to see him. O how I love him. I feel much better now.

Nov 1893

Wed 1 Geo has gone to South Ala[bama]. This is his last trip this season & I will be so glad when they are all ended.

Mon 6 Have felt a little worried to day. What if Geo should get hurt? Have a large amount of mail to answer today.

Wed 8 Geo & Bro K came last night and I was so glad to see them but how frightened I was when I heard that they were nearly killed last Sunday night by a mob.

Fri 10 Helping Geo with his work. I am so happy here and consider myself greatly blessed.

Dec 1893

Sun 24 The day before Christmas and the sun is shining lovely. Geo & I went down town without wraps & found it very warm walking in the sun. How grateful we should be for the blessings we enjoy

Sun 31 . . . The last of 93. What will next year bring to us? Just so we are happy as now I ought not to complain. All of this year we have spent in the South.

Feb 1894

Fri 2 Was busy in the office most of the morning. My darling came home at noon & how glad I was to see him.

Fri 9 Elders Halliday & Payne returned from Cassandra where they had been for one week awaiting instructions to go on. Word received that Elder [Walter H.] Barton is quite sick.

Sat 10 Elder Barton no better & Geo left tonight for his field of labor to see if he was dangerous. Hope he will soon recover.

Fri 16 Geo returned this morning but his patient is still quite ill. I do hope he will be alright.

Sun 18 This morning I was sick & didn't get up. At noon word came that Elder B was dead. I had to get up & make his burial clothes. Jennie & Mrs Mason assisted me. At night I was limp as a cloth from my exertion. God gave me strength to do it. Geo left at 8 P.M. for McComb.[14]

Tues 20 Just think I slept alone last night but wasn't very nervous over it after all. I am getting brave.

Sat 24 Received a telegram. Geo is in Salt Lake City. Wish he could stay awhile but how would I stand it. Went for my treatment & came home in a snow storm.

Sun 25 This morning there was seven inches of snow on the ground. Such a novelty for Chattanooga. It has snowed this whole day long. I went for the mail & could hardly get back.

Mon 26 Received a letter from Geo written at Colorado Springs also one from Nebeker & Jones saying they were alright which relieved me very much as they had been threatened by a mob. Went for treatment.

Feb 1894

Thurs 1 Would like to attend fast meeting once at home but I enjoy my labor here so much and I have learned so much about my church & faith.

Mar 1894

Thurs 1 My sweetheart is coming in the morning. I am both sorry and glad. Sorry he couldn't stay home longer & delighted to know I shall see him so soon.

After serving faithfully in the Southern States Mission, they were released and returned to Salt Lake City in June 1894, settling in the Seventeenth Ward. The couple struggled to have children in the early years of their marriage. When visiting with her grandfather Wilford Woodruff in the spring of 1895, Lucy burst into tears and confided her fears of being barren. President Woodruff comforted her by giving her a blessing and prophesied that she would soon become a mother.[15] Less than a year later, Lucy gave birth to her first child. George and Lucy eventually became the parents of two daughters and a son.[16]

As her journals show, Lucy was often plagued by health issues and easily fell sick. This did not impede her desire to serve in the Church, however, and she was especially active in the Young Ladies' Mutual Improvement Association (YLMIA). She was the Seventeenth Ward YLMIA president before being called to serve as a counselor and then president of the Salt Lake Stake YLMIA.

In October 1908 she was called to the general board of the YLMIA and held this position until the time of her death.[17] As a board member, she represented the organization at the 1920 International Council of Women held in Oslo, Norway. In addition to her YLMIA service, she frequently accompanied her husband on his travels as an apostle, a position to which he was called in 1903. While her husband presided over the European Mission from 1919 to 1921, Lucy became the president of the Relief Societies of the European Mission, leading the organization from her home in Liverpool, England.[18]

Some of Lucy's notable civic activities included being a charter member of both the Daughters of Utah Pioneers and the Utah State Society of Daughters of the American Revolution and an active

Sigma Chi[19] mother. As the wife of an apostle, and later president of the Church, she kept their home "open to relatives and friends alike," and the Smiths were noted for their generosity.[20] In addition, Lucy took pleasure in the births of her six grandchildren. She was diagnosed with arthritis and neuralgia in 1932, which left her in almost constant pain to her life's end. Lucy Emily Woodruff Smith suffered a heart attack in April 1937 and died seven months later, on November 5, 1937. She was buried in the Salt Lake City Cemetery.[21]

On the day Lucy died, George recorded in his journal of his companion of forty-five years: "I am of course bereft of a devoted helpmeet and will be lonely without her. . . . She has been a devoted, helpful, considerate wife and mother."[22] Many years earlier, while a missionary in the Southern States, Lucy expressed that she was "trying to do a little good in a weak way" but was unsure if she could succeed.[23] She need not have worried; her life was one of goodness, and her dedication to faith and family was anything but "little."

Chapter 19

"No Matter How Severe the Trial"

Ida Frances Hunt Udall (1858–1915)
by Kristin Owens

"I was born in a wagon," Ida Frances Hunt Udall wrote in her memoirs, "and it seems to have fallen to my lot to be a traveler ever since, much as I dislike that kind of life."[1] Ida's first wagon ride was traveling to Utah from the Latter-day Saint community at San Bernardino, California. Ida's father, John Hunt, settled in San Bernardino as a young man after his family accompanied the Mormon Battalion to California.[2] Ida's mother, Lois Barnes Pratt Hunt, stayed in San Bernardino after her family returned from Tahiti, where they had served as missionaries.[3] Ida was born on March 8, 1858, a year after her parents' marriage.

"No girl has a happier childhood to look back upon than I," wrote Ida.[4] Most of her youth was spent in Beaver, Utah, where she was surrounded by a large and loving family in a town humming with sociability, cultural events, and opportunities for education. In her late teens, Ida and her family left Beaver to pioneer in Utah's Sevier Valley and in Savoia, New Mexico, until her father was called in 1878 to serve as bishop in the new settlement of Snowflake, Arizona.

Ida was a talented, accomplished young woman remembered for her great capacity for friendship and for her alto voice and accompanying guitar playing—both were fixtures in the communities where she lived.[5] She served as president of the first Young Ladies' Mutual Improvement Association in Snowflake, as well as in the Relief Society and Primary presidencies. She taught school for several years and at other times earned money by sewing, copying court records, and bookkeeping.[6]

Ida met David K. Udall, the new bishop in St. Johns, Arizona, shortly after breaking off an engagement to her sweetheart in Beaver—a decision that her daughter writes was influenced by her testimony of the principle of plural marriage.[7] She became David Udall's second wife on May 25, 1882, the same year the United States Congress passed the antipolygamy Edmunds Act.[8] After two years of keeping their marriage hidden, David was charged with practicing polygamy, and Ida was forced to flee Arizona. She spent over two years in hiding with relatives in Utah.

From 1882 to 1886, Ida Hunt Udall kept a journal recording the details of her first two years of marriage and the following two years of life in hiding. Selected excerpts from these writings follow. Preceding Ida's first journal entry is correspondence between Ida and Eliza Luella (Ella) Udall, David's first wife, before Ida and David became engaged.

> Snowflake, Jan 29th 1882
> Mrs E. L. Udall
> St. John, A.Z.
> Dear Sister:
>
> I feel that I cannot allow another day to pass by without writing you, to ascertain if possible, your true feelings upon a subject, which is, no doubt, one painful to us both, but one which, I realize, must be disposed of sooner or later,

Ida Frances Hunt Udall (1858–1915)

*Ida Hunt Udall about the time of her
marriage to David K. in 1882.*

viz: the possibility or probability of my becoming at some distant day a member of your family. I trust you will not consider it presuming in me, addressing you without permission. In doing so I have consulted only my own sense of duty and right, feeling that I cannot allow the matter to go farther, without first having received some assurance of your willingness to such a step being taken; at least that you have no more serious objections to me, than you would to any other under like circumstances.

During my stay in St John, I learned to love you as a sister, and the very thought that I may have been the cause of bringing unhappiness to you has troubled me day and night, and nothing but *pride* kept me from writing this letter long ago. But I have finally become convinced that such humilliation is nothing compared to that of receiving the attentions of any man contrary to the wishes of his wife.

I trust, dear sister, that you will appreciate my true motive in writing and favor me with an answer if only a few words. I believe in this matter, it is not only your right, but your imperative duty to state plainly any objections you may have in your feelings, and I beg you will not hesitate to do so, for I promise you I shall not be offended, but on the contrary, shall thank you for it all ~~the d~~ my life, and I believe you will not have written in vain, for, unless it meets with your approval, I shall never listen to another word on the subject.

May the Lord bless you, and help you to decide in this matter, is the earnest prayer of

Your true friend
Ida Hunt[9]

St. John March 12th 1882.
Miss I. F. Hunt,
Snowflake, A.Z.
Dear Friend,

I received your letter bearing date Jan 29th some weeks ago, but my health has been so very poor, I have felt unable to reply sooner, and hardly feel equal to the task now.

The subject in question is one which has caused me a great amount of pain and sorrow, more perhaps than you would imagine, yet I feel (as I have done from the beginning) that if it is the will of the Lord, I am perfectly willing to try to endure it; and trust it will be overruled for the best good of all. My feelings are such that I cannot write but briefly on this subject—

With kind regards to all, I remain your friend
E. L. Udall[10]

With Ella's reluctant blessing, Ida and David moved forward with plans to marry. Ida's journal begins:

Ida Frances Hunt Udall (1858–1915)

May 6th 1882 On the evening of Sat. May 6th 1882 I left my dearly loved home in Snowflake, Apache Co. Arizona, in company with Bro and Sister D. K. Udall, and their baby Pearl to make a short visit to Utah. We started about 4 p.m. traveled about seven miles, and made a dry camp for the night, which proved to be a wet one before morning, it having rained incessantly all night.[11]

21st Sunday: was a beautiful day. The bright fields of lucern, green orchards, and singing birds made Kanab seem almost like a paradise. . . . After meeting repaired to Ella's sister Sarah's, wife of L[awrence] C. Marriger, where we partook of a bounteous repast. . . . Spent a pleasant evening, in conversation, songs and music. But with all the merriment, I felt lonely and depressed. Like a stranger in a strange land. The sorrow another was passing through seemingly on my account, though I was powerless to help it; the constant strain my mind had been on during the whole journey lest by word or look I should cause her unnecessary unhappiness, had weighed upon my spirits greatly, and I retired from the scene that evening with a feeling of dread and fear at my heart impossible to describe. Afterwards was greatly reassured by a moonlight walk and conversation with the one dearest on earth to me, who brought light and hope to my heart once more, with his loving encouraging words. So that I finally went to bed, feeling that in striving to obey the commandments of God, with a pure motive I had everything to live for. No matter how severe the trial, what a privilege to pass through it, in such a glorious cause.[12]

Thursday, May 25th 1882 This afternoon at half past 5 oclock in the Holy Temple of the Lord, I was sealed for Time and all Eternity to David King Udall, the only man on Earth to whose care I could freely and gladly entrust my future; for better, for worse. Ella and Bro and Sister Farnsworth walked down to the Temple with us, and after a talk with Prest. J. D. T. McAllister, (by whom the ceremony was performed,) she, Ella seemed to feel much cheered. Oh! if she could only feel happy and reconciled, I should feel that my life was indeed a happy one. Why is it, that in carrying out the commandments of God, his children need be so sorely tried? Today I have made the most solemn vows and obligations of my life. Marriage, under ordinary circumstances is a grave and important step, but entering into Plural marriage, in these perilous times is doubly so. May Heaven help me to keep the vows I have made sacred and pure and may the deep unchangeable love which I feel for my husband today increase with every coming year helping me to prove worthy of the love and confidence which he imposes in me, and to always be just and considerate to those the Lord has, and may give unto him in a similar way. When he bade me goodnight, the sacred name of *wife* was whispered for the first time in my ear, causing my heart to flutter with a strange new happiness. During the night, Ella, being unable to sleep, and thinking likely I was the same, came into my room, and mentioned for the first time to me our relationship to each other, and we talked long and earnestly of our hopes and desires for the future, both feeling much happier for the same.[13]

27th Started from St George at three p.m. arriving in Kanab Monday May 29th feeling much happier than I did when I left it, which I beleive was the case with all the party. After our visit to the Temple there seemed to be a feeling of peace and union between us which had not existed before. On the road home Ella and I had several long confidential talks. Told over our mutual trials and sorrows, and got to understand each other better. O, if we could always be frank and open with each other, how many heart-aches would be saved.[14]

[June] 25th. . . . We had a pleasant camp just below Brigham City with nice water, grass, wood, and good company. Thus passed the first month of my married life. It had been clouds and sunshine intermingled, with more happiness, in the mane, than I had anticipated. I can say truthfully that I beleive we are all three far happier, than we were one month ago today, which is indeed encouraging.[15]

27th. . . . We arrived [at Snowflake] about dusk. . . . Found the dear ones at home all well and anxiously looking for us. . . . Oh! it seemed so pleasant to get back home again, to father, mother, brothers & sisters.

28th. . . . David, Ella and little Pearl left for their home in St Johns, I to remain in Snowflake till we see which way the wind blows, and some arrangements can be made for my safe-keeping.[16]

Aug 23rd Dade [David] arrived in Snowflake, this time coming with the intention of taking me to St Johns to live. He felt that the sooner he got his family together, under each others influence, the better it would be for all parties.

24th We left S[nowflake] about 3 p.m. I felt very sorrowful at parting with my parents, brothers and sisters, and in leaving the old home, never to return on exactly the same footing. But I was happy in the thought that I left home with their approval and blessing, and also perfectly happy in the love of my good kind husband. We came that night to the Cedar Ridge. Talked long and earnestly of our past lives and our hopes for the future. Camped by the light of a beautiful moon. . . .

25th . . . Reached St Johns about 8 p.m. Little Pearl was at the door to give me a welcome, but no one else. That was a night never to be forgotten. In nearing the town, it seemed that all the powers of darkness were arrayed against me, whispering me "it was no use, I could not stand the test" of going to share another womans home and husband, even though it was her earnest desire that we should live together. Our neighbors on three sides were mexicans, and I felt that the wicked influence and spirit surrounding the place had something to do with the forebodings I had, but on reaching the house, and finding Ella in the depths of despair, with no welcome for me, my feelings can better be imagined than described: I cried earnestly unto the Lord for help and strength, and He is the friend that never forsakes us in the hour of sorest need. I felt greatly comforted in seeing a great change in Ella's feelings the next day, which we spent in arranging things for my comfort.[17]

1884 March During this month the persecutions of our enemies also became seemingly unbearable. A newspaper was published in St Johns, by one [George] McCarter, whose sole mission was to misrepresent and vilify our people. The "Secrets of the Endowments" were claimed to be exposed, and every issue contained low vulgar articles about some of our leading men's private affairs. My name frequently came out in glowing colors, calling me a prostitute, mistress etc. This was very hard for our brethren to bear, but they treated it with silent contempt, and quit reading the paper altogether.[18]

[August] 16th . . . David was arrested on a charge of Polygamy, an indictment having been found against him. . . . He gave bonds in the sum of $2,000.00.[19]

September 15th . . . When David related to me all . . . the many falsehoods the Evil One, had put it into the hearts of these wicked men to testify to before the Grand Jury, I was greatly exercised. It opened my eyes to the great power of the *Adversary* and I realized that I would not be safe to stay with my friends or relatives in any part of that country, and I tried to reconcile myself to do cheerfully whatever David thought was for the best. He prayed about the matter, that he might be directed aright, and . . . decided to send me back to Nephi, Utah, his old home, to stay with his father and Aunty [his father's third wife, Eliza Rebecca May Udall] until after his trial in November. The thought of going so far from home, among people I had never met, almost broke my heart.[20]

28th Sunday Morning, I parted with my dearest boy [her husband], with a heavy heart, and started for Holbrook in company with Bro Hatch. We took train at 1 oclock. In reaching the passenger coach, I had to pass through a large crowd of staring men, but being thickly veiled, I think no one recognized me. I merely had the chance of shaking hands with pa, just as the train started. This was a sorrowful hour for me. I was leaving home and dear ones for an indefinite length of time, expecting to travel hundreds of miles, to tarry among relatives whose acquaintance I had yet to make, until the persecutions of our enemies should cease sufficiently to allow me to remain at home. . . . I kept my veil pulled closely down to hide the great tears that chased each other down my cheeks.[21]

In Nephi, Ida was able to live fairly openly much of the time, hiding only when federal marshals came searching for polygamy case witnesses. She gave birth to a baby girl, Pauline, in March 1885 and received a visit from David shortly thereafter. In August that year David was convicted on a charge of perjury, as evidence was lacking for the polygamy charge, and he was sentenced to three years in prison in Detroit.[22]

[September] 10th, [1885]. I answered [Ella's] letter immediately, for I was much pleased to receive it, being the first and only one from Ella, since I left home. I said all in my power to comfort her, for I realized how sorely tried she was. But I also told her, I could not see where mine was the enviable position, or where there was hope for me and none for her, as she expressed. If David was pardoned; as she had faith he would be, she could look forward to having a husband, home, and a *name*, which were blessings I might never enjoy in this life certainly not in the near future, and I could not even enjoy the companionship of my father, brothers & sisters. But still I do not feel to murmur. The Lord can make the heaviest burden light if we lean on Him.[23]

[October] 13th Tues. . . . There was every thing to make the *ball* an enjoyable one. A nice crowd in attendance and the loveliest music I ever listened to, but the very first strain that reached my ear, sent a chill to my heart. Beautiful music always effects me like an eloquent sermon, either joyfully or the reverse. Tonight it seemed to picture to my mind, as nothing had ever done before the exact position of my poor boy. Banished far from home, and all that is dear, buried, as it were, in the confines of that dreary prison. Oh! how my heart ached. I could no more have danced, than I could laugh at a funeral. I sat shivering on the seat a little while, and begged of Charley to bring me home, which he did. Oh Dade, I never missed you as I do tonight! Will this great unquenchable longing in my soul for your society and companionship never, never be satisfied? The world seems so lonely so loveless without you. How long will the Lord require his poor weak children to be thus tried? . . . But I am not all alone, for I have my precious babe. My treasure sent from Heaven to comfort me. I clasp her in my arms and she seems to warm my heart through. Thank God for the blessings I do enjoy.[24]

After four months' imprisonment, David Udall was freed by presidential pardon but still faced the charge of polygamy.[25]

Jan 7th [1886] . . . How I rejoiced that [David] was once more at home among friends, and that they manifested their love for him so plainly, for I know how worthy he is of it. But oh! how lonely and homesick it makes me to think

I can join in none of the rejoicings over the return of my *own husband*. . . . I have felt that his *liberty* was all I could ask, but now that boon is granted, the desire to see his face absorbs every other thought. Oh! what have I done that I should be thus cruelly exiled, banished from all that is nearest & dearest to me, except my babe. Her sweet bright little face is the only thing that serves to cheer the flight of the weary days, weeks, and months. O Lord, help me to be ever mindful of the blessings I enjoy, and to bear patiently and humbly every trial thou seeest fit to send upon me.[26]

[February] 26th. Pauline is eleven months old. . . . Dear little "refugee." How she would love her papa if she could ever have the privilege of making his acquaintance. But how utterly she is exiled from his heart, for it is impossible to love a child whom you never see, as you do those whose sweet, cute little looks & ways are constantly before us. I feel sometimes that my babe's beauty and sweetness is all lost, when her father knows nothing about it.[27]

Mon [September] 13th Rece[ive]d letter from David written on his birthday. . . . He was so full of business he did not know whether he would be able to come to Utah before November or not. O! how angry this last sentence made me. He never said he was sorry to disappoint me, nor made any particular excuse, but talked as though it would be all right with me, whenever it suited his convenience to come. For months past I had wondered if I could possibly endure life till September, when he had led me to beleive I would surely see him. Now when the time was nearly up, to have all my fond hopes blighted, without one word of palliation by the one I had thought so true and tender—O it seemed more than I could bear. I sat down immediately and while I was still in a passion, wrote a most cruel reply, and took good care to send to post before I had time to relent. I told him he need not worry about coming at all on my account. That

I expected to go south to meet my father in St George before Nov. and I thought I had fooled around long enough, for some one who did not care a snap for me, etc. etc. Also told him that I had written some lines for his birthday but was too *mad* to send them.

Who but the Evil One could have prompted me to write such words to one I loved dearer than life? I had so many examples, that I saw daily around me, where men professing to be the best of Latter Day Saints would send their plural wives away from them, and seemingly take no more care or trouble about them, than they would mere acquaintances, and the *law* furnished them a cloak under which to neglect and mistreat their families and break the holy covenants they had made. And I was ready to judge my husband by such men. I had no dear wise mother to council me not to write until I had got over being angry. Aunty only gloried in my spunk. 'Said he deserved a good going over, while Father remonstrated with me, saying that while to us it would appear that David was rather neglectful, we did not know his circumstances, and could not understand his motives. He knew it would all be made right some day. I never admitted to Aunty that I was sorry for what I had done but I felt very unhappy, and laid awake many an hour weeping and praying over the matter.[28]

Sun 26th In the depths of humility I wrote to David asking him if he could ever forgive me for the hasty cruel words I had written. Telling him how I had suffered with remorse but it had taken me all this time to thoroughly repent; and I now felt if there was any thing I could do to attone for that wrong, I would be glad to do it. I also enclosed the birthday lines and sent them off. That night our friend and neighbor Mercy Wright gave a birthday party for her husband Jos. I was invited and went feeling very sad, but there was such a merry musical crowd there, that I had to lay aside my sorrows and join in the merriment. I sang and played a great many times during the evening. . . .

Mon 27th I received a letter from pa in which he takes me severely to task for writing as I did to David. He had just returned from St Johns. D. had given him my letters to read and had also unburdened his heart to him, and pa was full of sympathy for him in his trials and lonely situation. I felt very guilty indeed but was glad pa had taken D's side instead of mine. I wrote and told him so, at the same time calling his attention to the fact that I had some just and sufficient reasons for writing as I did. . . . O what trying gloomy times those were. I prayed to the Lord with all the earnestness of my soul that my husband might have the strength and courage to be true to all parts of his family.[29]

In March 1887, four months after the dismissal of his polygamy case, David went to Nephi to take Ida back home. Rather than taking her to St. Johns immediately after his polygamy charges were pardoned, he took her to Snowflake, where she lived with family for a year and gave birth to the second of her six children. In the spring of 1888, she and her two children moved to a farm and gristmill that David acquired.

After returning from exile, Ida found her life as a second wife to be one of nearly unremitting challenges. The Udall family was dogged by financial difficulties, but the privations of poverty often fell most heavily upon Ida and her children.[30] Visits from Ella and her children revealed the difficulties of sharing a husband on a day-to-day basis. Ida returned to Snowflake for another fifteen months, where she was supported by her father.[31] She went back to the farm for a time but was soon sent to spend the better part of another year in nearby Eager, where she kept the co-op store and supported her children.

Ida spent most of the next decade living on the farm. Ella maintained her home in St. Johns but spent stretches of time living on

Ida Hunt Udall and her six children, ca. 1898. Back row, left to right: John Hunt Udall, Pauline Udall, Grover Cleveland Udall. Front row, left to right: Gilbert Douglas Udall, Ida Hunt Udall, Don Taylor Udall (on lap), Jesse Addison Udall.

the farm as well, while David was away a great deal with his Church and civic responsibilities. David became president of St. Johns Stake and called his first wife, Ella Stewart, as stake Relief Society president. Ella was the wife who shared David's public life, accompanied him to conferences and on ward visits, and entertained visitors in their home. Ida, on the other hand, was frequently moving from place to place, often supporting herself or being supported by her father, and spending isolated years homesteading with her children.[32]

After the farm was foreclosed in 1899, Ida settled her own homestead on the Little Colorado River. She managed operations of the ranch and a way station, where she boarded travelers on the mail route. In 1906, she suffered the first of three strokes, and her daughter, Pauline, a schoolteacher, used her college savings to buy Ida a house near the family in St. Johns. In 1908, a third stroke left Ida partially paralyzed and a semi-invalid. Pauline and other family members helped care for her and her young sons until her death on April 26, 1915. Ella died in 1937, and David in 1938.

In the midst of her trials, Ida continued to find relief in the Lord and joy in her family. Her writings manifest a faithful woman of remarkable loyalty, grace, and resilience, retaining in all things her commitment to the restored gospel of Jesus Christ. She was, her friend Julia Murdock Farnsworth wrote, "always loyal to her friends and family, patriotic to her church and people, generous to others' failings, loving and constant toward all."[33]

Chapter 20

"Her Very Presence Is a Sermon"

Mere Mete Whaanga (1848–1944)
by Marjorie Newton

European missionaries introduced the Maori of New Zealand to Christianity beginning in 1814. Members of many Maori tribes thus came to believe that they were descendants of the house of Israel, a belief that spiritually prepared them to accept the Book of Mormon as a history of their ancestors.[1]

Although whalers and missionaries visited these South Pacific islands for many years, organized British settlement of New Zealand did not begin until 1840. Twenty years later, the British colonists outnumbered the Maori, and tensions over land ownership led to a decade of war between aggrieved Maori tribes and the British troops sent to quell them. Some Maori tribes, however, including many of the Ngati Kahungunu, remained loyal to the British.

About the time the wars were ending, twenty-one-year-old Mere Mete (the Maori pronunciation of "Mary Smith") married Hirini Te Rito Whaanga. Mere Mete, born February 15, 1848, in Nuhaka, Hawkes Bay, New Zealand, was one of a large family of children of a German whaler named Hachem Schmidt (John Smith) and

Mere Mete Whaanga (1848–1944)

Parapara Kurekure, a Maori. Hirini, who was about forty, had been widowed twice before marrying Mere; he was an influential leader of the Ngati Kahungunu tribe, of which his father had also been an important chief. In his youth, Hirini had spent some years working in the whaling trade, but by the early 1880s he was a successful sheep farmer and a prominent chief in the Mahia district of northern Hawkes Bay, where he was well respected by all who knew him.[2] Mere and Hirini became the parents of a son and three daughters, although the son and one daughter did not survive childhood.[3]

Missionaries of The Church of Jesus Christ of Latter-day Saints first preached in the Mahia Peninsula, on the northern boundary of the Hawkes Bay district, in 1884. The Maori villages of Hawkes Bay area proved a fruitful field for these pioneering Mormon elders, and among those they taught there were Hirini and Mere Whaanga. Mere's heart was touched first, and she persuaded Hirini to listen to the missionaries.[4] Membership records show that their daughters, Mihi and Katarina, were baptized into the Church at Kopuawhara on October 31, 1884, and that Mere and Hirini were baptized on November 30, 1884.[5] Within weeks, more than two hundred of their tribe followed them into the waters of baptism.

The missionaries organized their new converts into branches with local branch presidents. As they had a large area to supervise, the elders visited each branch for just one week at a time before moving on to the next branch. Hirini and Mere Whaanga built a special *whare,* or rush house, at their home for the missionaries, and the Whaanga home became the center of Latter-day Saint missionary work in Nuhaka for the next ten years.[6] Hirini served as branch president, speaking often at sacrament meetings and district conferences, and Mere's wise counsel was often sought by the sometimes bewildered American missionaries as they tried to deal with problems that arose from their lack of understanding of the Maori language and culture.[7]

Hirini and Mere both came from large extended families, and Hirini acted as patriarch and counselor to all. They frequently

*Hirini Te Rito Whaanga (1828–1905), a leader
of the Ngati Kahungunu Maori tribe.*

attended family weddings, funerals, and similar functions in other Maori *pa* (villages), both near and far. Maori culture is very family oriented, and attendance at these functions, even those held for distant relatives, is expected, even obligatory, to this day. But once she joined the Church, nothing was ever again as important to Mere Whaanga as the Lord's work and caring for the Lord's servants. Nearly half a century later, Elder Louis G. Hoagland related that when it was the elders' week to be in Nuhaka, Mere would leave such important Maori gatherings as *tangihanga* (funeral rites) "and ride back to her home so as to have the home ready and clean for the elders."[8]

As their knowledge and understanding of the gospel deepened, the Maori Saints learned of the principles of gathering and temple work. Many desired to gather to Zion to receive their own temple ordinances and to perform them for their deceased ancestors. Foremost among those who wanted to gather were Mere and Hirini Whaanga.

John T. Smellie, who spent his three-year mission (1887–90) among the Maori, recounted: "The day before I left N[u]haka [to return to Utah], my dear Maori parents, Hirini and Mere Whaanga, came to me and desired a blessing before I left. I told them it was the duty of a patriarch and not mine, but they insisted so that I in fear consented. I laid my hands upon their heads and among other promises, said they would gather to Zion and work in the House of the Lord, etc. When I had done I trembled over it, but it had been given to me. Well several years later a special permission was given them to gather to Zion and I met them in the temple and did work with them. They then reminded me of the promise."[9]

Church president Wilford Woodruff was reluctant to allow the gathering of Maori Saints, as Polynesian Saints from Hawaii had encountered many problems in Utah. He was concerned that the harsh climate in Utah would not suit the Maori people and that work would be hard to find in the economic depression then prevailing. The First Presidency also recognized that the time foreseen by Brigham Young had come when Zion should be built up in places other than Utah.[10] The First Presidency had therefore begun to encourage Saints everywhere to stay and build up the Church in their homelands.

Instead of inviting a mass migration of Maori Saints, which in any case the New Zealand government would never have allowed, the First Presidency suggested that one or two Maori families might come and live in Utah. If the experiment proved successful, more would be permitted to come.[11] Accordingly, Hirini and Mere Whaanga were the first Maori Saints to gather to Utah. Both were leaders, capable, and sufficiently well-to-do to be able to afford their fares and support themselves in Utah. They were well respected and were judged, as a later record testified, by all mission presidents and missionaries who knew them to be "among the best Maori Saints who ever joined the Church, and amongst the best immigrants who have ever come to Zion."[12] The First Presidency appointed John C. Stewart of Kanab, who had baptized Mere and Hirini during his mission to New Zealand (1883–86), to watch over them. It was thought the warmer climate in Kanab would be more suited to the Whaanga family than the colder climate of Salt Lake City.

So it was that on May 21, 1894, almost ten years after joining the Church, Hirini and Mere Whaanga left their home in Nuhaka for the long journey to Utah. They took with them Hirini's sister-in-law Apikara (Abigail) Whaanga and two of her sons, Ihaia (age twelve) and Ihaka (age four). Apikara's eldest son, Pirika, had gone to Utah eight years earlier with the returning Elder Stewart. Mere and Hirini also took with them their grandson Sidney Whaanga Christy (age eleven), Mere's nephew Watene Mete (known as Walter Smith, also eleven), and an adopted daughter, Edna Pomare (twelve).[13]

Mere suffered almost overwhelming sorrow at leaving her parents, her daughters and her siblings, but she held fast to her purpose despite pressure from family members to remain in New Zealand. "Our children never stopped crying or pleading with us to change our minds," she wrote later. "But to come to Zion was still the most prominent thought in our minds." She testified to her mother, saying, "Please don't cry any more, stop right now, for I know that my going with my husband to Zion is the right thing to do. Have patience for all things lie in the hand of God. he will bless us that someday, sometime, somewhere, we will meet again."[14]

There were nearly 450 members and eight branches in the Mahia Conference (District) when Mere and Hirini Whaanga left to sail across the Pacific to America in 1894. Instead of selling their home in Nuhaka or leaving it for the use of members of their extended family, Mere and Hirini directed that it should be kept as a permanent "Elders' house" for the missionaries.

They accomplished the first stage of their journey on horseback, riding across primitive, muddy trails from Nuhaka to the larger seaside town of Gisborne. From Gisborne, Mere, Hirini, Apikara, and the children traveled by coastal steamer to the major port of Auckland, where they boarded the SS *Monowai*. They sailed for

California on June 15 in the company of three returning American missionaries.[15]

The little company landed in San Francisco on July 7, 1894, but they were unable to proceed to Utah immediately, owing to a train strike. They spent several days in San Francisco, drinking in the sights. Mere, Hirini, Apikara, and the children stared in amazement at the "horseless cars" (cable trams) that ran up and down hills by themselves, but ten days in town were enough. Although bemused by the size of the city, the new arrivals were less than impressed with the prevailing lifestyle. They were shocked at the number of stores open for business on Sundays, contrasting this state of affairs unfavorably with Sabbath observance in New Zealand and Australia.[16]

After arriving in Salt Lake City by train on July 19, the Whaanga party were to be met at the corner of West Temple and Second South Streets. For half an hour they sat on their luggage or, in the case of the children, on the curbstone, while they waited for transport to their Valley House accommodation. Although by that time most Maori wore European-style clothing, the Maori party nonetheless presented an exotic appearance on the streets of Salt Lake City. Both Mere and her sister-in-law Apikara had the traditional blue Maori facial tattoo (*moko*) on their lips and chins, and a crowd soon collected to stare at them. It must have been a humiliating introduction to Utah society for these high-ranking, refined Maori women.[17]

Later that day, the new arrivals were driven around Salt Lake City, showing especially great interest in the temple. The children sampled ice cream for the first time: young Walter Smith tried to spread it on his bread, thinking it was butter.[18] That evening the Whaanga family was warmly welcomed at a reception held in the Fourteenth Ward assembly rooms, where they were greeted by former New Zealand missionaries. Many of those attending had fond memories of Mere caring for them during their missions, cooking their meals, and laundering their clothing. The proceedings at the reception were conducted in Maori, and the dinner, the Maori music, and warm fellowship must have done much to make the Whaanga family feel welcome.¹⁹

A week after their arrival in Salt Lake City, the Whaanga family traveled by train and covered wagon to complete their long journey from Nuhaka to Kanab in southern Utah.²⁰ There Hirini planned to raise sheep. Unfortunately, during the next year, two returned missionaries took over from John C. Stewart the task of helping the Whaanga family with their financial affairs. They apparently mismanaged the family's funds and were accused of defrauding them. Mere and Hirini suffered severe disillusionment from this trial, but their faith never wavered. When news of this situation reached members of the First Presidency, they assigned former New Zealand mission president William Paxman to go on a short mission to Kanab to investigate the rumors and take whatever action was necessary.²¹ As a result, members of the newly organized Zion's Maori Association, a society formed by returned missionaries who had served in New Zealand, relocated the Whaanga family to Salt Lake City. The association procured a house for them in the Forest Dale Ward close to the home of Benjamin Goddard, who was then vice president and later president of the association.

On October 9, 1895, Hirini and Mere Whaanga were endowed and sealed for time and all eternity. From that time forward, Mere, Hirini, and Apikara spent most of their time in the Salt Lake Temple and were very happy in performing ordinances for their own ancestors and the ancestors of Maori Saints still in New Zealand. Full of gratitude for temple blessings, Hirini wrote a letter to the New Zealand Mission encouraging the Maori Saints to remain faithful and testifying of the blessings he and Mere and their family had received since gathering to Zion. His letter was read to the Maori Saints all over the mission during subsequent conferences and was listened to with great interest.²²

Soon after settling in the Forest Dale Ward, Mere learned to write. Years later, she described how she had "prayed to God to send me just a little light and knowledge to enable me to write to

Maori Saints and missionaries outside a traditional marae *in New Zealand, ca. 1885–87.*

my children, parents, and loved ones, also tell them of my love for them. . . . I struggled very hard [and] I at last completed my first letter home. But I knew that I did not accomplish this big thing on my own. The Lord heard my heart crying for help to enable me to contact my children and parents and I received what I had asked for. . . . My heart was filled with happiness and joy."[23]

Just over two years later, in 1898, Hirini sailed back to New Zealand as "a messenger of salvation to his people,"[24] his mission financed by the Zion's Maori Association. He traveled with a new mission president, Elder Ezra T. Stevenson, and they arrived just in time for the annual conference (*Hui Tau*) of the New Zealand Mission at Papawai, Wairarapa, beginning Sunday, April 3, 1898. Hirini was welcomed with joy by the Maori Saints. He addressed the conference, bearing testimony of the mission of Joseph Smith. He went on to emphasize work for the dead and asked his people to gather their genealogies and send them to him and Mere to have the temple work done for their deceased ancestors.

President Stevenson noted the good effects of Hirini's mission in a letter to Church president Wilford Woodruff:

In company with Elder Whaanga we have visited the Mahia District his old home and adjoining districts. Have been everywhere well received, the natives showing very great pleasure, both members of the Church and others, in seeing their old friend back again. . . . His faithful testimony and mild reproof to those who have stepped aside from duty seem to have an encouraging effect, and we feel that much good is being done through his visit here.[25]

Some weeks later, President Stevenson wrote again to the First Presidency. "On a recent trip north," he recounted, "we had the pleasure of being entertained and performed baptisms in a village where a few years ago the Elders were driven out with orders never to return." He attributed this success "to Bro. Hirini's testimony. His is a fine appearance and happy countenance while the spirit he manifests is of itself a testimony and they cannot say nay."[26]

Hirini, aged seventy-one, was released in April 1899. He returned to his family in Salt Lake City, where he died six years later on October 17, 1905. There was great mourning among Maori, Pakeha (New Zealanders of European descent), and missionaries alike when his death became known in New Zealand. "Many were the hearts that were saddened and eyes that were stained with tears in behalf of one that we had all learned to love," wrote one American missionary.[27]

Eighteen months after her husband's death, Mere Whaanga served a full-time mission among the Maori people of New Zealand. While there, Mere visited every Latter-day Saint conference on the North Island as well as the Wairau Conference on the South Island to bear testimony of the restored gospel and tell of life in Utah.[28] Her missionary service was highly valued by her mission president, Rufus K. Hardy. The New Zealand Mission minutes tell of her visit to the South Island: "And here as everywhere Mere Whaanga has been, she did much good among the people. The people honor her and her words mean much to them."[29]

Mere Mete Whaanga (1848–1944)

Mere Mete Whaanga and five generations of her family in New Zealand. From left to right: Isabella Henrietta Christy, Sidney Whaanga Christy, and Mihi Whaanga. Seated is Mere Whaanga with her great-great grandson Makeanui Tinirau Ariki Solomon.

Just three weeks later, Mere, about to mark her sixtieth birthday, was in Kaikohe in the Bay of Islands District, having traveled some six hundred miles (one thousand kilometers) in the intervening weeks. President Hardy reported: "Sister Mere Whaanga did much good among her people in the north of New Zealand. They see in Mere Whaanga what the Gospel will do for them if they live it faithfully, and her very presence among them is a sermon."[30]

The mission minutes constantly praised the Maori widow. "Mere Whaanga since her arrival in New Zealand, March 28, 1907, has been a most humble, obedient and faithful missionary among her people and her influence for good will never be forgotten. Too much praise cannot be accorded her."[31] Mere was released at the Hui Tau in April 1908, sailing from Auckland on the *Aorangi* in the company of a missionary wife who was returning to America.

A month after Mere's departure, President Hardy wrote to former New Zealand missionary and mission president Louis G. Hoagland: "Mere will be home when this reaches you. Keep up her courage for she deserves a great deal from us, and Mere, after having visited so many people in the Island, has it in her power to constantly hold the people together with a little encouragement and advice. . . . She herself does not realize this as I do. She has stepped practically into the place of Hirini in the minds of the people."[32]

Mere settled down again in her home in Forest Dale Ward, but in 1917 her sister-in-law Apikara died, leaving her without both husband and female companionship.[33] Both her grandson Sid Christy and her nephew Walter Smith were now married. Walter had returned to New Zealand in 1913, becoming a beloved music teacher at the Latter-day Saint Maori Agricultural College. In 1918, as World War I drew to a close, Sid and Kate Christy wanted to take their children home to live in New Zealand.

Mere decided to accompany them. They received a tremendous Maori welcome when they finally arrived in Nuhaka—still, as time passed, Mere yearned to be back in Salt Lake City. She was growing old and, above all, she wanted to be buried beside her beloved Hirini. It was to take many years and the help of successive mission presidents, as well as United States senator Reed Smoot and Utah Congressman Don B. Colton,[34] before the United States government finally issued a visa allowing her to return to Utah in 1938. She lived quietly but happily, keeping busy into old age. At the age of ninety-five, five years after her return, Mere presented to Church president Heber J. Grant a quilt she had made for him as a birthday gift, but the birthday was hers, not his.[35]

On May 11, 1944, at the age of ninety-six, this faithful and devoted Maori Latter-day Saint died. Two days later she was laid to rest in the same grave as her husband, Hirini, in the Salt Lake City cemetery. A beautiful and dignified monument erected by her beloved missionary "sons," members of Zion's Missionary Association,[36] marks their grave. Mere Mete Whaanga was a true pioneer of the restored gospel of Jesus Christ in far-off New Zealand, and her name is honored in the annals of the Church there to this day.

Chapter 21

"If It Is the Truth, I Must Do So"

Anna Karine Gaarden Widtsoe (1849–1919)
by Kiersten Olson and Clinton D. Christensen

The tiny island of Frøya, the westernmost fragment of the Norwegian coast, fostered a people who knew how to survive, how to commit, and how to treasure what was truly precious. One of Frøya's daughters, Anna Karine Gaarden Widtsoe, brought those qualities to her faith, family, and service in Latter-day Saint communities in both Norway and Utah.

Anna Karine was born on June 4, 1849, the first child of Peder and Beret Haavig Gaarden, a prosperous and educated couple. Four years later, her sister, Pertroline Jørgine, completed the family circle. Anna learned to read and write early and attended school whenever the traveling teacher visited her small village of Titran. Further educational prospects appeared to dissolve after her mother died, however, leaving the nearly twelve-year-old Anna to run the Gaarden household. Providentially, that same year a new schoolteacher, John Anders Widtsoe, arrived in Titran. He recognized Anna's intelligence and tutored her privately. Mutual admiration grew, and six years later the couple became engaged. After John completed his university degree, the couple married, on December 29, 1870.

On January 31, 1872, Anna gave birth to John Andreas Widtsoe. The family moved to Namsos, on the Norwegian mainland, where she bore a second son, Osborne John Peder, on December 12, 1877. Tragedy struck two months later when Anna's husband died of a sudden illness in the dark depths of a Norwegian winter. The heartbroken twenty-eight-year-old widow, whose father had also died a few years before, felt lost and very alone. Standing by the grave, watching her little boy drop a crimson rose onto the casket, Anna received no hope of a future reunion from the priest's words "Dust thou art, to dust returnest." Turning to prayer and the Bible, she found some comfort and an increasing nearness to God, but true solace continued to elude her.

The Shoemaker

Pained by lingering memories and driven by her resolve to educate her two sons and shape their lives as a legacy to her husband, Anna moved to Trondheim, the old capital city of Norway, where she felt the boys' opportunities for schooling would be improved. She established herself as a dressmaker and gradually auctioned off her husband's vast library to provide for her family. Fortunately, she came into contact with some of her husband's friends, and at their urging the government gave her a small lifetime pension in recognition of her husband's service in education, including provision for her sons' education. Their future seemed assured.[1]

In the spring of 1879, Anna sent a pair of young John's shoes to Olaus Johnsen, the local shoemaker, for repair. When the shoemaker's son delivered the mended shoes, Anna found some religious tracts tucked inside. When Anna needed another pair of shoes repaired, she walked to the shoemaker's shop and, after concluding her business, asked the meaning of the tracts. The brave shoemaker said,

"You may be surprised to hear me say that I can give you something of more value than soles for your child's shoes."

Anna was cautious but curious. Olaus replied, "If you will but listen, I can teach you the Lord's true plan of salvation for His children. I can tell you whence you came, why you are upon earth, and where you will go after death. I can teach you, as you have never known it before, the love of God for His children on earth."[2]

Her hope turned quickly to horror when she learned that the shoemaker was a Mormon, and she left the premises immediately. Prejudice against Mormons ran deep in Norway. When the shoes were returned, though, more tracts were tucked inside. Nor was that the last time Olaus Johnsen courageously and modestly offered her the truths of the restored gospel of Jesus Christ.

Curiosity eventually drew Anna to attend a meeting in a room on the upper floor of the shoemaker's house. As the daughter of a well-respected family and the widow of a university-trained teacher, she initially resented the primitive environment and the humble nature of the Saints. Joining them, she felt, would be a step downward socially. But after months of inner struggle pondering these new doctrines and beginning to perceive the rightness in them, Anna said to the Lord, "Must I step down to that? Yes, if it is the truth, I must do so."[3]

Elder Anthon L. Skanchy broke the ice on the Trondheim fjord and baptized Anna on April 1, 1881. Throughout her life, she claimed to have felt only warmth on her baptismal day.[4]

But Anna's fears were also borne out. News of her conversion spread like wildfire from Trondheim to Frøya. Doors closed to her. Family and friends stopped speaking to her. Even her sister refused to understand. Her husband's friends turned away from her family, and her widow's pension was cut off.[5]

The Trondheim branch became Anna's new family. Shut out from the world that had once welcomed her, Anna turned her devotion and many gifts to blessing the Saints. Her testimony, intelligence, experience, and creative energies helped to invigorate the branch. Before long, she was called to serve in the Relief Society presidency, and in honor of a Relief Society celebration, Anna composed a poem that was framed and hung in the Trondheim meeting place for many years:

> *Jesus, our Brother, is King,*
> *For us He the victory won;*
> *Rejoice, dear brethren and sisters,*
> *In the newfound light and life.*
> *Our Zion awaits the Savior.*
> *We hope to meet Him there;*
> *His bride He will fetch to His home,*
> *Only be humble and true.*[6]

Gathering to Zion

The urge to gather to Zion, where prophets and apostles and thousands of believers lived and where temples were built, began to burn in Anna's soul. But her roots in Norway went deep—her forefathers, parents, and husband were buried there, and her loved ones, particularly Petroline, still pulled at her heart, even though they rejected her religion. Still, Anna's faith and desire to be with the Saints won out. Combining her meager savings with contributions from former missionary friends, she bought passage and sailed from Norway with her sons and twenty other Saints on October 20, 1883. About three weeks later, they arrived safely in Logan, Utah.[7]

Anna resumed her dressmaking trade, working far into the night despite the strain to her eyes. Though the family struggled with poverty, scarcity, severe cold, and injury, she held fast to her faith that the Lord would always provide, and He did, through both the Church organization and the generosity of neighbors.[8] Years later, assistant Church historian Andrew Jenson would say that "Sister Widtsoe [was] one of those strong characters who had set her face like flint to do that which was right."[9]

The blessings of Zion proved to be worth the struggle. Her son John was baptized, requesting the ordinance himself.[10] The completion of the Logan Temple in 1884 was a particularly sweet event.

Anna entered the temple to receive the ordinances for herself and have them performed vicariously for her deceased husband—at last the hope of a heavenly reunion was a reality. Anna's joy overflowed when she received the news that her sister had accepted the gospel and been baptized.[11] As Petroline prepared to follow her to Utah, Anna sent her a letter, dated May 7, 1885, asking her to bring along a piece of their homeland:

> In this letter I send you five dollars, which use as you desire, but . . . if you can, buy and bring with you . . . two myrtles with strong roots, several bulbs of Mrs. Rian's white lilies, as many bulbs as you can secure of Jacob's lilies, and as many rare flowers as you can conveniently secure. Place them in a tight cigar box containing right good garden soil. Water them carefully on the way. . . . I hope this box will not give you any more trouble than John and Osborne caused me.

Continuing, she also shared her testimony of Zion:

> The Lord has blessed this desert so that the poor among His children who come here in faith, are not disappointed. . . . I desire to bear witness to you, my dear sister of the covenant, that this gospel that we have accepted is of God, and I say to you and all members of the Church, be faithful in the midst of your tribulations and a glorious and beautiful day will dawn for you . . . This work is the last call to the earth from the King of glory.[12]

Education in the Wilderness

The Widtsoe family, including Aunt Petroline, who lived with them for a time, labored and prospered as John and Osborne assimilated into Utah's culture. Anna learned English, but she still preferred her native tongue, especially in writing her poetry.

Never losing sight of her goal to educate her sons, Anna ensured that they attended school. She sent Osborne to the regular school and arranged private lessons for John. Eager that they should also acquire cultural polish, she provided both with lessons in music and painting. She also looked forward to helping them pursue higher education.[13]

Some who knew of her dreams thought she was unwise to emphasize education above employment for her sons. One bishop criticized her, warning that her sons would become lazy and insisting that they should be doing hard work in the canyons. Anna graciously listened, but she concluded that "the Lord had given the boys to her and not to the bishop. They were her responsibility, not his. She had obligations to the living and the dead which he did not know about." She predicted that the community would one day admit that she was right to educate her boys.[14]

Years later, Elder Albert E. Bowen, a member of the Church's Quorum of the Twelve Apostles, described the traits that made the Widtsoe family successful and in doing so fulfilled Anna's prediction:

> More than forty years ago, there came to this state two women, leading by the hands two little, fatherless, immigrant boys. They had no wealth, no possessions . . . but they were rich in purpose and in faith, and in those qualities which go to make manhood and womanhood. . . . And in this strange land, among strange people with new ways and a new tongue, they set themselves down to fight out life's battle.[15]

Their mother's determination enabled the Widtsoe boys to fulfill their father's legacy, even in frontier conditions. In 1891, John graduated from Brigham Young College in Logan and left to further his education at Harvard University. The family worked and sacrificed to pay for his studies. Three years later, John graduated with honors and returned and accepted a teaching position at Utah State Agricultural College.[16] Osborne graduated as valedictorian of his class at Brigham Young College and looked forward to entering Harvard himself.

Anna Karine Gaarden Widtsoe (1849–1919)

Anna Karine Gaarden Widtsoe with sons, John Andreas Widtsoe (left) and Osborne Widtsoe (right), ca. 1883.

Feeling that they owed the Lord some service in return for the many blessings they had enjoyed, the family decided that one of the boys should volunteer for missionary service. They planned to send John; however, John was told that, before undertaking missionary service, he should "lay the foundation for a family," so he continued teaching.[17] Osborne had planned to attend Harvard in the fall of 1897; a week before he was to leave, however, he was called to preach the gospel in the Sandwich Islands (Hawaii). He accepted the call and served faithfully for forty months, returning in 1901.[18] Mother, aunt, and brother all helped defray Osborne's expenses.

Anna's and Petroline's sacrifices for the boys' education continued to bear fruit. John taught briefly at Brigham Young University (1905–1907) and eventually served as president of Utah State Agricultural College in Logan (1907–1916) and the University of

Utah in Salt Lake City (1916–1921). Osborne also became a teacher and later president of the Latter-day Saints' University in Salt Lake City.[19] Further fulfilling Anna's prediction that the community would recognize the value of her sons' education, Elder Albert Bowen said: "These two little boys . . . have left a mark among the peoples of this state and of surrounding states and of this country, which anybody would be proud to have made."[20]

Mission to the Land of the Midnight Sun

In April 1903, when Anna and her sister, Petroline, were in their early fifties, they attended a special meeting of Scandinavian Saints at which Patriarch Ola Liljenquist presided. They each requested and received a patriarchal blessing in which, to their surprise, they learned that "they should go back to the land of their nativity and preach the Gospel of life and salvation." On concluding, the patriarch immediately asked Arnt Engh, who recorded the blessing, if he really had made such a prophecy. Three weeks later, a mission call came from Joseph F. Smith, president of the Church. Anna and Petroline agreed to serve as some of the first single sister missionaries in the Church and in Norway.[21]

Upon arriving in Copenhagen, Denmark, the sisters sought out the headquarters of the Scandinavian Mission. There they met the mission president, their old friend Anthon L. Skanchy, who had baptized Anna. He assigned them to serve in Norway, where prejudice against Mormons had increased in the years of their absence. Rumors circulated that missionaries gathered young women to Utah for immoral purposes, making the Norwegians very hostile toward the Saints. The testimony of two native women who had gone to Utah and returned to share their faith made a great impression, doing much to change the prevailing attitude toward the Church. It was said of these new sister missionaries: "They awakened interest everywhere. Men might lie, said the people, but these women were likely to tell the truth."[22]

The Scandinavian Mission history records: "On request of several of the ladies of the town Sister Widtsoe and Gaarden held a women's meeting on which occasion they had the opportunity to address about 200 of the finest ladies in the little city [of Vardö]."[23] While they were in Vardö, one of the northernmost cities in the world, the elders organized a new branch. Ten people were baptized, and the record states, "The Lord assisted the sisters so that they had great influence among the people."[24]

The *Millennial Star* printed a letter from the sisters, dated June 28, 1904, in which they wrote of their experiences:

> The Lord has been with us and blessed us both in our conversations and our public meetings, and with His continued help we feel that we can do some good in the furtherance of the truth.
>
> At Vardö the brethren welcomed us gladly, and we had a splendid time. People came by the hundreds to hear us speak. At the request of many of the ladies of the town we held a meeting last Monday afternoon. We sang, prayed, sang and then one of us spoke for about an hour. After another song, the other spoke for an hour and a half. The last speaker tried to close her remarks a number of times, but the audience urged her to continue, as they wished to hear more. There were present nearly two hundred of the town's "finest" ladies, besides a few men. . . .
>
> We have had fine weather on our journey, and were well treated on board, although we did not travel first class. We made many friends on the boats, had many Gospel conversations, gave away tracts and books, and collected a good many addresses of people living at Trondhjem.
>
> At Vardö we visited the fishing stations and the whale oil factories. We found many good people, and the brethren laboring there have a large field.

These women are believed to be Anna Gaarden Widtsoe and her sister, Petroline Gaarden, on their mission in Norway, 1903–1907.

After we have rested a little here, we shall continue our journey southward. We are trying to use our time well. . . . Well, we are here to do whatever the Lord requires, and we hope to live in such a way that we can praise the Lord for His goodness to us in our mission.[25]

Anna kept in close contact with her family during her mission. In a birthday letter to her five-year-old granddaughter Anna, named in her honor, she shared her love and rich testimony:

Grandma Congratulite you on ÿour berthdaÿ and wich ÿou to lev and bi a Ladÿ and one of Sions preachers, and manÿ other tings ÿou most bi, that vi can not speak of to a little girl jet. O jes ther ar samthings more I can tell you that I vant ÿou to do, ÿou most have a "Mission" to Europe, wer ther jet are so manÿ ho do not know God as hie shoud (skulde) bi knowen (kjenett). . . .

Dear Anna Gaarden vi antÿ and I, send ÿou som Silkribbon for your hair, vi have herd about a little girl ho vanthet her hearribbon change eweÿ other daÿ, and vi thought perhaps som ribbon from norway wood bi a real chang. . . .

Dearest Anna wath a grand place you leve ind, beend your little knees ewery day and thank the Lord for it. . . .

Maÿ dearest little Anna Anna I hope you ar good to Mama Marsel and Pappa. Now I wont you to rite mi a long big lether, it vas sonts a long nice one ÿou rothe mi last time and many thanks for that and kisses. Tell mi all about, Papa Mama Marsel ÿourselv, and alsaa abaut dear Grandma [Susa Young] Gates. O jes allso about (Jok) Rosa og Hazel and let mi se oh jes tel mi allso about Rosas Sister I have herd you ar in love veth her.

Tel mi if you pray to Jesus the Lord. And hwen ÿou praÿ remember os her ind the far "Nort" and allso Grandma Gates and all your dear ones. Vi send our love to you Mama Marsel and Papa Grandma Gates and all our dear ones. Vi wont you to remember haw much vi love ÿou all.

God bless mÿ little girl. Many xxxxxxxxxxx from Grandma to you all.[26]

The sisters served as missionaries for four and a half years, during which time they delivered many lectures, attempted to teach family and friends, and gathered their family's genealogy from the old Protestant church on the island of Hitra. Their efforts and faith yielded unexpected success, and they testified that their prayers had been answered many times. John and Osborne supported their mother and aunt financially, and a small miracle increased their resources, enabling them to serve longer than they'd anticipated—a boyhood friend of Anna's deceased husband, who was then serving in Parliament in Norway, successfully petitioned the government to restore her widow's pension, including payment for the intervening years since she became a Latter-day Saint.[27]

At the conclusion of her mission, Anna had one last visit to make. "With courage in her heart," explained her son John, "she went on August 14, 1907, to the cemetery and stood long by the grave of the schoolmaster, her husband. 'Memories of the past filled my heart and overflowed,' she [wrote] in her journal."[28]

Anna's life had now come full circle, and she cherished the knowledge that her temple covenants would one day reunite her family for eternity.

Poetess

During her later years, Anna enjoyed a full life, delighting in her grandchildren, tending her flower gardens, and expressing her creativity through poetry in her native tongue. She founded the Norwegian literary society *Norroenna Laget*. She joined the Utah Woman's Press Club, a group of Utah women writers.[29] She shared her poetry in a Norwegian Latter-day Saint publication called *Bikuben (The Beehive)*.[30] Although a translation cannot adequately reflect the full richness and musicality of Anna's original composition, the depth of her faith and joy in the gospel is still evident in her verse, including the following poem titled "Easter Morning":

> *Easter morning, glorious day!*
> *Now is the ancient accusation broken,*
> *Now is the Serpent's crucial evidence crushed;*
> *Resurrected is Christ the Lord!*
>
> *Sing, o sing with jubilant tones,*
> *He is resurrected, our Atoner!*
>
> *The Message Mary bore the world,*
> *The Hero of Heaven, has now conquered;*
> *The seal broken, and the stone turned,*
> *Was greater news/joy*[31] *ever known on the earth?*
>
> *Sing, o sing with jubilant tones,*
> *He is resurrected, our Atoner!*

Anna Karine Gaarden Widtsoe (1849–1919)

That matchless grief,
Like mothers' hearts pierced through:
Good Friday's bitter sting and woe,
Now flows away like melted snow.

Sing, o sing with jubilant tones,
He is resurrected, our Atoner!

Our way to Heaven is now secured,
Delight is heard among Heaven's host,
All the world's children raise sounds of exultation,
Sing out freely your Easter song.

Sing, o sing with jubilant sounds,
He is resurrected, our Atoner![32]

Anna Widtsoe's final years were warmed by the joy of seeing her sons obtain prestigious positions at the University of Utah and serve on the general board of the Young Men's Mutual Improvement Association. She would not, however, live to see John's call as an apostle in 1927.[33]

In 1919 after an illness, Anna asked John, "Do you think that this means death?" John described his mother's reaction to his denial: "The wise eyes of the widow glowed as she said, 'I'm not so sure of that. In case this is my last illness, I want to tell you that the most glorious thing that came into my life, was the message delivered to me by Shoemaker Johnsen of Trondheim. The restored gospel has been the great joy of my life. Please bear that witness for me to all who will listen.'"[34]

Anna died on July 11, 1919, at the age of seventy. At her funeral, Church president Heber J. Grant said of her:

> When we think that the gospel found our sister away up in the northern country of Norway, and that it brought to her sufficient strength and force of character, that with the obstacles that would naturally come to her as a widow, yet she succeeded . . . and [spent] her life in the service of the Lord.[35]

Chapter 22

"THE POWER AND INFLUENCE OF WOMAN"

CLARISSA SMITH WILLIAMS (1859–1930)
by Andrea H. Maxfield

Clarissa Smith Williams was the first native Utahn to be called as the general president of the Relief Society of The Church of Jesus Christ of Latter-day Saints. A leader in woman suffrage and a promoter of human rights worldwide, she served for many years in general Relief Society leadership, beginning in 1901 when she became treasurer and continuing through the term of her presidency, April 1921 through October 1928. When she was called to be Relief Society general president, the *Salt Lake Telegram* said of her, "Mrs. Williams is gifted with rare executive ability . . . and is a natural leader of women, being endowed with the highest qualities of mind and heart."[1]

Clarissa was the daughter of George A. Smith and his wife Susan Elizabeth West Smith. The first of the couple's five daughters, she was born April 21, 1859, in their home on South Temple Street, which doubled as the Church Historian's Office. Her mother was George A.'s seventh wife, and they lived in the home with his first wife, Bathsheba W. Bigler Smith, who served as general Relief

Society president from 1901 to 1910.² Clarissa, who found in Bathsheba a second mother, later reminisced: "I began my Relief Society work when I was sixteen years old, going around the block as an assistant teacher, and I feel that the experience I gained at that time has been most valuable and formed the foundation for much of the work that I have been able to do since."³

Growing up at the center of Salt Lake City offered Clarissa and her sisters many opportunities, both social and educational. The young girls received music and art lessons and went to the nearby Salt Lake Theater. They also attended the well-known Miss Cook's School held in the Social Hall and studied reading, writing, and arithmetic. In later years Clarissa attended the University of Deseret, which became the University of Utah. She was part of the first graduating class, having earned a teaching certificate.⁴

In 1875 Clarissa met William Newjent Williams, who had journeyed with his family from Wales to Utah when he was ten. Their courtship led to marriage two years later, on July 17, 1877, just one day before he left to serve a mission in his native Wales. Ten days later, Clarissa posted a letter to her new husband:

> Darling old Will, if you only could imagine how badly I want to see you you would come right straight back to me. . . . Oh! Will, when I think that I won't see you again for two years, it nearly drives me wild, and I don't expect you back in less than that. . . .
>
> The Sunday after you went away was the most lonesome day I ever spent. . . . On the Twenty Fourth I went to the Jubilee and then came home and cut me out a new dress and got the seams all sewn when several of the girls called. Then Sade came down and said that John Henry wanted Maggie and I to go to the party with him; He was "boss" now, and it was better to go and see folks than to stay home and mope. . . . I never realized my darling Will, how much

Clarissa Smith Williams began her service in the Relief Society at sixteen years of age.

you contributed to my happiness until that party. It was worse than eating beefstake without salt.

Do you know Will, this is the first letter I ever wrote to you? Well it won't be the last for now you are my hus____. I can't write the rest it makes me blush.[5]

Two years later William returned home, and the two made their home at 37 N. West Temple Street in Salt Lake City. There Clarissa gave birth to eight daughters and three sons.[6] Three of their eleven children died before reaching adulthood: one as an infant, another at age five of diphtheria, and the third at eighteen of rheumatic heart disease.[7]

The Williamses believed strongly in having an equal partnership in their marriage. William fulfilled civic and Church responsibilities, including service as a state senator and member of the University of Utah's board of regents, and he encouraged and supported Clarissa in her own interests. She served in numerous Church and public positions and was a charter member of both the Daughters of Utah Pioneers and the Daughters of the American

Clarissa Smith Williams (1859–1930)

Revolution, president of the Authors' Club, state chairman of the Woman's Committee of the Council of National Defense during World War I, and delegate for the National and International Councils of Women.[8]

In May 1914 in Rome, Italy, Clarissa joined women from around the world in representing their countries as delegates to the International Council of Women. This conference was in no way a mere social gathering of the gentler sex; these women had serious agendas that concerned the social and political welfare of their world. The two-week conference discussed suffrage, education, moral standards, peace and arbitration, public health, immigration, and the legal protection of women.[9]

The International Council of Women had been formed in 1888 by May Wright Sewell with her close friend Rachel Foster Avery after they approached Susan B. Anthony with the idea to organize as women and address issues plaguing the world. As a result, the new organization came to life at a meeting of the U.S. National Woman Suffrage Association. Called the National Council of Women, it invited women's organizations throughout the nation to become members. Among the charter organizations of the International and National Councils were two groups from The Church of Jesus Christ of Latter-day Saints: the Relief Society, in which Clarissa was deeply involved, and the Young Ladies' Mutual Improvement Association. Along with the others, these two groups paid annual membership dues and regularly sent representatives to the meetings to help promote the values of the council.[10]

At its first meeting, the National Council of Women adopted a constitution. Its mission was defined in the preamble:

> We, women of all nations, sincerely believing that the best good of humanity will be advanced by greater unity of thought, sympathy and purpose, and that an organized movement of women will best conserve the highest good of the family and the state, do hereby band ourselves together

in a confederation of workers committed to the overthrow of all forms of ignorance and injustice, and to the application of the golden rule to society, custom and law.[11]

Twenty-six years later, Clarissa Smith Williams, having been nominated and accepted by the National Council of Women as an International Council delegate, was in Rome for the convention. She was at that time first counselor to general Relief Society president Emmeline B. Wells. Clarissa's years of involvement with the Relief Society organization had prepared her well to address the issues overshadowing a world on the brink of war.

Women's prayers for peace were a regular topic on the agenda of the International Council for years; however, the real threat of a world war had not yet been realized. Clarissa had been accompanied by her husband to Rome, and they had planned to tour Europe after the conference. After visiting Italy, Switzerland, France, Germany, and England, they made their way to Wales to visit William's family home in Brechfa. Then on June 28, Archduke Franz Ferdinand of the Austro-Hungarian Empire, and his wife, Sophie, were assassinated in Sarajevo. Europe was quickly embroiled in the early stages of World War I, and William and Clarissa were forced to return home.[12]

An editorial published in the *Relief Society Bulletin* a few months later beautifully articulates a concern weighing on many minds at the time: "Our heart contracts, and we mothers know at once how the mothers of those Serbian, German, French and English soldiers feel at even the suggestion of war. Men may fight and kill, but women must suffer and weep."[13] The United States was soon involved in the war effort, and Clarissa's commitment to humanity quickly increased her public service. She became a member of the Red Cross Civilian Relief Committee and the state chairman of the Women's Committee of the National Council of Defense. Both the International Council of Women and the Relief Society provided

Under Clarissa Williams's leadership, the Relief Society became heavily involved in the Red Cross. Relief Society sisters in Ogden, Utah, marched in a parade to raise funds to aid victims of World War I, 1918.

ways for Clarissa to put into action her lofty ideals during a time of great public need.[14]

During World War I, the U.S. government prohibited groups and individuals from storing food. This meant that the wheat the Relief Society had been storing for years had to be converted into cash. Under Clarissa's direction, the trust fund resulting from the sale of the wheat was placed in the Presiding Bishopric's Office, and the interest earned from it each year was used to meet women's health and maternity needs.[15]

Clarissa held out her hand to those in need in both her public pursuits and in her personal life. Her daughter Eva Williams Darger recounted, "As a little girl I remember the many hobos, vagrants or tramps who would knock at the back door for a 'handout.' One summer day when three or four men had come to the door for food, Mama asked, 'Where are these men coming from?' The hungry hobo said, 'Ma'am, there is a mark on the tree in your front yard that tells us that you are generous with your food. We have marks that let our friends know about mad dogs, gun crazy men and good victuals. You ought to be proud, Ma'am, of your generous reputation.'"[16]

Clarissa sought ways to advocate the principles embraced by the Relief Society. Finding that the aims of the National and International Councils of Women aligned with those of her own organization, Clarissa enthusiastically carried out her responsibilities in connection with the councils. In 1925 she was again honored to serve as a delegate to the International Council, this time in Washington, D.C. She was delighted to mingle with "many notable and interesting, as well as picturesque, characters . . . women who have gained high rank in their respective countries in the field of education and human welfare work."[17]

Her excitement over the conference was poured across a ten-page report in the *Relief Society Magazine.* The many paragraphs of praise for prominent women and their accomplishments worldwide contained only a sentence about her own involvement, which praised the state of Utah more than herself. Speaking of a breakfast held in honor of state delegates who had worked to raise money to cover costs of "the great meeting," the sentence read, "An outstanding feature of the breakfast was the report that Utah was the first state to raise its quota, and the detailed account by Mrs. Clarissa S. Williams, chairman of the Utah State committee, as to how the quota was raised."[18]

Clarissa reported enthusiastically on the events and issues discussed:

> Probably the most interesting of the general sessions was the evening meeting devoted to the reports of the work of the various National Councils. It was indeed inspiring to hear of the efforts being put forth by women to make the world better and safer for humanity.
>
> New Zealand reported among other things the lowest death rate among children in all the world; Australia, the great results from their maternity program, which with the

assistance of trained social workers and public health nurses, has become very effective. Denmark reported improvement in police work since the introduction of police women. Sweden reported five women in parliament; and Holland, eight women in parliament. In Holland equal pay for equal work is the rule in many professions. Hungary has received great benefit from the recent tuberculosis campaign. . . . In Chile the women are training themselves and are being trained for suffrage.[19]

Clarissa enjoyed a variety of activities at the convention. "There were also excursions to the historic places in and about Washington," she wrote, "such as Arlington, Gettysburg and Mt. Vernon, where a wreath was placed on the tomb of Washington, in the name of the women of the world." But she found that "the reports of standing committees were most interesting and inspiring" in the areas of education, equal moral standards, trades and professions, emigration, suffrage, child welfare, and peace and arbitration.[20]

She particularly enjoyed the speech of Ishbel Hamilton-Gordon, known as Lady Aberdeen, president of the council, in which she explained "that the main object of the existence of the International Council is not to promote propaganda but to form a center around which all women's societies can gather, confer, and make the voice of organized womanhood heard regarding various subjects of world interest."[21] During Clarissa's leadership years in the Relief Society, it sent delegates annually to the National Council meetings to report the organization's initiatives and to report back to her and the general board on international issues.

At the 1920 session of the International Council of Women, Lady Aberdeen said, "Mothering power is what the world must have to bring it back to faith and love."[22] The women of the council understood the power of their nature to set a standard for the world.[23] Clarissa was a champion for women's issues, yet she was careful to balance her public causes with her private calling of motherhood. Her family remained important to her. Those who knew her declared, "Although Mrs. Williams has given much valuable service to her church and to the public, she is typically a home woman and is a loving, patient and devoted mother to her large family."[24] At the dinner table, Clarissa "always sat at her husband's right so they could hold hands," and "dinner conversation centered around the children and what they were doing and the day's activities."[25] Clarissa's cousin Alice Merrill Horne remembered:

> At noon times, each child curled, clean-bibbed and fresh-aproned, sat up at a table, ready for the father's entrance with his loving kisses at the stroke of 12:00. When the mother finished the weekly ironing of 28 starched dresses—the weekly allowance for the girls adorned the ample clotheshorse. The writer often wondered how the children were up and dressed with such promptness and she one morning witnessed the method: Uncle Will and Aunt Clarissa chose up sides and ran races to see which side should be dressed first, and every child was washed and smiling dressed and up to the breakfast table almost before I could say "Jack Robinson."[26]

For much of the lives of her younger children, Clarissa held a calling in general Relief Society leadership. She was treasurer from 1901 to 1910 and first counselor from 1910 to 1921.

When Clarissa was called to preside over the Relief Society in April 1921, she addressed her sisters on having a purpose larger than themselves.

"I greet you this morning, my dear sister workers," she said, "in behalf of the General Board of the Relief Society. . . . We have looked forward to the same goal, our vision has always been in the future, our purpose has been to do the things which would be for the best good of humanity, not for ourselves alone, but for the communities in which we live, whether they be of us or not of us. . . . as time goes on, and we see the needs of humanity at large, our hearts will swell, and we will be given the inspiration to do the things which shall build up those about us."[27]

Clarissa emulated the examples of the influential women who preceded her. In a 1921 issue of the *Young Woman's Journal* that featured her new, "wonderfully strong presidency," an editorial rehearsed past achievements of women: "Few women of today," it said, "realize what struggles have taken place, what time and effort and money have been expended that they might have equal rights with men—equal rights before the law, equal opportunities for education, equal pay for equal work, equal political rights, in short that they might stand side by side sharing in the world's work, having a voice in government, and receiving equal recognition for ability and accomplishment. . . . The wonderful change has come since 1842, the year in which the Prophet Joseph Smith organized the Relief Society and when he said, 'I turn the key for women.' . . . It has shown the power and influence of woman, her obligations and opportunities, and it has extended to her every right and privilege with which her Creator has endowed her."[28]

Clarissa Smith Williams held high these ideals, believing that the betterment of humanity worldwide was intertwined with the promotion of women. Soon after being sustained as general president of the Relief Society, she recommended memorial funds be established in the names of past presidents. The purpose of these funds was two-fold: first, to honor the past presidents, and second, to foster growth in women. The memorials established were the Eliza R. Snow Relief Society Memorial Prize Poem Fund, which provided first and second prizes annually for poetry; the Zina D. H. Young Relief Society Memorial Nurse Loan Fund, which provided loans to help undergraduate nurses pay for hospital courses; the Bathsheba W. Smith Relief Society Memorial Temple Grant, which provided means for temple work to be performed, thus advancing women's spiritual welfare; and the Emmeline B. Wells Relief Society Memorial Loan Fund, which made loans to upper-division students at Brigham Young University.[29]

In 1926 the women of Relief Society decided to show appreciation for Clarissa's great efforts by recommending another memorial fund, this one in her name, and requesting that she determine its use. Clarissa chose for the fund to provide loans for the education of public health nurses in the hope that eventually every community would have at least one such nurse.[30] This honor, like previous ones, she accepted in her usual modest way. "There are many people in the world who have honors given to them," Elder George Albert Smith said of her, "but I cannot think of any who have received honor with more humility, and carried it with more dignity than has Aunt Clarissa."[31]

At the Relief Society conference held on October 4, 1928, Clarissa remarked that "it was not her desire to remain in active service indefinitely" and that she had "always advocated that Relief Society women do not hold office too long, as there are many capable women" willing to serve. Three days later she was released at general conference. At the close of her many years in public service, Clarissa reminisced about her experiences and her husband's support:

> After I was married and had seven children, I was asked to be a secretary of the Seventeenth ward Relief Society. I felt that I could not do this with all my little babies. But my husband said, "My dear, you must do it; it is the very thing you need; you need to get away from the babies, and I will help you all I can." . . . I felt that I couldn't refuse then, so I consented. . . . I had occupied this position of secretary between seven and eight years when I was asked if I would accept the position of president of the ward. And I did not know how I could do that either.

Clarissa accepted that calling and succeeding ones with increasing responsibility as she continued to lead Latter-day Saint women. Less than two years before her death on March 8, 1930, she was able to look back and say, "Now, I like to feel that I have no regrets, that I have done my work as well as I could."[32]

Clarissa, through the support of a loving husband, balanced fulfilling her home duties while maintaining her commitment to public service. At the Relief Society general conference in April 1922, she said: "The greatest thing in the world is love. And if we keep that always in our hearts, and give it as a message to those about us, we will be blessed and will be instruments in blessing those with whom we associate."[33]

Clarissa Smith Williams was a remarkable role model. She focused on the humanity of the world, employing her gifts as a mother and a leader. She honored woman as an equal companion to man and expanded her influence to an international arena. She was a leader of leaders. Her "varied experience in religious, patriotic, civic and social activities very properly qualifie[d] her for the responsible position" she filled.[34]

Chapter 23

"How Thankful We Should Be"

Cohn Shoshonitz Zundel (1863–1949)
by Patricia Lemmon Spilsbury

Cohn Shoshonitz was born in 1863 in the Bear River region of northeastern Utah.[1] Her parents, members of Great Basin Shoshone family bands, were named Yellow Shoshonitz and Tic-a-Marrack or Nab-it-not-a-ci.[2] Cohn was raised in a cohesive family group of the Northwestern Shoshone tribe. They traveled during the year, following traditional hunting and gathering cycles in areas that include what is now northern Utah, southwestern Wyoming, southern Idaho, and eastern Nevada.[3]

Cohn was born during a period of great change for native peoples in the western United States and for the Northwestern Shoshone in particular. In January 1863, ten months before her birth, Cohn's people were nearly annihilated at their traditional winter camp near the Bear River in southern Idaho during an attack led by U.S. Army Colonel Patrick Connor, an event now known as the Bear River Massacre. In the years following that horrendous event, the Northwestern Shoshone faced the stark reality that their traditional food-gathering migrations were no longer possible because of the tremendous influx of settlers who, through land occupation and cultivation, limited access to seasonal camps and consumed natural resources that the Shoshone depended on for subsistence. Thus the Shoshone began the difficult transition from their traditional lifestyle to the more settled existence of the Euro-Americans.[4]

According to the Washakie Ward history, sometime during the early 1870s, Egipbetche (John), son of Moembugie, one of the tribal leaders, suggested that the tribe "tak[e] up some land somewhere and farm like white people."[5] They eventually settled on a site near the Malad River in present-day Box Elder County, Utah. The settlement was named Washakie, in honor of the revered Shoshone chief from Wind River, Wyoming.[6]

During this transition, many Shoshone joined The Church of Jesus Christ of Latter-day Saints. Cohn's family was among them, and she was baptized on May 5, 1873, at age nine.[7] Both her parents were full participants not only in their native community but also in Church activities.

Following the Shoshone tradition of taking a new name when a significant life event occurs, Cohn's parents and the young man who later became Cohn's husband took new names when they joined the Church.[8] Her mother, Tic-a-Marrack or Nab-it-not-a-ci, took the name Sarah. Her father, Yellow Shoshonitz, became Alma. Another tribe member, Tru-Ow-Wutsey, took the name Moroni and the surname Zundel, honoring Isaac D. Zundel, bishop of the Washakie Ward. Cohn married Moroni about 1877, and they were sealed on December 7, 1882, in the Endowment House in Salt Lake City.[9] Cohn thus became Cohn Shoshonitz Zundel, the name she kept throughout her life. She gave birth to her first child at age fifteen and with Moroni had six children, only two of whom lived to maturity.[10]

Though the earliest branch records of Washakie were lost in a fire, the names of Cohn and her mother, Sarah, appear frequently on the extant rolls of the Washakie Ward Relief Society. Cohn's father, Alma, was identified by Isaac Zundel as a "leading man" at Washakie in 1884.[11] An 1887 photograph in the diary of John Hess identifies Alma as both a recognized leader of his people and a participating member of the Church. Hess's diary described a mission he and Isaac Zundel undertook to visit Washakie, chief of the Snake, or Shoshone, then living in the Wind River Range of Wyoming. The photograph shows Alma with five others, all identified as "Shoshone Members of the Church."[12]

In July 1883, Eliza R. Snow wrote about a visit she made with her brother Lorenzo Snow and his son Alphonso to Brigham City and areas north. In particular, she described her trip to Washakie, to "the Indian Farm" in Box Elder County, where she participated in the organization of a Relief Society. Elizabeth Jane Zundel, wife of Bishop Zundel, was sustained as president, with Malissa Hunsaker as first counselor, and "Kohn," described as a Lamanite, as second counselor.[13] Thus began Cohn's more than thirty-five years of service in the Relief Society. In fact, Cohn served as first or second counselor to four presidents in the Washakie Ward Relief Society from 1883 until 1918. She served as an interpreter on occasion, offered prayers, bore testimony, and conducted Relief Society meetings. While she was serving in Relief Society, her husband, Moroni Zundel, was sustained in 1890 as superintendent of the Washakie Sunday School.[14]

Along with attending Relief Society, Cohn made regular monetary donations to the organization, including extra contributions in 1904 and 1905 to fund the construction of a building to house the women's auxiliaries at Church headquarters.[15]

The secretary of the Washakie Relief Society, Mary Ann Ward, with the assistance of Cohn's daughter Lucy Peyope,[16] recorded synopses of testimonies shared during their monthly testimony meetings. The depth of Cohn's testimony, frequently borne, and the issues foremost in her mind and heart were preserved in these records. The following excerpts from the minutes are of comments Cohn made between 1906 and 1926:[17]

Cohn Shoshonitz Zundel (1863–1949)

Washakie Relief Society, 1918, as identified by Mae Parry in 1999. Standing, left to right: Cohn Zundel, Lewis Jones Neaman, Positze Norigan, Sadie Peyope, Towenge Timbimboo, Yampitch Timbimboo, Mary Ann Ward, Helen Young (schoolteacher at left center), Amy Timbimboo, unknown, Ivy Hootchew Bird, Annie Hootchew, unknown, Minnie Woonsook, Hitope Joshua, Hazel Timbimboo (child). Seated, left to right: Po ne Nitz, Boe be nup, Jane Pabowena, Mary Woonsook, Anzie Wagon with Eddie Wagon on her back in a cradleboard.

Mar. 17, 1906 1 C[ounselo]r Chon Zundle a short time explained the great changes that have been Wrou[gh]th upon the sisters since the Relief Society work has been introduced unto them, showing how thankfull we should be for the priviledges that we are permited to enjoy. also the advantages of living a good life.

Jan. 11, 1908 1 Cr. Chon Zundle spoke for some time to the young sisters that were present upon the laws of Virtue, encouraged each and every one to do right.

Mar. 6, 1908 1st Cr Chon Zundle spoke about the [illegible] Meeting day of R.S. also bore her testimony.

May 31, 1908 1 Cr Chon Zundle said she glad to bee to meeting but was sorry she could not under stan more of what the Stk authorities had to tell us when they come to visit us.

July 11, 1908 1 Cr Chon Zundle said she did not understand all of the lecture [on mother's work] but what she did thought it was good for us sisters.

Sept. 5, 1908 1st Cr Chon Zundle encouraged to live good lives so that when we leave this stage of life we might [go] to our Father in Heaven.

Apr. 17, 1909 1 Cr Chon Zundle felt wel in the work of the Lord & thought these Lectures [on mother's work and in the Relief Society Conference] would be good for us if we would try to remember & put it into practice.

June 12, 1909 1st Cr Chon Zundle announced that today is our testimony meeting while upon her feet bore here testimony encouraged the sister[s] to live their religion & when they have done a wrong to any one to go to them & make it right.

Nov. 8, 1909 Chon Zendle encouraged the Sistes to put the instructions that they have heard in to practice.

Jan. 8, 1910 1st Cr Chon Zundle bore her testimony & encouraged the sistes to attend to our dutties.

June 2, 1910 Cr Cohn Sundle said she did not understand much and she could not talk much. She w[a]s not very well acquainted with any of the sisters but Philine [Hall] but she felt prayerful. Spoke of its condition of her ancesters. She always felt well to attend meeting.

July 7 [n.d.] Chon Zundle spoke of the goodness of the Lord unto us.

April 6, 1926 Chon Zundle bore her testimony and said that she believes Joseph Smith to be a prophet of God.

November 16, 1926 Sister Chon Zundle bore her testimony said She was glad to be home so she can come to meetings again.

December 28, 1926 Sister Chon Zundle said she has been sick that why she did not pay all of her donations for the year.

Despite her final statement, there appear in the records six different occasions during 1926 on which she made donations to the

Relief Society, including contributions to a bazaar, funds for benches for the meetinghouse, charity donations, and her annual Relief Society dues.[18]

Donating money was likely a sacrifice for Cohn. Her life was vastly different from the life lived by her grandparents, and although more stationary, it was far from easy. The members of her tribe worked many hours on their farms, but, because of weather conditions, harvests were not always optimal. At such times, residents sought work in surrounding areas.

The minutes of the Relief Society reflect a similar situation on November 21, 1908. After the roll was taken and only ten members were found to be present, President Mary A. Ward bore her testimony and then said she wished "to have seen more of the sisters present but as they are away from home working in the beet fields it cannot be helped." Cohn was not recorded as being present at that meeting or the next one. But she did attend the December 5 meeting, at which Sister Ward stated that "she was please to see so many of the sister back hom from the beet fields so they can come to meeting again."[19] This comment suggests that Cohn may have been among those sisters who went to the beet fields to work.

Cohn was not spared from tragedy while cultivating the land. When community members worked on surrounding farms, it was not uncommon for them to take their own equipment, such as threshing machines, to assist other farmers. On one such occasion, her young son, Nephi, was playing near a threshing machine while others were working. His pant leg was caught in the universal joint of the drive shaft, which mangled his leg before the horses and machinery could be halted. Nephi's leg had to be amputated, and afterward he walked with a homemade crutch.[20] He retained his independence, however, and census records later indicate that his occupation was farmer and mail carrier.[21]

Cohn was left a widow with two children when her husband, Moroni Zundel, passed away on February 8, 1892, at age thirty-seven, from typhoid fever aggravated by influenza.[22] On January 14,

1893, Cohn married Johnny Annebooey Quedup (Indian Johnny or Johnny Fly) and had three additional children, two of whom survived to adulthood.[23] He died on December 30, 1899, leaving her a widow for the second time, now with four surviving children.[24]

Cohn lived nearly fifty years as a widow.[25] During this time, she lived with her son, Nephi, and frequently visited her daughters and grandchildren. She encouraged them to care for one another and shared her testimony in word and action. Cohn was described by her descendants as being a good provider for her family and a skilled homemaker. She kept "a barrel of apples in the upstairs room and also one of dry meat." In her cellar she kept "onions, turnips, parsley, red beets, potatoes and some apples and watermellon . . . and some sugar beets that she baked in the oven in the afternoons and let us eat it on evenings after we come from school. She had bottles of fruit." Cohn had three cows she milked daily and thirty-five chickens, as well as ducks, turkeys, and geese. In addition, Cohn baked bread, pies, and cakes, skills she learned from her Relief Society sisters. Her granddaughter Marjorie related that Cohn was careful with her resources and taught her family to be the same way. "She remembered one year we had a hard winter, but she said don't worry about things. Our prayers will be answered, then we will have things to buy."

Cohn had a good sense of humor. Marjorie related, "The funniest thing happened. She made soup and she put a bottle of tomatoes in it. The tomatoes had sugar in it and the soup was sweet. She laughed at us. She said half of her bottles of tomatoes had sugar in them, and she didn't mark them. She was always good to us."

Marjorie also described Cohn as loving to dance, whether square dancing, old folk's dances, or Shoshone dances. Cohn loved sports and enjoyed watching baseball and basketball games. She also enjoyed more traditional Shoshone work—tanning hides, doing beadwork, and making moccasins, gloves, purses, and belts.[26]

Cohn shared her heritage and her testimony with her grandchildren. "She [Cohn] would call us and tell us about what came before," recalled Rios Pacheco, Cohn's great-grandson. She would "tell us stories and she would sing Indian songs." She said, "It is time you be good. The years are changing now. . . . Have faith and read. If you are good, you will see me. Jesus is coming, then he will say 'I am Jesus.' While you are waiting, go do your work and read and learn all you can." Her favorite hymn was "Come, Come, Ye Saints."[27]

Cohn's leadership position in Relief Society allowed her, in Rios's words, "to help her people and let them know how much the gospel was important to them, but also let them know that their role was equally as important as their husbands' role . . . that without [their husbands], they would be the caretakers of their part in the priesthood bringing up their male and female children. Both roles are spiritual parts."[28]

Released from her long-standing position as counselor in the Relief Society presidency in 1918, Cohn continued to be active in the Washakie Ward, attending and participating in meetings. Marjorie remembered that the whole family got up early to go to Sunday School together; Rios said his grandmothers "were in Church every Sunday . . . they would make sure we were there by the time Church was starting, [and] we lived in Perry. [They] made sure [we] were at priesthood [meetings]."[29]

Willie Ottogary, a Shoshone journalist living in the Brigham City area, wrote a column for various newspapers in northern Utah and southern Idaho.[30] In several columns, Ottogary made reference to Cohn and her activities:

> Washaki, May 13, 1919 Miss Cohn Zundel laid up with cold and under Doctor treatment. She is little improved now. I hope she will get over it.
> Washaki, September 22, 1924 Mrs. John [Cohn] Zundel and family been down [to] Peach Day, too.[31]
> Washaki, November 24, 1924 Mrs. Cohn Zundel and family been up [to] Idaho Reservation and visiting her granddaughter up there. She was return home last week.

Even into her old age, Cohn Zundel enjoyed tanning hides and doing beadwork. She made moccasins, gloves, purses, and belts of deerskin.

Washakie, April 22, 1925 Mrs. Cohn Zundell and her daughter motoring over Cache valley some time go last week.

Washaki, August 25, 1926 Mrs. or (Miss) Ethel Perdash was took sick last . . . she have a appendicitis. . . . She improving pretty nicely now. She doing pretty fine and her grandma, Miss Cohn Zundel was visit her last Monday too.

Washaki, January 12, 1927 Mrs. John [Cohn] Zundel received a bad news from Fort Washakie, Wyoming. Her uncle was died out there about two week ago. But he was well know this part of this country. His name was Mr. Pa-zo-quita. I expect he was about 75 year of age.[32]

Cohn Shoshonitz Zundel died at Washakie on November 17, 1949. Her funeral was attended by many of the early pioneers of Washakie, who gathered home to honor her in her passing. They included Mary Ann Ward, the Relief Society president with whom she had served for many years, and her former bishop, George A. Ward.[33]

Although relatively little written information remains about this valiant woman, she lived a life of faith worthy of remembrance. Taught during her childhood the traditions and lifeways of her forebears, Cohn lived during a period of great transition among the Shoshone, and she demonstrated resilience, diligent service, and faithfulness in helping to pave the way for future generations.

Notes

Chapter 1: Maud May Babcock

1. "Babcock Resigns Position as 'U' Speech Head," *Utah Daily Chronicle,* April 21, 1938.
2. Roy Webb, "Dramatis Personae," *Continuum* 20, no. 3 (Winter 2010–11), 48. Other brief accounts of Babcock's career include Ann Garner Stone, "Maud May Babcock: 'Understand the Thought, Hold the Thought, Give the Thought,'" in *Sister Saints,* ed. Vicky Burgess-Olson (Provo, UT: Brigham Young University Press, 1978), 263–72; David G. Pace, "Maud May Babcock: Speak Clearly and Carry a Big Umbrella," in *Worth Their Salt: Notable but Often Unnoted Women of Utah,* ed. Colleen Whitley (Logan: Utah State University Press, 1996), 148–57; "A Dramatic Leader: Maude May Babcock, 1867–1954," Teacher Resources, Utah State History, accessed July 2, 2013, http://ilovehistory.utah.gov/people/difference/babcock.html.
3. "Family Record," Holograph, Maud May Babcock Papers, Special Collections, J. Willard Marriott Library, University of Utah, Salt Lake City, hereafter cited as Babcock Papers; "Woman's Hygiene Reform Class," *Young Woman's Journal* 7, no. 9 (June 1896): 425–27; [Maud May Babcock], "Physical Culture," in Hannah Sorensen, *What Women Should Know* (Salt Lake City, UT: George Q. Cannon and Sons, 1896), 158–68; Stan Russon, "Call It a Day, or Idiot's Delight," Maud May Babcock Celebration, October 8, 1981, Typescript, Babcock Reading Arts Society, Babcock Papers. A display at the Social Hall Heritage Museum in Salt Lake City includes photographs and a replica of her gymnasium clothing.
4. Remarks of Mary Johnson Webster, Maud May Babcock Celebration, October 8, 1981, Typescript, Babcock Reading Arts Society, Babcock Papers.

5. Dudley Allen Sargent, *An Autobiography*, ed. Ledyard W. Sargent (Philadelphia: Lea & Febiger, 1927), 196–98, 208, 219; Betty Spears, "The Philanthropist and the Physical Educator," *New England Quarterly* 47, no. 4 (December 1974): 594–602; "Biographical Sketch of Maud May Babcock, B.E.," *Young Woman's Journal* 5, no. 9 (June 1894): 410–13; "Maud May Babcock," *Woman's Who's Who of America, 1914–1915*, ed. John William Leonard (New York: American Commonwealth, 1914), 63. See also Maud May Babcock, "Personal Record," Babcock Papers.
6. Harvard Summer School of Physical Education Records, Harvard University Archives, Cambridge, Massachusetts.
7. J. M. Tanner to F. M. Lyman, and J. M. Tanner to Emily Richards, September 16, 1892, Holographs, Babcock Papers.
8. Pace, "Maud May Babcock," 150.
9. Herbert B. Maw, Remarks at Maud May Babcock Celebration, October 8, 1981, Babcock Reading Arts Society, Babcock Papers.
10. "Woman's Hygiene Reform Class," *Young Woman's Journal*, 425–27.
11. Maud May Babcock, "Loyalty," *Improvement Era* 8, no. 3 (January 1905), 178–83.
12. Young women in YLMIA ages fourteen through sixteen.
13. "Officers' Notes: Hints on Presenting a Lesson to Juniors," *Young Woman's Journal* 20, no. 7 (July 1909): 341–42.
14. She took these lines from Alfred Lord Tennyson, "The Golden Year," which can be found in many editions, including *The Poetical Works of Alfred Tennyson* (New York: Harper's, 1871), 57. The full passage reads as follows:

> *Ah! when shall all men's good*
> *Be each man's rule, and universal Peace*
> *Lie like a shaft of light across the land,*
> *And like a lane of beams athwart the sea,*
> *Thro' all the circle of the golden year?"*

15. Maud May Babcock, Prayer before the Utah State Senate, February 14, 1945, Babcock Papers.
16. Maud May Babcock, Prayer before the Utah State Senate, March 7, 1945, Babcock Papers.

Chapter 2: Martha Maria Hughes Cannon

1. For published materials relating to Martha Hughes Cannon, see Jean B. White, "Dr. Martha Hughes Cannon: Doctor, Wife, Legislator, Exile," in *Sister Saints,* ed. Vicky Burgess-Olson (Provo, UT: Brigham Young University Press, 1978); Constance L. Lieber, "'The Goose Hangs High': Excerpts from the Letters of Martha Hughes Cannon," *Utah Historical Quarterly* 48, no. 1 (Winter 1980): 37–48; Shari Siebers Crall, "'Something More': A Biography of Martha Hughes Cannon" (honor's thesis, Brigham Young University, 1985); Constance L. Lieber and John Sillito, eds., *Letters from Exile: The Correspondence of Martha Hughes Cannon and Angus M. Cannon, 1886–1888* (Salt Lake City, UT: Signature Books, 1989); Mari Graña, *Pioneer, Polygamist, Politician: The Life of Dr. Martha Hughes Cannon* (Guilford, CT: TwoDot, 2009).
2. Barbara Replogle (ca. 1858–?) was married to William Dent Atkinson in 1890; they had one child, Ruby Louise, in 1894. Barbara held the chair of elocution at Hedding College in the 1890s and was a noted temperance lecturer who listed her hometown as Abingdon, Illinois.
3. Carroll Smith-Rosenberg, "The Female World of Love and Ritual: Relations between Women in Nineteenth-Century America," in *Disorderly Conduct: Visions of Gender in Victorian America* (New York: Oxford University Press, 1986), 53–76.
4. Letters in this chapter are transcribed from holographs in the Martha H. Cannon Collection, 1883–1912, Church History Library, The Church of Jesus Christ of Latter-day Saints, Salt Lake City, Utah, hereafter cited as Church History Library.
5. A house physician was a junior doctor who lived on site and was not compensated for his or her labor.
6. Martha M. Hughes to Barbara Replogle, September 18, 1884.
7. William Shakespeare, *Macbeth,* act 1, scene 7.
8. Hughes Cannon to Replogle, February 10, 1884.
9. Hughes Cannon to Replogle, May 1, 1885.
10. Hughes Cannon to Replogle, March 21, 1885. Because Mattie could not be located and questioned in court, Angus was acquitted of the charge of unlawful cohabitation with her. He was, however, found guilty of unlawful cohabitation with Amanda Mousely Cannon and Clarissa V. Mason Cannon.

11. On Mormon polygamy during this period, see Carmon Hardy, *Solemn Covenant: The Mormon Polygamous Passage* (Urbana: University of Illinois Press, 1992).
12. Hughes Cannon to Replogle, May 1, 1885.
13. Polygamists and their wives who chose to remain in Utah (the great majority) lived so as to render themselves as inaccessible as possible to federal marshals. They may have resided in their own homes, but they had networks established so they were warned of coming raids and could go elsewhere to hide. Such men, among them President John Taylor and other Church leaders, including Angus M. Cannon, rotated among the homes of their wives and children in Salt Lake City and outside it.
14. Martha Hughes Cannon to Angus M. Cannon, March 19, 1888, Holograph, Angus M. Cannon Collection, Church History Library; Lieber and Sillito, *Letters from Exile,* 269.
15. Ella Wheeler Wilcox, *Poems of Pleasure* (New York: Belford, 1888), 75–76.
16. Parley P. Pratt, *Key to the Science of Theology: As Designed As an Introduction* (Liverpool: F. D. Richards, 1855), 160–61.
17. Hughes Cannon to Replogle, July 22, 1886. Mattie was writing from Stratford-upon-Avon, her place of residence.
18. Hughes Cannon to Replogle, September 9, 1886.
19. Hughes Cannon to Replogle, April 28, 1887. Mattie's letter was written from London. In her letters to her husband, Angus, during this period, Mattie repeatedly instructed him to burn her letters. Lieber and Sillito, *Letters from Exile,* 66, 74, 79, 87, 191, 239, 259.
20. Hughes Cannon to Replogle, July 22, 1886.
21. Hughes Cannon to Replogle, July 22, 1886.
22. Hughes Cannon to Replogle, December 15, 1886.
23. Closing lines from philosopher George Berkeley's poem "Verses on the Prospect of Planting Arts and Learning in America," first published in 1752.
24. Hughes Cannon to Replogle, August 6, 1887.
25. Hughes Cannon to Replogle, November 10, 1888.
26. Hughes Cannon to Replogle, August 10, 1888.
27. Highcockalorum is a children's game, but it was also used as a term to denote pretensions to great importance.
28. Hughes Cannon to Replogle, September 18, 1889.

29. We have not been able to identify the writings of Harriet Beecher Stowe that Mattie quoted in this letter.
30. Louisa "Lula" Greene Richards, "Corneel," *Woman's Exponent* 4, no. 13 (December 1, 1875): 97. In the original poem, Lula writes "man *never* proves." Hughes Cannon to Replogle Atkinson, May 5, 1890. Barbara was married on February 14, 1890.
31. It is not clear from what source Martha Cannon is quoting in this letter.
32. Hughes Cannon to Replogle Atkinson, June 6, 1891. Mattie wrote this letter from San Francisco.
33. Mattie and Angus's children were Elizabeth Rachel Cannon McCrimmon (1885–1972), James Hughes Cannon (1890–1950), and Gwendolyn Hughes Cannon Quick (1899–1928).
34. Young Women's Mutual Improvement Association Minutes and Records, September 1, 1876, Tenth Ward, Park Stake, Holograph, p. 159, Church History Library.

Chapter 3: Mary Elizabeth Woolley Howard Chamberlain

1. Mary Elizabeth Woolley Chamberlain, "A Sketch of My Life," in *Mary E. Woolley Chamberlain: Handmaiden of the Lord,* comp. Farel Chamberlain Kimball (Provo, UT: privately published, 1981), 21. Kimball's volume supplements Mary's original *Sketch of My Life,* privately published circa 1936, with tributes and memories provided by Chamberlain family members.
2. Chamberlain, "Sketch of My Life," 222.
3. Chamberlain, "Sketch of My Life," 352–53.
4. Chamberlain, "Sketch of My Life," 21–22.
5. Chamberlain, "Sketch of My Life," 24–25.
6. Chamberlain, "Sketch of My Life," 46.
7. Kanab city.
8. Chamberlain, "Sketch of My Life," 90.
9. Chamberlain, "Sketch of My Life," 93–97.
10. Chamberlain, "Sketch of My Life," 98–99.
11. Chamberlain, "Sketch of My Life," 102–3.
12. Utah was granted statehood on January 4, 1896. Mary's life sketch includes a description of statehood celebrations in Kanab, noting, "This was a great day and was celebrated from one end of the Territory to the other." Chamberlain, "Sketch of My Life," 109.

13. Chamberlain, "Sketch of My Life," 150–52.
14. Thomas Chamberlain had previously been convicted of unlawful cohabitation in 1888 and paid the full penalty under the Edmunds Act—six months served in the penitentiary and fines amounting to $320. See "Released from Prison," *Deseret News [Weekly]*, May 25, 1889.
15. Thomas Chamberlain had served as bishop in Orderville and as president of the communal United Order there. Mark A. Pendleton, "The Orderville United Order of Zion," *Utah Historical Quarterly* 7 (October 1939): 141–59.
16. Elinor Angeline Hoyt (1856–1928); Laura Sumner Fackrell (1856–1936); Ann Elizabeth Carling (1859–1894); Ellen Alvira Carling (1863–1951); and Chastie Ellen Covington (1867–1942).
17. Contrary to Mary's statement, plural marriage was in fact illegal in Mexico, though Mexican authorities agreed not to enforce the law in order to encourage immigration of Latter-day Saints. B. Carmon Hardy, *Solemn Covenant: The Mormon Polygamous Passage* (Urbana: University of Illinois Press, 1992), 175–76. When Mary became pregnant with her first child, which served as evidence that she was a plural wife, she went into hiding. Chamberlain, "Sketch of My Life," 170, 172–73, 175–76.
18. Chamberlain, "Sketch of My Life," 181–82.
19. Royal Reward Chamberlain (1902–1951) and Edwin Dilworth "Dee" Chamberlain (1905–1999).
20. "On Sunday, October 29, 1916, I asked the secretary of the Sunday School, Ila Hamblin, to change my name on the roll and call it that day, which she did. And I want to say right here that it was an embarrassing ordeal for all of us, and it took a lot of stamina to face the music. But I was more than thankful to have it over with and to be recognized as my real self, after living under an assumed name for sixteen long years." Chamberlain, "Sketch of My Life," 223.
21. Mary W. Howard to Susa Young Gates, October 19, 1913, Holograph, p. 6, listed as "Kanab Woman Mayor, 1913," Correspondence, History of Women Files, Susa Young Gates Papers, 1870–1933, Church History Library, The Church of Jesus Christ of Latter-day Saints, Salt Lake City, Utah, hereafter cited as Church History Library.

22. Mary is mistaken in this claim. While her leadership of the first all-female town council is undisputed, the title of "first female mayor" belongs to Susanna Madora Salter of Argonia, Kansas, elected in 1887. See Kylie Nielson Turley, "The Politics of Politics: Remembering Mary Woolley Chamberlain, Mayor of Kanab," in *New Scholarship on Latter-day Saint Women in the Twentieth Century*, ed. Carol Cornwall Madsen and Cherry B. Silver (Provo, UT: Joseph Fielding Smith Institute for Latter-day Saint History, 2005), 40.
23. The other members of the board included Ada Pratt Seegmiller and Blanche Robinson Hamblin; Tamar Stewart Hamblin, clerk; Luella Atkin McAllister, treasurer. Vinnie Farnsworth Jepson was initially elected to the town council but resigned at the first meeting of the new board and was replaced by Seegmiller. Caroline Roundy also served briefly as town clerk. See Kylie Nielson Turley, "Kanab's All Woman Town Council, 1912–1914: Politics, Power Struggles, and Polygamy," *Utah Historical Quarterly* 73 (Fall 2005): 309.
24. Mary W. Howard, "An Example of Women in Politics," *Improvement Era* 17 (July 1914): 865–68. The original letter is listed as "Kanab Woman Mayor, 1913," History of Women Files, Susa Young Gates Papers, 1870–1933, Church History Library. It includes a comprehensive list of the improvements and ordinances enacted under Mary's leadership. In her letter to Susa, Mary remarked: "It is a noted fact that nine tenths of the people never knew before who the members of the Town Board were or that there even was a Board, but you can ask any child on the street who the present Board is and they can tell you every one of our names for we are discussed in every home for good or *ill*."
25. Chamberlain, "Sketch of My Life," 212–13, 219.
26. Chamberlain, "Sketch of My Life," 229–30.
27. Chamberlain, "Sketch of My Life," 243–53.
28. See Kimball, *Handmaiden of the Lord*, 11–12.
29. Turley, "Politics of Politics," in *New Scholarship*, 39–49.
30. A reference to the story "The Last Leaf" by O. Henry, pen name of William Sydney Porter (1862–1910).
31. Chamberlain, "Sketch of My Life," 222.

Chapter 4: Ruth May Fox

1. Ruth May Fox, "My Story," 1953, Photocopy of original typescript, Church History Library, The Church of Jesus Christ of Latter-day Saints, Salt Lake City, Utah, hereafter cited as Church History Library. An annotated volume of Ruth's autobiography and diaries, tentatively titled *Carry On: The Personal Writings of Ruth May Fox,* ed. Brittany A. Chapman (Salt Lake City: University of Utah Press), is forthcoming. For additional information regarding Ruth's migration to Utah, see Ruth May Fox, "From England to Salt Lake Valley in 1867," *Improvement Era* 38, no. 7 (July 1935): 406–9, 450.
2. Ruth May Fox, "An Acrostic to My Husband," 1889, May Blossoms Volume Two, comp. Leonard Grant Fox (unpublished manuscript, 1966), p. 450, Church History Library. Before the Salt Lake Temple was completed in 1893, several buildings in Salt Lake City were used for the administration of temple ordinances. One such building was the Endowment House, which was in operation from 1855 to 1889. Lamar C. Berrett, "Endowment Houses," in *Encyclopedia of Mormonism*, ed. Daniel H. Ludlow, 4 vols. (New York: Macmillan, 1992), 2:456.
3. Jesse May Fox (1874–1947), Eliza May Fox (1876–1878), George James Fox (1877–1959), Ruth Clare Fox Taylor (1879–1961), Feramorz Young Fox (1881–1957), Hyrum Lester Fox (1883–1978), Esther Vida Fox Clawson (1885–1976), Frank Harding Fox (1887–1975), Lucy Beryl Fox Evenson (1890–1972), Leonard Grant Fox (1892–1983), Florence Marie Fox MacKay (1894–1982), and Emmeline Blanche Fox (1896–1914).
4. Fox, "My Story," 31.
5. Florence Fox MacKay, Interview by William G. Hartley, July 1, 1981, Salt Lake City, Utah, Typescript, p. 7, Church History Library. In her autobiography, Rosemary Johnson Fox included a detailed description of events preceding her marriage. Rosemary Johnson Fox Johnson, "Highlights from the Life of Rosemary Johnson Fox Johnson," comp. Edith Ivins Lamoreaux, in *Three Lives Reach Forward in Time: Ruth May Fox, Jesse Williams Fox Jr., Rosemary Johnson Fox Johnson,* ed. Merilyn Fox Alexander (West Valley City, UT: privately printed, 1996), sec. 3:21. Original letters written by Jesse to Rose during their courtship and early marriage are extant

and in private possession. Typescripts of the letters are published in Alexander, *Three Lives Reach Forward in Time*, sec 3:43–211.
6. See *Salt Lake City Directory* (Salt Lake City, UT: R. L. Polk, 1884–1914, 1924–1928); 1880–1900 U.S. Federal Census, Salt Lake City, Salt Lake County, Utah; 1910 U.S. Federal Census, Farmer, Salt Lake County, Utah.
7. Ruth May Fox, Notes, n.d., Holograph, p. 1, Book of Remembrance, vol. 2, private possession.
8. Fox, "My Story," 68.
9. Fox, "My Story," 70. For an account of Ruth's experience writing "Carry On," see Rachel Grant Taylor and Elsie Hogan Van Noy, "The Story of 'Carry On,'" in Ruth May Fox, "My Story: Supplemented by Miscellaneous Articles Pertaining to Her Life," comp. Leonard Grant Fox, 1973, Church History Library.
10. Fox, "My Story," 57.
11. Fox, "My Story," 72.
12. The name of the Young Ladies' MIA was changed to Young Women's MIA in 1934.
13. Albert E. Bowen, "The Paradise of the Pacific Welcomes the M.I.A.," *Improvement Era* 39 (October 1936): 603.
14. Ruth May Fox, "My Hawaiian Trip," 1936, Holograph, Book of Remembrance, vol. 2, private possession.
15. Ruth's children Hyrum Lester Fox and Lucy Beryl Fox Evenson lived in the Los Angeles area with their families.
16. Jeanette Hyde, a member of the Relief Society general board from 1913 to 1929, died unexpectedly "in the meetinghouse on Saturday afternoon as she sat with the Relief Society sisters in their conference." Bowen, "Paradise," 604.
17. In 1915, Ruth wrote a poem entitled "A Temple in Hawaii." It was published in the *Improvement Era* and set to music by Orson Clark, a missionary laboring in the Hawaiian Mission. It became a popular anthem among the Hawaiian Saints as the temple was being built; it was dedicated in 1919. Dean Clark Ellis, "A Temple in Hawaii" (paper, Annual Meeting of the Mormon Pacific Historical Society, Laie, Hawaii, March 20, 2010). Ruth M. Fox, "A Temple in Hawaii," *Improvement Era,* December 1915, 116; Conference Report, April 1916, 36–37. For words and music, see "A Temple in Hawaii," *Young Woman's Journal* 31, no. 2 (June 1916): 383–84.

18. Emma Lucy Gates Bowen, daughter of Susa Young Gates, accompanied her husband, Albert, to the Hawaiian Islands. Emma Lucy had had a successful career as an opera singer in Europe and North America and recorded with Columbia Records.
19. W. Frank Bailey, president of the Hawaiian Mission, and his wife, Cassander Debenkam Bailey.
20. Green and gold were the colors of the Mutual Improvement Associations.
21. "Much of the time we were high above the clouds," Albert Bowen wrote. "Always far below were the sparkling waters of the blue Pacific. As Sister Fox expressed it, 'the world was upside down.'" Bowen, "Paradise," 605.
22. From 1921 to 1922, Hugh J. Cannon, editor of the *Improvement Era*, a Church magazine, and David O. McKay, then an apostle, toured around the world to meet with the Latter-day Saints in the South Pacific, Europe, and the Middle East. While in Hawaii on February 8, 1921, they, with two other missionaries, prayed powerfully under a pepper tree and received a sacred vision of Cannon's father, George Q. Cannon, and Joseph F. Smith, two former missionaries in Hawaii. George Q. Cannon himself had prayed under a tree as a young missionary in Hawaii and saw "the greatness of the work to be done among the native inhabitants of those islands." "A Faith Promoting Incident on the Hillside of Haleakala," in *Cherished Experiences from the Writings of President David O. McKay*, comp. Clare Middlemiss (Salt Lake City, UT: Deseret Book, 1955), 50–52; Bowen, "Paradise," 605–6.
23. YWMIA class for young women aged seventeen to twenty-three.
24. See chapter 1 herein. Maud May Babcock was on an extended visit to Hawaii.
25. Ed was Edwin Evenson, husband of Ruth's daughter Beryl; "Katharan" was Cathie Irene Evans, wife of Ruth's son Lester.
26. Young women aged fourteen through sixteen.
27. Fox, "My Story," 75.
28. Ruth May Fox, June 8, 1937, "M.I.A. Trails," in Treasures of Truth, 2 vols. (unpublished manuscript), private possession, 2:5.
29. Fox, "My Story," 75.
30. Speaking in the MIA June conference just hours before the Centennial Party departed, Ruth "expressed her great pleasure at being permitted

to return to visit her native land. She had left England as a child of eleven. She said all her life she had longed again to travel the green lanes of England and to see the beautiful green fields with their buttercups and daisies." Lucy Grant Cannon, "The Log of a European Tour with President Grant and the Centennial Party," *Improvement Era* 40 (August 1937): 482.

31. "On this occasion," wrote Amy Brown Lyman, then first counselor in the Relief Society general presidency, Ruth "gave such an eloquent and stirring address that it thrilled the souls and touched the hearts of all of us who had the good fortune to be in attendance, and brought tears to the eyes of many." Amy Brown Lyman, quoted in Fox, "My Story," 76.

32. For additional information about the European Tour, see Lucy Grant Cannon, "The Log of a European Tour," *Improvement Era* 40 (August 1937): 482–83, 517; (September 1937): 533, 578, 589, 590–91; (October 1937): 598–99, 627, 644, 648, 650–51; (November 1937): 688–89, 697, 708–10, 712; Parry D. Sorensen, "After One Hundred Years in Britain," *Improvement Era* 40 (September 1937): 540–42, 576; Heber J. Grant, Conference Report, October 1937, 123–34; Clarissa A. Beesley Collection, 1863–1973, Church History Library.

33. Fox, "My Story," 76.

34. Young Women General Board minutes, November 3, 1937, Church History Library.

35. Young Women's Mutual Improvement Association Minutes and Records, August 21, 1905, Saint Johns Arizona Stake, Church History Library.

36. Young Women's Mutual Improvement Association Minutes and Records, August 25, 1901, Vernal Utah Uintah Stake, Church History Library.

37. Ninetieth birthday party placard, 1943, private possession.

Chapter 5: Susa Amelia Young Dunford Gates

1. Susa Young Gates, "Lucy Bigelow Young," Typescript, pp. 53–54, Susa Young Gates Papers, 1852–1932, Utah State Historical Society, Salt Lake City, Utah, hereafter cited as Utah State Historical Society.

2. Susa Young Gates to Zina D. H. Young, May 5, 1888, Holograph, Susa Amelia Young Gates Papers, ca. 1870–1933, Church History

Library, The Church of Jesus Christ of Latter-day Saints, Salt Lake City, Utah, hereafter cited as Church History Library.

3. "Original S.S. letter abt. Testimony," Typescript, n.p., Susa Young Gates Papers, 1852–1932, Utah State Historical Society.
4. The children of Susa and Alma Dunford were Leah Eudora Dunford Widtsoe (1874–1965) and Alma Bailey Dunford Jr. (1875–1895).
5. The children of Susa and Jacob Gates were Emma Lucy Gates Bowen (1880–1951), Jacob Young Gates (1882–1887), Karl Nahum Gates (1883–1887), Simpson Mark Gates (1885–1885), Joseph Sterling Gates (1886–1891), Brigham Cecil Gates (1887–1941), Harvey Harris Gates (1889–1948), Sarah Beulah Gates (1891–1898), Franklin Young Gates (1893–1979), Heber Gates (1894–1894), Brigham Young Gates (1896–1900).
6. Susa Young Gates to Young Ladies' Mutual Improvement Association Presidency, August 24, 1888, Holograph, Susa Amelia Young Gates Papers, ca. 1870–1933, Church History Library.
7. Susa Young Gates, Diary, October 1, 1888, Holograph, Susa Amelia Young Gates Papers, ca. 1870–1933, Church History Library.
8. Alma 34:27.
9. Gates, Diary, October 28, 1888.
10. Gates, Diary, November 6, 1888. Susa was about six months pregnant at this time.
11. Gates, Diary, February 14, 1888. It is not clear whether he meant coal oil or consecrated oil. Susa frequently mentions in her diary using consecrated oil as a healing balm.
12. Gates, Diary, entry dated "Wednesday" [February 22, 1888].
13. Gates, Diary, entry dated "Sunday" [February 26, 1888]. Karl died on March 2.
14. Gates, Diary, February 22, 1888.
15. "The Little Missionary," chapter XVIII, *Juvenile Instructor* 34, no. 19 (October 1, 1899), 595. "The promise" Susa refers to in the Word of Wisdom—the Latter-day Saint code of health—is that "the destroying angel shall pass by them [those that keep the Word of Wisdom], as the children of Israel, and not slay them." Doctrine and Covenants 89:21.
16. "The Little Missionary," chapter XIX, *Juvenile Instructor* 34, no. 21 (November 1, 1899), 653–54. This installment appears to be mislabeled, as the previous one is also numbered chapter XIX.

17. A contemporary diary entry by a fellow missionary corroborates Joseph F. Smith's dream. Matthew Noall journal, March 9, 1887, Matthew Frederick and Claire Wilcox Noall Papers, Special Collections, J. Willard Marriott Library, University of Utah.
18. Susa Young Gates, Typescript, pp. 9–10, Susa Young Gates Papers, 1852–1932, Utah State Historical Society.
19. Gates to Young, May 5, 1888.
20. Susa Young Gates, "Hail and Farewell," *Young Woman's Journal* 40, no. 10 (October 1929), 676.
21. Susa Young Gates, *Why I Believe the Gospel of Jesus Christ* (Salt Lake City: Deseret News Press, n.d.), 3, Utah State Historical Society.
22. Gates, *Why I Believe*, 27.
23. Gates, *Why I Believe*, 28.

Chapter 6: Sarah Ann Taylor Howard

1. Sarah Ann Taylor Howard, "History of Thomas Taylor and Mary Ann Danley (Taylor)," 1931, Typescript, p. 4, private possession.
2. Howard, "History of Thomas Taylor and Mary Ann Danley (Taylor)," 2; "Jedediah Morgan Grant," Joseph Smith Papers, The Church of Jesus Christ of Latter-day Saints, accessed April 16, 2013, http://josephsmithpapers.org/person/jedediah-morgan-grant.
3. Lee R. Taylor, "A History of Zachariah Sherdick Taylor," 1951, Typescript, p. 9, private possession.
4. Howard, "History of Thomas Taylor and Mary Ann Danley (Taylor)," 2.
5. Sarah Ann Taylor Howard, "Some Events of My Life," ca. 1933, Typescript, 1, private possession. For reasons unknown, Sarah was not baptized until age fourteen in Payson, Utah, on August 4, 1870.
6. Leonidas DeVon Mecham, "Life Sketch of Sarah Ann Taylor Howard," ca. 1929, Typescript, 3, private possession.
7. Howard, "History of Thomas Taylor and Mary Ann Danley (Taylor)," 2. See also Henry G. Boyle to Editor, *Deseret News,* July 3, 1869, in "Correspondence," *Deseret News [Weekly],* July 21, 1869. Sarah traveled with nearly one hundred members of the Surry County Branch, which included members of the Taylors' extended family.
8. Before the Salt Lake Temple was completed in 1893, several buildings in Salt Lake City were used for the administration of temple ordinances. One such building was the Endowment House, which

was in operation from 1855 to 1889. Lamar C. Berrett, "Endowment Houses," in *Encyclopedia of Mormonism*, ed. Daniel H. Ludlow, 4 vols. (New York: Macmillan, 1992), 2:456. Howard Street received its name from the many children and grandchildren of Samuel's parents, Joseph and Ann Shelton Howard, who built homes on the street. Originally part of Woods Cross, Utah, the area became known as South Bountiful about 1896. Fifty years later, in 1946, Howard Street became Main Street in North Salt Lake, Utah.

9. Mecham, "Life Sketch," 4; Nina Howard Gerber, Interview by Karol G. Chase, 1995, Bountiful, Utah.
10. Sarah Howard Cheney, Interview by Karol G. Chase, 2010, Kaysville, Utah.
11. Samuel Cyrus Howard (1878–1941), Lydia Ann Howard Schulthies (1880–1969), William Henry Howard (1882–1945), Royal Franklin Howard (1885–1885), Arthur Lee Howard (1886–1961), David Edward Howard (1889–1957), and Amasa Ray Howard (1891–1971).
12. Lydia Ann Howard Schulthies, "Notes from a History Written by Lydia Ann Howard Schulthies," 1954, Typescript, p. 4, private possession.
13. Schulthies, "Notes," p. 4.
14. "W.S.A. Reports," *Woman's Exponent* 20, no. 19 (April 15, 1892): 150. Samuel, also a woman's rights advocate, attended the first meeting of the South Bountiful Woman Suffrage Association, where he said he "was willing that his wife should stand side by side with him in 'equal rights.'"
15. Mecham, "Life Sketch," 4.
16. Daughters of Utah Pioneers, South Davis County Company, *East of Antelope Island*, 3rd ed. (Salt Lake City, UT: Publishers Press, 1969), 348.
17. Schulthies, "Notes," 2.
18. Howard, "Some Events of My Life," 1.
19. Mecham, "Life Sketch of Sarah Ann Taylor Howard," 3.
20. In 1890, Wilford Woodruff delivered a manifesto advising Latter-day Saints "to refrain from contracting any marriage forbidden by the law of the land." This Manifesto led to the end of the practice of plural marriage in the Church. Doctrine and Covenants, Official Declaration 1. Plural marriages entered into after the Second

Manifesto in 1904 were viewed with particular disdain. According to his grandson, Samuel was severely reprimanded by ecclesiastical leaders for his post-Manifesto marriage, but, for unknown reasons, he was not excommunicated as other men had been. D. Hatch Howard, Interview by Karol Gerber Chase, 2010, Woods Cross, Utah.

21. *1909 Salt Lake City Directory* (Salt Lake City, UT: R. L. Polk, 1909). Samuel's second marriage "was not looked on with favor by . . . the children and created some distance between Samuel and his family although there was still visits and communication between him [and] other family members." Paul L. Howard, "Samuel Shelton Howard—A Brief History," 1986, Typescript, private possession.

22. For example, in her journal, Sarah wrote on October 3, 1925, "Willie & his father came out to paint fence in front of house." On October 9, she wrote, "Sammie, Willie, David & their father had dinner with me, they were looking at some sheep at Stock Yards." Sarah A. Howard, Journal, 1919–1927, Holograph, private possession.

23. The California Mission, like other Latter-day Saint missions of the time, was divided into several large districts, called conferences, each led by its own president.

24. Mutual was the weekly meeting of the Young Men's and Young Ladies' Mutual Improvement Associations, the Church's organizations for adolescent youth, now known simply as Young Men and Young Women.

25. Wilford W. Richards was president of the San Francisco Conference.

26. Joseph W. McMurrin was president of the California Mission from 1919 to 1932.

27. Sarah A. Howard, Journal, 1919–1927, Holograph, private possession. See also California Los Angeles Mission, Manuscript History and Historical Reports, 1846–1973, vol. 3, Church History Library, The Church of Jesus Christ of Latter-day Saints, Salt Lake City, Utah.

28. Howard, "Some Events of My Life," 2.

Chapter 7: Lorena Eugenia Washburn Larsen

1. Bent Franklin Larsen, *Memories of My Father, Bent Rolfsen Larsen* (Provo, UT: n.p., 1963), 2.
2. Lorena Eugenia Washburn Larsen, "Life Sketch of Lorena Eugenia Washburn Larsen," ca. 1939, Holograph, p. 79, Willard and Celia

Luce Collection, L. Tom Perry Special Collections, Harold B. Lee Library, Brigham Young University, Provo, Utah. Because the manuscript was a work in progress, pages were added in places after the initial drafting, requiring such pagination as 145–1 and 145–2, meaning that for a page added between 144 and 146, the first side would be numbered 145–1 and the second side 145–2. After page 155, Lorena started over with page 146. Thus 149 [159] means that the page is marked with page number 149 but is actually page 159.

3. Larsen, "Life Sketch," 144.
4. L. E. W. Larsen, "Mother Reminiscences," unpublished manuscript, p. 327, private possession.
5. Larsen, "Life Sketch," 88–1.
6. Larsen, "Life Sketch," 144, 145–1.
7. Larsen, "Life Sketch," 97.
8. Larsen, "Life Sketch," 145–1, 146.
9. Lorena Larsen to Bent Rolfsen Larsen, June 4, 1882, Holograph, private possession.
10. Larsen, "Life Sketch," 114.
11. Larsen, "Life Sketch," 117.
12. Larsen, "Life Sketch," 125.
13. Larsen, *Memories of My Father*, 2–3.
14. Larsen, "Life Sketch," 130, 131–1.
15. Larsen, "Life Sketch," 149.
16. Larsen, "Life Sketch," 149 [159].
17. Larsen, "Life Sketch," 151–2, 152.
18. Larsen, "Life Sketch," 164–65.
19. Larsen, "Life Sketch," 168.
20. Larsen, "Life Sketch," 205.
21. Larsen, "Life Sketch," 198.
22. Larsen, "Life Sketch," 214–15.
23. Larsen, "Life Sketch," 239–41.
24. Bent Franklin Larsen (1882–1970), Ida Lorena Larsen Bartholomew (1885–1918), Charlottie Eugenia Larsen Robison (1886–1963), Enoch Rolf Larsen (1889–1972), Floy Isabel Larsen Turner (1892–1973), Pearl Larsen Bartholomew (1893–1955), Ella Almeda Larsen Turner (1896–1969), Clarence Abraham Larsen (1898–1950), Fern Emma Larsen Mellor (1901–1999).
25. Larsen, *Memories of My Father*, 12.

26. Floy L. Turner, *Lorena Eugenia Washburn Larsen, a Mother in Israel* (Provo, UT: J. Grant Stevenson, 1969), 36g.
27. Bent Franklin Larsen, "Memories of My Father, Bent Rolfsen Larsen," draft manuscript, ca. 1962.
28. Larsen, *Memories of My Father,* 24.
29. Larsen, *Memories of My Father,* 24–25.
30. Turner, *Lorena Eugenia Washburn Larsen,* 70.
31. Turner, *Lorena Eugenia Washburn Larsen,* 50.
32. Glen H. Turner, comp., *Memories of Grandma Larsen* (n.p.: privately printed, ca. 1970), 27–28.
33. Larsen, "Life Sketch," 170–76 [180–86].
34. Bent Franklin Larsen, "My Mother, Lorena Eugenia Washburn Larsen," in Loretta Luce Evans, *Lorena Eugenia Washburn Larsen, 1860–1945* (Provo, UT: n.p., 2008), 155.
35. Larsen, "Life Sketch," 177 [187].

Chapter 8: Mary Roselia Cook McCann

1. Mary had two brothers, David Savage Cook (1858–1924) and Joseph Cook (1866–1867), and a large number of half-siblings. Her mother, Amanda Polly Savage Cook, was a plural wife of Phineas W. Cook. Mary was a twin; her sister died a month after their birth.
2. Mrs. Hyrum J. McCann, "A Sketch of My Life for Jean," Holograph, Utah State Historical Society, Salt Lake City, Utah, 2.
3. McCann, "Sketch of My Life," 3.
4. McCann, "Sketch of My Life," 3–5.
5. The Logan Temple was dedicated in May 1884, giving thousands of members of the Church easier access to temple ordinances. The only other temple in operation at the time was the St. George Temple, in southern Utah.
6. McCann, "Sketch of My Life," 6–9, 11, 14–16. On blessing by women, see Jonathan A. Stapley and Kristine Wright, "Female Ritual Healing in Mormonism," *Journal of Mormon History* 37, no. 1 (Winter 2011): 1–85.
7. McCann, "Sketch of My Life," 18.
8. McCann, "Sketch of My Life," 34–35.
9. McCann, "Sketch of My Life," 39.
10. A half brother to Hyrum, Thomas Newell Ravenhill McCann was the son of Elizabeth Sant McCann, another wife of Thomas Ravenhill

McCann, father of Hyrum and Tom. Eunice Teeples McCann, Tom's wife, was the daughter of one of Mary's half sisters.
11. McCann, "Sketch of My Life," 40–42, 45–46, 52–56, 59–60, 62–70.
12. Hyrum David McCann (1884–1959), Joseph Arthur McCann (1885–1894), Stella McCann Spencer (1887–1975), Rozella McCann Erickson (1890–1966), Vera McCann Erickson (1892–1979), Laurence McCann (1894–1976), Loys McCann (1896–1982), Lorell McCann (1899–1967), and Jean McCann Obray (1904–1994).
13. McCann, "Sketch of My Life," 73–77.
14. "Chauncey Loveland Dustin (1863–1937) and Mrs. Mary Roselia Cook Mccann," Utah, County Marriages, 1887–1937, Index, FamilySearch, The Church of Jesus Christ of Latter-day Saints, accessed April 17, 2013, https://familysearch.org/pal:/MM9.1.1/X21F-VJG.
15. The immediate cause of death was cardiovascular disease.
16. 1880 U.S. Census, Garden City, Rich County, Utah; 1900 U.S. Census, Cokeville, Uinta County, Wyoming; 1910 U.S. Census, Garden City, Rich County, Utah; 1920 U.S. Census, [n.p.], Cache County, Utah; 1930 U.S. Census, Logan, Cache County, Utah; 1940 U.S. Census, Logan, Cache County, Utah.

Chapter 9: Elizabeth Ann Claridge McCune

1. Polly Aird, "Bound for Zion: The Ten- and Thirteen-Pound Emigrating Companies, 1853–54," *Utah Historical Quarterly* 70, no. 4 (Fall 2002): 300–25.
2. S. George Ellsworth, *Samuel Claridge: Pioneering the Outposts of Zion* (Logan, UT: n.p., 1987), 12–35; Samuel Claridge, Autobiography, ca. 1910, Typescript, Church History Library, The Church of Jesus Christ of Latter-day Saints, Salt Lake City, Utah, hereafter cited as Church History Library.
3. "The Story of Telegraphy," in *Heart Throbs of the West,* ed. Kate B. Carter, 4 vols. (Salt Lake City, UT: Daughters of Utah Pioneers, 1947), 4:182–87.
4. "From an Adobe Hut to a Mansion of Brick and Stone," *Deseret Evening News,* June 6, 1903.
5. "From an Adobe Hut." The better-known account of this experience comes from Susa Young Gates, *Memorial to Elizabeth Claridge McCune: Missionary Philanthropist, Architect* (Salt Lake City, UT:

n.p., 1924), but the account in the *Deseret Evening News* is much earlier and less heavily edited, thus preserving Elizabeth's voice more accurately.

6. Elizabeth's mother and sister remained in Nephi the first year while Elizabeth, her brother, and her father and his second wife made a home for their family.
7. "From an Adobe Hut."
8. "From an Adobe Hut."
9. Ann M. Cannon, "Our New Home," *Young Woman's Journal* 21, no. 4 (April 1910): 181. A hod is a box often used for carrying mortar.
10. Gates, *Memorial*, 17. See chapter 5 herein.
11. Before the Salt Lake Temple was completed in 1893, several buildings in Salt Lake City were used for the administration of temple ordinances. One such building was the Endowment House, which was in operation from 1855 to 1889. Lamar C. Berrett, "Endowment Houses," in *Encyclopedia of Mormonism*, ed. Daniel H. Ludlow, 4 vols. (New York: Macmillan, 1992), 2:456.
12. Alfred and Elizabeth's children were Alfred William McCune (1873–1923), Harry Berthrand McCune (1874–1874), Earl Vivian McCune (1875–1906), Raymond McCune (1878–1955), Sarah Fay McCune Naylor (1880–1966), Frank Claridge McCune (1882–1887), Lottie Jacketta McCune Quealey (1884–1964), Matthew Marcus McCune (1889–1939), Elizabeth Claridge McCune Trower (1891–1967).
13. George M. McCune, ed., *Matthew McCune Family History*, vol. 2AB (Salt Lake City, UT: McCune Family Association, 1993), 382–91.
14. See Gates, *Memorial*, 85; John P. Hatch, ed., *Danish Apostle: The Diaries of Anthon Lund* (Salt Lake City, UT: Signature Books, 2006), 433.
15. Gates, *Memorial*, 84.
16. For a life sketch of Elizabeth interwoven with a tour of the home, see Carol Ann S. Van Wagoner, "Elizabeth Ann Claridge McCune: At Home on the Hill," in *Worth Their Salt: Notable but Often Unnoted Women of Utah*, ed. Colleen Whitley (Logan: Utah State University Press, 1996), 89–100.
17. Susa Young Gates, "Biographical Sketches: Mrs. Elizabeth Claridge McCune," *Young Woman's Journal* 9, no. 8 (August 1898): 339.
18. Gates, "Biographical Sketches," 342–43.

19. "Biographical Sketches: Jennie Brimhall and Inez Knight," *Young Woman's Journal* 9, no. 6 (June 1898): 245. For more on Elizabeth's missionary experience in England, see Matthew S. McBride, "I Could Have Gone into Every House," Church History, The Church of Jesus Christ of Latter-day Saints, accessed July 10, 2013, http://history.lds.org/article/elizabeth-mccune-missionary.
20. Gates, "Biographical Sketches," 339–40.
21. Elizabeth C. McCune, "Peru and Pioneer Life," *Improvement Era* 6, no. 10 (August 1903): 755.
22. McCune, "Peru and Pioneer Life," 755.
23. Elizabeth C. McCune to Susa Young Gates, ca. 1922, Holograph, Susa Young Gates Papers, Church History Library.
24. Gates, *Memorial*, 79.
25. While some have assumed Alfred W. McCune was not a Latter-day Saint, he was baptized in Nephi in November 1857. He and Elizabeth were married in the Endowment House in Salt Lake City on July 1, 1872. This privilege required a letter of recommendation from Bishop Joel Grover of Nephi attesting that the two were "members of the Church and worthy" of the privilege. See McCune, *Matthew McCune Family History*, 457n5, 458n23. For most of his adult life, however, Alfred was not a practicing member and chose to remain aloof from the Church.
26. Elizabeth Claridge McCune to Julia Claridge Ellsworth, November 25, 1923, Typescript, Samuel Claridge Research Files, S. George Ellsworth Papers, Special Collections and Archives, Merrill-Cazier Library, Utah State University, Logan.
27. Susa Young Gates to Alfred W. McCune, April 26, 1918, Carbon copy, Susa Young Gates Papers.
28. Elizabeth Claridge McCune to Susa Young Gates, August 28, 1918, Susa Young Gates Papers. The letter sent by Susa highlighted remarks of Don B. Colton, president of the Uintah Stake.
29. Gates, *Memorial*, 27.
30. Claridge, Autobiography, 13–16. For more on genealogical missions, see Jessie L. Embry, "Missionaries for the Dead: The Story of the Genealogical Missionaries of the Nineteenth Century," *BYU Studies* 17, no. 3 (1977): 355–60.
31. Samuel Claridge to Elizabeth Claridge McCune, June 4, 1907, Holograph, Susa Young Gates Papers.

32. Samuel Claridge to Elizabeth Claridge McCune, March 27, 1902, p. 4, Typescript, Samuel Claridge Research Files.
33. Claridge to McCune, March 27, 1902, p. 3.
34. Orson F. Whitney, "Elizabeth Ann Claridge McCune," *History of Utah,* 4 vols. (Salt Lake City, UT: George Q. Cannon & Sons, 1904), 4:606.
35. Claridge to McCune, March 27, 1902, 2.
36. "Elizabeth Ann Claridge McCune," in Andrew Jenson, *Latter-day Saint Biographical Encyclopedia,* 4 vols. (Salt Lake City, UT: Andrew Jenson History Company, 1901–36), 2:668; Lula Greene Richards, "A Happy Remembrance," *Relief Society Magazine* 11, no. 10 (October 1924): 496; Gates, *Memorial,* 27.
37. Susa Young Gates, untitled typescript, Susa Young Gates Files, Church History Library. The typescript is a draft history of genealogical work by women in Utah. For more information about the Relief Society's role in the expansion of genealogical research in the Church, see James B. Allen and Jessie L. Embry, "Provoking the Brethren to Good Works: Susa Young Gates, Genealogy, and the Relief Society," *BYU Studies* 31 (Spring 1991): 115–38. For instances of Elizabeth's teaching genealogical courses, see "Lecture Tomorrow," *Deseret News,* February 25, 1908, and "The April Conference," *Relief Society Magazine* 3, no. 6 (June 1916): 311–12.
38. "Mrs. M'Cune Talks to Mesa People," undated news clipping accompanying letter from Elizabeth C. McCune to Susa Young Gates, March 15, 1907, Susa Young Gates Papers.
39. Elizabeth C. McCune to Susa Young Gates, October 18, 1918, Holograph, Susa Young Gates Papers. One Sunday in September each year was set aside for the discussion of genealogy and temple work. See "Suggestions for Genealogical Sunday," *Utah Genealogical and Historical Magazine* 7, no. 3 (July 1916): 153.
40. Elizabeth Claridge McCune to Susa Young Gates, August 28, 1918, Holograph, Susa Young Gates Papers.
41. Susa Young Gates to Elizabeth Claridge McCune, September 4, 1918, Carbon copy, Susa Young Gates Papers.
42. Hatch, *Danish Apostle,* 267.
43. Fay Tarlock, "The Visitors," *Relief Society Magazine* 35, no. 3 (March 1948): 170.

44. Ann M. Cannon, "Our New Home," *Young Woman's Journal* 21, no. 4 (April 1910): 179–81.
45. Elizabeth C. McCune to Susa Young Gates, November 13, 1919, Holograph, Susa Young Gates Files.
46. Elizabeth C. McCune to President Heber J. Grant and Counsel, October 7, 1920, Draft copy, Susa Young Gates Files. The next day, an official donation letter with slightly different wording was read over the pulpit in general conference and signed "A. W. McCune, Elizabeth A. C. McCune." This earlier draft clearly identifies Elizabeth as the instigator of the donation. "President Heber J. Grant," Conference Report, October 1920, 2.
47. "President Heber J. Grant," Conference Report, October 1920, 2.
48. Emmeline B. Wells et al. to Mr. and Mrs. A. W. McCune, November 10, 1920, Susa Young Gates Files.
49. Susa Young Gates to Elizabeth C. McCune, November 26, 1920, Susa Young Gates Files.
50. See "President Heber J. Grant," Conference Report, April 1921, 141; Donald George Schaefer, "Contributions of the McCune School of Music and Art to Music Education in Utah, 1917–1957" (master's thesis, Brigham Young University, 1962).
51. For a report of Elizabeth's funeral and burial services, see Gates, *Memorial*, 59–71.

Chapter 10: Tsune Ishida Nachie

1. Alma O. Taylor to Sanford W. Hedges and William R. Fairbourn, July 26, 1905, Japan Mission letterpress copybooks, Church History Library, The Church of Jesus Christ of Latter-day Saints, Salt Lake City, Utah, hereafter cited as Church History Library. See also Alma O. Taylor to Erastus L. Jarvis, August 3, 1905; Alma O. Taylor to Yoshiro Oyama, August 4, 1905; and Alma O. Taylor to Augusta W. Grant, August 4, 1905, Japan Mission letterpress copybooks.
2. Alma O. Taylor to Joseph E. Featherstone, September 15, 1905, Japan Mission letterpress copybooks.
3. Reid L. Neilson, "The Japanese Missionary Journals of Elder Alma O. Taylor, 1901–1910" (master's thesis, Brigham Young University, 2001), July 30, 1905, hereafter cited as Alma O. Taylor journal.

4. Alma O. Taylor to Augusta W. Grant, August 4, 1905, Japan Mission letterpress copybooks.
5. Fred A. Caine to John W. Stoker and others, October 3, 1905, Japan Mission letterpress copybooks.
6. Alma O. Taylor journal, August 22, 1905. Taylor's entry for September 26, 1905, records that Tsune had asked for baptism some weeks before, probably during her first conversation with Caine.
7. Alma O. Taylor journal, December 17, 1903.
8. Fred A. Caine to John W. Stoker and others, October 3, 1905, Japan Mission letterpress copybooks.
9. Alma O. Taylor to First Presidency, October 26, 1905, Japan Mission letterpress copybooks.
10. Alma O. Taylor to Sandford W. Hedges and William R. Fairbourn, October 26, 1905, Japan Mission letterpress copybooks.
11. Alma O. Taylor to John W. Stoker and others, December 8, 1905, Japan Mission letterpress copybooks.
12. Alma O. Taylor to Sandford W. Hedges and William R. Fairbourn, December 27, 1905, and Alma O. Taylor to John W. Stoker and others, January 1, 1906, Japan Mission letterpress copybooks.
13. Alma O. Taylor journal, December 19, 1906. The entry for January 5, 1908, records Tsune Nachie's "retirement" from teaching Sunday School.
14. Alma O. Taylor journal, September 23, 1906.
15. Alma O. Taylor journal, December 19, 1907. At the time he consecrated the oil, Elder Taylor believed it was the first time that it had been done in Japanese. He later learned of one earlier instance.
16. Alma O. Taylor journal, January 1, 1908.
17. Alma O. Taylor journal, March 17, 1906.
18. Alma O. Taylor journal, January 12, 1908.
19. Alma O. Taylor journal, March 26, 1908.
20. Joseph H. Stimpson to Edwin J. Allen, March 11, 1916, Japan Mission letterpress copybooks, in which Tsune declined to hire additional help for the Tokyo office.
21. Joseph H. Stimpson to Val W. Palmer, April 10, 1918, Japan Mission letterpress copybooks.
22. Joseph H. Stimpson to Val W. Palmer, June 6, 1918, Japan Mission letterpress copybooks.

23. Joseph H. Stimpson to Bryan L. Wright, March 31, 1920, Japan Mission letterpress copybooks. In this case, Tsune had been asked by a girl's mother "to look after her, and she has done so," and unless certain conditions were met, "she (Sister Nachie) will not let her return" to Kofu and her former employment there. "It seems to me that Sister Nachie's argument is pretty well founded . . . and I know Sister Nachie has her welfare at heart," Stimpson wrote.
24. Joseph H. Stimpson to Elders, April 26, 1916, Japan Mission letterpress copybooks, with similar warnings in the programs for other years.
25. Alma O. Taylor journal, November 30, 1905.
26. Joseph H. Stimpson to Joseph S. Pyne, September 23, 1920, Japan Mission letterpress copybooks.
27. Japan Mission missionary area journals, 1905–1924, Kofu, Japan Mission, Church History Library.
28. Alma O. Taylor journal, December 26, 1907 and December 28, 1908.
29. Alma O. Taylor journal, December 4 and 13, 1906.
30. Joseph H. Stimpson to Brother Takanashi, October 7, 1916; Joseph H. Stimpson to Alma O. Taylor, September 7, 1917; Joseph H. Stimpson to Elbert D. Thomas, July 24, 1918. Japan Mission letterpress copybooks are among many examples of Tsune Nachie's *yoroshiku* messages.
31. Stimpson to Thomas, July 24, 1918.
32. Alma O. Taylor journal, September 17, 1907.
33. General Minutes, Tokyo District, Japan Tokyo Mission, 1921–1923, Church History Library. Available minutes from 1920–1922 are probably representative of her contributions throughout her Church membership and show her participation virtually every week. For nightly Book of Mormon study in 1919, see General Minutes, Japanese Mission, 1901–1955, Church History Library.
34. Alma O. Taylor journal, March 17, 1906.
35. Joseph H. Stimpson to Alma O. Taylor, August 3, 1916, Japan Mission letterpress copybooks.
36. Joseph H. Stimpson to Joseph F. Smith, March 21, 1917, Japan Mission letterpress copybooks. Hisa Udagawa's vicarious baptism was performed in the Laie Hawaii Temple on June 5, 1923—the same day Tsune Nachie received her endowment there.

37. Lloyd O. Ivie to Whom It May Concern, June 26, 1922, Japan Mission letterpress copybooks. This letter was a request for permission from the Japanese government for Tsune Nachie's emigration.
38. Lloyd O. Ivie to Hilton A. Robertson, June 14, 1922, Japan Mission letterpress copybooks.
39. Honolulu, Hawaii, Passenger and Crew Lists, 1900–1959, Ancestry.com, accessed July 22, 2013, www.ancestry.com.
40. "Ishida Tsune Nachie," Family Search, The Church of Jesus Christ of Latter-day Saints, accessed October 19, 2013, https://new.familysearch.org.
41. "Hawaiians Adopt Former Japanese Mission Mother," *Church News*, November 25, 1933.
42. 1930 U.S. Census, Koolauloa, Honolulu, Hawaii. Tsune is identified as "missionary for a church."
43. Edward Lavaun Clissold, interview by R. Lanier Britsch, 1976, Salt Lake City, Utah, Typescript, Church History Library.

Chapter 11: Emily Sophia Tanner Richards

1. Annie Wells Cannon, *In Memoriam: Emily Sophia Tanner Richards* (Salt Lake City, UT?: n.p., 1929), 7, Church History Library, The Church of Jesus Christ of Latter-day Saints, Salt Lake City, Utah, hereafter cited as Church History Library; "Willard Richards Company, 1848," Mormon Pioneer Overland Travel Database, The Church of Jesus Christ of Latter-day Saints, accessed October 22, 2013, http://mormontrail.lds.org.
2. "Emily S. Richards," in Andrew Jenson, *Latter-day Saint Biographical Encyclopedia*, 4 vols. (Salt Lake City, UT: Andrew Jenson History Company, 1901–36), 2:701.
3. Cannon, *In Memoriam*, 12.
4. Cannon, *In Memoriam*, 8.
5. Cannon, *In Memoriam*, 15. See also Virginia H. Pearce, "'In Blessing Others We Are Blessed': Sarah Melissa Granger Kimball," in *Women of Faith in the Latter Days, Volume 1, 1775–1820*, ed. Richard E. Turley Jr. and Brittany A. Chapman (Salt Lake City, UT: Deseret Book, 2011), 115–28.
6. See Meghan M. Mathews, "'She Went About Doing Good': Jane Snyder Richards," in *Women of Faith in the Latter Days, Volume 2,*

1821–1845, ed. Richard E. Turley Jr. and Brittany A. Chapman (Salt Lake City, UT: Deseret Book, 2012), eBook edition, 524–39.

7. Charles C. Richards, "Funeral Services," August 22, 1929, in Cannon, *In Memoriam*, 38.
8. Jane S. Richards, Jane S. Richards Autobiographical Sketch, 1881, Microfilm of holograph, Church History Library, 7; Richards, "Funeral Services," 39.
9. Richards, "Funeral Services," 39.
10. Richards, Autobiographical Sketch, 8.
11. Richards, Autobiographical Sketch, 8.
12. Richards, Autobiographical Sketch, 12; Cannon, *In Memoriam*, 10.
13. Young Women's Mutual Improvement Association Minutes and Records, July 20, 1882, North Ogden Ward, Ben Lomond Stake, Church History Library.
14. Cannon, *In Memoriam*, 11.
15. Cannon, *In Memoriam*, 12.
16. Emily S. Richards, "General Conference Relief Society," *Woman's Exponent* 30, no. 7 (December 1, 1901): 54.
17. Cannon, *In Memoriam*, 23.
18. Cannon, *In Memoriam*, 11.
19. "Emily S. Richards," in Brigham Young University Building Dedication Files, 1892–2006, 21, L. Tom Perry Special Collections, Harold B. Lee Library, Brigham Young University, Provo, Utah. For additional information about the 1886 memorial, see Orson F. Whitney, *History of Utah*, 4 vols. (Salt Lake City, UT: George Q. Cannon and Sons, 1895): 4:589; "'The Rotunda'—Kirtland—the 'Memorial,'" *Woman's Exponent* 14, no. 22 (April 15, 1886): 169–70.
20. Jean Bickmore White, "Women's Suffrage in Utah," *Utah History Encyclopedia*, ed. Allan Kent Powell (Salt Lake City: University of Utah Press, 1994), accessed July 10, 2013, http://www.uen.org/utah_history_encyclopedia/w/WOMENS_SUFFRAGE_IN_UTAH.html
21. For a history of Utah women's entrance into national suffrage associations, see Carol Cornwall Madsen, ed., *Battle for the Ballot: Essays on Woman Suffrage in Utah, 1870–1896* (Logan: Utah State University Press, 1997); Carol Cornwall Madsen, *An Advocate for Women: The Public Life of Emmeline B. Wells, 1870–1920* (Provo, UT: Brigham Young University Press; Salt Lake City, UT: Deseret Book, 2006);

Lola Van Wagenen, *Sister-Wives and Suffragists: Polygamy and the Politics of Woman Suffrage 1870–1896* (Provo, UT: BYU Studies and the Joseph Fielding Smith Institute, 2003); and Jill Mulvay Derr, Janath Russell Cannon, and Maureen Ursenbach Beecher, *Women of Covenant: The Story of Relief Society* (Salt Lake City, UT: Deseret Book Company; Provo, UT: Brigham Young University Press, 1992): 132–38.

22. Cannon, *In Memoriam,* 17; see also Jenson, *Latter-day Saint Biographical Encyclopedia,* 2:700.
23. Cannon, *In Memoriam,* 21.
24. Cannon, *In Memoriam,* 22.
25. Cannon, *In Memoriam,* 22.
26. For a copy of the endorsement, see Wilford Woodruff, George Q. Cannon, and Joseph F. Smith to "Whom It May Concern," May 9, 1893, Elmina S. Taylor Collection, Church History Library. For reference to Emily's receiving a similar letter, see Jenson, *Latter-day Saint Biographical Encyclopedia,* 2:700.
27. Andrea G. Radke-Moss, "Mormon Women, Suffrage and Citizenship at the 1893 Chicago World's Fair," in *Gendering the Fair: Histories of Women and Gender at World's Fairs,* ed. T. J. Boisseau and Abigail M. Markwyn (Urbana: University of Illinois Press, 2010), 104.
28. Emily S. Richards, "The Legal and Political Status of Woman in Utah," in *The World's Congress of Representative Women,* ed. May Wright Sewall (Chicago, IL: Rand, McNally, 1894), 913–15.
29. *Chicago Inter Ocean,* June 18, 1893, in Newspaper Clippings, Charles E. Johnson Collection, Special Collections and Archives, Merrill-Cazier Library, Utah State University, Logan.
30. Cannon, *In Memoriam,* 25.
31. Cannon, *In Memoriam,* 25.
32. Kathryn L. MacKay, comp., "Chronology of Woman Suffrage in Utah," in *Battle for the Ballot: Essays on Woman Suffrage in Utah, 1870–1896,* ed. Carol Cornwall Madsen (Logan: Utah State University Press), 316.
33. Cannon, *In Memoriam,* 16.
34. For more on Emily's and other Utah suffragists' participation in the Utah constitutional convention, suffrage discussions, political alignments and disagreements, see Madsen, *Battle for the Ballot*; Madsen, *An Advocate for Women,* 324–55; Van Wagenen, *Sister-Wives and*

Suffragists; and Beverly Beeton, *Women Vote in the West: The Woman Suffrage Movement, 1869–1896* (New York: Garland Publishing, 1986).

35. Emily S. Richards, "Woman Suffrage in Utah," *Deseret News [Weekly]*, February 15, 1896; reprinted in *Collected Discourses: Delivered by President Wilford Woodruff, his Two Counselors, The Twelve Apostles, and Others, 1886–1898*, ed. Brian H. Stuy, vol. 4 (Burbank, CA: B.H.S. Publishing, 1991), 419–23.
36. Cannon, *In Memoriam*, 17.
37. Cannon, *In Memoriam*, 12.
38. Cannon, *In Memoriam*, 12.
39. Cannon, *In Memoriam*, 13.
40. The Mothers' Congress of Utah (1903) was the Utah chapter of the National Congress of Mothers, organized in 1897 by Alice McLellan Birney and Phoebe Apperson Hearst to foster American mothers' involvement in educational reform, improved child rearing, and the Kindergarten movement. It was the forerunner to the National Parent-Teacher Association.
41. Cannon, *In Memoriam*, 14. For more on the National Congress of Charities and Corrections, see John E. Hansan, "National Conference of Charities and Correction (1874–1917): Forerunner of the National Conference of Social Welfare," The Social Welfare History Project, accessed July 10, 2013, http://www.socialwelfarehistory.com/organizations/national-conference-of-charities-and-correction-the-beginning/.
42. The Reapers' Club (1892–1912) was a women's literary organization founded by Emmeline B. Wells and dedicated to the "social and intellectual development" of its members. "Utah Federation of Woman's Clubs," *Woman's Exponent* 25 (June 1, 1896): 1; Sharon Snow Carver, "Salt Lake City's Reapers' Club," *Utah Historical Quarterly* 64 (Spring 1996): 108–20; "A Historic House," *Woman's Exponent* 21 (December 15, 1892): 92.
43. "Emily S. Richards," in BYU Building Dedication Files, 21; Cannon, *In Memoriam*, 14.
44. Emily S. Richards and Minnie J. Snow to Stake Presidents of Relief Society and Young Ladies Mutual Improvement Associations, May 1, 1907, Relief Society Circular Letter, Church History Library, Salt Lake City, Utah. The circular included a suggested program outline

for local peace meetings, advising on décor, music, and poetry, and questions for discussion.
45. Jenson, *Latter-day Saint Biographical Encyclopedia*, 2:704.
46. Franklin S. Richards, "Address Delivered to the High Priests Quorum of Ensign Stake," November 13, 1932, Typescript, p. 38, Church History Library.
47. "Emily Sophia Richards," 1929, State of Utah Death Certificate, no. 1489.
48. Jenson, *Latter-day Saint Biographical Encyclopedia,* 2:704.

Chapter 12: Sarah Louisa Yates Robison

1. Janath R. Cannon, "Louise Yates Robison," in *Encyclopedia of Mormonism*, ed. Daniel H. Ludlow, 4 vols. (New York: Macmillan, 1992), 3:1237–38; Janet Peterson and LaRene Gaunt, *Faith, Hope, and Charity* (American Fork, UT: Covenant Communications, 2008), 138.
2. Thomas J. Yates, "Elizabeth Francis Yates," Church History Library, The Church of Jesus Christ of Latter-day Saints, Salt Lake City, UT, hereafter cited as Church History Library; Our Families Roots, accessed Dec. 6, 2013, http://ourfamiliesroots.org/sketches/1901.htm. Thomas J. Yates, "Thomas Yates," Our Families Roots, accessed June 17, 2013, http://www.ourfamiliesroots.org/sketches/5180.htm.
3. Louise Yates Robison, Address, March 1944, Relief Society Birthday Party, Sunset Ward, San Francisco Stake, pp. 1–2, Gladys R. Winter Scrapbooks, Church History Library.
4. Manuscript History and Historical Reports, 1861–1983, Scipio Ward, Millard Stake, Church History Library.
5. Robison, Address, March 1944, 2–3; Dorothy R. Bosquet, "Louise Yates Robison," in *History of Relief Society: General Presidents of the Relief Society* (Salt Lake City, UT: Corporation of the President of The Church of Jesus Christ of Latter-day Saints, 1987), 1.
6. Robison, Address, March 1944, 1; Peterson and Gaunt, *Faith, Hope, and Charity,* 126–27, 30.
7. Bosquet, "Louise Yates Robison," 1; Peterson and Gaunt, *Faith, Hope, and Charity,* 128.
8. Robison, Address, March 1944, 3.
9. Robison, Address, March 1944, 3; Peterson and Gaunt, *Faith, Hope, and Charity,* 126–27.

10. Robison, Address, March 1944, 4.
11. Robison, Address, March 1944, 4; Peterson and Gaunt, *Faith, Hope, and Charity,* 129.
12. Robison, Address, March 1944, 4–5.
13. Peterson and Gaunt, *Faith, Hope, and Charity,* 132–33.
14. Peterson and Gaunt, *Faith, Hope, and Charity,* 131.
15. Bosquet, "Louise Yates Robison," 1.
16. Gladys R. Winter, "Mother in Her Home," Gladys R. Winter Scrapbooks, 7, Church History Library.
17. "Louisa Y. Robison," Heritage Halls biographical sketches, 1, Church History Library.
18. Robison, Address, March 1944, 5.
19. Peterson and Gaunt, *Faith, Hope, and Charity,* 132.
20. Robison, Address, March 1944, 5; Bosquet, "Louise Yates Robison," 5; "Louisa Y. Robison," Heritage Halls biographical sketches, 2; Peterson and Gaunt, *Faith, Hope, and Charity,* 130, 133.
21. Bosquet, "Louise Yates Robison," 6; Robison, Address, March 1944, 6. The Gardo House, once located immediately south of the Beehive House on the corner of South Temple and State Streets, was an elegant home designed as an official residence for Brigham Young. It was not completed until after his death, however, and although John Taylor lived in the home at one point, it was later turned over to the city. In 1917, the Red Cross occupied the building. Sandra Dawn Brimhall and Mark D. Curtis, "The Gardo House," in *Brigham Young's Homes,* ed. Colleen Whitley (Logan: Utah State University Press, 2002), 173–201.
22. Jennie Brimhall Knight, "Louise Yates Robison," *Relief Society Magazine* 16 (January 1929): 4–5.
23. Winter, "Mother in Her Home," 7.
24. Gladys R. Winter, "Mother in the General Presidency of the Relief Society," Gladys R. Winter Scrapbooks, [1], Church History Library.
25. Winter, "Mother in the General Presidency," [1]; Robison, Address, March 1944, 5.
26. Winter, "Mother in the General Presidency," [1].
27. Relief Society Women's Auxiliary of the Church of Jesus Christ of Latter-day Saints, *A Centenary of Relief Society, 1842–1942* (Salt Lake City, UT: General Board of Relief Society, 1942), 31; Jill Mulvay Derr, Janath Russell Cannon, Maureen Ursenbach Beecher, *Women*

of Covenant: The Story of Relief Society* (Salt Lake City, UT: Deseret Book; Brigham Young University Press, 1992), 262–64; Peterson and Gaunt, *Faith, Hope, and Charity,* 132; Cannon, "Louise Yates Robison," 3:1238; Knight, "Louise Yates Robison," 5.
28. Knight, "Louise Yates Robison," 5.
29. Derr, Cannon, and Beecher, *Women of Covenant,* 248.
30. Belle S. Spafford, Interview by Jill Mulvay Derr, 1975–76, Salt Lake City, Utah, Typescript, p. 40, Church History Library.
31. Kate M. Barker, "Louise Y. Robison," *Relief Society Magazine* 27 (February 1940): 79.
32. "The Fundamental Purpose of Our Work Days," *Relief Society Magazine* 23 (January 1936): 51.
33. "Officers' Meeting," *Relief Society Magazine* 22 (May 1935): 272.
34. Louise Y. Robison, "Official Instructions," *Relief Society Magazine* 19 (November 1932): 653.
35. "Tribute to Louise Y. Robison," Given at a luncheon for Sister Robison by the Relief Society board, May 26, 1945, Church History Library.
36. Louise Y. Robison, "The Spirit of Relief Society Work," Radio address given on KSL Radio, March 20, 1938, Church History Library; Peterson and Gaunt, *Faith, Hope, and Charity,* 136; *A Centenary of Relief Society,* 32; Thomas J. Yates, "Thomas Yates," Church History Library.
37. Winter, "Mother in the General Presidency," [4]; Helen Bay Gibbons, "Highlights in the History of Mormon Women and Music," Church History Library.
38. "To the Relief Society," *Relief Society Magazine* 19 (December 1932): 703.
39. Derr, Cannon, and Beecher, *Women of Covenant,* 262–64; Winter, "Mother in the General Presidency," [7].
40. "Sister Louise Y. Robison," Conference Report, October 1929, 84.
41. "President Louise Y. Robison Speaks at General Conference," *Relief Society Magazine* 17 (January 1930): 27–28. The other two women to bear testimony were Ruth May Fox, president of the Young Ladies' Mutual Improvement Association, and May Anderson, president of the Primary Association.
42. Peterson and Gaunt, *Faith, Hope and Charity,* 132–33.

43. Robison, Address, March 1944, 6; "Louisa Y. Robison," Heritage Halls biographical sketches, 3.
44. Janet Peterson and LaRene Gaunt, *Elect Ladies* (Salt Lake City, UT: Deseret Book, 1990), 124.
45. Robison, Address, March 1944, 7; Peterson and Gaunt, *Faith, Hope, and Charity,* 138; Kate M. Barker, "Louise Y. Robison," *Relief Society Magazine* 27 (February 1940): 77–80.
46. "Funeral Services for Louise Yates Robison," Church History Library; Winter, "Mother in the General Presidency," [11–12]; "Mrs. Robison, Church Leader, Dies on Coast," *Deseret News,* April 1, 1946; "Mrs. Robison's Funeral Slated for Tomorrow," *Deseret News,* April 3, 1946.
47. Barker, "Louise Y. Robison," 80; Peterson and Gaunt, *Faith, Hope, and Charity,* 139.
48. Barker, "Louise Y. Robison," 80; "Tribute to Louise Y. Robison."
49. Spafford, Interview by Derr, 40.

Chapter 13: Annie Marie Woodbury Romney

1. Eleanor Farnsworth Bentley, "A Glimpse into the Life of Annie Marie Woodbury Romney" (unpublished manuscript, private possession, n.d.), introduction.
2. Ella J. Seegmiller, "Reminiscences of Annie M. W. Romney," 1928, Typescript, International Society Daughters of Utah Pioneers, Pioneer Memorial Museum, Salt Lake City, Utah.
3. Jennifer Moulton Hansen, ed., *Letters of Catharine Cottam Romney, Plural Wife* (Urbana: University of Illinois Press, 1992), xi.
4. Miles and Annie Romney's children were Ann Cannon Romney Clayson (1879–1955), Alice Lambert Romney Hurst (1881–1923), Orin Nelson Romney (1884–1965), Erastus Snow Romney (1886–1920), Eleanor Romney Farnsworth (1888–1956), Ivie Romney Richardson (1890–1975), Erma Romney Haymore (1893–1922), and Frank Romney (1897–1983).
5. Thomas Cottam Romney, *Life Story of Miles P. Romney* (Independence, MO: Zion's Printing, 1948), 113; Hansen, *Letters,* 32.
6. Romney, *Life Story,* 114.
7. Annie Romney Call, comp., *Life and Family of Orin Nelson Romney and Alberta Farnsworth Romney, 1884–1965* (Provo, UT: privately printed, 1984), 8.

8. Call, *Life and Family,* 9–10. Annie's letters have been photocopied and bound with life sketches of herself and her children. The original letters, however, have not been available since the 1980s. Apparently Ella Farnsworth Bentley was the last keeper of these letters, but since her death, their whereabouts are unknown.
9. Call, *Life and Family,* 10.
10. Annie Woodbury Romney to Eleanor Woodbury Jarvis, August 31, 1884, in Call, *Life and Family,* 11.
11. Call, *Life and Family,* 10.
12. Hansen, *Letters,* x.
13. Bentley, "Glimpse," 6.
14. Nelle Spilsbury Hatch, *Colonia Juarez: An Intimate Account of a Mormon Village* (Salt Lake City, UT: Deseret Book, 1954), 150; Albert Kenyon Wagner and Leona Farnsworth Wagner, *The Juarez Stake Academy, 1897–1997: The First One Hundred Years* (Colonia Juarez, Mexico: The Academy, 1997).
15. Call, *Life and Family,* 17.
16. Call, *Life and Family,* 21.
17. This earthquake did in fact result in additional much-needed water in the Mormon colonies. Call, *Life and Family,* 21. For more on this topic, see Annie R. Johnson, *Heartbeats of Colonia Diaz* (Salt Lake City, UT: Publishers Press, 1972), 85.
18. Call, *Life and Family,* 24.
19. Call, *Life and Family,* 25.
20. Bentley, "Glimpse," 11.
21. Bentley, "Glimpse," 12.
22. Call, *Life and Family,* 31.
23. Bentley, "Glimpse," 13–14.
24. This quotation and those that follow are from Ella Farnsworth Bentley, "Life Story of Wilford Martindale Farnsworth and Eleanor Romney Farnsworth" (unpublished manuscript, private possession, ca. 1990), 14–16.
25. Bentley, "Glimpse," 27.
26. Bentley, "Life Story," 19.
27. Bentley, "Glimpse," 24.
28. Hansen, *Letters,* xiii.

29. Emily Harmon, "Biographical Sketch of Annie M. W. Romney" (student paper, Dixie Normal College, 1917–1918), International Society Daughters of Utah Pioneers.
30. Hansen, *Letters,* xiii.

Chapter 14: Ellis Reynolds Shipp

1. "Ellis Reynolds," Mormon Overland Travel Database, 1847–1868, The Church of Jesus Christ of Latter-day Saints, accessed July 8, 2013, http://mormontrail.lds.org.
2. The Walker War (1853–1854) was a conflict between the Ute Indians and settlers in the small communities of central Utah. The Ute leader's name was Wakara, pronounced "Walker" by some.
3. Ellis R. Shipp, "In the Year of 1852," biographical fragment, Holograph, p. 9, Ellis Reynolds Shipp Papers, 1875–1955, Utah State Historical Society, Salt Lake City, hereafter cited as Shipp Papers.
4. Ellis R. Shipp, "Sketches from the Student Life of Ellis R. Shipp, M. D.," Typescript, April 1, 1881, p. [1], Shipp Papers.
5. Shipp, "Sketches from Student Life," 4; Ellis R. Shipp, Autobiography, Holograph, pp. 11–14, Shipp Papers.
6. Ellis R. Shipp, "Third Book of Life Sketches: All in the Rough," Holograph, p. 12a, Shipp Papers. Ellis wrote this life sketch in an account book whose facing pages have the same page number. To distinguish one page from another, they are cited "a" and "b."
7. Shipp, "Third Sketch," 9b–10a.
8. Shipp, "Sketches from Student Life," 1.
9. Shipp, "Third Sketch," 12a.
10. Milford Bard Shipp (1867–1919), William Austin Shipp (1868–1868), Richard Asbury Shipp (1869–1936), Anna Shipp (1872–1872), Bert Reynolds Shipp (1873–1879), Olea Shipp Hill (1877–1954), Ellis Reynolds Shipp Musser (1879–1966), Ambrose Pere Shipp (1882–1883), Paul Elbert Shipp (1885–1885), Nellie Shipp McKinney (1889–1966).
11. Shipp, "Third Sketch," 17a.
12. Ellis R. Shipp, "The Diary (1871 to 1878)," in *While Others Slept: Autobiography and Journal of Ellis Reynolds Shipp*, ed. Ellis Shipp Musser (Salt Lake City, UT: Bookcraft, 1985), 69.
13. Shipp, "Third Life Sketch," 50a.
14. "The Diary (1871–1878)," *Her Diary,* 172.

15. Shipp, "Life of Dr. Ellis Shipp," Typescript, p. 8, Shipp Papers.
16. Shipp, "Life," 5.
17. Ellis Shipp to Ellis Musser, 1935, Typescript, p. 12, Shipp Papers.
18. Shipp, "Third Life Sketch," 49b–50a.
19. Shipp, "Third Life Sketch," 50a.
20. Shipp, "Life," 6–7.
21. Shipp, "Third Sketch," 52b; "Life of Dr. Ellis Shipp," 7.
22. Ellis R. Shipp, "Late Autobiography (1878–1939)," in *Her Diary: The Early Autobiography and Diary of Ellis Reynolds Shipp, M.D.*, ed. Ellis Shipp Musser (Salt Lake City, UT: Deseret News Press, 1962), 285.
23. "Late Biography," *Her Diary,* 282–83.
24. Handwritten sheet by Olea Shipp Hill, Ellis Reynolds Shipp Manuscript Collection, Utah State Historical Society, Salt Lake City, Utah, as quoted in Susan Evans McCloud, *Not in Vain* (Salt Lake City, UT: Bookcraft, 1984), 186.
25. "Love Divine" in *Life Lines: Poems by Ellis Reynolds Shipp, M.D.* (Salt Lake City, UT: Skelton Publishing, 1910), 40.

Chapter 15: Edith Ann Smith

1. "The Unveiling," *Improvement Era* 21, no. 10 (August 1918): 856. Originally, Junius Wells had planned for his daughter, Abbie, to unveil the monument. "President Smith and Party at the Dedication Ceremonies," *Deseret Evening News,* December 23, 1905. This "telegraphic" report was probably prepared before the dedication.
2. Susa Young Gates, "Memorial Monument Dedication—I," *Improvement Era* 9, no. 4 (February 1906): 317.
3. Edith's obituaries state that there were fifteen siblings in the family. Lucy Brown Smith had four children, of whom Edith was the youngest. The other eleven appear to have been the children of Edith's father's plural wife, Amy Jane King Smith. In addition, Edith mentioned that her mother took in and raised a Swiss boy named Rudolph Zupinger. Edith Ann Smith, Descendants of John and Edith Atterton Brown, ca. 1947, Holograph, p. 6, Church History Library, The Church of Jesus Christ of Latter-day Saints, Salt Lake City, Utah, hereafter cited as Church History Library.
4. Elias Smith, Journal, August 5, 1861, comp. Sarah C. Thomas, Typescript, vol. 1, Church History Library.

5. Manuscript History and Historical Reports, September 17, 1873, Seventeenth Ward, Salt Lake Stake, Church History Library. When the young girls of the Seventeenth Ward (Edith presumably among them) initially went to their bishop requesting that they might be organized into their own society, the bishop met their first request "somewhat coldly" and with a bit of confusion. The girls returned a second time, and he agreed and allowed them to form their Juvenile Relief Society. Though the details are somewhat limited, 1873 appears to be the year of its organization. This was after the reorganization of the Relief Society in 1867 and the formal organization of the Young Ladies' Department of the Ladies' Cooperative Retrenchment Association in 1870. The Primary was not organized until 1878, though all three organizations were closely related. "R. S. Reports," *Woman's Exponent* 6, no. 18 (February 15, 1878): 138; Carol Cornwall Madsen and Susan Staker Oman, *Sisters and Little Saints: One Hundred Years of Primary* (Salt Lake City, UT: Deseret Book, 1979), 3–4.
6. "R. S. Reports," 138.
7. Elias Smith, Journal, October 30, 1876. Edith was fifteen; her sixteen-year-old half sister, Rebecca Jane Smith, received her endowment the same day. This practice was not unusual at that time. Emmeline B. Wells noted in her diary that her daughters Elizabeth Ann Wells and Louise Martha Wells received their endowment at the age of fourteen. Emmeline B. Wells, Diary, September 14, 1874, and October 13, 1876, L. Tom Perry Special Collections, Harold B. Lee Library, Brigham Young University, Provo, Utah, hereafter cited as BYU Special Collections. During the years before the Salt Lake Temple was dedicated in 1893, several buildings were used for the administration of temple ordinances. One such building was the Endowment House, which was in operation from 1855 to 1889. LaMar C. Berrett, "Endowment Houses," in *Encyclopedia of Mormonism*, ed. Daniel H. Ludlow, 4 vols. (New York: Macmillan, 1992), 2:456.
8. "Honoring our beloved grandfather Joseph F. Smith and his wife 'Aunt' Mary Taylor Smith and 'Cousin' Edith A. Smith," 1949, n.p., BYU Special Collections; Isaac B. Ball, "Pioneering Families of Joseph Smith's Uncles," *Improvement Era* 53, no. 3 (March 1950): 235; Richard R. Lyman, "The Indians and the Wild West," *Improvement Era* 27, no. 1 (November 1923): 5; *Deseret News,* June 28, 1954;

Salt Lake Tribune, June 28, 1954; Gates, "Memorial Monument Dedication," 317. Edith's short autobiographical sketch is the foundation for this biographical sketch and is supplemented by other sources. Smith, Descendants, 16–17.

9. Edith A. Smith, *A Sit Down Strike for Love* (Salt Lake City, UT: Mutual Improvement Association, Deseret News Press, n.d.).
10. Edith Ann Smith, Journal and Scrapbook, Holograph, p. 108, Church History Library.
11. A memorial cottage was built on the original site of the Smith home in Sharon, Vermont, and functioned as a visitors' center for tourists. The hearth stone was thought to have been "saved from the ruins of the old [Smith] home." Angus J. Cannon, "The Joseph Smith Memorial Farm," *Improvement Era* 32, no. 3 (January 1929): 196.
12. The Joseph Smith Memorial Monument is a granite obelisk thirty-eight and a half feet high, each foot representing one year of Joseph Smith's life. A program preceded the ceremonial unveiling of the monument, with Joseph F. Smith offering a dedicatory prayer. The monument is now called the Joseph Smith Birthplace Memorial.
13. Junius F. Wells, a member of the Young Men's Mutual Improvement Association general board, directed the construction of the monument.
14. Edith Ann Smith, Journal, pp. 1, 19–22, 32–33, 36–37. For more information about the monument and its dedication, see Conference Report, April 1906, 52–58; *Proceedings at the Dedication of the Joseph Smith Memorial Monument* ([Salt Lake City, UT?], 1906?); Gates, "Memorial Monument Dedication," 308–19; Susa Young Gates, "Memorial Monument Dedication—II," *Improvement Era* 9, no. 5 (March 1906): 375–89; Kathleen Flake, "Re-placing Memory: LDS Use of Historical Monuments in Narrative in the Early 20th Century," *Religion and American Culture: A Journal of Interpretation* 13, no. 1 (Winter 2003): 76–82, 92–94.
15. Edith Ann Smith, Journal, 100–9.
16. Edith Ann Smith, Journal, 193.
17. Gates, "Memorial Monument Dedication," 378.
18. When Edith's father, Elias, died on June 24, 1888, Edith observed that the funeral was, fittingly, held on June 27. The date was obviously meaningful to her.

Chapter 16: Ellen Johanna Larson Smith

1. Ellen Johanna Larson Smith, "Life Sketch of Mons Larson," ca. 1940, Microfilm of typescript, p. 5, Church History Library, The Church of Jesus Christ of Latter-day Saints, Salt Lake City, Utah, hereafter cited as Church History Library.
2. Smith, "Life Sketch," 7.
3. Ellen Johanna Larson Smith, [Autobiography], in *The Kinsman* 19, no. 2 (February 1965): 4.
4. Ellen J. Smith, Autobiography, 1962 July–August, Transcription of oral history, p. 4, Church History Library.
5. Melvin Frost and Ethel S. Randall, comp., "Ellen Johanna Larson Smith," 1959, Typescript, p. [2], in Ellen Smith, *Original & Selected Poems* (privately printed, 1959), Church History Library.
6. Smith, "Life Sketch," 4.
7. Smith, [Autobiography], in *The Kinsman*, 5; Silas Derryfield Smith, "Life Story," in *Silas Derryfield Smith, 1867 to 1956: Memories of a Mormon Pioneer*, comp. Derryfield N. Smith, Ethel Smith Randall, and Seraphine Smith Frost (Mesa, AZ: privately printed, 1970), 33.
8. Smith, "Life Story," in *Silas Derryfield Smith*, 34.
9. Smith, "Life Story," in *Silas Derryfield Smith*, 34–35.
10. Ellen Johanna Larson Smith, [Personal History], 1958, Transcription of sound recording, p. 2, in author's possession.
11. Smith, "Life Story," in *Silas Derryfield Smith*, 37.
12. Smith, "Life Story," in *Silas Derryfield Smith*, 32.
13. Ellen and Silas's children were Silas Reuel Smith (1887–1920), Ethel Smith Randall (1889–1976), Seraphine Smith Frost (1891–1989), Charity Smith (1893–1900), Mons Larson Smith (1895–1989), Alof Omni Smith (1898–1926), Josephine Smith Hackett (1900–1935), Mae Smith Pilon (1905–1986), Ellen Smith Lyon (1910–1999).
14. Smith, "Life Story," in *Silas Derryfield Smith*, 40.
15. Frost and Randall, "Ellen," in *Original & Selected Poems*, [1].
16. Smith, "Life Story," in *Silas Derryfield Smith*, 62.
17. Smith, "Life Story," in *Silas Derryfield Smith*, 41.
18. Ellen Smith Lyon, [Reminiscences of Her Mother], 1958, Transcription of sound recording, p. 4, private possession.
19. Ellen L. Smith to Silas D. Smith, May 20, 1906, Holograph, private possession. See also Smith, [Autobiography], in *The Kinsman*, 5.
20. Smith, Autobiography, 8.

21. Collections of her glass plate negatives and photographs are located at the Church History Library in the Snowflake, Arizona, Glass Plate Negative Collection, ca. 1890–1915, and in the Silas and Ellen Smith Family Papers, ca. 1909–1970. Her work still hangs in homes of Snowflake residents and is found in family scrapbooks—a tribute to her ingenuity.
22. Silas D. Smith to Ellen L. Smith, July 1, 1930, Holograph, private possession.
23. Mae Smith Pilon, [Reminiscences], in *The Kinsman* 19, no. 2 (February 1965): 11.
24. Frost and Randall, "Ellen," in *Original & Selected Poems*, [2].
25. Ida S. Hendrickson, "Ellen Johannah Larson Smith," in *Silas Derryfield Smith*, 79.
26. Lyon, [Reminiscences], 4.
27. Derryfield N. Smith, *Maria Elizabeth Bushman Smith: The Life Story of Our Mother* (Altamonte Springs, FL: Maria E. B. and Silas D. Smith Family Association, 1982).
28. Ellen L. Smith to Silas D. Smith, July 17, 1930, Holograph, private possession.
29. Ellen L. Smith to Silas D. Smith, March 22, 1931, Holograph, private possession.
30. Ellen L. Smith to Silas D. Smith, May 8, 1930, Holograph, private possession.
31. Smith, Autobiography, 10.
32. Hyrum A. Hendrickson, "Life Sketch, Snowflake," January 15, 1965, Ellen Johanna Larson Smith Funeral Services, Transcription of sound recording, p. 1, in possession of author.
33. Clarence A. Frost, "Life Sketch, Utah," January 15, 1965, Ellen Johanna Larson Smith Funeral Services, 4.
34. Ida S. Hendrickson, "Ellen Johannah Larson Smith," 80. Dryland farming relies on natural rainfall without irrigation. It requires careful crop rotation and specialized tilling methods.
35. Proverbs 10:4. Hendrickson, "Life Sketch," [3].
36. Ellen L. Smith to Silas D. Smith, January 1, 1941, Holograph, private possession.
37. Smith, [Personal History], 3.
38. Lyon, [Reminiscences], 4.
39. Smith, "Life Story," in *Silas Derryfield Smith*, 68.

40. Smith, Autobiography, p. 10.
41. Henry L. Smith, "Life Sketch, Mesa," January 15, 1965, Ellen Johanna Larson Smith Funeral Services, 6–7.
42. Smith, Autobiography, 10.

Chapter 17: Julina Lambson Smith

1. "Alfred Boaz Lambson," *Utah Genealogical and Historical Magazine* 6 (1915): 145.
2. "Autobiography of Bathsheba W. Smith (1822–1910)," Typescript, Church History Library, The Church of Jesus Christ of Latter-day Saints, Salt Lake City, Utah, hereafter cited as Church History Library.
3. Julina Smith, March 15, 1927, Holograph Addendum written at the end of "Autobiography of Bathsheba W. Smith (1822–1910)," Typescript, p. 123, Church History Library.
4. Smith, Addendum, 123–24.
5. Julina Smith, "A Loving Tribute to Sarah Ellen Richards Smith," *Relief Society Magazine* 2 (May 1915): 215.
6. For a description of Joseph's relationship with Levira, see Scott G. Kenney, "Before the Beard: Trials of the Young Joseph F. Smith," *Sunstone* (November 2001): 28–35.
7. Smith, Addendum, 130.
8. In an 1867 letter to Brigham Young, Levira said Joseph F. Smith physically mistreated her. Joseph F. replied that he was trying to keep her from hurting herself. Whatever the nature of their relationship, Levira sued for divorce shortly after Joseph married Julina, claiming that he had taken a concubine and nullified their marriage. Julina's son Joseph Fielding Smith later said Levira divorced his father because she was disillusioned with polygamy. Joseph Fielding Smith, *Life of Joseph F. Smith* (Salt Lake City, UT: Deseret Book, 1999), 231; Levira Annette Smith to Brigham Young, 1867, Brigham Young Incoming Correspondence, quoted in Kenney, "Before the Beard," *Sunstone*, 30–31.
9. Julina L. Smith, Diary, Holograph, vol. 1, Julina L. Smith Papers, 1870–1933, Church History Library.
10. "The April Conference," *Relief Society Magazine* 3 (June 1916): 311.
11. Julina Lambson Smith to Sarah Ellen Richards Smith, May 20, 1885, Photocopy of holograph, Sarah Ellen R. Smith Collection, Church

History Library. Holograph photocopies of all letters to Sarah Ellen are located in the Sarah Ellen R. Smith Collection, Church History Library.
12. Smith, "Loving Tribute," 215.
13. Joseph F. Smith to Sarah E. Richards Smith, October 22, 1884.
14. Julina Lambson Smith to Joseph F. Smith, March 8, 1874, Holograph, Joseph F. Smith Papers, Church History Library.
15. Julina Lambson Smith to Joseph F. Smith, March 8, 1874.
16. Julina Lambson Smith to Joseph F. Smith, March 15, 1874, Holograph, Joseph F. Smith Papers, Church History Library.
17. Julina Lambson Smith to Sarah Ellen Richards Smith, August 12, 1886.
18. Julina Lambson Smith to Sarah Ellen Richards Smith, January 29, 1886.
19. Julina Lambson Smith to Sarah Ellen Richards Smith, May 20, 1885.
20. Julina Lambson Smith to Sarah Ellen Richards Smith, December 18, 1886.
21. Although federal marshals knew Joseph was a polygamist, they needed depositions and witnesses to prove that he was. The raids were meant to find evidence and to capture women and children who could then be questioned and forced to testify. During raids on individual houses, wives and children were forced to lie about their identities and hide in attics, cellars, and ditches to escape detection.
22. Joseph F. Smith to Sarah Ellen Richards Smith, March 11, 1885.
23. Julina L. Smith, Diary, February 21, 1886, Holograph, vol. 3, Julina L. Smith Papers, Church History Library.
24. Julina L. Smith, Diary, March 7, 1886.
25. Julina L. Smith, Diary, June 6, 1886.
26. Joseph F. Smith to Melissa Jane and Edna Lambson, June 12, 1870, copy at back of Julina L. Smith, Diary, after 1920s entries.
27. Julina Lambson Smith to Sarah Ellen Richards Smith, December 18, 1886.
28. Francis M. Gibbons, *Joseph F. Smith: Patriarch and Preacher, Prophet of God* (Salt Lake City, UT: Deseret Book, 1984), 153.
29. Joseph F. Smith, Diary, March 15, 1887, quoted in Gibbons, *Joseph F. Smith*, 153.
30. Gibbons, *Joseph F. Smith*, 156.
31. Smith, "Loving Tribute," 215.

32. Gibbons, *Joseph F. Smith*, 173–74.
33. Smith, "Loving Tribute," 216.
34. Smith, "Loving Tribute," 215.
35. Julina gave birth to Mercy Josephine (1867–1870), Mary Sophronia (1869–1948), Donette (1872–1961), Joseph Fielding (1876–1972), David Asael (1879–1952), George Carlos (1881–1931), Julina Clarissa (1884–1923), Elias Wesley (1886–1970), Emily Jane (1888–1982), Rachael (1890–1986), and Edith Eleanor (1894–1987). She adopted Edward Arthur (1858–1911) and Marjorie Virginia (1906–1994). Julina also considered herself the mother of the children of her sister wives. Sarah Ellen Richards had eleven children and Edna Lambson Smith ten; Alice Ann Kimball had four biological children and three adopted children; and Joseph's final wife, Mary Taylor Schwartz, had seven children.
36. Julina Lambson, "Journal," submitted to International Society of the Daughters of the Utah Pioneers, 3, quoted in Honey M. Newton, *Zion's Hope: Pioneer Midwives and Women Doctors of Utah* (Springville, UT: Cedar Fort Press, 2013), n.p.
37. Smith, "Loving Tribute," 215.
38. "Passing of Julina L. Smith," *Relief Society Magazine* 23 (February 1936): 130.
39. Smith, "Loving Tribute," 216.

Chapter 18: Lucy Emily Woodruff Smith

1. Lucy's mother, Emily Jane Smith Woodruff, passed away on May 8, 1878, in Salt Lake City. See "Emily Jane Woodruff," Utah Death Registers, 1847–1966. Lucy's paternal grandfather, Wilford Woodruff, at the time of her birth a member of the Quorum of the Twelve Apostles, later became president of The Church of Jesus Christ of Latter-day Saints. Her maternal grandfather, Elias Smith, was a cousin of the Prophet Joseph Smith. "Elias Smith," in Andrew Jenson, *Latter-day Saint Biographical Encyclopedia*, 4 vols. (Salt Lake City, UT: Andrew Jenson History Company, 1901–36), 1:719–22.
2. According to Francis M. Gibbons, Lucy lived with her paternal grandparents in Salt Lake City and was neighbor to George Albert Smith. Francis M. Gibbons, *George Albert Smith: Kind and Caring Christian, Prophet of God* (Salt Lake City, UT: Deseret Book, 1990), 5, 166. The 1880 United States Census indicates that Lucy lived with

her maternal grandparents. It apparently was not uncommon for her family members to reside in multiple households alternatively, for her youngest brother, Asahel, is recorded twice in the 1880 U.S. Census, first as living with his father and his father's second wife, Julia Spencer Woodruff, and second as living with his maternal grandparents. 1880 U.S. Census, Salt Lake City Ward 17, and Salt Lake City Ward 14, Salt Lake City, Utah.

3. George Albert Smith's father, John Henry Smith, had been called to serve a mission in England, and George was needed at home to help support the family. Gibbons, *George Albert Smith*, 5–6.
4. Lucy Woodruff, Journal, February 5, 1888, George Albert Smith Family Papers, University of Utah, quoted in *George Albert Smith*, Teachings of Presidents of the Church series (Salt Lake City, UT: The Church of Jesus Christ of Latter-day Saints, 2011), xv.
5. Lucy seldom used punctuation at the end of her sentences in her correspondence and journal, but she indicated the beginning of a new sentence by capitalizing the first letter of the first word. She also tended to omit the apostrophe with such words as "don't" or "won't." Punctuation has been added for ease of reading.
6. Lucy E. Smith to George Albert Smith, June 28, 1891, Photocopy of holograph, Church History Library, The Church of Jesus Christ of Latter-day Saints, Salt Lake City, Utah, hereafter cited as Church History Library.
7. Lucy E. Woodruff Smith, Diary, 1893 January–1894 February, Photocopy of holograph, Church History Library.
8. Lucy assisted George in his responsibilities as mission secretary by organizing and answering correspondence and performing other such tasks. Because she made entries in her diary every day, ellipsis points have not been used to indicate omitted entries.
9. A small town in Walker County, Georgia.
10. The Salt Lake Temple was dedicated on April 6, 1893, by President Wilford Woodruff.
11. The post–Civil War South was notorious for its anti-Mormon sentiment and its violence against missionaries, including the murder of one missionary, Joseph Standing, in 1879. Patrick Mason, *The Mormon Menace: Violence and Anti-Mormonism in the Postbellum South* (New York: Oxford University Press, 2011).

12. Lucy did not elaborate on her ailment or what operation she had to undergo.
13. A hospital designed for recuperation from surgery.
14. George accompanied the body of Elder Walter H. Barton back to Salt Lake City.
15. Gibbons, *George Albert Smith*, 34.
16. George and Lucy's three children: Emily Smith Stewart (1895–1973), Edith Smith Elliott (1899–1977), and George Albert Smith Jr. (1905–1969).
17. Susa Young Gates, *History of the Young Ladies' Mutual Improvement Association* (Salt Lake City, UT: Deseret News Press, 1911), 313–14.
18. See Lucy Emily Woodruff Smith, "Address of the President: To the Officers of the Relief Society of the European Mission," January 20, 1921, Church History Library.
19. Sigma Chi, founded in 1855, is one of the largest Greek-letter collegiate social fraternities in the United States. Lucy was likely a Sigma Chi mother for the chapter at the University of Utah.
20. "Rites for Mrs. Smith Will Be Held Tuesday," *Deseret News*, November 6, 1937; Gibbons, *George Albert Smith*, 158–59.
21. "Rites for Mrs. Smith"; "Lucy Emily Woodruff Smith," 1937, State of Utah Certificate of Death, file no. 1920.
22. George Albert Smith, Journal, November 5, 1937, George Albert Smith Family Papers, University of Utah.
23. Lucy Woodruff Smith, Diary, April 6, 1893.

Chapter 19: Ida Frances Hunt Udall

1. Ida Frances Hunt Udall, Journal, Holograph, p. 3, David King and Ida F. Hunt Udall Family Papers, 1800–1938, Special Collections, Merrill-Cazier Library, Utah State University, Logan. The first portion of the Ida Hunt Udall journal is an autobiography.
2. John Hunt's father, Charles Jefferson Hunt, was a captain in the Mormon Battalion. Charles Jefferson and Celia Mounts Hunt became prominent members of the San Bernardino community.
3. See Louisa Barnes Pratt, Journal and Autobiography, 1850–1880, Holograph, Louisa Barnes Pratt Collection, Church History Library, The Church of Jesus Christ of Latter-day Saints, hereafter cited as Church History Library; Alisha Erin Hillam, "'Be Still and Know That I Am God': Louisa Barnes Pratt," in *Women of Faith in the Latter*

Days, Volume 1, 1775–1820, ed. Richard E. Turley Jr. and Brittany A. Chapman (Salt Lake City, UT: Deseret Book, 2011), 246–58.
4. Udall, Journal, 4.
5. Maria S. Ellsworth, *Mormon Odyssey: The Story of Ida Hunt Udall, Plural Wife* (Chicago: University of Illinois Press, 1992), 225, 30.
6. Ellsworth, *Odyssey*, xi.
7. Ellsworth, *Odyssey*, 41.
8. David King Udall (1851–1938) was one of the most prominent Latter-day Saint pioneers in Arizona. Andrew Jenson, "David King Udall," *Latter-day Saint Biographical Encyclopedia, 4* vols. (Salt Lake City, UT: Andrew Jenson History Co., 1901–36), 1:325–28.
9. Ida Hunt to Eliza Luella Udall, January 29, 1882, Holograph, Udall Family Correspondence Collection, 1859–1950, Church History Library.
10. Eliza Luella Udall to Ida Frances Hunt, March 12, 1882, Holograph, Udall Family Correspondence Collection, 1859–1950, Church History Library.
11. Udall, Journal, 22.
12. Udall, Journal, 25–26.
13. Udall, Journal, 27–28.
14. Udall, Journal, 28–29.
15. Udall, Journal, 33.
16. Udall, Journal, 34.
17. Udall, Journal, 35–36.
18. Udall, Journal, 49.
19. Udall, Journal, 62.
20. Udall, Journal, 64–65.
21. Udall, Journal, 67–68.
22. Udall, Journal, 109–10, 128, 131.
23. Udall, Journal, 148.
24. Udall, Journal, 154.
25. Udall, Journal, 170.
26. Udall, Journal, 175.
27. Udall, Journal, 180.
28. Udall, Journal, 206–8.
29. Udall, Journal, 209–10.
30. Ellsworth, *Odyssey*, x.
31. Ellsworth, *Odyssey*, 189.

32. Ellsworth, *Odyssey*, x; David King Udall and Pearl Udall Nelson, *Arizona Pioneer Mormon, David King Udall: His Story and His Family, 1851–1938* (Tucson, AZ: Arizona Silhouettes, 1959), 264.
33. Ellsworth, *Odyssey*, xi.

Chapter 20: Mere Mete Whaanga

1. See Marjorie Newton, *Tiki and Temple: The Mormon Mission in New Zealand, 1854–1958* (Salt Lake City, UT: Greg Kofford Books, 2012).
2. Peter J. Lineham, "Hirini Te Rito Whaanga (1825–1905)," *Dictionary of New Zealand Biography*, *Te Ara—The Encyclopedia of New Zealand*, accessed April 24, 2013, http://www.teara.govt.nz/en/biographies/2w13/whaanga-hirini-te-rito.
3. Katarina Whaanga, Mihi Whaanga, Ihaka Whaanga, Heneriata Whaanga.
4. Louis G. Hoagland to M. C. Woods, May 11, 1937, Louis Gerald Hoagland Papers, 1915–1941, Church History Library, The Church of Jesus Christ of Latter-day Saints, Salt Lake City, Utah, hereafter cited as Church History Library.
5. Membership Records, Nuhaka Branch, New Zealand Mission, Microfilm of holograph, Family History Library, The Church of Jesus Christ of Latter-day Saints, Salt Lake City, Utah, hereafter cited as Family History Library.
6. Edward H. Anderson, "Events and Comments," *Improvement Era* 9, no. 4 (January 1906), 261–62.
7. William M. Douglass Jr., Journal, June 16, 1891, and September 24, 1893, Microfilm of holograph, Family History Library.
8. Hoagland to Woods, May 11, 1937.
9. Elder Smellie became fluent in the Maori language and learned to love the generous, warm-hearted Maori Saints wholeheartedly. "Indeed I became as one of them, their joys were mine, their sorrows were mine," he wrote some years later. John Taylor Smellie, Autobiography, Photocopy of typescript, p. 9, Church History Library.
10. "Second General Epistle of the First Presidency," in James R. Clark, *Messages of the First Presidency of The Church of Jesus Christ of Latter-day Saints*, vol. 2 (Salt Lake City, UT: Bookcraft, 1965), 33; Wilford Woodruff, George Q. Cannon, Joseph F. Smith to William Paxman,

February 1895, copied into William Gardner, Diary, April 2, 1895, Church History Library.
11. Woodruff, Cannon, and Smith to Paxman, February 1895.
12. "Departure of Mere Whaanga and Party for Nuhaka," *Deseret Evening News,* November 2, 1918.
13. Walter Smith, "From the Leaves of an Old Family Bible: 'The First Maoris to Emigrate to Zion,'" *Te Karere* 35 (May 1941): 658.
14. "From the Diary of Mere Whaanga, Transcribed by one of the mokopuna (grandchildren)," [5–8], in Kia Ngawari Trust Collection, Temple View, New Zealand. Copy courtesy of Robert Joseph. Although this document is termed a diary, it appears to be a memoir written by Mere Mete Whaanga in 1902.
15. Smith, "From the Leaves of an Old Family Bible," 658.
16. "Hirini Whaanga, the Maori Chief," *Deseret News [Weekly]*, February 19, 1898; Smith, "From the Leaves of an Old Family Bible," 658.
17. "Hirini Whaanga Is Here," *Salt Lake Tribune,* July 20, 1894.
18. Smith, "From the Leaves of an Old Family Bible," 658; "Maori Meeting," *Deseret Evening News*, July 21, 1894.
19. "Maori Meeting," *Deseret Evening News*, July 21, 1894.
20. Smith, "From the Leaves of an Old Family Bible," 658.
21. Woodruff, Cannon, and Smith to Paxman, February 1895; John E. Magleby to George Reynolds [Secretary to First Presidency], April 25, 1902, New Zealand Mission, Minutes, Church History Library.
22. New Zealand Mission, Minutes, November 12–13, 1895.
23. "From the Diary of Mere Whaanga," [5–8].
24. New Zealand Mission, Minutes, April 3, 1898.
25. Ezra T. Stevenson to President Wilford Woodruff, June 9, 1898, New Zealand Mission, Presidents' Correspondence, 1897–1900, Church History Library.
26. Ezra T. Stevenson to First Presidency, August 24, 1898, New Zealand Mission, Presidents' Correspondence, 1897–1900.
27. William Frank Atkin, Papers and New Zealand Mission Journals, 1903–1906, 1916–1918, entry of November 21, 1905, L. Tom Perry Special Collections, Harold B. Lee Library, Brigham Young University, Provo, Utah.
28. Rufus K. Hardy to Louis G. Hoagland, November 22, 1907, Louis Gerald Hoagland Papers, 1905–1938, Church History Library.
29. New Zealand Mission, Minutes, December 20, 1907.

30. New Zealand Mission, Minutes, January 11–12, 1908.
31. New Zealand Mission, Minutes, April 4, 1908.
32. Rufus K. Hardy to Louis G. Hoagland, May 1908, Louis Gerald Hoagland Papers, 1905–1938, Church History Library.
33. *Deseret Evening News,* August 6, 1917.
34. John Ephraim Magleby, New Zealand Mission Diary, 1928–1929, 43, entry of February 26, 1929.
35. On February 20, 1943, the *Church News* published an article and photograph featuring Mere with her quilt.
36. Now known as the New Zealand Missionary Society.

Chapter 21: Anna Karine Gaarden Widtsoe

1. John A. Widtsoe, *In the Gospel Net: The Story of Anna Karine Gaarden Widtsoe* (Salt Lake City, UT: Improvement Era, 1942), 60–61.
2. Widtsoe, *Gospel Net,* 65.
3. Widtsoe, *Gospel Net,* 67.
4. Widtsoe, *Gospel Net,* 67–68.
5. Widtsoe, *Gospel Net,* 108.
6. Widtsoe, *Gospel Net,* 71–72.
7. Widtsoe, *Gospel Net,* 74–78.
8. Widtsoe, *Gospel Net,* 78–81.
9. Andrew Jenson, Remarks, "Funeral Services of Mrs. Anna K. Widtsoe," July 13, 1919, Typescript, p. 13, Widtsoe Family Papers, 1824–1953, Church History Library, The Church of Jesus Christ of Latter-day Saints, Salt Lake City, Utah, hereafter cited as Church History Library.
10. Widtsoe, *Gospel Net,* 88.
11. Widtsoe, *Gospel Net,* 133.
12. Widtsoe, *Gospel Net,* 84–85.
13. Widtsoe, *Gospel Net,* 93.
14. Widtsoe, *Gospel Net,* 93–94.
15. Albert E. Bowen, Remarks, "Funeral Services for Sister Petroline Gaarden," April 14, 1929, Widtsoe Family Papers, Church History Library.
16. Widtsoe, *Gospel Net,* 94–96.
17. Widtsoe, *Gospel Net,* 99.
18. Widtsoe, *Gospel Net,* 94–97, 99–101.
19. Widtsoe, *Gospel Net,* 101, 118, 127.

20. Bowen, Remarks.
21. Arnt Engh, Remarks, "Funeral Services for Sister Petroline Gaarden."
22. Widtsoe, *Gospel Net,* 105–6.
23. Scandinavian Mission, Manuscript History, August 3, 1904, Church History Library.
24. Scandinavian Mission, Manuscript History, February 25, 1904, Church History Library.
25. "Lady Missionaries in Norway," *Millennial Star* 66, no. 32 (August 11, 1904): 508–9.
26. Anna K. G. Widtsoe to Anna G. Widtsoe, March, 11, 1904, Holograph, Widtsoe Family Papers, Church History Library.
27. Widtsoe, *Gospel Net,* 108–9.
28. Widtsoe, *Gospel Net,* 116.
29. Widtsoe, *Gospel Net,* 120.
30. Widtsoe, *Gospel Net,* 123.
31. The word Anna used, *Nyt,* can be translated as either *news* or *joy.*
32. "Paaskemorgen," *Bikuben,* April 4, 1912, translation by Lilly Christensen and Kiersten Olson.
33. Widtsoe, *Gospel Net,* 127.
34. Widtsoe, *Gospel Net,* 127–28.
35. "Funeral Services of Mrs. Anna K. Widtsoe," 26.

Chapter 22: Clarissa Smith Williams

1. "Is Chosen by Head Church Official," *Salt Lake Telegram,* April 2, 1921; Amy Brown Lyman, "Clarissa S. Williams," *Relief Society Magazine* 15 (December 1928): 639.
2. See Heidi S. Swinton, "'Peace Be with You': Bathsheba Wilson Bigler Smith," in *Women of Faith in the Latter Days, Volume 2: 1821–1845,* ed. Richard E. Turley Jr. and Brittany A. Chapman (Salt Lake City, UT: Deseret Book, 2012), 349–365.
3. "Is Chosen by Head Church Official"; Amy Brown Lyman, "Semi-Annual Conference of the Relief Society," *Relief Society Magazine* 15 (December 1928): 668; Janet Peterson and LaRene Gaunt, *Elect Ladies* (Salt Lake City, UT: Deseret Book, 1990), 98–99, 112.
4. "Is Chosen by Head Church Official"; Peterson and Gaunt, *Elect Ladies,* 112–13.
5. Clarissa S. Williams to William N. Williams, July 27, 1877, in *Mission to Wales, 1877–'79: Being an Account of William Newjent*

Williams's Two Years as a Missionary for the Church of Jesus Christ of Latter-day Saints in Wales, comp. Richard W. James (Salt Lake City, UT: privately printed, 1987), 40.

6. Clarissa Williams Van Law (1880–1931), Susan Smith Williams (1882–1882), William Newjent Williams (1883–1888), Sarah Smith Williams Wilson (1885–1950), Josephine Williams (1887–1919), Hetty Smith Williams (1889–1907), Eva Williams Darger (1890–1969), Georgia Williams James (1892–1935), George Albert Williams (1894–1981), Bathsheba Smith Williams (1896–1960), Lyman Smith Williams (1899–1971).
7. "Is Chosen by Head Church Official"; Peterson and Gaunt, *Elect Ladies,* 101–3.
8. "Is Chosen by Head Church Official"; Lyman, "Clarissa S. Williams," 640, 643; Peterson and Gaunt, *Elect Ladies,* 104–5.
9. "The International Council of Women at Work," *Courier Home Circle,* July 1, 1914; "The International Council of Women," *Relief Society Magazine* 8 (January 1921): 21–24; Clarissa S. Williams, "International Council of Women Quinquennial Meeting," *Relief Society Magazine* 12 (August 1925): 397, 404–5.
10. "International Council of Women," 21–22.
11. "International Council of Women," 23.
12. Peterson and Gaunt, *Elect Ladies,* 107–8.
13. "War! War! And Why War?" *Relief Society Bulletin* 1 (September 1914): 4–5.
14. Peterson and Gaunt, *Elect Ladies,* 105.
15. Lyman, "Clarissa S. Williams," 641–42.
16. Personal history of Eva W. Darger, quoted in Janet Peterson and LaRene Gaunt, *Faith, Hope, and Charity: Inspiration from the Lives of General Relief Society Presidents* (American Fork, UT: Covenant Communications, 2008), 117–18.
17. Williams, "International Council of Women Quinquennial Meeting," 397–98.
18. Williams, "International Council of Women Quinquennial Meeting," 407.
19. Williams, "International Council of Women Quinquennial Meeting," 402.
20. Williams, "International Council of Women Quinquennial Meeting," 403–7.

21. Williams, "International Council of Women Quinquennial Meeting," 403.
22. "International Council of Women," 25.
23. "International Council of Women," 21.
24. "Is Chosen by Head Church Official."
25. Peterson and Gaunt, *Faith, Hope, and Charity*, 115.
26. Alice Merrill Horne, "Sketch of the Home Life of Clarissa S. Williams," p.1, qtd. in Peterson and Gaunt, *Faith, Hope, and Charity*, 115–16.
27. Amy Brown Lyman, "General Conference of Relief Society," *Relief Society Magazine* 7, no. 12 (December 1921): 695–96.
28. "Woman's Victory," *Young Woman's Journal* 32 (1921): 378–79. Joseph Smith said: "I now turn the key to you in the name of God and this Society shall rejoice and knowledge and intelligence shall flow down from this time—this is the beginning of better days to this Society." Nauvoo Relief Society Minute Book, April 28, 1842, Church History Library, also available at josephsmithpapers.org.
29. Lyman, "Clarissa S. Williams," 642.
30. Lyman, "Clarissa S. Williams," 642–43.
31. George Albert Smith, Clarissa Smith Williams Funeral Address, March 1930, Church History Library.
32. Lyman, "Semi-Annual Conference of the Relief Society," 668–69.
33. "General Conference of Relief Society," *Relief Society Magazine* 9 (June 1922): 312.
34. "Is Chosen by Head Church Official."

Chapter 23: Cohn Shoshonitz Zundel

1. Later in her life, Cohn identified her birthplace as Bear River, Box Elder County, Utah. At her death, reflective of changing jurisdictions and boundaries, her family members reidentified her birthplace as Willard, Box Elder County, Utah. Endowment House Sealings: Sealing of Couples, Living and by Proxy, 1857–1889, December 7, 1882, Special Collections, Family History Library, The Church of Jesus Christ of Latter-day Saints, Salt Lake City, Utah. "Cohn Zundel," 1949, Utah Certificate of Death, file no. 49–020128.
2. Record of Members Collection, 1931–1941, Washakie Ward, Malad Stake, Church History Library, The Church of Jesus Christ of Latter-day Saints, Salt Lake City, Utah, hereafter cited as Church History

Library; "Moroni Tro-ou-wutsey Zundel and Conn Shoshonitch," Family Group Record, Pedigree charts and personal records of descendants, private possession; Paula Watkins, Interview by Patricia L. Spilsbury, 2013, Salt Lake City, Utah.
3. Scott R. Christensen, *Sagwitch: Shoshone Chieftain, Mormon Elder, 1822–1887* (Logan: Utah State University Press, 1999), 2–3.
4. Christensen, *Sagwitch,* 70–102.
5. "Washakie Ward History," Manuscript History and Historical Reports, Washakie Ward, Box Elder Stake, History, p. [2] Church History Library.
6. Christensen, *Sagwitch,* 139–88.
7. "Moroni Tro-ou-wutsey and Conn Sho-sho-nitch," Family Group Record, Pedigree charts and personal records of descendants, private possession.
8. Scott R. Christensen, Oral communication with Patricia L. Spilsbury, 2012, Salt Lake City, Utah.
9. Endowment House Sealings, December 7, 1882. Before the Salt Lake Temple was completed in 1893, several buildings in Salt Lake City were used for the administration of temple ordinances. One such building was the Endowment House, which was in operation from 1855 to 1889. LaMar C. Berrett, "Endowment Houses," in *Encyclopedia of Mormonism,* ed. Daniel H. Ludlow, 4 vols. (New York: Macmillan, 1992), 2:456.
10. Nephi Zundel (1878–1951), Harriet Zundel (1884–1885), Lehi Zundel (1886–?), Lucy Zundel Peyope Elk/Alex (1889–1966), Alexander Zundel (1891–?), (unnamed) Zundel (1893–?).
11. "Bishop Zundell's Wards. The Shoshones' Progress toward Civilization," *Deseret Evening News,* September 9, 1884.
12. Jedediah Morgan Hess, "John W. Hess Family History, 2005," Church History Library; "Washakie Ward History," Manuscript History and Historical Reports, 1847, p. [2], Washakie Ward, Box Elder Stake History, Church History Library.
13. "An Interesting Trip," *Woman's Exponent* 12, no. 3 (July 1, 1883): 20; Manuscript History and Historical Reports, 1883, Washakie Ward.
14. He chose Ammon Pubigee and Alfred Wahnee as counselors. Manuscript History and Historical Reports, Associations, Sunday School, p. [1], Washakie Ward.

15. Delayed for a number of decades, a building dedicated solely to the women's auxiliaries of the Church, called the Relief Society Building, was completed in 1956 and is adjacent to Temple Square.
16. Cohn's daughter Lucy married George Peyope on January 24, 1903. Mary Ann Ward was the president of the Washakie Ward Relief Society and also, with an assistant, functioned as the secretary.
17. Washakie Ward Minutes, 1883–1910, pp. 97, 121, 124, 127, 129, 131, Washakie Ward, Box Elder Stake, Church History Library.
18. Washakie Ward minutes, 1883–1910.
19. Washakie Ward minutes, 1883–1910, 97.
20. LaVerd and Flora Hill John, comp. *The Community of Portage Then and Now, 1855–1995* (n.p.: privately printed, 1995), 157.
21. 1900 U.S. Federal Census, Indian Population, New Portage Precinct, Box Elder County, Utah; 1910 U.S. Federal Census, Indian Population, New Portage Precinct, Box Elder County, Utah. Cohn's great-grandson Rios Pacheco, born after Nephi's death in 1951, recounted hearing as a child of "a man with one leg who rode around on a horse." Rios stated that during this time, "most farming was done on horseback or on a wagon, so it is possible [Nephi] could have still farmed." Grant Perry confirmed Rios's identification of Nephi Zundel as the son of Cohn who lost his leg and used a horse for mobility. Rios Pacheco, Interview by Paula Watkins, April 18, 2013, Brigham City, Utah. Nephi's identification was confirmed during an oral communication between Grant Parry and Paula Watkins in June 2013.
22. Record of Members, Washakie Ward.
23. Ceasor Anneboey (1893–1894), Jessie Anneboey Perdash (1896– ca. 1990), Emily Anneboey Zundel Perdash (1898–?).
24. Records of Marriage Licenses, Box Elder County, Utah, Book 1, 1888–1899, no. 256; Washakie Branch Record of Members, Records of Members Collection, 1836–1970, Church History Library.
25. Record of Members Collection, Washakie Ward; Box Elder County Clerk, Records of Marriage Licenses for Box Elder County, Utah, 1887–1966, Book 1:124.
26. Marjorie Alex Pacheco, Interview by Helen Chappell Taylor and Albert Jay Taylor, ca. 1975, Brigham City, Utah, Typescript, private possession.
27. Pacheco, Interview by Watkins.

28. Pacheco, Interview by Watkins.
29. Pacheco, Interview by Watkins; Pacheco, Interview by Taylor and Taylor.
30. Matthew E. Kreitzer, ed., *The Washakie Letters of Willie Ottogary: Northwestern Shoshone Journalist and Leader, 1906–1929* (Logan: Utah State University Press, 2000).
31. Peach Days were begun in Brigham City in 1904 to celebrate "an abundance of the best peaches in Utah." Peach Days is held every September on the weekend following Labor Day.
32. Kreitzer, *Washakie Letters*, 90, 152, 154, 192–93, 200.
33. General Minutes, 1905–1962, Washakie Ward, Box Elder Stake, p. 148, Church History Library.

Contributors

BRITTANY A. CHAPMAN holds a bachelor's degree in humanities from Brigham Young University and a master's degree in Victorian Studies from the University of Leicester in Leicester, England. She works at the Church History Library of The Church of Jesus Christ of Latter-day Saints, where she specializes in women's history. Brittany edited the autobiography and journals of her great-great-grandmother Ruth May Fox, forthcoming from the University of Utah Press. She lives in one of Ruth's historic homes in Salt Lake City, Utah.

KAROL GERBER CHASE received her bachelor of science degree in chemistry and math education from the University of Utah, where she met her husband, Richard P. Chase. They raised four sons in Salt Lake City, Utah. After Richard died from a brain tumor, she spent the next decade watching her sons receive advanced education, fulfill LDS missions, and marry. She enjoys watching her grandchildren and compiling and sharing family histories. She is the great-granddaughter of Sarah Ann Taylor Howard.

CLINTON D. CHRISTENSEN graduated from Brigham Young University with bachelor's and master's degrees in English. He also earned a master's degree in library and information science and archival administration from Wayne State University in Detroit, Michigan. He worked as college archivist at Hanover College in Indiana before joining the Church History Department of The Church of Jesus Christ of Latter-day Saints, where he specializes in international Church history. He and his wife and two sons live in Willard, Utah.

CHRISTINE T. COX earned her bachelor's degree in child development and family relations from Brigham Young University and a master's degree in library science from the same institution. She presently manages the public service division of the Church History Library of The Church of Jesus Christ of Latter-day Saints, where she has worked for forty years. Christine was introduced to Ellen Larson Smith through her photographs, which, in turn, intrigued her to learn more about the woman behind the camera. Christine lives in Salt Lake City, Utah, and has four children and six grandchildren.

LORETTA LUCE EVANS graduated from Brigham Young University with a degree in elementary education and a minor in history. She taught third grade for six years. Loretta began researching her family history in college and returned to it when her youngest children started school. She began working as an accredited professional genealogist in 1997. She has written articles for the *Ensign, Crossroads, Ancestry,* and *Heritage Quest* magazines and has presented lectures at local and national conferences. She and her husband, Bob, are the parents of five grown children. They are serving for the second time in the Family and Church History Mission in Salt Lake City, Utah. Loretta is the great-granddaughter of Lorena Eugenia Washburn Larsen.

AMANDA HENDRIX-KOMOTO attended the College of Idaho, where she earned a bachelor's degree in history, music, and religion. After graduation, she participated in Teach for America and earned a master's degree in elementary education from the University of Nevada–Las Vegas. She is currently a PhD candidate in history at the University of Michigan and lives in Ann Arbor with her husband, Jordan, and daughter, Eleanor.

Contributors

Janelle M. Higbee holds a master's degree in English rhetoric and composition from Brigham Young University and a bachelor's degree in English from the same institution. She is a writer, editor, and researcher based in Pleasant Grove, Utah. Her professional specialties include marketing, training, technical communications, and nineteenth-century Mormon women's history. One of her current projects is editing a documentary history of the first fifty years of Relief Society, forthcoming from the Church History Department of The Church of Jesus Christ of Latter-day Saints. She is also a managing editor for the Mormon Women Project digital library. Janelle is a great-great-granddaughter of Mary E. Woolley's husband, Thomas Chamberlain.

Alisha Erin Hillam earned a master's degree in antebellum American history from Purdue University, where she focused her research on the early history of The Church of Jesus Christ of Latter-day Saints. She received a bachelor's degree in creative and professional writing, also from Purdue, and taught Church history at the Purdue LDS Institute of Religion. She resides in Phoenix, Arizona, with her husband, Jeff, where she is a stay-at-home mother of two children and a freelance writer and poet.

Jeff Hillam received a bachelor's degree in Jewish studies at Purdue University. He began his career in international business in Latin America and the Middle East. He received an MBA from Thunderbird School of Global Management in December 2013. He and his wife, Alisha, and their two children live in Phoenix, Arizona. He is proud to be the great-great-great-grandson of Mary Roselia Cook McCann.

Janiece Johnson earned a bachelor's degree in political science from Brigham Young University and holds master's degrees in American history and in theology from BYU and Vanderbilt University, respectively. She is the general editor of the Mountain Meadows Massacre Legal Papers for the Church History Department of The Church of Jesus Christ of Latter-day Saints and has published a variety of journal articles. Janiece has also taught as adjunct faculty in Religious Education at BYU. She is a PhD candidate in American history at the University of Leicester in Leicester, England.

KESHIA LAI, originally from Singapore, graduated from Brigham Young University with a bachelor's degree in history. She is a second year PhD student in the history department at Ohio State University in Columbus. Her areas of interest include twentieth-century Asian and American history, women's history, and the history of The Church of Jesus Christ of Latter-day Saints in Singapore. Prior to entering graduate school, she worked as an intern in the Church History Department of The Church of Jesus Christ of Latter-day Saints.

CONSTANCE L. LIEBER holds a bachelor's degree in history from the University of Utah, a master's degree in Germanic and Slavic languages from Brigham Young University, and a PhD degree from the University of Utah in languages and literature. She discovered Martha Hughes Cannon's letters to her husband while working as an archivist at the Church History Library in 1975. She co-edited a volume with John Sillito entitled *Letters from Exile: The Correspondence of Martha Hughes Cannon and Angus M. Cannon, 1886–1888,* published by Signature Books in 1989. She is writing a biography of Martha. She divides her time between homes in Salt Lake City, Utah, and Frauenfeld, Switzerland.

ANDREA H. MAXFIELD is a project specialist in the Church History Department of The Church of Jesus Christ of Latter-day Saints, where her responsibilities include historical research and management of Church history publication projects. She is working on a bachelor's degree in history with a minor in English from the University of Utah and plans to earn a master's degree in cultural communication. Andrea and her husband, Michael K. Maxfield, are the parents of four grown children.

MATTHEW S. MCBRIDE earned a bachelor's degree in business management from the University of Utah and is currently pursuing a master's degree in history at the same institution. He is a web strategist for the Church History Department of The Church of Jesus Christ of Latter-day Saints. In addition to articles and reviews in the *Ensign* and the *Journal of Mormon History,* Matthew wrote *A House for the Most High: The Story of the Original Nauvoo Temple,* published by Greg Kofford Books in 2007. He enjoys his life in American Fork, Utah, with his wife and four children.

SUSAN EVANS MCCLOUD has published more than forty books in a variety of genres and was honored in 2011 with the Whitney Lifetime Achievement Award. A columnist on mormontimes.com, Susan is a contributor to "History of the Hymns" and creator of "Poets of the Restoration," both on radio.lds.org. She has written lyrics for several seminary and Young Women programs and is well known for her lyrics to two hymns in the 1985 LDS hymnal: "Lord, I Would Follow Thee" and "As Zion's Youth." For several years Susan taught English and creative writing at a private school in Provo, Utah. She is a thirty-five-year member of Daughters of Utah Pioneers and has served on the Provo Area Board of that organization. She and her late husband, James, are the parents of six, grandparents of nine, and great-grandparents of one.

BARBARA E. MORGAN received a bachelor's degree in American studies and a master's degree in educational leadership with an emphasis in international development from Brigham Young University. She earned a PhD in instructional psychology from Utah State University. She is an assistant professor of religion at BYU. Previous to teaching there, she taught seminary and institute and worked as a researcher for the Church Educational System of The Church of Jesus Christ of Latter-day Saints. She enjoys her family of twelve siblings, parents, fifty-four nephews and nieces, and other family and friends. Barbara resides in Provo, Utah.

MARJORIE NEWTON earned her BA, MA (Hons.), and PhD from the University of Sydney. She is the author of *Southern Cross Saints: The Mormons in Australia* (1991), *Hero or Traitor? A Biographical*

Study of Charles Wesley Wandell (1992), and *Tiki and Temple: The Mormon Mission in New Zealand, 1854–1958* (2012), plus numerous articles. Her doctoral dissertation on Mormonism and the Maori is forthcoming from Greg Kofford Books. Marjorie is an Australian who was born in Sydney and lives in Hobart, Tasmania.

KIERSTEN OLSON earned a bachelor of arts degree in music from Brigham Young University. She served a mission in Norway and developed a deep respect for the Widtsoe family by associating closely with many Latter-day Saints whose ancestors' lives were touched by Anna's missionary service. Kiersten works as an administrative assistant at the Church History Library of The Church of Jesus Christ of Latter-day Saints and lives in Cottonwood Heights, Utah.

ARDIS E. PARSHALL is a historian and freelance researcher specializing in Mormon history. On her Mormon history blog, *Keepapitchinin,* Ardis highlights the stories of lesser-known Latter-day Saint women and men. She co-edited with Paul Reeve *Mormonism: A Historical Encyclopedia,* published by ABC-CLIO in 2010. She works for the Church History Department of The Church of Jesus Christ of Latter-day Saints as a historian and writer and resides in Salt Lake City, Utah.

ANDREA G. RADKE-MOSS is a professor of history at Brigham Young University–Idaho. She received a bachelor's degree in history education and a master's degree in history from Brigham Young University and a PhD in history from the University of Nebraska–Lincoln. Her *Bright Epoch: Women and Coeducation in the American West* was published by the University of Nebraska Press in 2008. She has published on Latter-day Saint women, higher education, schoolteaching, and material culture in the Great Plains and American West. Andrea lives in Rexburg, Idaho, with her husband, Stephen, and two children.

PATRICIA LEMMON SPILSBURY received a bachelor's degree in English and journalism from the University of Arizona and a master's degree in curriculum and instruction from the University of Nevada–Las Vegas. She taught second and third grades for twelve years and was a literacy specialist for eight years in Las Vegas, where she raised seven lively children. She is the grandmother of twelve and serves as a full-time missionary for The Church of Jesus Christ of Latter-day Saints, assigned to the Church History Library in Salt Lake City, Utah.

JONATHAN A. STAPLEY received his doctorate from Purdue University and works with a firm that is industrializing his graduate work. He is an independent historian and serves on the board of the Mormon History Association. He is married and has four children.

LISA OLSEN TAIT received a PhD in American literature from the University of Houston and works as a historian and writer for the Church History Department of The Church of Jesus Christ of Latter-day Saints. She researches late nineteenth- and early twentieth-century LDS women's history and is working on a biography of Susa Young Gates. She has published articles in several journals and collections. Lisa serves on the executive committee of the Mormon Women's History Initiative Team (MWHIT) and works with several other projects to promote research and awareness of the field of Mormon women's history. Lisa and her husband, Mike, have four children and two dogs and enjoy hiking, biking, and spending time in the mountains.

LAUREL THATCHER ULRICH, a fifth-generation Latter-day Saint, completed an undergraduate degree in English at the University of Utah, a master's degree in English at Simmons College (Boston), and a PhD in history at the University of New Hampshire. She and her husband, Gael Ulrich, live in Cambridge, Massachusetts, where she is a member of the faculty at Harvard University. She grew up hearing stories about Maud May Babcock because her father, John Kenneth Thatcher, was a member of the Babcock Varsity Players in the 1920s.

Image Credits

Except as noted below, images are courtesy of the Church History Library, The Church of Jesus Christ of Latter-day Saints, Salt Lake City, Utah. All images are used by permission.

Images of Maud May Babcock, pages 1 and 3; Edith Ann Smith, page 183; Lucy Emily Woodruff Smith, page 228; courtesy of Special Collections Department, J. Willard Marriott Library, University of Utah.

Images of Martha Hughes Cannon, page 26; Emily Sophia Tanner Richards, page 131; courtesy of Utah State Historical Society, all rights reserved.

Images of Elizabeth Ann Claridge McCune, pages 107 and 119; Ida Frances Hunt Udall, pages 237, 239, and 250; courtesy of Special Collections & Archives, Merrill-Cazier Library, Utah State University.

Page 46: Image of Ruth May Fox courtesy of Kathryn MacKay Jones.

Pages 69 and 74: Images of Sarah Ann Taylor Howard courtesy of Karol Chase.

Page 75: Image of Sarah Ann Taylor Howard from *Liahona, the Elder's Journal* 18 (December 7, 1920): 229; public domain.

Pages 82, 88, and 94: Images of Lorena Eugenia Washburn Larsen courtesy of Loretta Luce Evans.

Page 96: Image of Mary Roselia Cook McCann courtesy of International Society Daughters of Utah Pioneers, Salt Lake City, Utah.

Page 98: Image of two young women at Bear Lake courtesy of Idaho State Historical Society, Browsing Collection.

Page 158: Image of Annie Marie Woodbury Romney courtesy of Barbara E. Morgan.

Pages 252 and 260: Images of Mere Mete Whaanga courtesy of Mel Whaanga.

Pages 288, 291, and 296: Images of Cohn Shoshonitz Zundel courtesy of Paula Watkins.

Index

Aberdeen, Lady, 283
Alex, Lucy Zundel Peyope, 350n10, 351n16
Anneboey, Ceasor, 351n23
Anthony, Susan B., 135–36, *140*, 279
Atkinson, Barbara Replogle, 14–15, 19–21, 23–24, 301n2
Atkinson, Ruby Louise, 301n2
Atkinson, William Dent, 301n2

Babcock, Maud May: legacy of, 1–2; fitness and, 2–3, 6–7; conversion of, 3–4; as teacher, 4–6, 7–11; political activism of, 11–12
Babcock, Sarah Jane Butler, 2
Babcock, William Wayne, 2
Bartholomew, Ida Lorena Larsen, *88*, 314n24
Bartholomew, Pearl Larsen, 314n24
Barton, Walter H., 234
Bear River Massacre, 288
Beekeeping, 92, 202
Bentley, Emma Geneva, 28, 30
Bigelow, Lucy, 29–30, 57–58
Bigler, Bathsheba, 211–12, 276–77
Bigler, Melissa Jane, 211
Bird, Ivy Hootchew, *291*
Birney, Alice McLellan, 326n40

Blackburn, Pat, 150
Bloomers, 31–32
Boe be nup, *291*
Book of Mormon, 128
Bountiful Dairy Company, 71
Bowen, Albert E., 45, 268, 270, 308nn18, 21
Bowen, Emma Lucy Gates, *60*, *64*, 308n18, 310n5
Bowman, Henry E., 33
Boyle, Henry G., 70
Brown, Lucy, 184, 223, 333n3
Bullock, Electa, 139
Bushman, Maria Elizabeth, 200, 201
Butler, Sarah Jane, 2

Caine, Frederick A., 124–25
Caine, John T., *136*
Caine, Margaret, 135, *136*
Cannon, Amanda Mousely, 301n10
Cannon, Angus M., *18*; Martha Maria Hughes marries, 17; plural marriage and, 22–23, 25–26, 301n10, 302n13; children of, 303n33
Cannon, Ann, 158, 159, 169
Cannon, Clarissa V. Mason, 301n10
Cannon, Elizabeth Rachel, 19, 27, 303n33

Cannon, George Q., 114, 308n22
Cannon, Gwendolyn Hughes, 25–26, 27, 303n33
Cannon, Hugh J., 308n22
Cannon, James Hughes, 27, 303n33
Cannon, Martha Maria Hughes: early years and education of, 13–15; as physician, 15–16, 22; on women and mothers, 16–17; as plural wife, 17–19, 21–26; on afterlife, 20–21; political and social activism of, 25, *140*; faith and final years of, 26–27; children of, 303n33
Chamberlain, Dee, *36*, 38
Chamberlain, Mary Elizabeth Woolley: early years of, 28–32; education of, 32–33; political service of, 33–34, 39–41, 305nn22, 24; courtship and marriage of, 34–38; final years of, 41–42
Chamberlain, Royal, *36*, 38
Chamberlain, Thomas, 34–38, 304nn14, 15
Chicago World's Columbian Exposition (1893), 136–39, 230
Child, Julia A., 152, *155*
Christy, Isabella Henrietta, *261*
Christy, Sidney Whaanga, 256, *261*, 262
Civil War, 69
Claridge, Charlotte Joy, 107
Claridge, Elizabeth Ann. *See* McCune, Elizabeth Ann Claridge
Claridge, Samuel, 107, 108, 109–10, 116–17
Clark, J. Reuben Jr., 55

Clark, Levira Annette, 212, 213, 338n8
Clawson, Esther Vida Fox, 306n3
Clayson, Ann Cannon Romney, 160, 330n4
Consecrated oil, 102, 126
Cook, Amanda Polly Savage, 96, 315n1
Cook, David Savage, 315n1
Cook, Joseph, 315n1
Cook, Mary Rosella. *See* McCann, Mary Rosella Cook
Cook, Phineas Wolcott, 96, 315n1
Coray, Howard, 70
Cottam, Catharine Jane, 159, 160, 161, 164
Cram, Charles, 31–32
Cumorah, 194–96
Curtis, Margaret, 174, 180

Danley, Mary Ann, 69, 70
Darger, Eva Williams, 281–82, 348n6
Death, of pure, 20–21
Divided skirts, 31–32
Drama, Maud May Babcock and, 1–2, 4–6
Dream(s): of Lorena Eugenia Washburn Larsen, 87–88, 94–95; of Mary Rosella Cook McCann, 101–2
Dunford, Alma Bailey Jr., 310n4
Dunford, Alma Bailey Sr., 58, 63, 310n4
Dunford, Leah Eudora, *64*, 310n4
Dunford, Susa Amelia Young. *See* Gates, Susa Amelia Young Dunford
Dustin, Chauncey L., 106

Index

Dustin, Mary Rosella Cook McCann. *See* McCann, Mary Rosella Cook

Egipbetche (John), son of Moembugie, 289
Elk, Lucy Zundel Peyope, 350n10, 351n16
Erickson, Rozella McCann, 100, 105, 316n12
Erickson, Vera McCann, 100, 316n12
Evans, Elizabeth, 13–14
Evenson, Lucy Beryl Fox, 306n3, 307n15

Faith: of Martha Maria Hughes Cannon, 26–27; of Mary Elizabeth Woolley Chamberlain, 29, 106; of Ruth May Fox, 56; of Susa Young Gates, 58–59, 61–67, 68; of Sarah Ann Taylor Howard, 81; of Lorena Eugenia Washburn Larsen, 91–92; of Mary Rosella Cook McCann, 100; of Elizabeth Ann Claridge McCune, 114; of Annie Marie Woodbury Romney, 162; of Ellis Reynolds Shipp, 178–81; of Edith Ann Smith, 185; of Ellen Johanna Larson Smith, 209–10; of Lucy Emily Woodruff Smith, 226–27; of Anna Karine Gaarden Widtsoe, 266, 267; of Cohn Shoshonitz Zundel, 290–93
Farnsworth, Eleanor Romney, 166, 167–68, 330n4
Farnsworth, Julia Murdock, 251
Farnsworth, Wilford, 169

Ferguson, Ellen B., 135
Financial responsibility, Mary Elizabeth Woolley Chamberlain on, 30
First Vision, 192–93
Fitness, Maud May Babcock and, 1–2, 6–7
Fox, Eliza May, 306n3
Fox, Emmeline Blanche, 306n3
Fox, Esther Vida, 306n3
Fox, Feramorz Young, 306n3
Fox, Florence Marie, 306n3
Fox, Frank Harding, 306n3
Fox, George James, 306n3
Fox, Hyrum Lester, 306n3, 307n15
Fox, Jesse May, 306n3
Fox, Jesse Williams Jr., 44
Fox, Leonard Grant, 306n3
Fox, Lucy Beryl, 306n3, 307n15
Fox, Rosemary Johnson, 44, 306n5
Fox, Ruth Clare, 306n3
Fox, Ruth May: migration of, 41–42; legacy of, 42–43; visits Hawaiian Islands, 45–51; visits Europe, 51–56, 308–9nn30, 31
Francis, Elizabeth, 146–48
Frost, Seraphine Smith, 205, 336n13

Gaarden, Anna Karine. *See* Widtsoe, Anna Karine Gaarden
Gaarden, Beret Haavig, 263
Gaarden, Peder, 263
Gaarden, Pertroline Jørgine, 263, 267, 270–74
Gardo House, 112, 220, 328n21
Gates, Brigham Cecil, 310n5
Gates, Brigham Young, 310n5
Gates, Emma Lucy, *60, 64,* 308n18, 310n5

Gates, Franklin Young, 310n5
Gates, Harvey Harris, 310n5
Gates, Heber, 310n5
Gates, Jacob F., 58–59, *60*, 310n5
Gates, Jacob Young, 59–62, 310n5
Gates, Joseph Sterling, *60*, 310n5
Gates, Karl Nahum, 59, *60*, 61, 310n5
Gates, Sarah Beulah, *64*, 310n5
Gates, Simpson Mark, 310n5
Gates, Susa Amelia Young Dunford: Maud May Babcock and, 3; Mary Elizabeth Woolley Chamberlain and, 40–41; childhood of, 56–57; missionary service of, 58–59; trials of, 59–63; spiritual search of, 63–67; activism of, 64–65; final years of, 67–68; Elizabeth Ann Claridge McCune and, 115, 116, 117, 118–19; Edith Ann Smith and, 197; children of, 310nn4, 5
Genealogy: Susa Young Gates and, 67–68; Elizabeth Ann Claridge McCune and, 116–19; Edith Ann Smith and, 184–85; Ellen Johanna Larson Smith and, 204; Mere Mete Whaanga and, 259
Gibbs, George F., *136*
Gleason, Flora Clarinda, 82–83
Grant, Heber J., 55, 76, 151–52, 275
Grant, Jedediah M., 70
Great Depression, 152–54

Haavig, Beret, 263
Hackett, Josephine Smith, 336n13
Hakii, Nami, 126

Hamblin, Blanche Robinson, *40*, 305n23
Hamblin, Tamar Stewart, *40*, 305n23
Hamilton-Gordon, Ishbel, 283
Harding, Mary Ann, 43
Hardy, Rufus K., 260–62
Hawaiian Islands: Ruth May Fox tours, 45–51; Susa Young Gates' mission to, 58–59; Tsune Ishida Nachie migrates to, 129–30; Joseph F. Smith's mission to, 215–19; Hugh J. Cannon and David O. McKay visit, 308n22
Hawley, Anna, 171, 172
Haymore, Erma Romney, 169, 330n4
Hayward, J. W., 103
Hearst, Phoebe Apperson, 326n40
Hendrickson, Hyrum A., 208
Hess, John, 289–90
Hill, Hannah Hood, 159, 164
Hill, Olea Shipp, 179, 182, 332n10
Hill Cumorah, 194–96
Hillstead, Mary Elizabeth, 174, 175
Hoagland, Louis G., 254
Hootchew, Annie, *291*
Horne, Alice Merrill, 284
Horne, Richard, 159
Howard, Amasa Ray, 312n11
Howard, Ann Shelton, 312n8
Howard, Arthur Lee, 312n11
Howard, David Edward, 312n11
Howard, Joseph, 312n8
Howard, Lydia Ann, 71, 312n11
Howard, Royal Franklin, 312n11
Howard, Samuel Cyrus, 71, 312n11
Howard, Samuel Shelton, 70, 71, 72, 312n14, 313nn20, 21

Howard, Sarah Ann Taylor: childhood of, 69–70; industriousness of, 70–71; political and social activism of, 71–72; education and church service of, 72; missionary service of, 73–80; final years of, 80–81; baptism of, 311n5
Howard, William Henry, 312n11
Hughes, Elizabeth Evans, 13–14
Hughes, Martha Maria. *See* Cannon, Martha Maria Hughes
Hughes, Peter, 13–14
Hunt, Celia Mounts, 342n2
Hunt, Charles Jefferson, 342n2
Hunt, Ida Frances. *See* Udall, Ida Frances Hunt
Hunt, John, 237–38, 249
Hunt, Lois Barnes Pratt, 237
Hurst, Alice Lambert Romney, 160, 169, 330n4
Hyde, Jeanette, 48, 307n16

International Council of Women, 135, 137, 279, 282–83
Ishida, Cho, 123
Ishikawa, Katsu, 126
Ivie, Lloyd O., 129

James, Georgia Williams, 348n6
Jarman, William, 113
Jenson, Andrew, 145, 266
Jepson, Vinnie Farnsworth, 305n23
Johnsen, Olaus, 264–65, 275
Johnson, Rosemary, 44, 306n5
Joseph Smith Memorial Monument, 183, 185–91, 335n12
Joshua, Hitope, *291*

Junior Relief Society, 82–83, 184, 334n5

Kato, Hisa, 126
Kimball, Alice Ann, 213, *219*, 340n35
Kimball, J. Golden, 226, 232, 233
Kimball, Mary C., *155*
Kimball, Sarah M., 132, *140*
King, Amy Jane, 333n3
Kurekure, Parapara, 253

Lambourne, Caroline, 159
Lambson, Alfred Boaz, 211, 212
Lambson, Edna, 211, 215, 219–20
Lambson, Julina. *See* Smith, Julina Lambson
Lambson, Mary Jane Martin, 212
Lambson, Melissa Jane, 211
Lambson, Melissa Jane Bigler, 211
Larsen, Bent Franklin, 85, 86, *88*, 92–93, 314n24
Larsen, Bent Rolfsen, 83–92
Larsen, Charlottie Eugenia, *88*, 314n24
Larsen, Clarence Abraham, 314n24
Larsen, Ella Almeda, *88*, 314n24
Larsen, Enoch Rolf, *88*, 89, 314n24
Larsen, Fern Emma, 314n24
Larsen, Floy Isabel, *88*, 92, 93, 314n24
Larsen, Ida Lorena, *88*, 314n24
Larsen, Julia, 83–84, 85
Larsen, Lorena Eugenia Washburn: early years of, 82–83; marriage and family of, 83–92; industriousness of, 92–93; spiritual manifestations given to, 93–94; final years of, 94–95

Larsen, Pearl, 93
Larson, Ellen Johanna. *See* Smith, Ellen Johanna Larson
Larson, Elna Olsson Malmstrom, 198, 199
Larson, Mons, 198
Lisonbee, Hugh, 93
Logan Temple, 266–67, 315n5
Loyalty, Maud May Babcock on, 7–10
Lund, Anthon H., 119–20
Lund, Julia A., *155*
Lyman, Amy Brown, 152, *155*, 309n31
Lyon, Ellen Smith, 336n13

MacKay, Florence Marie Fox, 306n3
Maeser, Karl G., 172
Malmstrom, Elna Olsson, 198, 199
Manifesto regarding plural marriage, 90–91, 220, 312–13n20
Manti Temple, 30, 85, 87
Maori, 252, 254–55
Marriage: Martha Maria Hughes Cannon on, 23–25; Elizabeth Ann Claridge McCune on, 115–16. *See also* Plural marriage
Martin, Ann E., 147–48
Martin, Mary Jane, 212
Mason, Clarissa V., 301n10
Maternity welfare program, 152
Maw, Herbert, 4–6
May, James, 43
May, Mary Ann Harding, 43
May, Ruth. *See* Fox, Ruth May
McAllister, Luella Atkin, *40*, 305n23
McCann, Elizabeth Sant, 315–16n10
McCann, Eunice Teeples, 316n10

McCann, Hyrum David, 316n12
McCann, Hyrum Johnston, 97, 98, 100, 101–2, 104
McCann, Jean, 103, 106, 316n12
McCann, Joseph Arthur, 99, 100–101, 316n12
McCann, Laurence, 100, 101, 105, 316n12
McCann, Lorell, 102, 105–6, 316n12
McCann, Loys, 101, 103, 105, 316n12
McCann, Mary Rosella Cook, 96–106, 315n1
McCann, Rozella, 100, 105, 316n12
McCann, Stella, 99, 316n12
McCann, Thomas Newell Ravenhill, 315–16n10
McCann, Thomas Ravenhill, 315–16n10
McCann, Vera, 100, 316n12
McCarter, George, 244
McCrimmon, Elizabeth Rachel, 19, 27, 303n33
McCune, Alfred William Jr., 317n12
McCune, Alfred William Sr., 110, 114–17, *119*, 120, 317n12, 318n25
McCune, Earl Vivian, 317n12
McCune, Elizabeth Ann Claridge: early years of, 107–8; in Nephi and Muddy River, 108–10; financial success of, 110–12; missionary service of, 112–15; relationships of, 115–16; genealogy and temple work and, 116–19; as homebuilder and philanthropist, 119–21; children of, 317n12

McCune, Elizabeth Claridge, 317n12

McCune, Frank Claridge, 110, 317n12

McCune, Harry Berthrand, 317n12

McCune, Lottie Jacketta, 317n12

McCune, Matthew Marcus, 317n12

McCune, Raymond, 317n12

McCune, Sarah Fay, 317n12

McCune Mansion, 112, 119–21

McKay, David O., 308n22

McKinney, Nellie Shipp, 179, 180, 332n10

McMurrin, William, 113, 114

Medicine: Martha Maria Hughes Cannon and, 14–16, 22–23, 25–26; Ellis Reynolds Shipp and, 175–82

Mellor, Fern Emma Larsen, 314n24

Memorial funds, 285–86

Mesa Temple, 117–18, 209, 210

Mete, Mere. *See* Whaanga, Mere Mete

Mete, Watene (Walter Smith), 256, 257, 262

Missionary work: Susa Young Gates and, 58–59; Sarah Ann Taylor Howard and, 72, 73–80; Lorena Eugenia Washburn Larsen and, 84–86; Elizabeth Ann Claridge McCune and, 112–15; Tsune Ishida Nachie and, 122–30; Ellen Johanna Larson Smith and, 209–10; Julina Lambson Smith and, 215–18; Lucy Emily Woodruff Smith and, 226–35, 341n8; Mere Mete Whaanga and, 253,

260–62; Anna Karine Gaarden Widtsoe and, 269, 270–74

Mormon Handicraft, 154

Motherhood: Martha Maria Hughes Cannon on, 16–17; Ellis Reynolds Shipp and, 173, 176–80; Julina Lambson Smith on, 214; Clarissa Smith Williams and, 283–84

Mothers' Congress of Utah, 142–43, 326n40

Mounts, Celia, 342n2

Mousely, Amanda, 301n10

Muddy River, Nevada, 108, 109–10

Murphy, Castle H., 129–30

Musser, Annie, 151

Musser, Ellis Reynolds Shipp, 179, 332n10

Nab-it-not-a-ci, 288, 289

Nachie, Ei, 122, 123, 126

Nachie, Sataro, 123

Nachie, Tsune Ishida, 122–30

National Council of Women, 135, 137, 156, 279–80, 282, 283

Naylor, Sarah Fay McCune, 317n12

Neaman, Lewis Jones, *291*

Nephi, Utah, 107–9

Norigan, Positze, *291*

Nutrition, Maud May Babcock and, 6–7

Nuttall, L. John, *136*

Obray, Jean McCann, 103, 106, 316n12

Oil, consecrated, 102, 126

Orphans' Home of Salt Lake City, 142

Ottogary, Willie, 295–96

Pabowena, Jane, *291*
Pacheco, Rios, 294–95, 351n21
Parsen, Pearl, *88*
Paxman, William, 258
Peace movement, 143–44
Peach Days, 352n31
Penrose, Charles W., *136*
Perdash, Emily Anneboey Zundel, 351n23
Perdash, Jessie Anneboey, 351n23
Peterson, Joseph, 202
Peyope, George, 351n16
Peyope, Lucy Zundel, 350n10, 351n16
Peyope, Sadie, *291*
Photography, 202–3
Physical culture, Maud May Babcock and, 1–2, 6–7
Pilon, Mae Smith, 203, 336n13
Plural marriage: Martha Maria Hughes Cannon and, 17–19, 21–24, 301n10; Mary Elizabeth Woolley Chamberlain and, 34–38; Ruth May Fox and, 44; Sarah Ann Taylor Howard and, 72; Lorena Eugenia Washburn Larsen and, 83–92; Emily Sophia Tanner Richards and, 133–34, 139; Annie Marie Woodbury Romney and, 159–62, 164, 167; Ellis Reynolds Shipp and, 174; Ellen Johanna Larson Smith and, 198, 199–200, 201; federal persecution regarding, 201, 302n13, 339n21; Julina Lambson Smith and, 212–22; Ida Frances Hunt Udall and, 238–50; Thomas Chamberlain and, 304n14; in Mexico, 304n15; end of, in Church, 312–13n20; Samuel Howard and, 313nn20, 21
Political service and activism: of Maud May Babcock, 11–12; of Martha Maria Hughes Cannon, 25; of Mary Elizabeth Woolley Chamberlain, 33–34, 39–41, 305n22,24; of Sarah Ann Taylor Howard, 71–72; of Emily Sophia Tanner Richards, 133–42; Clarissa Smith Williams on, 285
Pomare, Edna, 256
Po ne Nitz, *291*
Pratt, Lois Barnes, 237
Pratt, Parley P., 20–21
Prayer: Lucy B. Young on, 29, 58; Brigham Young on testimony and, 63
Prescott, Augusta, 139

Quealey, Lottie Jacketta McCune, 317n12
Quedup, Johnny Annebooey, 294
Quick, Gwendolyn Hughes Cannon, 25–26, 27, 303n33

Randall, Ethel Smith, 336n13
Reapers' Club, 326n42
Relief Society: Emily Sophia Tanner Richards and, 134; peace activism and, 143–44; Sarah Louisa Yates Robison and, 151–57; Anna Karine Gaarden Widtsoe and, 265–66; Clarissa Smith Williams and, 276–77, 280–81, 284–86; National Council of Women and, 279; Cohn Shoshonitz Zundel

INDEX

and, 290–93, 295; Joseph Smith and, 349n28
Relief Society Monument, 155
Replogle, Barbara, 14–15, 19–21, 23–24, 301n2
Reynolds, Anna Hawley, 171, 172
Reynolds, Ellis. *See* Shipp, Ellis Reynolds
Reynolds, William Fletcher, 171–72
Richards, Emily Helen, 132
Richards, Emily Sophia Tanner: early years of, 131–32; marriage and family of, 132; callings of, 132–33; political activism of, 133–42; social activism of, 142–43; peace activism of, 143–44; final years of, 144–45; Lucy Emily Woodruff Smith and, 230
Richards, Franklin D., 132
Richards, Franklin Dewey, 132, *133*
Richards, Franklin S., 132, 133, 135, *136*, 145
Richards, Jane Snyder, 132
Richards, Joseph Tanner, 132, *133*
Richards, Sarah Ellen, 213, 214–22, 340n35
Richards, Wealthy Lucile, 132
Richards, William Snyder, 132, *133*
Richardson, Ivie Romney, 330n4
Robinson, Joe, 33
Robison, Charlottie Eugenia Larsen, *88*, 314n24
Robison, Dorothy, 149
Robison, Gladys, 149, 151, 152
Robison, Joseph Lyman, 148, 156
Robison, Rulon, 149–50
Robison, Sarah Louisa Yates: early years of, 146–48; marriage and family of, 148–50; callings and service of, 150–56; legacy of, 156–57
Robison, Winifred, 149–50
Romney, Alice Lambert, 160, 169, 330n4
Romney, Ann, 169
Romney, Ann Cannon, 160, 330n4
Romney, Annie Marie Woodbury: early years of, 158–59; marriage and family of, 159–60; trials of, 160–62; in Mexico, 162–69; final years of, 169–70; children of, 330n4
Romney, Caroline Lambourne, 159
Romney, Catharine Jane Cottam, 159, 160, 161, 164
Romney, Eleanor "Ella," 166, 167–68, 330n4
Romney, Emily "Millie" Eyring Snow, 159–60
Romney, Erastus Snow, 163, 330n4
Romney, Erma, 169, 330n4
Romney, Frank, 169, 330n4
Romney, Hannah Hood Hill, 159, 164
Romney, Ivie, 330n4
Romney, Miles Park, 159–60, 162, 165, 168, 330n4
Romney, Orin Nelson, 160, 162, 330n4
Roundy, Caroline, 305n23

Sacrament, 29
Sacred Grove, 193–94
St. George Temple, 30
Sakazaki, Tome, 123
Salt Creek, Utah, 107–9
Salt Lake Temple, 117
Sant, Elizabeth, 315–16n10

Sarah Daft Home for the Aged, 142
Sargent, Dudley Allen, 2
Savage, Amanda Polly, 96, 315n1
Saxton, Clara, 43
Saxton, Mary Ann Thompson, 43
Scandinavian Mission, 270–74
Schmidt, Hachem (John Smith), 252
Schulthies, Lydia Ann Howard, 71, 312n11
Schwartz, Mary Taylor, 213, *219*, 340n35
Seegmiller, Ada, *40*, 305n23
Servility, Maud May Babcock on, 8
Sharon, Vermont, 185–97
Shaw, Anna Howard, 135, *140*
Shipp, Ambrose Pere, 332n10
Shipp, Anna, 175, 332n10
Shipp, Bert Reynolds, 332n10
Shipp, Ellis Reynolds: early years of, 171–72; marriage and family of, 172–74; education of, 174–79; occupation of, 179–80; later years of, 180–82
Shipp, Ellis Reynolds (daughter), 179, 332n10
Shipp, Margaret Curtis, 174, 175, 180
Shipp, Mary Catherine Smith, 174
Shipp, Mary Elizabeth Hillstead, 174
Shipp, Milford Bard, 172–76, 177, 180, 332n10
Shipp, Nellie, 179, 180, 332n10
Shipp, Olea, 179, 182, 332n10
Shipp, Paul Elbert, 332n10
Shipp, Richard Asbury, 332n10
Shipp, William Austin, 332n10
Shoshone, 288–89
Shoshonitz, Cohn. *See* Zundel, Cohn Shoshonitz

Shoshonitz, Sarah (Tic-a-Marrack/Nab-it-not-a-ci), 288, 289
Shoshonitz, Yellow (Alma), 288, 289–90
Sigma Chi, 342n19
Singing Mothers, 154
Skanchy, Anthon L., 265, 270
Skirts, divided, 31–32
Smellie, John Taylor, 255, 344n9
Smith, Alice Ann Kimball, 213, *219*, 340n35
Smith, Alof Omni, 336n13
Smith, Amy Jane King, 333n3
Smith, Bathsheba Bigler, 211–12, 276–77
Smith, Bathsheba W., 134
Smith, Charity, 204, 336n13
Smith, Clarissa. *See* Williams, Clarissa Smith
Smith, David Asael, 340n35
Smith, Donette, 340n35
Smith, Edith Ann: life and legacy of, 183–85, 197; journal of, 185–93; visits Sacred Grove, 193–94; visits Hill Cumorah, 194–96; receives endowment, 334n7
Smith, Edith Eleanor, 340n35
Smith, Edna Lambson, 211, 219–20
Smith, Edward Arthur, 340n35
Smith, Elias, 184, 223, 335n18, 340n1
Smith, Elias Wesley, 340n35
Smith, Ellen, 336n13
Smith, Ellen Johanna Larson: early years of, 198–99; marriage of, 199–201; self-reliance and diligence of, 201–4; final years of, 204–5; correspondence of, with Silas Smith, 205–7; moves

to Tanglewood, Utah, 207–8; church service of, 209–10; children of, 336n13
Smith, Emily, 342n16
Smith, Emily Jane, 223, 340n1, 340n35
Smith, Ethel, 336n13
Smith, George A., 212, 276
Smith, George Albert: Relief Society Monument and, 155; Lucy Emily Woodruff Smith and, 223–26, 228, 230–35, 236; on Clarissa Smith Williams, 286; children of, 342n16
Smith, George Albert Jr., 342n16
Smith, George Carlos, 340n35
Smith, Jesse N., 199
Smith, Joseph, 191–93, 349n28. *See also* Joseph Smith Memorial Monument
Smith, Joseph F.: Susa Young Gates and, 62; as lobbyist for Utah statehood, *136*; Edith Ann Smith and, *186*; Joseph Smith Memorial Monument and, 191; visits Hill Cumorah, 195; Julina Lambson Smith and, 212–13, *221*; missionary service of, 215–19; with family, *219*; plural marriage and, 220; Hugh J. Cannon and David O. McKay's vision of, 308n22; divorces Levira Smith, 338n8
Smith, Joseph Fielding, 338n8, 339n21, 340n35
Smith, Josephine, 336n13
Smith, Julina Clarissa, 340n35
Smith, Julina Lambson: early years of, 211–12; marriage of, 212–13; daily life of, 213–14; plural marriage and, 214–15, 219–20; in Hawaii, 215–19; final years and legacy of, 220–22; children of, 340n35
Smith, Levira Annette Clark, 212, 213, 338n8
Smith, Lucy Brown, 184, 223, 333n3
Smith, Lucy Emily Woodruff: early years of, 223–24, 340–41n2; courtship and marriage of, 224–26; missionary service of, 226–35, 341n8; final years and legacy of, 235–36; children of, 342n16
Smith, Mae, 203, 336n13
Smith, Maria Elizabeth Bushman, 200, 201
Smith, Marjorie Virginia, 340n35
Smith, Mary Catherine, 174
Smith, Mary Sophronia, 340n35
Smith, Mary Taylor Schwartz, 213, *219*, 340n35
Smith, Mercy Josephine, 218, 340n35
Smith, Mons Larson, 205, 336n13
Smith, Rachael, 340n35
Smith, Rachel Winter, 131
Smith, Rebecca Jane, 334n7
Smith, Robert, 217–18
Smith, Samuel B., 19
Smith, Sarah Ellen Richards, 213, 214–22, 340n35
Smith, Seraphine, 205, 336n13
Smith, Silas Derryfield, 199–203, 205–10, 336n13
Smith, Silas Reuel, 204, 336n13
Smith, Susan Elizabeth West, 276

Smith, Walter (Watene Mete), 256, 257, 262
Snow, Emily "Millie" Eyring, 159–60
Snow, Lorenzo, 113
Solomon, Makeanui Tinirau Ariki, *261*
Spafford, Belle, 153
Spencer, Stella McCann, 99, 316n12
Statehood, for Utah, 139–40, 303n12
Stevenson, Ezra T., 259–60
Stewart, Eliza Luella "Ella," 238–46, 249–50, 251
Stewart, Emily Smith, 342n16
Stewart, John C., 255–56
St. George Temple, 30
Stimpson, Joseph H., 128–29, 322n23
Suffrage. *See* Women's suffrage

Tai, Fude, 126
Tanner, Emily Sophia. *See* Richards, Emily Sophia Tanner
Tanner, Joseph Marion, 3
Tanner, Nathan, 131
Tanner, Rachel Winter Smith, 131
Taylor, Alma O., 122, 123–24, 126
Taylor, John, 302n13, 328n21
Taylor, Mary Ann Danley, 69, 70
Taylor, Ruth Clare Fox, 306n3
Taylor, Sarah Ann. *See* Howard, Sarah Ann Taylor
Taylor, Thomas, 69, 70
Teeples, Eunice, 316n10
"Temple in Hawaii, A" (Fox), 307n17
Temple work: Lorena Eugenia Washburn Larsen and, 93;
Elizabeth Ann Claridge McCune and, 116–19; Tsune Ishida Nachie and, 128–30; Edith Ann Smith and, 184; Ellen Johanna Larson Smith and, 209, 210; Mere Mete Whaanga and, 254–55, 258, 259
Testimony: Maud May Babcock on, 10–11; of Brigham Young, 63; of Susa Young Gates, 65–67, 68; of Sarah Ann Taylor Howard, 81; of Edith Ann Smith, 185; of Hirini Te Rito Whaanga, 260; of Anna Karine Gaarden Widtsoe, 267; of Cohn Shoshonitz Zundel, 290–93
Theater, Maud May Babcock and, 1–2, 4–6
Thompson, Lizzie Yates, 148, 151
Tic-a-Marrack, 288, 289
Timbimboo, Amy, *291*
Timbimboo, Hazel, *291*
Timbimboo, Towenge, *291*
Timbimboo, Yampitch, *291*
Tokizo, Ando, 123
Trials: of Susa Young Gates, 59–63; of Lorena Eugenia Washburn Larsen, 83, 84–92; of Mary Rosella Cook McCann, 99–100, 101, 104; of Mary Elizabeth Woolley Chamberlain, 106; of Annie Marie Woodbury Romney, 160–62, 165–66, 167, 169–70; of Ellis Reynolds Shipp, 173, 175; of Ellen Johanna Larson Smith, 201–2, 204; of Lucy Emily Woodruff Smith, 226–27, 230–33, 235; of Ida Frances Hunt Udall, 241–50; of Mere

Mete Whaanga, 256, 257, 258; of Anna Karine Gaarden Widtsoe, 264, 265, 266; of Cohn Shoshonitz Zundel, 293–94
Trower, Elizabeth Claridge McCune, 317n12
Turner, Ella Almeda Larsen, *88*, 314n24
Turner, Floy Isabel Larsen, *88*, 92, 93, 314n24
Turner, Glen, 93–94

Udagawa, Hisa, 129, 322n36
Udall, David King, 238–50, 251
Udall, Don Taylor, *250*
Udall, Eliza Luella "Ella" Stewart, 238–46, 249–50, 251
Udall, Eliza Rebecca May, 245, 248
Udall, Gilbert Douglas, *250*
Udall, Grover Cleveland, *250*
Udall, Ida Frances Hunt: early years of, 237–38; plural marriage and trials of, 238–49; final years of, 249–51
Udall, Jesse Addison, *250*
Udall, John Hunt, *250*
Udall, Pauline, 245, 247, *250*, 251
Utah: women's rights in, 113, 137–42; statehood for, 139–40, 303n12
Utah State Council of Women, 141
Utah Woman Suffrage Association, 135

Van Law, Clarissa Williams, 348n6

Wagon, Anzie, *291*
Wagon, Eddie, *291*
Walker War, 172, 332n2

Ward, Mary Ann, *291*, 293, 297, 351n16
Washakie settlement, 289–90
Washburn, Abraham, 82, 83, 94
Washburn, Flora Clarinda Gleason, 82–83
Washburn, Lorena Eugenia. *See* Larsen, Lorena Eugenia Washburn
Wells, Elizabeth Ann, 334n7
Wells, Emmeline B., 134, 135, *140*, 326n42
Wells, Junius F., 190, 335n13
Wells, Louise Martha, 334n7
West, Josephine R., 135
West, Susan Elizabeth, 276
Whaanga, Apikara (Abigail), 256, 256–57, 257, 262
Whaanga, Hirini Te Rito, 252–60
Whaanga, Katrin, 253
Whaanga, Mere Mete: marriage and family of, 252–53; church service of, 253–54; immigrates to Utah, 254–59; missionary service of, 260–62; final years of, 262
Whaanga, Mihi, 253, *261*
Widtsoe, Anna Karine Gaarden: early years and marriage of, 263–64; conversion of, 264–66; immigrates to Utah, 266–67; emphasizes education for her sons, 267–70; missionary service of, 270–74; poetry of, 274–75; final years of, 275
Widtsoe, John Anders, 263–64
Widtsoe, John Andreas, 264, 266, 267–70, 273, 275
Widtsoe, Leah Eudora Dunford, *64*, 310n4

Widtsoe, Osborne John Peder, 264, 267–70, 273, 275
Williams, Bathsheba Smith, 348n6
Williams, Clarissa, 348n6
Williams, Clarissa Smith: as Relief Society president, 151, 284–86; early years of, 276–77; marriage of, 277–78; activism of, 278–83; as mother, 283–84; legacy of, 286–87
Williams, Eva, 281–82, 348n6
Williams, George Albert, 348n6
Williams, Georgia, 348n6
Williams, Hetty Smith, 348n6
Williams, Josephine, 348n6
Williams, Lyman Smith, 348n6
Williams, Sarah Smith, 348n6
Williams, Susan Smith, 348n6
Williams, William Newjent, 277–78, 286, 348n6
Wilson, Sarah Smith Williams, 348n6
Woman's Exponent, 14
Women: Martha Maria Hughes Cannon on role of, 16; Mary Elizabeth Woolley Chamberlain on, 32; condition of, in Utah, 113, 137–39; Clarissa Smith Williams' activism for, 278–83; Clarissa Smith Williams on rights for, 285. *See also* Women's suffrage
Women's suffrage: Martha Maria Hughes Cannon and, 25; Sarah Ann Taylor Howard and, 71–72; Emily Sophia Tanner Richards and, 134–42; Samuel Howard and, 312n14

Woodbury, Ann Cannon, 158, 159, 169
Woodbury, Annie Marie. *See* Romney, Annie Marie Woodbury
Woodbury, Eleanor, 159
Woodbury, Orin, 159
Woodbury, Orin Nelson, 158, 159
Woodruff, Asahel, 341n2
Woodruff, Emily Jane Smith, 223–24, 340n1
Woodruff, Lucy Emily. *See* Smith, Lucy Emily Woodruff
Woodruff, Phebe Whittemore Carter, 223
Woodruff, Wilford Jr., 223
Woodruff, Wilford Sr., 223, 235, 255, 340n1
Woolley, Edwin Dilworth Jr., 28, 30
Woolley, Emma Geneva Bentley, 28, 30
Woolley, Louie, 33
Woolley, Mary Elizabeth. *See* Chamberlain, Mary Elizabeth Woolley
Woonsook, Mary, *291*
Woonsook, Minnie, *291*
World's Fair (1893), 136–39, 230
World War I, 105–6, 280–81

Yates, Elizabeth Francis, 146–48
Yates, Sarah Louisa. *See* Robison, Sarah Louisa Yates
Yates, Thomas, 146–48, 154
Young, Brigham: Susa Young Gates and, 57, 63; calls Samuel Claridge to settle Muddy River, 108–9; Ellis Reynolds Shipp and, 172, 176
Young, Helen, *291*

Young, Lucy Bigelow, 29–30, 57–58
Young, Susa. *See* Gates, Susa Amelia Young Dunford
Young, Zina D. H., 58, 134, *140*
Young Ladies' Mutual Improvement Association: Ruth May Fox and, 44–45, 56; Emily Sophia Tanner Richards and, 132–33; peace activism and, 143–44; Sarah Louisa Yates Robison and, 150; Lucy Emily Woodruff Smith and, 235; National Council of Women and, 279
Young Woman's Journal, 64

Zion's Maori Association, 258
Zundel, Alexander, 350n10
Zundel, Cohn Shoshonitz, 288–97, 349n1
Zundel, Emily Anneboey, 351n23
Zundel, Harriet, 350n10
Zundel, Isaac, 289–90
Zundel, Lehi, 350n10
Zundel, Lucy, 350n10, 351n16
Zundel, Moroni (Tru-Ow-Wutsey), 289, 290, 293
Zundel, Nephi, 293, 294, 350n10, 351n21
Zupinger, Rudolph, 333n3